HANDEL

HANDEL

A SYMPOSIUM

edited by

GERALD ABRAHAM

LONDON
OXFORD UNIVERSITY PRESS
NEW YORK   TORONTO

Oxford University Press, Amen House, London, E.C.4

GLASGOW NEW YORK TORONTO MELBOURNE WELLINGTON
BOMBAY CALCUTTA MADRAS KARACHI LAHORE DACCA
CAPE TOWN SALISBURY NAIROBI IBADAN ACCRA
KUALA LUMPUR HONG KONG

First published 1954
Reprinted 1963

Printed in Great Britain

PREFACE

OF all the master musicians of the very first rank, none, not even Haydn, is now so proportionately unknown to the general musical public as Handel is. Even the once-worshipped oratorios, after all only a part of his work, have one by one dropped out of the normal round, so that only *Messiah* remains. Yet *Messiah*, as Professor Bukofzer says in his admirable chapter on Handel's style in his *Music in the Baroque Era*, 'is not musically superior to the best choral dramas and its fame is due more to its universal religious appeal than to its musical excellence', though Mr. Herbage will be found making a higher claim for it in the present book. Whether or not *Messiah* is the supreme peak of Handel's art, the general public does not know it as such. The object it worships—and worships largely from habit and custom—is a species of religious monument, disfigured by generations of editors and conductors, frequently defiled by the casual, thoughtless irreverence that springs from over-familiarity. On a much smaller scale, the same fate has befallen one among the innumerable lovely songs in the operas; as the late W. G. Whittaker remarked in the Preface to his admirable edition of 'Ombra mai fù', 'it is a curious anomaly that the one piece of music of Handel's which the British public has placed on an equality with the most loved oratorios has been the first aria of his only comic opera, and that it has been turned into "sacred song", anthem, organ voluntary, and what not, mostly in incorrect versions'.

The only way to rescue *Messiah* from its religious pedestal in the choral-society box-office is to remove the filth of two centuries and perform it, as we ought to perform all Handel's music, in the Handelian manner or as nearly as we can get to it: with due proportion of voices and instruments, with continuo instruments and without the accretions that have crept in to take their place, and with at least enough ornamentation to shock audiences into realizing that they are listening to living music and not to a petrified object of devotion. A number of most praiseworthy attempts have been made in that direction and, thanks very largely to the lead given by the B.B.C., not only *Messiah* but Handel's music generally is beginning to be performed in England in something like a Handelian style. This is our modern *Händel-Bewegung*, in contrast with the German one of the period between the wars, which consisted of the furbishing up and revival of the operas.

We need not only to get to know the operas, or the best of the music in them, but the oratorios which our grandparents would be astounded to know have been allowed to drift away into oblivion. They are very far from deserving oblivion, and it is hoped that this book will draw attention once again not only to these half-forgotten masterpieces but to the innumerable other beauties of Handel's music. It will also draw attention to the pressing need for a 'Handel concordance' showing his numerous borrowings and innumerable self-borrowings.

G. A.

CONTENTS

CHAPTER I

HANDEL THE MAN

By PERCY M. YOUNG

IT is to be regretted that Dr. Johnson left no recorded observation on the subject of Handel. This lacuna is perhaps surprising in view of his particular friendship with the enthusiastic Burney. Johnson and Handel, the great chams of letters and music respectively, were complementary figures. Each bestrode his department of art and dominated his corner of society; each respected his family obligations and displayed loyalty, though with reservations, to the twin pillars of the constitution—the church and the monarchy; each was jealous of independence and sufficiently and richly characteristic to become—handing, accordingly, hostages to unscrupulous biographers—a 'character'. The individual artistic style of each is in truth the man himself so that the music of the one and the literature of the other can hardly be misattributed even by the unmusical and the unliterary. Without these two great artists who were, equally, great citizens, eighteenth-century England would have been infinitely the poorer.

Popular history has an unfortunate capacity for enshrining in the memory those facets of character which are the least typical. Thus the brusque Handel—he who snapped off the heads of opinionated singers, terrified the Princess of Wales by passionate outbursts at rehearsal at Carlton House, and cursed the governing body of the Foundling Hospital when it was proposed to ratify his generosity by parliamentary procedure—is remembered. But the opposite pole of temperament is forgotten. 'When he did smile', comments Burney, 'it was his sire the sun, bursting out of a black cloud. There was a sudden flash of intelligence, wit, and good humour, beaming in his countenance, which I hardly saw in any other.' Here Burney condenses a whole biography. By implication we learn of the specific qualities of sympathy, shrewdness, culture and comedy which made Handel what he was. Confined piety does further dishonour to the immortal memory. The middle-aged composer of 'sacred oratorio' is recollected, as in the severity of Hudson's and Kneller's portraiture, while the voluptuous imagery of Hogarth and the refinement of the early miniature by Platyer are overlooked.

This latter was made on the occasion of Handel's first visit to Italy when he was just of age. The young Saxon who conquered the fashionable fraternities of Florence, Rome, Naples, and Venice had social gifts which were appreciable. It was not only skill in composition, supported by irresistible testimonials from the Abbate Steffani, which won for him a place in Italian affections; it was a capacity for doing in Rome as the Romans did. The classical culture of a Lutheran *Gymnasium* in Halle qualified the apt student for intellectual collaboration with such excellent scholars as the Cardinals Panfili and Grimani, two of Handel's most distinguished librettists, and the strong faculties of jurisprudence and theology at the new University of Halle ensured a facility in dialectic which was useful when proselytizing prelates endeavoured to provoke secession from 'heretical' beliefs.

As a matter of musical interest, Catholic ritual impressed itself on Handel's mind, always alive to colour and pageantry, in no uncertain terms. The *Salve Regina* is an unmistakable act of chivalrous devotion before the Queen of Heaven. Handel was, of course, catholic: he might well have become a Catholic had his post-graduate course in Italy been prolonged beyond a three-year term.

Handel in Italy was as an Italian just as in England he was as an Englishman. He was the true cosmopolitan, able to adjust himself to the conditions of any society in which he might happen to be living. The restlessness of the born traveller—Handel continually preferred the hazards of eighteenth-century transport to the monotonous prospect of provincial immurement—was tempered by a rare appreciation of the fact that although language may appear to divide, considerations of humanity unite all men of goodwill. Handel, possessing an abiding affection for his fellow men, was a citizen of the world. He left the narrow limits of advancement in Halle for the fresher life of Hamburg. There he immediately stepped out of German society into the little world presided over by the bibulous John Wych, English Resident. In Hamburg too he met Giovanni Gastone de' Medici, who proposed the charms of the warm south. And so to Italy.

A basic reason for Handel's affection for travel was an unconscious state of rebellion with the rigid, authoritarian strictures of his father's upright but dull outlook. Georg Handel died when his son was a schoolboy, but his was the sort of influence which leaves permanent impression. The desire to control was part of his nature, as indeed it was of his son's, and we can well imagine that the early peregrinations, as those of Wolfgang Mozart, would have been subject to superintendence. One can imagine that alarm would have been occasioned, and much acrimony, had some unfriendly informer conveyed news of the sequence of amorous experiments—with Mlle Sbülens (this is implied in the correspondence of Georg Friedrich), with one or other of the more celebrated Italian singers, and with the nearly anonymous Spanish or Portuguese princess, the Donna Laura. Handel, as a young man, shook a loose leg from time to time, and in his excursions, both physical and mental, we may detect with independence more than a grain of defiance.

Experience in human intercourse inevitably bred a cultivation of modern languages. German was the mother tongue, French the necessary mode of polite communication (the social standing of his brother-in-law may be reckoned by the fact that Handel wrote to him as a rule in French), and Italian the official language of music. All of these Handel spoke and wrote as a matter of course. When a new language was required it was learned. By midsummer 1711, Handel, presuming return to London which in the previous year he had conquered as effectively as previously he had captivated Italy, is hard at work with English. 'J'ai fait', he writes to his fellow countryman, Andreas Roner, 'depuis que je suis parti de vous, quelque progrés dans cette langue.' In 1712 Handel is back in England, where he remains for the remainder of his life—the best part of half a century. One memorial to biographic convention requires removal. Handel may have retained in speech guttural traces of German origin, he may have stimulated sluggish colleagues with fiery broadsides of intermingled Italian, French, and German oaths, but no law of probability can be adduced to support the fiction that he spoke the pidgin English of common ascription.

Whatever Handel's accent, there is no doubt of his lively intellectual interest in literary affairs. He was a member, soon after his arrival, of the Burlington House coterie. Gay, Pope, Swift (who is interestingly reported to have commented on the skill with which Handel concealed his petticoat peccadillos), and Arbuthnot were his intimates. With Gay, to whose collected works in 1730 he was a subscriber, he could discuss music as well as literature. But with Pope there was only literature. Reading between the lines, it is possible to reconstruct some of the topics of friendly conversation. The classics, whence emerged the fact that *Aci, Galatea e Polifemo* had been composed for Italian consumption and the project which culminated in the delicious fancy of *Acis and Galatea*; contemporary

French drama, the influence of which was potent in theatrical circles
—the spur to *Esther*; the decline and fall of English opera—the
greatness of Addison could not disguise the poverty of invention in
Rosamond; and art and architecture, for Kent was patronized under
the same roof.

Literature and the literary permanently attracted Handel. His
friends included John Hughes, poet, fiddler, and dramatist; Henry
Carey; James Miller, who disgraced his cloth by writing plays which
displeased his ecclesiastical overlords; Dr. Morell, scholar and
antiquarian; and, above all, Aaron Hill. To Hill, whose collected
works also formed part of Handel's library, we are, in part at least,
indebted in that he urged strongly that English should supplant
Italian as the Englishman's operatic *lingua franca*. Some Shakespeare—Handel was a particular friend of James Quin and Mrs.
Cibber, both prominent as Shakespearean actors, and a regular
patron of the drama—a little Ben Jonson, a good deal of Milton, some
Dryden, the Authorized Version, and the fashionable books of the
not undistinguished age in which he lived gave not only a wide
general knowledge, but also much material for musical consideration.
One assumes that Richardson and Smollett were not unknown as
authors to Handel, for they were generous in observation on him;
the synoptic vision of these great novelists is the synoptic vision of
Handel in another medium. Read the one and you understand the
other.

From the musical standpoint, Handel is in one sense untypical
of his period, for, following Purcell, he was a master of verbal
dexterity. He possessed a discriminating ear in accentuation (which
undercuts the theory that he misunderstood our language) and
accordingly allowed the subtle music of language place within the
ambit of more absolute music. One further point emerges from a
consideration of Handel's acquaintance with books and authors.
Messiah may have been, in fact, provoked by the title and sources
from Isaiah of Pope's ode of 1712.

Dr. Busby, Sir John Hawkins, and many others commented on
Handel's general scholarship. If he had a particular interest, it was
pictorial art. It is well known that he possessed two Rembrandts,
but it is less well known that the Governors of the Foundling Hospital
consulted him over the details of the interior decoration of the chapel,
and that when Hogarth himself was a Governor. . . . Interest in art
(and there is a moral in this) found expression in the everyday details
of life. Handel bought charming furniture—his bookshelves (now in

the Fitzwilliam Museum), most lovely in proportion and design, are a case in point. In 1736 Handel wrote to his brother-in-law regarding his niece's wedding present:

I have taken the liberty of sending to her husband a small wedding present in the form of a gold watch of Delharmes, a gold chain and two seals, one of amethyst and one of onyx. Allow me to send at the same time as a wedding present to my dear niece, a diamond ring containing a single stone weighing something over seven grains, flawless and of the first water.

The jewellery may have been purchased either from Lewis Morel of Fleet Street or Edward Shewell of Lombard Street, both of whom figured as beneficiaries in Handel's will. Handel was well known in business circles; he had many friends in the financial world, some who assisted him in the investment of his capital. Here it might be said that Handel was capable of dealing with the business fraternity on equal terms and (despite popular tradition) he was never bankrupt or anywhere near it.

The particular letter to Michaelsen to which I have referred throws light on one major and one minor facet of personality. Taking the latter first, we have a reference to the value of the niece's 'good education' as an assurance of happiness. Handel apparently was progressive with regard to the higher education of women. And then we come upon his affection for family connexions. He, like Johnson, respected his mother—even though he seldom saw her. 'Her memory', he records, 'will always stay by me, until we are united after this life, which I hope the Good God may grant us through His mercy.' But piety did not stop with reverence for the dead. There were the living to consider. 'I see from the accounts you sent that Frau Händelin, who lives in the house, pays 6 *Reichstaler* a year rent; I would like her in future not to pay anything and she can stay there as long as she likes.'

It is surely this loyalty to the family which affects the domestic equations in the operas and the oratorios. Drama with Handel more often than not centred round commitments and pleasures which conflict or appear to conflict with family duty. In *Admeto* matrimonial complications, through absence on active service, in *Hercules* wifely jealousy, in *Samson* and *Deidamia* paternal love and pride are subtly and marvellously delineated. This eminent humane skill principally distinguishes Handel from his lesser contemporaries. He wrote not only with more certainty of style, but also with conviction about the thing he most valued: human relationships.

And here lies the enigma and the paradox. Handel loved children
—Mary Granville, with the wisdom of ten years of age, appreciated
this—but had none of his own. He admired, respected, and loved
women, but he never married. He loved his art too well not to love
life also, and the pious asseveration that he sacrificed All for Art will
not bear scrutiny in the face of Swift's reported aside, the rumours
which tied his name with those of Vittoria Tesi and Tarquini in
Italy, his dalliance in Hamburg with Mlle Sbülens, in London with
Strada and others, his affection for Mrs. Cibber, and his long
devotion to the estimable, attractive and affectionate Mrs. Delany.
The enigma and the paradox remain.

Handel was a many-sided genius and his friendship was bestowed
with appropriate generosity. Moreover, he had, as in family affairs, a
code of honour. Telemann and Mattheson maintained long contact
after the dispersal which followed their neighbourly studenthood.
Zachow was remembered after his death by means of a gracious act
of charity towards his widow. When in 1716 Handel went to Anspach
—he followed his old mentor Steffani some part of the diplomatic
way, for this was an unexpected tour, at the behest of the Princess
Caroline, in the character of a plenipotentiary—he came across
J. C. Schmidt. Schmidt, being poor, was transferred (as 'Smith'),
complete with family, to London as a permanent pensioner, and a useful one, in Handel's household.

Generosity stirred Handel both publicly and privately. To the
unrecorded acts of charity we have the moving testimonial of the
memorialist: 'he was liberal even when he was poor, and remembered
his former friends when he was rich'. The Foundling Hospital, the
Decayed Musicians, the Dublin charities which reaped rich harvests
from Handel's generous intentions, reveal the composer as a
citizen to be honoured by the side of General Oglethorpe, Captain
Coram, Henry Fielding, and many others in the van of social welfare
who made their generation not ignoble in respect of humanitarian
zeal. Once again Handel the man and Handel the musician integrate:
the Foundling Hospital Anthem demonstrates by its text a moral
purpose, just as the Funeral Anthem enshrines the character of a
friend and a queen in a particular manner. The second part of
Solomon directly springs from the building of the Foundling Hospital
chapel. *Messiah* itself, if one accepts the story of the commission
to produce an *ad hoc* work for the Dubliners (and I think the evidence
just sufficient), contains apt and frequent textual hints as to the
nature of the charities embraced in the directors' general scheme. In

performance of *Messiah* such relevance (and the musical philosophy of the age was towards 'reality') warms our reading of the score and our interpretation.

A study of the circle of Handel's English friends yields one more significant musical point. Handel, like Haydn (only in greater degree), was what Dr. Einstein calls an 'open-air' composer. Handel is master of the pastoral style. He falls into the English lyrical tradition of the pastoral poets and echoes what his contemporaries, such as Dyer, Matthew Green, and Collins, were trying to achieve. The music of *L'Allegro*, of *Susanna*, of the superbly impressionistic nightingale chorus of *Solomon*, is not only the music of a man paying decorous lip service to the pastoral deities: it is the music of one who knew the countryside in intimate detail. The sights, the sounds, the people are all there. Handel the metropolitan is but one aspect, to which we may return after consideration of Handel in rustication. We find him, from time to time, taking the waters with the fashionable and the valetudinarians at Tunbridge Wells, at Bath, at Cheltenham; in Wiltshire with the Harrises; in Kent with Wyndham Knatchbull; in Leicestershire with the faithful, industrious, opinionated, and long-suffering Jennens; in Cheshire with Colonel Legh; near Stafford with the Littletons and at Calwich in the same county with Bernard Granville. Here, in country sacred to the shades of Walton, Rousseau, Tom Moore, and George Eliot, he was within half an hour (by horse) of Johnson's home from home at Dr. Taylor's lovely house in Ashbourne. We add to the English peregrination a visit to Ireland and, legend has it, one to Wales. We may remark that ears as well as eyes were continually open so that Handel may be discovered transcribing Irish folk-melodies and imitating the pattern in his lost *Forest Music*, while on the Welsh side there is a connexion between the movement 'Happy we' from *Acis and Galatea* and the traditional song, 'Codiad yr haul'. *Acis and Galatea* dates from the days at Cannons, when among the occasional employees of the princely Chandos was to be found the harper Powell.

The biographer must find the contrasts, the inconsistencies, the frequent antitheses which constitute character. Handel was personally richer in contrast than almost any Englishman of his generation. Not being English by birth, he had obvious cause to examine the conditions of the country of his adoption.

The spirit of England is frequently taken to be the spirit of London; and the spirit of London, just because it is in some mysterious way the spirit of England, is best appreciated by those who are not Londoners: Dunbar, Shakespeare, Johnson, Handel—strangers all. Handel left imperishable monuments to the memory of a city which he loved. There are his pageant music, his *desipere in loco* orchestral music, and his oratorios. These latter are at once metropolitan in thought but, equally, national in significance. The green fields, the sights of the country are there; the city crowds; the governors of the realm; the aspirations of a proud nation (read 'England' for 'Israel') approaching imperial power and prestige and high commercial prosperity. All these facets of the Georgian outlook on life are sublimely represented by one who saw the fierce dignity of Parliament and heard its spacious orators, who applauded the Erastian Church with its wise latitudinarianism, and approved the familiar and sometimes tragi-comic place in society of the naturalized (or shall we say nationalized?) Hanoverian monarchy.

London was essentially a city which would appeal to Handel. It retained sufficient of its ancient character to attract a sentimentalist. It was in possession of new buildings which demonstrated the strength of combined wealth and taste; St. Paul's, a favourite resort of Handel, was completed in the year in which he first came to England. The city had open spaces which enticed rich and poor to nightly entertainment. The coloured lights of Vauxhall, of Ranelagh, of Marylebone contrasted with the dim-lit thoroughfares of the city and gave that mystery and pageantry to life without which the spirit is starved. Handel loved the physical face of London. He attended service at St. Paul's and found congenial company at the Queen's Arms. Often his music was to be heard in the Cathedral, and the manner in which he followed Purcell's example with the *Birthday Ode* and the Utrecht *Te Deum* showed early in his career how thoroughly he understood the appropriate qualities of English Church-cum-State ceremonial. There were other churches which Handel frequented. He went to St. Martin-in-the-Fields, built by James Gibbs in 1725, to hear Kelway at the organ, and to St. George's in Hanover Square. This church, by John James, a pupil of Gibbs, was Handel's parish church, and here he attended to his private devotions.

It may be convenient at this point to advert to Handel's religious beliefs, so far as we can penetrate them. We should understand that the Bach (religious)-Handel (secular) antithesis is based on half-truths and misconceptions regarding the substance as opposed to the shadow of religious thought. Handel would appear to have had an affection for the institution of the Church, whether Lutheran,

Calvinist, Roman, or Anglican; this, in view of his early environment and his education in the theological atmosphere of the new University of Halle, is not surprising. He had no wish to be a Church musician, largely because he preferred to be independent of the enclosed *musical* routine and the narrow interests of the clergy. He prided himself on knowledge of the Bible and declined to accept the Bishop of London's choice of words for the Coronation Anthems. Handel had many friends in orders—in Rome he resisted their attempts at proselytization—and was inevitably *au fait* with orders of procedure. This has nothing to do with the religious sense. It is not to the point that he had the capacity for realizing the best in the rival creeds. The beauty and imaginative mystery of Rome found expression in Roman church music; the strong tragic sense of the German Protestant is apparent in climactic moments in the setting of Brockes' *Passion* (a work which attracted Bach), in *Saul*, in *Israel in Egypt*, in *Messiah*, and elsewhere. We notice that the divinity of Christ seldom appears, whereas the humanity of Christ does; that erring mortals are contemplated with vast sympathy and with some consciousness of the inexorability of supernatural agents. The treatment of *Saul* is Hardyesque; the emphasis is on the unfair weighting of the scales against mankind. The *via dolorosa* in Handel's thought is a human way. Each of us makes his individual way to his separate Calvary. The greatness of God (and Handel subscribed to the conventional findings of theology only as a criterion by which he might assess his own judgement) finds exalted expression often enough, but in the manner of the Establishment. In the great choruses Handel feels with his fellows and speaks for them: in the recitatives and arias he speaks for himself. Handel believed in justification by works. He befriended the poor and—here there is analogy with Johnson—took the orphan into his house. He loved his fellow men.

This man of religion—and any great humanitarian must be a man of religion—was also a man of the world. His music was the man and is still the best token of his essential personality. Therefore we must remark that part of his output which belonged to the atmosphere of Vauxhall—the atmosphere so charmingly described by Fanny Burney in *Evelina*. Tyers, the proprietor of the Gardens, appreciated the impetus which *concerti grossi*, airs from the 'favourite' operas and oratorios and many specimens of miscellaneous balladry afforded to his profits and had the master

plac'd marmoric in the vocal grove.

B

The statue which presided over the love-feasts of Vauxhall was by Roubiliac, who also designed the Handel monument in Westminster Abbey. Handel was often to be seen at Vauxhall himself. Like Hogarth and others of distinction he had his particular and embossed ticket of admission, bearing the symbol of an Arion bestride a dolphin. Leisure—and Handel was inclined to rigorous separation of work and pleasure—was often spent in contemplative strolls in Hyde Park or Marylebone Gardens. At Marylebone he would, in old age, sit with Mr. Fontayne discussing the merits, or, rather—in Handel's view—the demerits of *Judas Maccabaeus* and, probably, watching the new pastime of cricket.

Outwardly Handel possessed all those qualities, later to be decried as bourgeois, which gave grace and dignity to the middle classes. By birth he was a member of this stratum of society, and he chose to live in a city where it was possible for his peers to retain both spiritual and economic independence. Democracy is a term both overworked and misunderstood: one either lives democratically or fails to perceive the significance of that way of life. Handel had excellent opportunities for examining the strength of English society at those celebrated evenings in 1710 which were spent in the comprehensive circle of Thomas Britton. This mutual-improvement society, with its array of peers and peeresses, justices and civil servants, merchants and artists, natives and aliens, was unique in the Europe of those days (as, unfortunately, it would probably be to-day), and the conclusion may be drawn that the possibilities of wide camaraderie were instrumental in engaging Handel's affection for the English. Pepusch, it will be remembered, felt very much as did Handel about residence here. He had left Germany through hatred of, and evidence of, tyranny. Hawkins reported Handel's observation that in England it was possible for a man to hold to whatever religious views he pleased without fear of molestation. This is a statement of significance.

Handel appreciated a man (or a woman) for his own sake and maintained throughout life a noble independence of sectarianism and chauvinism. He admired, personally, Whigs and Tories alike; Catholics, Anglicans, Dissenters, and Jews. He moved as an equal with princes and nobles and with commoners. He treated his royal clients with firmness, with kindness or with humour, according to the warrant of the occasion. He stood higher than kings when, by the natural right of innate affection for children, he stroked the head of the infant who was to become George III, observing that he was a good boy and prophesying that he would, as indeed he did through all the vicissitudes of long kingship, protect the reputation of Mr. Handel. It may be observed that court associations directly infected the music. In addition to the obvious examples, we may glimpse the varied pageantry of royalty and satellite nobility in the represented courts of Belshazzar and Solomon. The former holds a moral; the latter a principle. On the one hand we have a reproof against dissipation, on the other a grave salutation to the monarchic doctrine. Handel, the patriot, did his part for the House of Hanover in 1745 by applying his talent to direct propaganda. Purcell and Lully had previously helped in the apotheosis of autocracy, but Handel was perhaps the first composer to show kings as other men. Unconsciously, Handel obeyed Aristotelean canon: he made likenesses 'true to life and yet more beautiful'.

Thus we can commemorate Handel as man and musician, the musician being the voice of the man. We recollect a citizen conscious of the obligations of citizenship; a prudent administrator of his own considerable estate and, perpetually, generous; a philosopher who, as Leigh Hunt observed, was at home both with pagan and Christian teaching—'for the beauties of all religions find room in his heart'; an exemplar of tolerance; an heroic battler against the odds of cerebral thrombosis and consequent blindness; a protagonist in the cause of amelioration of the most dismal conditions of human welfare. 'He was', and we may conclude by stretching his vast character beside Johnson's,

steady and inflexible in maintaining the obligations of religion and morality; both from a regard for the order of society, and from a veneration for the GREAT SOURCE of all order; correct, nay stern in his taste; hard to please and easily offended; impetuous and irritable in his temper, but of a most humane and benevolent heart, which showed itself not only in a most liberal charity, as far as his circumstances would allow, but in a thousand instances of active benevolence . . . a man whose talents, acquirements, and virtues were so extraordinary, that the more his character is considered, the more he will be regarded by the present age, and by posterity, with admiration and reverence.

CHAPTER II

THE OPERAS

By Edward J. Dent

Of all Handel's works, his operas, nearly fifty in number, are the least accessible to the modern musician. Those which have survived have been printed in full score by the German Handel Society under the editorship of Chrysander, but this edition is hardly to be found anywhere now except in a few public libraries. A small number have been printed in vocal score in Germany, but these editions are not always trustworthy, and some have only a German version of the original Italian words. Since 1920 a good many have been put on the stage in Germany, where for a few years there was a sudden craze for them; but the fashion was short-lived and hardly penetrated to other countries. Even in Germany they soon reverted to the status of museum pieces, revived only at special Handel festivals of more or less academic character. None of them has ever come to be regarded as belonging to the standard repertory, like the well-known operas of Gluck, or has even been cherished as a national classic, like *Dido and Aeneas* in England.

There are many reasons for this lack of practical interest in them. The standard operatic repertory of the present day, even if we accept it at its widest, taking into consideration the operas commonly performed during the present century in France, Germany, and Italy, is historically based almost exclusively on principles that are French and German by origin. This may sound strange to admirers of Verdi and Puccini, but even those two owed much to Wagner and still more to Meyerbeer and Massenet, not so obviously in such details as melody, harmony, orchestration, and methods of musical continuity as in general construction, both of libretto and music. The standard repertory begins with Gluck, and from Gluck onwards the line is continuous throughout all French opera. Romantic opera in all three countries arose out of the mixture of elements from French *grand-opéra* or *tragédie lyrique* and French *opéra-comique*; we can trace this influence even in such apparently nationalistic works as *Maritana*, *Halka*, and *The Bartered Bride*. The last opera in which we can trace some sense of continuity with the Italian operas of Handel's period is *Semiramide*, and even that shows French principles, first in its derivation from a drama of Voltaire, and secondly in the building up of its great ensembles and in its copious employment of the ballet. The older Italian opera, the *dramma per musica* or *opera seria*, originating with Cavalli and his librettist, Busenello, ending with Metastasio and the innumerable composers who set his librettos to music, was killed by the *opera buffa* or *dramma giocoso* in the Italian theatres both of Italy and elsewhere. Wherever there was opera in the native language, French *opéra-comique* became the dominating influence, and eventually Italy herself yielded to it. *Lucrezia Borgia* and *Rigoletto*, to name two of the most typical Italian romantic operas, are based on plays of Victor Hugo, and contain many elements of French comic opera.

The comic element had always been conspicuous even in the most sumptuous of the seventeenth-century Venetian operas, but as the librettists came more and more under the influence of Racine, it was first reduced to the limitations of *intermezzi* and then finally eliminated altogether. At the time Handel began to write for the Italian stage, *intermezzi* were being freely transferred from one opera to another, according to the requirements of the particular theatre. This system of comic *intermezzi* has been often misunderstood by musical historians. The presence of comic servants in the older Venetian operas is not in itself any more absurd or inartistic than their presence in Shakespeare's plays. If we remember that it was not until the middle of the eighteenth century that the curtain fell at the end of each act, these *intermezzi*, in which the two comic characters have a little scene all to themselves, always at the ends of the first and second acts, and just before the end of the third, are analogous to the dances and comic turns between the acts in the English theatre (cf. *The Knight of the Burning Pestle*), and could be regarded as things quite apart from the main drama, like any entr'acte music or even a visit to the bar. We may note that there are comic *intermezzi* after the Italian manner in Addison's English imitation of an Italian opera, *Rosamond*; but by the time Handel's first Italian opera came out in London audiences apparently did not want them, as they probably could not appreciate the natural Italian humour of them. Nor did they want the sort of comedy-operas which Alessandro Scarlatti had composed in his early days, mostly for performances in private, as, for instance, in the Roman palace of Queen Christina of Sweden, based not on ancient history or medieval romance, but on

Spanish comedies. London wanted the heroic alone, and it was only in later life that Handel made experiments in comedy.

The most distinguished librettists of Handel's period were Apostolo Zeno (writing, 1695–1734), Pietro Pariati, who often collaborated with Zeno (1706–34), and Pietro Metastasio (1724–52). All three spent many years of their lives at Vienna in the service of Charles VI and Maria Theresa. Handel, living first at Hamburg and later in London, had no direct contact with any of them, and was always at the mercy of minor literary hacks who had no interest in raising the whole level of operatic drama, as these three had, but merely manufactured opera-books for commercial use by 'altering' the librettos of earlier writers. Zeno, Pariati, and Metastasio, even in Vienna, had patrons and audiences who could appreciate their merits; Hamburg and London enjoyed no princely subsidies for opera and depended on the box-office alone. Italian opera there was neither a courtly nor a native entertainment, and in Handel's Hamburg days the librettos were adapted by Germans from Italian originals, set to music by Germans and sung in a mixture of both languages, often with recitatives in German and arias in Italian. London also had tried a mixture of languages, but soon gave it up for Italian alone, whereas Hamburg did eventually settle down to opera in German. Several of Handel's London Italian operas were performed in Hamburg in German translations.

The Venetian opera of the seventeenth century was overcrowded with both incidents and characters; its arias were numerous and mostly short; the eighteenth-century type established by Zeno and perfected by Metastasio had fewer incidents, fewer characters, and fewer songs, and the result of that was that the separate songs all became much longer, and entirely new musical forms were invented for them. This is the period of the extended *da capo* aria, the horror of modern audiences and the delight of our ancestors. We can trace the whole history of this change in the operas of Alessandro Scarlatti, who seems to have been the chief standardizer of the *da capo* form. But the longest *da capo* arias of Scarlatti in his latest operas are not nearly so long as those of his followers, such as Leo, Pergolesi, and Hasse, and his early ones, belonging to the period before 1700, are shorter still; one hardly notices the *da capo*—it is nothing more than a pleasing return to the first strain after a short contrasting one. The *da capo* aria before 1700 is merely one among many quite different musical forms.

The standardization of the aria fits in quite naturally with the standardization of the dramatic form. It is true that this arose not solely from a purification of literary style; we may feel sure that it coincided with an intenser interest in virtuoso singers. The ever-increasing admiration of the virtuoso in the post-Scarlattian period must certainly have been the cause of the lengthening of the arias, but for Scarlatti's own time (about 1680–1720) it is rash to distinguish between causes and effects. Adoration of the virtuoso is at all times an artistic evil, but we cannot justly say that of the composer's desire to extend the range of his purely musical forms.

Compared with the librettos of the modern repertory, those of Zeno and Metastasio may well seem absurdly formal. They deal with classical and heroic subjects drawn from sources often quite unfamiliar to modern audiences. The background may be historical, but the plots are curiously complicated, although there is very little action or incident. Disguises, often including women disguised as men, are frequent, and the motives of conduct often seem to us utterly improbable, especially as they are expressed in very formal language liberally seasoned with dramatic irony. The story of the play is told entirely in *recitativo secco*; the arias each concentrate on the expression of one single emotion. The characters, whatever their names may be, never seem to be real persons with a possible existence outside the opera, like Don Giovanni, Rigoletto, or Falstaff; they are merely puppets going through a series of emotional experiences— love, hatred, jealousy, ambition, suffering, triumph. One might perhaps say the same thing of the characters in *Così fan tutte*, but these are at least the sort of men and women whom we might meet in ordinary life, or might have met in the life of their period. Characterization of this kind was possible only after the development of comic opera. Another defect is that there is never any dramatic movement, physical or psychological, within a musical number; this again was not possible before comic opera had created its technique. The whole drama is in the recitative, which is barely different from speech; the arias, and even the few ensembles, are completely static. We can approach Handel's operas only by accepting these conventions.

There is yet another convention which we must accept, and it is perhaps the hardest of all—the employment of *castrati* for the leading male parts. We cannot enter here into discussion of the moral and social aspects of this problem; it is difficult enough for us of today to understand why our ancestors liked to associate the noblest heroes of antiquity with high soprano voices, relegating

tenors and baritones to subordinate parts, and basses to those of
tyrants or sages. The Handelian *castrato* cannot be ignored, and in
modern revivals of Handel's operas it is generally fatal to give his
parts to tenors or baritones to sing an octave lower. Nor was the
adoration of him confined to the Handelian age; Mozart wrote for
castrati—equally irreplaceable—in *Idomeneo* and *La Clemenza di
Tito*. Rossini openly deplored the abolition of the *castrati*, and
during the first quarter of the nineteenth century many heroic male
parts were written for soprano or contralto voices in Italy, although
we have the evidence of the librettos that they were sung by women.
A leading soprano like Pasta always claimed in her contracts the parts
of *primo uomo* as well as those of *prima donna*. The mezzo-soprano
in male parts went on still longer, as in *Lucrezia Borgia* (Orsini),
Rienzi (Adriano), and *Faust* (Siebel); and *Der Rosenkavalier* positively
reverts to Handelian practice with a soprano hero, tenors and a
baritone in secondary parts only, and a bass who is an expanded
Polyphemus. In the early years of the Italian opera in London male
soprano parts were sung by women when *castrati* were not available;
they were never transposed for men, and such a transposition would
have been unthinkable throughout almost the whole century.[1] I can
only offer the suggestion that the male soprano voice bore some resemblance to the sound of the trumpet, which was always associated
with heroism, and was also an instrument of outstanding virtuosity
in the time of Scarlatti, Handel and Bach.

Handel's first contact with opera began at Hamburg, where he
joined the theatre orchestra as a violinist in 1703. The operas of
Keiser, partly in German, partly in Italian, were naturally his model
for *Almira* (1705), the libretto of which was a bilingual adaptation
by Feustking of an Italian one of earlier date, itself probably based
on a Spanish play, as the scene is laid in Spain in the days of the
Moors. The story begins with Almira being crowned Queen of
Castile. Her previous guardian, Consalvo, Prince of Segovia, gives
her a letter from her deceased father, instructing her to marry one of
Consalvo's family. She is secretly in love with her secretary,
Fernando, a young man of unknown origin who is equally in love
with her, but too modest to reveal the fact. Needless to say, he is
discovered at the end to be the long-lost son of Consalvo. As in all
the operas of the period, the drama results from a perpetual series

---

[1] Gluck's transposition of the part of Orpheus for Paris may be cited as an
exception, but in this case the transposition was from contralto to tenor, sometimes
a fifth lower, sometimes less, never a whole octave.

of understatements and misunderstandings, because every character acts at once on impulse without ever asking for explanations, let alone listening to them or using elementary common sense as a basis of action, such a thing being quite incompatible with the exalted principles of chivalry.

Almira differs from the usual Venetian type of libretto in having a good deal of dance music. Ballets were often part of an Italian operatic evening, but they were not integral to the opera and were generally danced to music by some other composer, probably to French music. It is curious to observe that Alessandro Scarlatti, a supreme master of the aria, seems utterly out of his element on the rare occasions when he writes dance music. Handel, on the contrary, is at home in it from the very beginning. He must have been well acquainted with French dance music and the whole French instrumental style before he went to Hamburg. Keiser was equally at home in it, and we notice too that the libretto of *Almira* uses French words in the course of its stage directions, e.g. (Act III, Scene 9) 'in der Ferne der Almiren *maison de plaisance*'. Another curious episode in *Almira* occurs at the beginning of Act III, which opens with a masque of the continents Europe, Africa, and Asia, represented by three of the male characters, with suites of dancers. The famous air in *Rinaldo*, 'Lascia ch'io pianga', comes in here as a dance of Asiatics. Keiser's own operas are an extraordinary jumble of all styles and effects, French, Italian, and German. He does not appear to have gone in for the elaborate scenic effects of the Venetians, probably not having the necessary machinery, but made up for it by every other resource that he could muster.

The recitatives of *Almira* are in German, and Handel sets them in a purely German style, using melodic outlines that to a modern reader suggest Bach's cantatas rather than Italian opera. Nor can we expect to find a truly Handelian style in the songs, some of which are in German and some in Italian. Handel is not likely to have had any great acquaintance with Italian opera scores at this period of his life. What is at once obvious is that he approaches composition as a violinist with a quite definite style of violin-playing, energetic rather than elegant or sentimental. The example from Act III on p. 18 is much more appropriate to the violin than to any human voice.

The general style of *Almira* is undistinguished, as one might expect from so inexperienced a composer with no very distinguished models to follow. Young Handel, like many Germans, tended to

think instrumentally rather than vocally; in his arias an over-
elaborated violoncello part often diverts too much attention from
the melody of the voice. Keiser, like all Germans, delights in showy
songs with trumpets or hunting horns; the Italians used trumpets
often enough, but horns are rare, and when they do appear they are
treated very differently. Handel naturally imitates Keiser, and this
is no doubt the reason why horns play such a large part in most of
his operas and in many of the oratorios too.

Ex.1

It is unfortunate that Handel's *Nero* is lost, for it would have
been interesting to compare it with Keiser's *Octavia*,[1] a setting of
the same libretto, composed after Handel's opera as a challenge to
Handel's success. It has often been said that Handel borrowed
copiously from *Octavia* in some of his later works,[2] but the resemblances quoted are really quite insignificant and amount to nothing
more than the use of a bar or two of instrumental figure, associated
with a vocal line that is entirely different. Handel undoubtedly
learned much from Keiser, but it is absurd to suggest that he
'borrowed' from him. It is necessary to emphasize this, because
Handel's undoubted 'borrowings' of a much later date have tempted
some researchers to suggest that Handel was a systematic 'borrower'
throughout his life, whereas he was no more indebted to Keiser than
Schubert was to Beethoven or Beethoven to Handel himself.

It is a complete change from *Almira* to *Rodrigo* (1707), an opera
about which we have very little information. It is supposed to
have been composed for performance at Florence, but the details of
date and place of performance are still an unsolved mystery. The
score is incomplete, and we cannot even be certain that *Rodrigo* was
its proper title. Librettos which have been remodelled are difficult

[1] Published as Supplement No. 6 to the Händel-Gesellschaft edition.

[2] Cf. Max Seiffert's Preface to *Octavia*; also Sedley Taylor, *The Indebtedness of
Handel to Works by other Composers* (Cambridge, 1906), pp. 167–71.

to trace to their origins, because although Handel's operas as a rule take their titles from the principal character, the earlier librettos very often have titles of a quite different kind, such as *L'infedeltà fedele* or *Gl'inganni felici*—to take names at haphazard without reference to Handel. A critical study of Italian librettos between 1650 and 1750 would require a lifetime of research. We can classify them roughly according to subjects—mythology, classical antiquity, later Roman Empire, which includes the history of Persia and Armenia, &c., as well as early medieval history; subjects taken directly from Ariosto and Tasso form a class by themselves, and there is further a class taken from Spanish sources, probably from Spanish drama rather than from purely historical sources such as were utilized by Gibbon. We have also to consider librettos from the point of view of dramatic construction, for no librettist ever troubled himself about historical accuracy. All librettos turn mainly on the two motives of *la gloire* and *l'amour*, political or military ambition and the various aspects of love. Here the moral atmosphere becomes interesting and varies at different periods. It is not necessary to pass ethical judgements on these dramas, and it is difficult to believe that Handel—as Leichtentritt and Dr. Percy Young seem to suggest[1]—deliberately chose librettos which exalted conjugal fidelity, thereby anticipating Beethoven, whose attitude to music was always that of a moralist. We have no evidence at all to show whether Handel discussed his operas with his poets (as he certainly discussed *Judas Maccabaeus* with Dr. Morell), or whether he simply took whatever they provided. Letters of the poet Paolo Rolli[2] tell us that he found Handel very difficult to deal with, but he never suggests that Handel collaborated with him, or against him, as Mozart did with Varesco and Da Ponte.

The music of Handel's day is so remote from us that it seems entirely devoid of that erotic quality which modern audiences easily find in Wagner or Richard Strauss; but we have some contemporary evidence that in Italy at any rate the arias of the seventeenth century were regarded as lascivious, and the sensuality of Italian poetry at that period has been remarked on by many critics of literature. A reaction towards a severer morality came later with Zeno and Metastasio, along with the trend towards a more dignified literary style and a firmer dramatic construction. The libretto of Keiser's

---

[1] See p. 5.

[2] R. A. Streatfeild, 'Handel, Rolli and Italian Opera in London in the Eighteenth Century', *The Musical Quarterly*, July, 1917.

Octavia has a sultry atmosphere; love is almost always physical desire in haste for immediate satisfaction. The German adapter may perhaps have made this plainer than in the Italian original. The gradual change of both moral atmosphere and literary style seems to be due to a preference for French rather than for Spanish models; in earlier librettos there is often a pronounced element of comedy from which humour is by no means excluded, whereas in the eighteenth century *opera seria* is rigidly heroic.

Handel's earlier librettos are interesting to analyse just because they are not new dramas written for music, like those of Metastasio, but adaptations, often of previous adaptations, and present curious vestigial traces of earlier dramatic methods.

Rodrigo, as far as one can judge, is a strong, dramatic libretto written in a good literary style. It has an unusually large amount of *recitativo secco*, the music of which runs fluently and easily in a definitely Italian manner; we may almost wonder whether Handel, at that date, was capable of composing it himself, for it shows no German traces. The songs are mostly taken from *Almira*. The background is Spanish. Rodrigo is the usual tyrant, in this case described as a lascivious one; he has a faithful wife, Esilena, who is all patience, devotion, and self-sacrifice—a common operatic type, ready to commit suicide in every act for the benefit of someone who has treated her abominably. Florinda is the energetic type of lady, thirsting for vengeance, since Rodrigo has seduced her and she has borne him a child. Such situations would never occur in Metastasio. Since it is a fundamental rule that all operas must have a happy end, Rodrigo finally returns to his wife, who has been forgiving him all the way through, and Florinda is married off to another character, the enemy captive prince, who is bursting with chivalry.

The next opera, *Agrippina* (Venice, 1709), was the making of Handel's fame. The libretto was by Cardinal Vincenzo Grimani; it is remarkably well written in a very clear style which studiously avoids poetic conceits and involutions, though its formalities of construction may well cause the modern reader to smile. The outstanding figures are Agrippina, wife of the Emperor Claudius, who is determined to secure the throne for her own son, Nero, and Poppea, the courtesan who is pursued by all the male characters and plays off one against the other. Agrippina has two courtiers, Pallante and Narciso, who are both in love with her; she merely utilizes them both to serve her own political ends, and they invariably appear one immediately after the other in strict and very comical symmetry.

Eventually they discover Agrippina's duplicity and agree to combine forces. The whole drama bears a certain resemblance to that of *Octavia*; there is no lady with any sort of noble sentiments, and Ottone, who eventually marries Poppea, is the only male with any approach to them. The Emperor is for the most part a mere puppet, and spends his spare time in running after Poppea. There is an amusing scene at the beginning of Act III where Poppea receives Ottone, hides him on the entrance of Nero, and hides Nero on the entrance of Claudio. The conversations which take place are almost unintelligible, as one never knows whether Poppea is telling the truth or not. The learned Cardinal must certainly have approached his task with a sense of humour, for at the end Claudio first tries to get matters settled by giving Poppea as wife to Nero and the succession to Ottone, to which Nero replies:

> Ubbidiente io sono alle tue voglie,
> Ma doppio mio castigo
> È il togliermi l'impero e darmi moglie.

Juno comes down from heaven to bless the nuptials, but there is only one happy pair (Ottone and Poppea) instead of the two, or even three, which are united at the end of most operas.

Agrippina was written mainly under the influence of Alessandro Scarlatti,[1] and it is therefore interesting to see how far Handel, at this period, was able to assert a style of his own. We can note at once a more vigorous handling of the orchestra than is common in Scarlatti, who even as late as this still seems to have regarded the violins as dangerously noisy. Handel is much less afraid of them, and he evidently writes as a practised violinist himself. We shall see in many later operas that Handel is more at home with the violin than with the voice, and that he is accustomed to a much more energetic and vigorous style of violin-playing than that of Corelli. The famous episode of his rudeness to Corelli at the rehearsal of *Il Trionfo del Tempo* is a further proof of this. The following example is not unlike Scarlatti, but the violin writing is much more forceful, and there is much more strength about the whole harmonic structure than we find in Scarlatti. It is not that Scarlatti's harmony is weak, still less unskilful, but his inspiration is more vocal and he regards the instruments as subordinate to the voice. Handel by comparison seems aggressive and sometimes almost brutal in his energy.

---

[1] On the relationship between *Agrippina* and the oratorio *La Resurrezione*, see p. 72.

Ex.2

A more striking anticipation of later Handelian effects occurs in the introduction to a song for Agrippina—'Pensieri, voi mi tormentate'— during which she comes on to the stage very cautiously, before making arrangements for three murders:

Ex.3

With *Rinaldo*, his first opera for London, both Handel and his manager were determined to startle their audiences. The libretto by G. Rossi is said to have been based on a scenario by Aaron Hill, the story being taken from Tasso. Armida's magical powers are exerted to the full, and provide abundant opportunity for scenic effects in the Venetian style. The libretto is inclined to literary affectations, but is generally clear, though undistinguished. It is evident that Rossi was instructed to keep recitative down to the barest minimum, as the English audience did not understand it. Paolo Rolli's letters tell us the same story. The only extended scenes of recitative are those of quick, dramatic dialogue in which the singers could show energetic delivery even if their words were unintelligible. Streatfeild justly makes fun of the Paynim chief Argante, who is made to enter with a bass song in Handel's most energetic style (taken from the Italian cantata, *Aci, Galatea e Polifemo*[1]) to words about Alecto's snakes and Scylla's barking, both of which are treated descriptively in the orchestra.

The arias of this period fall into three main classes. The best in every way are always those which express a direct personal emotion of the character, especially when they are addressed to another character on the stage. A less satisfactory type is the 'sententious' aria, the words of which make a general philosophical statement in the form of an aphorism or epigram. In *The Beggar's Opera*, Gay often makes this type very pointed and witty, but in the Italian operas such words are seldom other than pompous or merely flat. From a dramatic point of view, the worst of all are the arias based on a simile (also amusingly caricatured by Gay); this was a comparatively new type in Handel's time. It appears just at the moment when arias begin to lengthen considerably and to exhibit a great deal of conventional coloratura; the result is showy and effective for the singer, and sometimes for an instrumental soloist as well, but it is often completely unsuitable to the dramatic situation.

Another operatic convention, observed regularly in Handel's time and traceable even before 1700, is that after singing an aria the singer must immediately leave the stage. This often leads to surprisingly sudden departures when one would expect the character to stay and talk to the lady for whom he has just energetically protested his love. This convention and various others are generally attributed to the writers of librettos, but it is obvious that they must have been forced on both poets and composers by the vanity of the singers, for whom their own applause was the only thing that mattered. An equally absurd convention was forced upon composers of the following century in order that all great arias, as far as possible, should be in the form of soliloquies, even if another character had to go out and come back again after the aria when common sense would have kept him on the stage the whole time.

Rinaldo contains various famous items, including the march with four trumpets borrowed in *The Beggar's Opera*. At the revival of

[1] See pp. 133–4.

Rinaldo in 1731 this march was omitted and another one substituted; one wonders whether the original march had become too much associated with Gay's highwaymen, or whether four trumpets were too expensive a luxury—the substituted march has one only. There is also another march, in B flat, which is curiously Purcellian in style, both for its melody and its rhythmical irregularities. As it is a march for the Paynims, it may have been an attempt at local colour.

Handel's next three operas, *Il Pastor Fido* (1712), *Teseo* (1713) and *Silla* (1714), are all rather experimental. *Il Pastor Fido* is more in the style of Scarlatti's early comedy operas; Handel's librettist, Giacomo Rossi, reduced Guarini's famous play so drastically that very little of its poetry is left, and Rossi's own arias contrast very awkwardly with the exquisite sixteenth-century language of Guarini. The music is mostly a *pasticcio* from previous works. Some of the arias are more like chamber-cantatas, and the maturity of the instrumental style suggests that the long overture was originally a concerto. Several of these early operas contain instrumental music in the concerto style, with conspicuous solos for single instruments, and many of the arias have obbligato parts which almost look as if they had been composed before the vocal line which adapts itself to that of the instrument.

Teseo is the only one of Handel's operas in five acts, and this suggests that it was adapted from a Venetian libretto by Girolamo Frigimelica-Roberti, author of two operas by Alessandro Scarlatti performed at Venice in Handel's time, both in five acts, as indeed are others by the same poet, who seems to have been the only librettist of his period who preferred five acts to three. The dialogue was obviously much cut down and the story is very confused. It turns mainly on the contrast between two types of female, the malignant sorceress and the virtuous wife or maiden; the same contrast appears in other operas of Handel.

Silla, which was possibly performed privately, is of little importance, so far as can be judged from a very fragmentary score.

Another opera of sorcery and magic is *Amadigi* (1715), in which more signs of the mature Handel begin to appear. We can still see the Scarlattian tendency to accompany many arias with the harpsichord alone, or with little additional instrumentation. The second act opens with a curious scene in which Amadigi is discovered alone in an enchanted cave, looking into a magical well from which he may learn whether his lady love is true to him or not. His aria,

'Susurrate, onde vezzose', has a descriptive accompaniment for strings and flutes, one of Handel's new experiments in instrumental effect. Here is the introduction:

Ex.4

In the water he sees a vision of the lady caressing his rival, on which he faints and goes into a trance. Handel's treatment of this is Scarlattian and curious to read, as there is nothing in the score but the figured bass. It shows clearly what is evident in all Handel's early works, a habit of thinking upwards from the bass rather than downwards from the melody, strange as it may seem to us of today.[1]

Ex.5

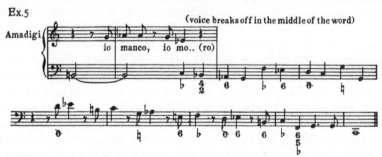

Five years intervened between *Amadigi* and Handel's next opera, *Radamisto* (1720), during which Handel's personal style came to maturity. There is very little change to be observed during the rest of his career, though he gradually achieved a more satisfactory balance between vocal and instrumental expression. He never adopted the new methods of the younger Neapolitans, such as Vinci, Leo, and Pergolesi; his music and theirs seem to belong to two entirely separate periods. If we compare an average aria of Handel in common time with one by Pergolesi, we shall find that for Handel the main harmonic time-unit is the quaver, whereas for Pergolesi it

[1] See also p. 269.

c

is more likely to be the minim. Naturally, there is a certain common ground of crotchets; Handel's eight quavers of moving bass sometimes carry no more than four harmonies. Pergolesi's minims are generally split up into four repeated quavers. But there can be no mistake about Handel's insistence on movement in the bass or about Pergolesi's tendency towards stagnation—the tendency of the whole 'classical' period of the eighteenth century. Handel treats all his upper instruments in the concerto style. All his overtures and many of his other 'symphonies' in the course of an opera are based on the concerto style, and it is the fundamental system of many of his arias, anthems, and oratorio choruses, as well as of his instrumental works. This is, of course, the clear line of demarcation between the whole age of Handel and the age of Haydn and Mozart; the basic form for the first is the *concerto-fugato* or, as some writers call it, ritornello form, that of the second 'sonata-form' derived from the Neapolitan operatic aria. The newer developments in the technique of orchestration are quite clearly the result of this change in both texture and structure.

Radamisto has the advantage of an unusually strong and well-designed libretto, published as the work of Niccolò Haym, but most probably adapted by him from an earlier source. It has no effects of magic and demands no scenery beyond what in those days would have been common operatic stock. The motives of the plot, as with most operas of the period, are confined to politics and love, though the hero and heroine are an already married couple, which is comparatively rare, and the villain is a married man too, though he treats his wife very badly. Handel seems to have taken unusual trouble with this work, with the result that his London audience found it rather beyond their comprehension. The first act begins at once with a startling effect; after an introduction for strings in unison and octaves, Polissena, the deserted wife of Tiridate the tyrant, enters with the following phrase unaccompanied:

Ex.6 *Largo*

Som - mi   De - i,

The arias in this opera are mostly on a large scale, with long introductions; the orchestration is much more elaborate than in any of Handel's previous works for the stage. Handel's arias for bass voices are always magnificent, even when the strings are mostly in unison with the voice. He almost always gives the bass voice the real bass of the harmony, if there is any, but it is a splendidly melodious

bass. Towards the end of Act I in this opera, Farasmane, the old
gentleman of the cast, has a fine song in which he invariably sings the
real bass, but accompanied with contrapuntal parts for strings
above; obviously the bass part must have been conceived first. The
technique of composition throughout the opera is most accomplished. In Act II there is a short and pathetic air for Zenobia, the
devoted wife of Radamisto, with a contrasting part for the oboe,
always in melodious counterpoint with the singer, no less beautiful
and expressive than the vocal line, but never standing in the way of
it. Zenobia throws herself into a river to escape from the persecution
of Tiridate, but is rescued and brought back to the stage a little later
in furious indignation, as she fears that she has been captured by one
of his minions. Her aria, 'Già che morir non posso', is an early
example of an air in binary form with two well-defined subjects.
The introduction, although apparently derived from the first vocal
phrase, looks as if it had been conceived first as an instrumental one.
It has itself three contrasting themes, each of which is subsequently
used separately with the voice, or by the voice too:

Figure *a* is introductory; figure *b* is used as an intermediate
ritornello, and does not come into the voice part until just at the
end, when it is played by the strings in unison and octaves, making
a great final climax, as in a concerto. Figure *c* is used only in the
second part of the song on which follows the *da capo*; it alternates
with the vocal phrases in *concertante* style, contrasting with them,
not accompanying them like a figure in a song of Schubert.

A song for Fraarte, a subsidiary character, shows the weakness of
the operatic convention. It is one of Handel's charming songs in
12/8, a style derived from Alessandro Scarlatti which he kept up
all his life; but it is quite inappropriate to both the character and the
dramatic situation. Fraarte had a right to a song, and Handel obliges

him with a very pleasing one which shows him off attractively, but the music is suggested merely by the opening words 'vaga e bella', which are really intended to be ironical. In most of Handel's operas the songs for the secondary characters are conventional concessions to the singer. Tiridate, who is passionately in love with Zenobia, offers her his kingdom in a fine aria, but operatic etiquette obliges him to leave the stage before she can make any reply. Radamisto manages to return to Zenobia in disguise, and they are left alone together to end the act with a rapturous duet. The resemblance of this scene to the similar situation in *Fidelio* has naturally been made the most of by modern German critics.

In Act III Tiridate, who, to do him justice, genuinely believes that Radamisto is dead, makes a formal proposal of marriage to Zenobia, offering her crown and sceptre as visible and tangible guarantees of good faith. As she refuses him with indignation, he prepares to resort to rape, but is prevented by the simultaneous entrance of several other characters. Polissena addresses her 'ungrateful spouse', accompanied by a very long and over-elaborate violin solo on the grandest scale—an error of judgement comparable to Mozart's 'Martern aller Arten'. Husband and wife are again left alone, and here we meet Handel's first example of a 'simile' song about a ship in a storm. Needless to say, the opera comes to a happy end, with forgiveness all round and an unusually long *coro*, i.e. a final ensemble for all the characters in block harmony to a brisk minuet with alternating passages in thirds for the two married couples.

For his next three operas Handel reverted to a much simpler and more obviously attractive style. *Muzio Scevola* (1721) is of little importance, as only the third act was composed by Handel. The libretto is by P. A. Rolli; it was his first attempt at an opera, and he was not very skilful in technique. Rolli also provided the libretto for *Floridante* (1721), the plot of which is less aggressively heroic than *Radamisto* and approaches more to the Spanish comedy style, although there is a prison scene with a cup of poison rather like that in Addison's *Rosamond*. Rolli was a man of literary ability; he eventually translated *Paradise Lost* into Italian verse. His dialogue is in good, clear Italian, but literary rather than dramatic, and he is not very expert in managing his entrances and exits. Handel's arias are very Scarlattian, but all very agreeable; the accompaniments are of the lightest, but admirable as regards style. There is a remarkable scene in Act II, where the heroine, Elmira, is waiting in a dark chamber for the approach of her lover. Both Streatfeild and Leichtentritt have pointed out the resemblance to Agathe's scena in *Der Freischütz*, but Handel's *arioso* and recitative, followed by a return to the *arioso*, very much in Scarlatti's manner, is far less pretentious than Weber's scena, and for that reason more dramatic; it is a masterly example of effect secured by the very simplest means.

The music of *Ottone* (1723) is mostly conventional, but effective. The gavotte which concludes the overture is one of the most familiar popular tunes of Handel. The libretto is an adaptation by Haym; the story is very confused, but supplies dramatic situations. The language is involved and obscure in the extreme, and the words of some of the songs are almost unconstruable. The characters are well drawn by Handel, especially the three women: Teofane, the usual suffering heroine, Matilda, something of an Amazon, and Gismonda, the intriguing mother of the villain. The most obviously effective songs are those for Emireno, the pirate who is eventually discovered to be the lost brother of the Princess Teofane (like the brigand chief in Lesueur's romantic opera, *La Caverne*); he is one of Handel's rollicking basses, and his first song, 'Del minacciar del vento', has always been a favourite with concert singers.

Haym was again responsible for *Flavio* (1723), a clumsily constructed libretto in very stilted language; the plot, which is amusing and sometimes quite definitely comic, seems to be taken from a Spanish source, as it turns on a 'point of honour'—a box on the ear given by one privy councillor to another. Both seem to be elderly gentlemen, as they are bass and tenor respectively. Politics have no part in this opera. Flavio, King of the Longobards, is a comparatively unimportant character; the intrigue turns on the love affairs of the son and daughters of the two councillors, whose quarrel puts one pair of lovers in a difficult position. The opening scene sets a rather Spanish atmosphere; the other pair of lovers are seen coming out of a house into a garden at night, and we are left in some doubt as to whether they are secretly married or not. Lotario, the aggressive councillor, is killed in a duel by the son of his rival; his daughter, who is in love with the young man, finds her father dead, and Leichtentritt at once points out the obvious resemblance to *Don Giovanni*.

These accidental resemblances to later well-known operas must be viewed with caution; such episodes occur in a great many old plays and operas, and we must not jump to the conclusion that Handel saw them with the eyes of a modern audience which has acquired an

exaggeratedly romantic view of Mozart, Beethoven, and Weber.
Handel in fact takes the story of Flavio quite light-heartedly, and the
libretto itself presents more similarity to a comedy of Goldoni
than to a heroic drama of Metastasio. There is nothing very notable
about the music, but it is all very agreeable and attractive.

Giulio Cesare (1724) has in recent years attained a certain notoriety
through frequent revivals in Germany, but the English reader must
be warned that the modern German vocal score is not by any means
reliable. The plot deals with Caesar's intrigue with Cleopatra, now
fairly well known to English readers through Bernard Shaw's play,
but there is little resemblance between that play and Handel's opera.
The libretto is ascribed to Niccolò Haym, but Haym probably
adapted it from some older version, possibly from G. F. Bussani's
Giulio Cesare in Egitto, first set by Antonio Sartorio for Venice
(1677), and used again by various composers from 1735 onwards.
Haym's libretto, like most of those set by Handel, shows signs of
having been much compressed. The best parts are those of Cleopatra and Cornelia, the long-suffering widow of Pompey; the male
parts are very conventional. It is during this middle period of
Handel's operatic career that we find so many long and elaborate
airs for *castrati*, especially for those with a contralto range. As a rule
they are utterly conventional in style and utterly undramatic,
especially when the singer compares himself to something or other,
and still more so when he utters some general statement in the
guise of a simile. These 'simile' airs always offered Handel great
opportunities for descriptive music in the orchestra and original
effects of orchestration, but they are nothing but concert pieces and
contribute nothing to the drama, as they express no sort of personal
emotion. A characteristic example is Caesar's 'Va tacito e nascosto'
in Act I.[1] Caesar, well aware of Ptolemy's intention to have him
assassinated at a banquet, observes that a hunter stalking his prey
conceals himself in silence; but as the word 'hunter' inevitably suggests a horn, Handel turns the song into a great display of virtuosity
for a solo horn-player. German stage managers expend all their
ingenuity in arranging some pantomimic illustration of this idea
among the numerous supers at the back of the stage, while Caesar
himself can do nothing but stand still and sing to the audience.
This opera has several outstanding scenes, such as Caesar's apo-
strophe to the murdered Pompey and Cleopatra's vision of Parnassus,
but on the whole the music is very conventional. The libretto supplies

[1] See p. 186.

plenty of rapid action, attempted murders, and sudden rescues, and also violent declarations of love, sometimes verging on rape. These effects point to an early Venetian original. Ptolemy's directness almost recalls that of Osmond in *King Arthur*:

> But if you will not fairly be enjoy'd,
> A little honest force is well employ'd.

Tamerlano (1724) is another adaptation by Haym from a Venetian libretto by Agostino Piovene, first set in 1710. Tamerlane, like Ptolemy, is the passionate barbarian who settles everything in a hurry without scruple. The finest part is that of Bajazet, the imprisoned Sultan, sung by a tenor (Borosini), which was something of a novelty, as tenors in those days were seldom employed except in minor parts, such as old men. Bajazet is in fact an old man, but his part is the most interesting in the whole drama. Some of his airs are almost in the style of Bach; the first of them, 'Forte e lieto a morte andrei',[1] exhibits a type of *coloratura* which is expressive rather than showy, more instrumental than vocal:

Ex. 8

con più va-lor

In Act II he has an intensely expressive air in a similar Bach-like style, 'A suoi piedi padre esangue',[2] depicting his heroic struggle against age and infirmity, and later in the act he takes part in a very dramatic trio. This style is fundamentally derived from Alessandro Scarlatti; the well-known air 'Cara tomba' from *Mitridate Eupatore*, which Handel no doubt heard in Venice, is the original model for it, as we can see clearly in the air of Asteria (Bajazet's daughter) in Act III, 'Cor di padre',[3] where it is amplified in the grandest Handelian style, and entirely free from virtuosity. We shall find that in all these operas of Handel's 'heroic' period the airs for the women are generally much finer and more seriously expressive than those for the men. Streatfeild points out that Handel, despite his celibacy, had an acute understanding of female character; but there is a more obvious and less romantic reason for this apparent devotion to the fair sex. The male characters, apart from occasional tenors, of whom

[1] There is a separate reprint in W. G. Whittaker's series of 'Arias from the Operas of G. F. Handel', published by the Oxford University Press, No. 27.
[2] No. 31 of Whittaker's series.
[3] No. 33 of Whittaker's series.

we shall meet others later, were either *castrati* or basses. The famous
castrati, such as Senesino, Farinelli, and Carestini, inclined more to
elaborate virtuosity than to dramatic expression as a rule, and the
basses were always given blustering songs in which they sang the
real bass of the harmony. Most of Handel's famous bass songs were
written for Boschi, who, as Pope tells us, was expected to be 'always
in a rage'. In that particular style they were no doubt magnificent,
but the style had its expressive limitations. However, the contralto
hero in *Tamerlano*, Andronico, is given a share in a beautiful and
pathetic duet with Asteria in Act III, Scarlattian again in method,
but completely Handelian in its elaboration. Just before the end of
the opera, Bajazet has a magnificent *scena*—after taking poison—
with a fine accompanied recitative and the famous air 'Figlia mia
non pianger, nò',[1] probably the first great scene of its kind ever
written for a tenor. It is followed at once by Asteria's tragic air,
'Padre amato'. Apart from these outstanding moments, *Tamerlano*
is a more than usually confused libretto, and none the clearer for a
large proportion of *secco* recitative.

The libretto of *Rodelinda* is said by Dr. Loewenberg to have been
adapted from a *Rodelinda* by Antonio Salvi, set by Perti for Pratolino
(the private theatre of Ferdinando de' Medici near Florence) in
1710, but unless inspection of that libretto proves him right, it seems
more probable that Handel's version, made by Haym, was derived
from a *Flavio Bertarido* by Stefano Ghigi, set by C. F. Pollarolo for
Venice in 1706, as the names of the characters are almost completely
identical. It is written in the usual Venetian style, much overbur-
dened with conceits and affectations, but clearer and more dramatic
than most. The plot is well constructed and there are fewer of the
usual operatic absurdities. The secondary parts are very conventional
but Rodelinda herself is well drawn and consistent, Grimoaldo the
typical operatic villain and usurper, and in that character thoroughly
effective. This opera has appealed very strongly to modern German
producers and critics because they find in it a resemblance to
Fidelio; Rodelinda, Queen of the Lombards, has been dispossessed
by Grimoaldo, and her husband, supposed at first to be dead, is
finally rescued by her from a dungeon. Rodelinda is the typical
suffering female and faithful wife; she is contrasted with Edvige,
her sister-in-law, who is the resolute and courageous young woman
determined to see her faithless lover (Grimoaldo) grovel at her
feet.

[1] No. 35 of Whittaker's series.

The music of *Rodelinda* is generally on a high level and shows a
sense of character, apart from a few airs of the 'simile' type which
are inevitably undramatic and sometimes inappropriate to the characters who sing them, because the style of the music is dictated by the
simile and not by the personality. Many such airs of Handel have
become favourites in the concert-room, and when taken out of their
context they can be enjoyed on their purely musical merits; but we
shall often find that airs of Handel which seem uninteresting in
themselves have a dramatic value in a complete opera by virtue of
their contrast with what precedes or follows them.

In modern performance the absence of *castrati* places Grimoaldo
at some disadvantage. Pollarolo in 1706 made Grimoaldo a *castrato*
part, and there are plenty of precedents for *castrato* usurpers, either
soprano or contralto; but the modern system makes him the principal
tenor, and to modern audiences it is unthinkable that a tenor should
be a villain, perhaps because villainy involves some intelligence.
In most of these old operas the only characters who show the
slightest ability to reason are the villains. Tyrants and usurpers are
now expected to be basses, and a tenor Grimoaldo, aping the rages of
Boschi in a higher register, often makes himself completely ridiculous.

The libretto of *Scipione* (1726)[1] is by P. A. Rolli after Apostolo
Zeno's *Scipione nella Spagna*, first set by Caldara at Vienna in 1710.
It has no connexion with Alessandro Scarlatti's opera of the same
name (Naples, 1714); the characters, apart from Scipio, are entirely
different. Handel's opera is remembered by the famous march, which
follows directly on the overture and opens the first act. As a whole,
the opera is dull and conventional, though there are some fine
moments for Berenice, the heroine, who belongs to the 'noble
captive' type. It is curious to note how during this period Handel still
sticks closely to the early Scarlattian style, full of short anapaestic
phrases, which the younger school of Naples had by now discarded.

Ex. 9

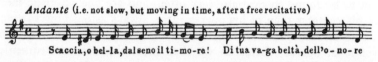

Andante (i.e. not slow, but moving in time, after a free recitative)

Scaccia,o bel-la,dal seno il ti-mo-ra! Di tua va-ga beltà,dell'o- no- re

[1] *Scipione* was revived in 1730, with the original alto title part rewritten for tenor,
that of Lelio (tenor) for an alto. On the differences between the two versions, and
the third in the Granville collection, and on the discrepancies between scores and
libretti, see R. A. Streatfeild, 'The Granville Collection of Handel MSS.' in
The Musical Antiquary for July, 1911, pp. 213-6.—*Ed.*

But Handel extends them, and he has a much stronger sense of harmony than Scarlatti, with a more frequent use of sequences. He provides too a more solid orchestral background when he needs it, but to the modern reader, familiar with Handel's opera songs only through those which are still sung at concerts, it is surprising to find how many are accompanied by the figured bass and nothing else.

Scipione must have been produced with some pageantry; at the beginning of Act II, Ernando, Berenice's father, arrives in a ship and disembarks to a symphony in the usual overture form with a good *fugato* in triple counterpoint. Berenice's air in the next scene, 'Com' onda incalza altr' onda', starts as a rather conventional song in 12/8, though always melodious and beautiful, but eventually passes through some very unexpected modulations:

Ex. 10

These modulations are typically Scarlattian, although they are not to be found in Scarlatti very often, and are characteristic more of his cantatas than of his operas. It is always astonishing to come across inspirations of this sort in the middle of otherwise very conventional operas. Later on we shall meet them more frequently, though they come as sudden flashes; one thinks of them as utterly un-Handelian, and yet no other composer of his time, not even Bach, could ever have conceived them.

The libretto of *Alessandro* (1726) seems to have been an original work of Paolo Rolli, and a most incompetent work too; its only merit is that it is written in simple and easy language without the usual conceits and inversions. Rolli provides a good many stage effects, one of them quite ludicrous, but he had no sense of drama. Streatfeild points out that this was the opera in which Faustina made her *début* in London, and says that 'the dramatic interest of the work is largely sacrificed to the necessity of keeping the balance even between her and Cuzzoni'. The two ladies, Rossane and Lisaura, are in fact both in love with Alexander. In Act III Rossane does her best to make friends with her rival, but Lisaura is not quite so amiable. Their recitative reads as if it was a deliberate jest of Rolli's at the pretensions of the rival singers:

> *Lis.* La resa libertà dunque, oh Rossane,
> A lasciarne t'alletta?
> E chi t'adora abbandonar potrai?

> *Ros.* Lasciam, Lisaura vaga,
> Le gelosie, l' insidie e gli artifici.
> Amiam del pari il vincitor del mondo.
> Sia d'Alessandro il core
> Conquista di chi avrà di noi più sorte
> In costanza amorosa e in vero amore.

> *Lis.* In generoso vanto vincermi tenti in vano.
> Si, l'eroe vittorioso amiam del pari;
> Sia più felice uno dei nostri affetti,
> Ma sian ambo egualmente illustri e rari.

As in many of Handel's operas, there is a good deal of fighting, and the assault and capture of a city with all the engines of war and a chorus of soldiers which includes sopranos and altos as well as tenors and basses. The absurd scene referred to above occurs in Act II. Alexander, seated on a throne under a canopy, divides his conquests between different generals. He calls himself the son of Jove, at which Clito, a Macedonian leader, is very sarcastic; he thanks him as son of Philip, but suggests that he is not much concerned about his mother's honour. (This sort of talk rather suggests an earlier Venetian model.) Alexander takes a spear to attack Clito, but Tassile, King of India, prevents him, and at this moment the canopy of the throne suddenly falls down 'per cospirazione', according to the stage direction. Alexander promptly ascribes his escape to a miracle of his divine parent. The canopy, alluded to as 'ruinosa mole', was evidently something heavy enough to have killed Alexander if he had not left his throne and stood up to attack Clito.

The best things in the otherwise conventional operas of this period, in which Handel was obliged to write for famous singers, are the little *ariosi* without *da capo* which occur at the beginnings of scenes (the word 'scene' is used here in the Continental sense); airs at the ends of scenes, after which the singer almost invariably left the stage, are on the full scale, and those at the ends of acts larger still. These *ariosi* are noticeably Scarlattian, and so are the accompanied recitatives, though Handel generally improves on his model. Here is an admirable example, sung by Rossane in Act I. Notice the introduction, and the curious crossings of the string parts, which add greatly to the effect. The repeat of the words at the end is typically Scarlattian (see opposite).

Admeto (1727) is supposed to be an adaptation by either Haym or Rolli from a much earlier opera called *L'Antigona delusa da Alceste*, first performed at Venice in 1660 (words by Aurelio Aureli, music by P. A. Ziani) and revived often elsewhere. This seems probable, as Antigona is a character in Handel's opera, though she does not come into Euripides' version of the story. The reader of Handel's operas who expects their plots to bear some resemblance to the lives of the heroes of antiquity after whom they are called will soon be disillusioned. It would be difficult to find a formula for all of them, but their system of intrigue is very much the same. The only novelty about *Admeto* is the introduction of an elaborate ballet in Act I. The plot may be summarized here as a specimen of how classical legend was habitually treated.

After a vigorous but conventional overture, we see Admetus lying ill and tormented by visions of furies. This is a really fine scene, with a beautiful recitative and air for Admetus. Orindo announces that Hercules has arrived and wishes to call upon Admetus; he further informs him that his brother Trasimede is in love with the portrait of an unknown lady. Hercules pays a polite visit to thank Admetus for his hospitality, and says that he is going off in search of further adventures. Admetus goes to sleep. Alcestis enters and is told by the voice of Apollo that Admetus must die unless someone dies for him. She makes up her mind to die for her husband, and takes a pathetic farewell of him in a most touching and beautiful song. The scene now changes to a wood. Antigona, a princess of Troy reduced to poverty after the siege, enters disguised as a shepherdess, along with Meraspe, her faithful old retainer, in similar dress. She is very indignant at having been deserted by Admetus, and regards his illness as a punishment from the gods. She tells

Ex. II

Vi-li-pe - se bel-lez-ze, lu - singhe disprez-za-te, ar-mi in-u-ti-li sie-te per vincer l'in-co-stanza. Voi mi deste spe-ran-za d'in-ca-te-nar so-lo per me quel co-re. Va - na speran-za, oh de-i! Voi mi man-ca-te, vi-li - pe - se bel-lez-ze, lu-singhe disprezza-te!

Meraspe to pass her off as his daughter in order to gain admission to the palace. Alcestis makes a short appearance to take leave of her women and goes out again; Admetus comes on with Hercules; he is now quite well again since Alcestis has made her sacrifice. Hercules congratulates him, but a mysterious voice is heard saying, 'O barbaro destino!' and Orindo comes out to say that Alcestis is dead. The scene opens showing her dead, with a dagger in her hand. She has left a letter which Admetus reads. He asks Hercules to go down to Hades and fetch her back; Hercules says he will do his best.

We now return to the wood. So far Handel is reasonably close to Euripides, but now the real business of the opera begins. Meraspe tells Antigona that Alcestis has committed suicide for some reason unknown, and that Admetus is restored to health. Now that he is a widower, he will no doubt be ready to marry Antigona. Enter Trasimede with a chorus of huntsmen, contemplating the mysterious portrait. He at once recognizes Antigona as the original, but she denies it and says she is a mere peasant girl, Rosilda by name. Trasimede at once engages her as a lady gardener, singing (to a gorgeous accompaniment of horns, oboes, and strings) that Diana must have come to earth in human form. Antigona ends the act with a hard and brilliant air; she is strongly contrasted with the tender and gentle Alcestis.

Act II opens in Hades, where Alcestis is chained to a rock and tormented by furies. Handel opens with a regular overture and a chromatic *fugato*. Hercules comes down with Cerberus on a lead, attacks the furies with his club and releases Alcestis; the furies fly away through the air and the scene disappears. The next scene is a garden. Antigona has had no success with Admetus. Orindo makes love to her; she repulses him indignantly. Orindo in an amusing air tells her not to lose her temper. Trasimede now makes love to Antigona, and throws away the portrait, which Orindo secretly picks up. Antigona is equally disagreeable to Trasimede.

Orindo now informs Admetus and shows him the portrait. Admetus says at once that it cannot be Antigona, as she was far more beautiful. Admetus is still thinking of Alcestis and hoping that Hercules will bring her back, but Antigona enters with Meraspe. Trasimede during this scene is watching unknown to the others. Antigona presents herself to Admetus as the lady gardener, but tells him that she has seen Antigona at Troy, and that Trasimede is in love with Antigona. Admetus shows her the portrait, but she tries to make him believe that it represents another lady. Admetus asks her if Antigona is still alive; she replies by asking him if he would in that case marry her. Admetus is embarrassed, Antigona enraged. Meraspe asks her why she does not reveal herself; she can only reply with a beautiful, pathetic air in Handel's usual 12/8 style.

We return to Hercules and Alcestis, who has now had time to change her dress, and appears disguised as a warrior in armour. She has done this because she suspects that Admetus has started a new love-affair; she tells Hercules to say to him that he was unable to fetch her out of Hades. Admetus enters and soliloquizes; he is in the uncomfortable situation of being in love with two ladies, both of whom are dead. He thinks he had better die himself too. Antigona, very indignant, as usual, is brought in by soldiers at the command of Trasimede. A page brings him a portrait, which Trasimede has asked him to steal from the King's apartments. But the stupid lad has brought a portrait of Admetus, not of Antigona; Trasimede sends him back, and as he goes out he drops the portrait. Antigona picks it up and is very glad to have it. Alcestis now enters (as a warrior) and talks to Antigona; neither knows who the other is. Antigona tells the warrior of her love for Admetus in a very pretty song about a tremulous star, which gives her great opportunities for shakes. Alcestis ends the act with the usual aria on the grand scale.

In Act III Meraspe and Orindo call on Admetus. Meraspe is much upset at Antigona having been carried off by Trasimede, and reveals that the lady gardener is not the peasant girl, Rosilda, but Antigona herself. He has a very pleasant air in which he assures the King of her fidelity to him. Orindo has already told Admetus that Hercules has come back from Hades alone. Admetus comments rather tiresomely on the situation with an air about the tigress and the turtle-dove. Just as he is making his orthodox exit at the end of it, Hercules appears and tells him of his supposed failure. Admetus goes out without a word, and Hercules is much puzzled at his indifference. The scene changes to a piazza. Antigona is admiring the portrait of Admetus. Alcestis enters, very angry, and snatches it away from her. Orindo arrests Alcestis, imagining her (still disguised as a warrior) to be the man who carried off Antigona. Enter Hercules, very indignant at seeing Alcestis in chains, but careful not to say who she is. He tells her that if she goes to the palace she will find it only too true that Admetus is in love with another woman. At the palace Antigona tells Trasimede that she is going to marry his brother Admetus, and reveals her own identity. Trasimede is in despair. Admetus enters and announces that he is going to marry

Antigona that day; they sing a duet, mostly in thirds. Trasimede
tries to kill Admetus; Alcestis snatches the sword out of his hand,
and he runs away. Admetus calls Orindo to arrest Alcestis, imagining
her to be the man who attacked him. She reproaches him indignantly,
and he now recognizes her. Hercules enters, remarking 'opportuno
qui giungo'; Alcestis explains; Trasimede begs forgiveness. Alcestis
is much surprised to meet Antigona, who adroitly hands over
Admetus to his lawful wife with a great show of magnanimity.
Alcestis returns to her husband with a very graceful and tender air,
and the opera comes to an end with the usual chorus (i.e. an ensemble
of all the principals).

From a musical point of view, *Admeto* is one of the best of Handel's
Royal Academy period. It inevitably contains a good deal that is
conventional, and the conventionality naturally falls mostly to the
lot of the chief *castrato* part, here, of course, Admetus. The airs for
Hercules (Boschi) are also conventional, but the fact remains that
Handel's bass songs are just those which have remained popular
concert songs to the present day. Perhaps it is their very conventionality which has secured them this immortality. The reader
may have found this detailed analysis of the plot extremely tedious,
but it is a convenient way of exhibiting the various stock devices
which are common, in various permutations, to all Italian operas of
the pre-Metastasian age. It is interesting to contrast the whole
psychological outlook of Handel's *Admeto* with that of Rutland
Boughton's *Alkestis*, which is based strictly on Euripides.

Rolli considered the libretto of *Riccardo Primo* (1727) to be
'almost entirely' his own. It conforms to the usual type, however,
though the hand of Rolli is certainly apparent in King Richard's
address to the English army:

> O voi, che meco del Tamigi in riva,
> Patria di libertà, virtù, valore, nati,
> Siete alle imprese di giustizia ed onore:
> Seguite il vostro re.

There is not much of musical interest in this opera. It opens with
a curious representation of a storm at sea; the first operatic storm
is generally supposed to be that of *Alcione*, by Marin Marais (1706),
though there is a still earlier one in Colasse's *Thétis et Pélée* (1689),
and storms were a common feature of French operas, though not of
Italian. In Act II Pulcheria has an interesting air, 'L' aquila altera',
very skilfully accompanied by strings in three independent parts,

making four-part harmony of a contrapuntal type with the voice. There is also a fine duet at the end of the act, long and elaborate, as usual in that position. Act III has some showy airs, almost caricatures of Handel, and towards the end a remarkable recitative for Costanza, Richard's long-suffering bride. Boschi had a great opportunity in this opera with raging bass songs.

With *Siroe* (1728) Handel made his first contact with Metastasio, although Haym cut down the dialogue ruthlessly for his London audience, thereby often ruining the drama. Nevertheless, *Siroe* still contains a good deal of *secco* recitative, and the *secco* scenes are extremely good, as Handel had really well-written dialogue to set to music. *Siroe* is an early work of Metastasio, his second libretto in fact, first set by Vinci for Venice in 1726. This was before Metastasio settled in Vienna as court poet, so that *Siroe* conforms more or less to the Venetian type of drama, more complicated and more violently exciting than those which he had to write for the ceremonial operas of the imperial court festivities. *Siroe* contains the usual two princesses, one faithful and long-suffering, the other disguised as a man and bursting for revenge, and both in love with the *castrato* hero. There are some good scenes of recrimination and irony almost verging on comedy. Handel's music is mainly conventional, but 'Mi lagnerò tacendo' is one of his famous songs and deserves its fame; Handel invariably ravishes us when he writes in 12/8 time. The bass part (Cosroe, father of Siroe) is pathetic rather than furious, and in Act III Cosroe has a most dramatic air of horror, 'Gelido in ogni vena'. We begin to notice in this opera a slight inclination towards a more modern style, such as had already made its appearance at Naples, where the methods of Alessandro Scarlatti were by this time completely out of date. But Handel remained faithful to Scarlatti all his life and hardly ever adopted the modern style, although he extended and amplified the style of Scarlatti in a way that is peculiarly his own. The Metastasians, as we might call them, for they all set Metastasio and hardly anyone else, are curiously alike in style; it is very difficult to tell one from another, at any rate in their serious operas. Handel stands entirely apart from them, and apart even from his own contemporaries.

The management of the Royal Academy was by this time in some difficulty, and after *Tolomeo* (1728) it came to an end. Its failure has generally been ascribed to the success of *The Beggar's Opera*, which came out in February 1728, but it is evident from Burney's account that the Italian Opera was on the decline before that. *Tolomeo* was also the last libretto written, or compiled, for Handel by Haym, who died in the following year. It is probably based on some earlier Venetian opera, but the original has not been traced. Recitative is reduced to the barest minimum; the opera is little more than a string of arias. The story is more than usually absurd and the management of entrances and exits often ludicrous. By far the best item is the overture, in which Handel makes very copious use of the horns, who have hardly a bar's rest in it. The *fugato* is based on an unusually long subject, elaborately developed, although for the sake of the horns it hardly ever leaves the key of F major. Most of the songs are dull and conventional, but there is a very charming air for Seleuce, Tolomeo's beloved, with flutes, and in Act III a most remarkable scene in which Tolomeo drinks poison and appears to die. Needless to say, he does not die, as he is the hero of the opera, but makes a very rapid recovery. After drinking, he sings a most expressive and dramatic aria in B flat minor, which has no *da capo* and breaks off abruptly as he collapses. It is difficult to estimate the exact length of Handel's operas, but *Tolomeo* appears to be unusually short.

Handel now started in management on his own account and opened his season in December 1729 with *Lotario*, based not on a libretto of Matteo Noris, as Burney says, but on Salvi's *Berengario*, which had been produced for the carnival of 1729 with music by Orlandini. The characters are the same as in Handel's opera, except that Lotario was originally called Ottone, and the London adapter, if not Handel himself, saw that this would lead to confusion with Handel's own *Ottone*, produced in 1723. We know that Handel was in Venice in March 1729, and if so, he probably heard Orlandini's opera, in which both Faustina and Senesino were singing; this may well have led him to secure a copy of the libretto for himself. For his London season he obtained new singers, who were not quite so famous as those of the Academy. Strada, the female soprano, he must have found at Naples; Bernacchi, the *castrato*, had sung in London in 1716–17, and was getting past his prime; Merighi, a woman contralto, he might have heard at Naples, and Bernacchi was singing there too at this time. Fabri, a tenor, was probably picked up at Bologna; he was an excellent musician and something of a composer. Mrs. Delany was charmed with him; 'he sings like a gentleman, without making faces, and his manner is particularly agreeable'. Bertolli, whose chief asset was her unusual beauty, was by way of singing male parts; she sang Ildeberto in *Lotario*, and a woman had sung the part at Venice.

It was hardly a brilliant cast, but it is necessary to name it here, because the engagement of these singers necessitated a considerable change in Handel's style, and also in his choice of librettos. Haym being dead, it is probable that Paolo Rolli was responsible for most of them; he stayed in England until 1744 and was the author of Handel's last opera, *Deidamia*. The libretto of *Lotario* (1729) is so much cut down as to be hardly more than a string of arias; the music on the whole is dull and conventional. There is, however, one magnificent character in it: Matilde, the wife of Berengario, and mother of Ildeberto. Handel is always at his best in depicting strong-minded and unscrupulous women, generally managing matriarchs. Streatfeild has pointed out that Storge in *Jephtha* is a typical 'heavy mother', but she is mild compared to those of the operas, generally the second consorts of kings, with sons by a previous husband whom they are determined at all costs to place on thrones. Matilde is secretly resolved that her son Ildeberto shall marry Adelaide, the dispossessed Queen of Italy, who is a prisoner in Berengario's hands, but her politics are so tortuous that her intrigues are very difficult to follow. She is nearly always in a towering rage, and one or two of her songs might almost have been written for Boschi. In Act II there is a dramatic prison scene for Adelaide, beginning with a noble air in B flat minor, 'Menti eterne che reggete'. Handel in these later operas shows a great partiality for B flat minor and its adjacent major keys; they had, of course, been used freely by Scarlatti. Clodomiro, an officer of Berengario, enters with two pages carrying covered basins; in one there is a dagger and a cup of poison, in the other a crown and sceptre. He offers Adelaide her choice, but on condition that she agrees to marry Ildeberto. She prefers dagger and poison, and starts on the latter, but is interrupted by Matilde, followed by Ildeberto. Matilde encourages her to drink the poison, but Ildeberto says that Matilde must slay him first. He demands the poison and then, while Adelaide is about to drink it, tries to stab himself, but Matilde prevents these simultaneous suicides by snatching away both dagger and poison and dashing them on the ground in a rage—a piece of stage business which must have required some rehearsal. Clodomiro re-enters to say that his army has been defeated and Berengario lost, on which Matilde makes a hasty exit, but not before singing a very sarcastic song at Ildeberto—'make love to her if you like, but she will only laugh at you!' This is a remarkably fine aria and admirably in character. Ildeberto and Adelaide are left alone together, and are so polite that the scene is quite ridiculous, especially as Ildeberto, of course, has to leave the stage as soon as he has sung his song. Adelaide follows with a dull 'simile' song to the effect that he is the disagreeable son of a disagreeable mother. After a series of violent and exciting scenes, Handel ingeniously ends the act with a song for Lotario which is in complete contrast, melodious, beautiful, and utterly tranquil. In Act III Matilde is driven to attempt suicide, but is prevented first by her son and again by Lotario, after a superb recitative, 'Furie del crudo Averno'.

With *Partenope* (1730) Handel breaks completely new ground. The libretto was originally written by Silvio Stampiglia and set by L. Manzo for Naples in 1699. It was altered for Venice in 1707 and was set by Caldara; for Venice the comic *intermezzi* indispensable at Naples were eliminated, though Caldara seems to have kept the comic bass, Beltrame, who does not appear in Handel's version. Beltrame must have been a *buffo*, as he was sung by G. B. Cavana, who sang in various Neapolitan operas round about 1700, including some by Scarlatti; he was often partnered by a tenor, Antonio Predieri, who appeared as a comic old woman. A Haymarket audience would hardly have appreciated that sort of humour; Mrs. Delany's comments on it might have amused a modern reader.

Stampiglia has generally found scant praise among the critics of musical drama, but *Partenope* is perhaps the best libretto that Handel ever had to set. It is a comedy opera, though not at all an *opera buffa*; it has nothing of the grand heroic style, and there is something quite Shakespearean about the atmosphere of it. Partenope is a Queen of Naples, courted by three suitors, Arsace, Prince of Corinth, Armindo, Prince of Rhodes, and Emilio, Prince of Cumae. The other female character is Rosmira, Princess of Cyprus, who has been deserted by Arsace and is now pursuing him in male disguise under the name of Eurimene. She combines passion with a considerable sense of humour and reminds us rather of Viola and Portia. Partenope herself is a delightful character, young, beautiful, and wayward, with a most exhilarating *joie de vivre*; she takes everything cheerfully, and when she becomes involved in a war she is at once ready to lead her troops into battle as an Amazon. In Act II there is a great deal of fighting, to the accompaniment of Handel's usual battle symphonies. This opera is an interesting hybrid between the Venetian heroic opera and the slighter type of opera, derived probably from Spanish comedy, which Scarlatti in his earlier period provided for more or less private entertainments.

The music is on a high level throughout. There are hardly any songs in that grand manner which Handel adopted for his previous constellation of stars; the style is simpler and much more concise, with frequent returns to the Scarlattian manner. The accompaniments are much more simple; Handel's English audiences always complained, as their descendants did of Wagner, that he drowned the voices with his noisy orchestra and his bewildering harmonies. From this period onwards we find more use of the chorus—though it is often difficult to guess whether the *coro* was sung by a full chorus, as would often be appropriate, or by the ensemble of the soloists, whose own personal names are generally mentioned in the score on these occasions, although for dramatic reasons one would not expect all of them to be on the stage together. There are also more trios and quartets, generally Scarlattian in style and very short.

Poro (1731) is adapted from Metastasio's *Alessandro nelle Indie*, first set by Vinci for Rome two years previously. Handel, having got rid of Bernacchi and secured Senesino in his place, with Montagnana for the bass parts, returns again to the grand manner. Most of the airs are rather conventional, and the two best are of that descriptive type which always inspired Handel to write solid music with novel and ingenious orchestration; but, as in the case of Julius Caesar's hunting song, they are utterly inappropriate to the drama.

Ezio (1732), another early drama of Metastasio, much reduced by Rolli, is a more than usually complicated and confused story of intrigue. The music is mostly rather conventional, but improves strikingly as the opera proceeds. But here again the drama suffers from too many 'simile' airs, even more so than its predecessor, *Poro*. As soon as one sees the word 'nocchiero' one knows at once what is coming; the steersman on a stormy sea is a stock feature of all these opera librettos. These airs cannot be excused as examples of the *Affektenlehre* much talked about by modern German critics, which simply amounts to the normal Handelian principle (and pre-Handelian too) of summing up the dramatic situation of a scene in a single song intended to express a single feeling such as grief, jealousy or courage. The 'simile' air never expresses the emotions of the character who sings it; it merely describes the external surroundings, and not even the feelings, of the object to which the singer compares himself. To the drama it is a perpetual obstruction, however admirable it may be as a mere piece of music.

Sosarme (1732) is another unsatisfactory opera, despite occasional moments. The libretto is said by Burney to have originally been called *Alfonso Primo*, a libretto which Dr. Loewenberg has identified as one by Matteo Noris set by Pollarolo, for Venice in 1694. Alfonso I was the first King of Portugal and died in 1185, and it may seem strange that he should have been converted into a King of Persia several centuries earlier. But Handel's autograph—which had been examined by Burney—shows that the first two acts were certainly composed to this libretto, or a later version of it. Handel calls the hero 'Fernando, Re di Castiglia', and the scene is laid at Coimbra. By the time Handel came to the third act, it was decided to change the names and site; Fernando became 'Sosarme, Re di Media', and the scene Sardis. These alterations are all in Handel's own hand. Why the change was made cannot be conjectured. Librettos of this period are so much alike in construction that it would make no appreciable difference.

Musically *Sosarme* is very unequal, but it has another of Handel's 'managing matriarchs', Erenice, whose airs are almost all of them admirably characteristic. There is also a duet for Elmira and Sosarme, 'Per le porte del tormento', which is singularly beautiful, though perhaps a little too long and too much in the duet-cantata style for its dramatic situation. In Act I occurs the famous song 'Rendi il seren al ciglio', and the *coro* at the end of the opera, a long barcarolle-like movement in 9/8, in *da capo* form, is a most unusual sort of conclusion, and also a fine piece of music. In this opera, and especially in the third act, we seem to see Handel trying to hurry the drama along in the arias, which are often short and terse, very much to the point; they may be quite uninteresting and commonplace considered by themselves as concert songs, but they have a distinct dramatic value for the sake of contrast with what precedes or follows.

The libretto of *Orlando* (1733) is another puzzle. It has been supposed to be derived from the *Orlando Furioso* of Grazio Braccioli, set first by G. A. Ristori for Venice in 1713 and later by Vivaldi and others; but the lists of characters do not agree. Braccioli's libretto brings in Bradamante, Alcina, and Astolfo, all important personages in Ariosto's epic, none of whom appears in Handel's version, and Handel brings in Zoroastro the magician, a most important personage, who does not come into the Venetian libretto and is never mentioned by Ariosto. All the same, it is a very good libretto, looking backwards to the older Venetian type of 'magical' opera and also forwards to the fairy plays (*fiabe*) of Carlo Gozzi, especially in its scenic effects. The moral aspect of this opera is interesting; the poet approaches his subject very much in the humorous spirit of Ariosto, almost in that of Voltaire. It is entirely different from the court operas of Zeno and Metastasio in its attitude towards love and chivalry. Orlando in his madness is rather like Don Quixote, half terrifying and half comic at the same time. Dorinda, the shepherdess, belongs to the pastoral convention, but she is never sentimental, like a shepherdess of Guarini or Tasso; she stands for frivolous common sense. Zoroastro anticipates Mozart's Sarastro, who is, of course, another incarnation of Zoroaster. Handel makes him impressive, especially in his opening scene, but cannot quite get away from the conventional style of an operatic *basso*. The libretto seems to assume in its audience some familiarity with Ariosto as a story-teller, and we must remember that even down to the present century it was customary for public readers to declaim Ariosto and Tasso aloud in the gardens of various Italian cities for the spontaneous enjoyment of quite humble people, many of whom probably could not read for themselves.

The overture, in the unusual key of F sharp minor, is full of character, though its *fugato* is not very fugal; it ends with a gigue, probably intended for a ballet of spirits on the rise of the curtain, which shows us Atlas on the summit of a mountain holding up the heavens on his shoulders. Zoroaster contemplates the stars and reads in them Orlando's destiny. Orlando enters, torn between glory and love; Zoroaster urges him to purge his heart of unmanly desires, and shows him the palace of Cupid, with the god enthroned and ancient heroes asleep at his feet. Orlando sings a song comparing himself to Hercules, richly scored with oboes and horns. The scene changes to a pastoral scene; Dorinda contrasts it with her own unhappiness, and asks, 'Can this be love?' There is a noise of fighting; Orlando rushes on with an unknown princess, whom he has rescued from her enemies. Dorinda recognizes him, but he has no time to talk to her and rushes out again for more fighting. Angelica enters in search of Orlando, but says she is in love with Medoro, who enters wounded. Dorinda has already had an affair with him and is very jealous at his pursuit of Angelica. She sings a charming gigue in a very original rhythm:

Ex. 12

Allegro

Oh ca-re pa-ro let-te, ohdol-ci sguar-di! Se
ben sie-te bu-giar-di, tan-to vi cre-de-rò.

Zoroaster warns Angelica of Orlando's jealousy; Orlando enters and makes love to her. Zoroaster, seeing Medoro approaching, causes a fountain to spring up, which conceals Medoro, and then changes the scene to a garden. Angelica tells Orlando to send away Isabella, the lady whom he has rescued (she has no part in the opera), if he wishes to obtain her own favours. He protests that he was nothing more than her rescuer, and sings a fine and very Handelian heroic aria. Angelica has a love-scene with Medoro which is interrupted by Dorinda. Angelica is quite open about it, and tries to pacify Dorinda by the gift of a jewel, which she regards as very inadequate. The act ends with a long and elaborate trio, rather in Scarlatti's manner, skilfully contrasting the sentiments of the characters, but developed in a typically Handelian style. It is a most charming and attractive movement and makes an admirable and musically beautiful conclusion of the act, completely true to the dramatic situation. It is the first example in Handel, or indeed in any opera of the period, so far as I am aware, of a trio as a finale to an act.

Act II begins with a nightingale song for Dorinda. She shows Orlando the jewel, which he recognizes as one which he once gave to Ziliante, another lady who does not appear at all in the opera. He is already beginning to go mad, thinks that Ziliante has betrayed him, and is furious with Angelica. The scene changes to a cave by the sea; Zoroaster warns Angelica and Medoro against the raving Orlando and promises to protect them. They decide to fly to the kingdom of Angelica's father, but before they can start Orlando appears and discovers their names cut in the bark of a tree. He pursues Angelica, and she is on the point of throwing herself into the sea when four genii carry her up into the air in a cloud. Orlando is now completely mad and has a remarkable *scena* in which he thinks he sees the boat of Charon and gets into it. Here occurs the famous passage in 5/8 time, but it is extremely short; there are only four bars of it altogether. It perhaps is intended to suggest a rather choppy crossing:

Ex. 13

This is followed by the aria *a tempo di gavotta*, 'Vaghe pupille', much broken up by contrasting moods of fury and grief, the main

theme recurring in rondo form. Orlando throws himself into the cave;
it explodes, and Zoroaster is seen to carry him off in a flying chariot.
It is conceivable that Handel was influenced in this scene by some of
Purcell's 'mad songs', as they were still sung at concerts in his day.
This ends the second act.

Act III begins with a short instrumental piece very much in the
manner of a Purcell act-tune. In his earlier operas Handel often
opens an act with instrumental music, but it is almost always a battle-
piece or a procession accompanying some visible movement on the
stage. It is only in these later operas that he tends more and more to
begin his second and third acts with a sort of act-tune, generally in
two repeated sections of about eight bars each, quite independent of
the stage business. They all have a distinctly Purcellian flavour.
Medoro, having lost Angelica, takes refuge with Dorinda, as previously agreed on by Angelica; they have an amusing little scene of
mild flirtation. Orlando now makes violent love to Dorinda, which
she is half inclined to accept, comparing the situation to that of
Jupiter and Leda. They sing a short and rather odd duet in contrasting styles; then Orlando breaks off and suddenly throws away
his helmet and sword, with another 'mad' song, again *a tempo di
gavotta*. Dorinda's shrewd comment is simply 'e vedo ben, che
amore è un grande imbroglio'.

Zoroaster appears with the genii and remarks to the audience,

> Impari ognun da Orlando
> Che sovente ragion si perde amando.

He orders the genii to change the scene to a horrid cavern and
wait in attendance; he will soon restore Orlando to sanity. This
gives him an opportunity for a great Handelian bass song. Angelica
and Dorinda are now in tears because Orlando has destroyed
Dorinda's *albergo*, as she calls her hut, and has buried Medoro under
the ruins. Orlando enters, madder than ever, and Angelica makes a
pathetic appeal to him, in a longish duet with strongly contrasted
phrases which are ingeniously combined in counterpoint. His only
reply is to seize her and throw her violently into the cavern, but it
suddenly changes to 'a most beautiful temple of Mars' in which
Angelica is seen sitting high up at the back, guarded by genii.
Orlando says that he has now rid the world of all its tyrants, and
wants to go to sleep, which he does after a short aria accompanied by
two *violette marine*, i.e. *viole d'amore*, played by the brothers Castrucci.

Zoroaster invokes Jupiter, who sends down an eagle with a cup of

a magical liquor, which Zoroaster throws on Orlando's face; all this
takes place to an instrumental symphony of thirty bars *pianissimo*,
after which Orlando awakes. According to the stage directions, he is
now sane, but his first act is to sing a short and exaggeratedly chivalrous air, after which he attempts suicide. Angelica prevents him,
telling him to live, in a phrase that might have been written by
Gluck, such is its touching simplicity:

Ex. 14

Orlando si muo-re! Deh, vi-ver an - co-ra, deh, vi-ver an-co- ra!

At this point a statue of Mars rises from below, with an altar on
which a fire is burning, and four little cupids fly about in the air.
Orlando makes a short speech, saying that he has conquered en-
chantments, battles, and monsters, and has now won a victory over
himself and over love; he gives Angelica and Medoro his good wishes
and leads off the usual finale, which in this case is a long bourrée,
very French in style.

It has been necessary to describe *Orlando* in some detail, as the
magical scenic effects are an essential feature of it. A concert performance of *Orlando* with neither scenery nor action would be a
disgraceful sacrilege.

Arianna (1734) is a lamentable falling-off after *Orlando*. The
libretto is ascribed to Francis Colman, but it is not known whether
he wrote it in Italian himself or had it translated, or whether he
merely adapted it from some older Italian libretto. Its language is
extremely obscure and it reads as if it had been a good deal cut down.
The minuet at the end of the overture was enormously popular in
the eighteenth century, and Streatfeild amusingly compares it with
the intermezzo from *Cavalleria rusticana*. At the present day it is
completely forgotten, and if any minuet of Handel's is now famous,
it is that from *Berenice*, which is far superior. The only outstanding
scene of *Arianna* is the dream of Theseus and his combat with the
Minotaur; otherwise the best one can say of the opera is that it is
generally good average Handel, of the conventional type.

Terpsicore, a ballet with songs, composed as a prelude to the
revival of *Il Pastor Fido* in 1734, is also disappointing, and even the
ballet music is not very distinguished.[1]

[1] See pp. 260–1.

The story of *Ariodante* (1735) is taken from Ariosto, and was freely adapted by Shakespeare in *Much Ado about Nothing*. It was first made into an opera by Antonio Salvi, whose *Ariodante*, set by Pollarolo for Venice in 1716, was adapted by Rolli for Handel's use. Salvi's libretto was used by various subsequent composers, often under the name of *Ginevra di Scozia*, and there are several operas on the same subject in the Romantic period, the most notable of which is Méhul's *Ariodant* (Paris, 1799). Handel's libretto is in this case thoroughly good, a dramatic story well planned for the stage and written in an exceptionally clear style.

The overture is remarkable for a long dance movement at the end, based on the same rhythm as the sailors' dance in *Dido and Aeneas*, and even ending with it:

Ex. 15

This dance is used later on at the end of the opera, as a long chorus and ballet. The whole opera shows considerable French influence, but the scene is laid in Scotland. Ginevra, the King's daughter, is betrothed to the knight, Ariodante, and her father approves cordially of the match. Ariodante, however, has a rival in Polinesso, Duke of Albany, whom she scorns. Polinesso arranges with her lady-in-waiting, Dalinda, who is more or less in love with him —in Ariosto she is his mistress—that she shall disguise herself as Ginevra and let him in at her window at night. Dalinda is admired by Ariodante's brother, Lurcanio, but repels his advances. The first act ends with a long ballet of nymphs and shepherds celebrating the betrothal of Ariodante and Ginevra. This scene is extremely pictur-esque and attractive as music.

The second act opens at night in the palace garden, where a secret door leads to Ginevra's apartments. Polinesso is on the watch, and a symphony of ten bars for strings, the melody rising through two octaves, seems to depict his excitement.[1] Ariodante enters, also much excited, but with pleasure, at the prospect of his marriage. Polinesso pretends to take it as a joke, and tells Ariodante that Ginevra has already granted her favours to himself. Ariodante is naturally furious, and challenges Polinesso to a duel, but Polinesso says he will furnish proof. Meanwhile, Lurcanio is secretly listening in the background. Polinesso knocks at the secret door; Dalinda,

---

[1] Burney, perhaps rightly, interprets it as the rising of the moon.

dressed as Ginevra, lets him in. Ariodante attempts suicide, but is
prevented by his brother, who tells him to live and punish the
traitor. After appropriate arias, they leave the stage, and there is a
short scene for Polinesso and Dalinda. The scene changes, and
Odoardo, a courtier, informs the King that Ariodante has thrown
himself into the sea; they next break the news to Ginevra, who faints
and is carried out. Lurcanio now presents himself. The King offers
condolences, but Lurcanio demands justice, and accuses Ginevra of
infidelity, on which the King collapses. Ginevra re-enters with
Dalinda, but she has by this time gone mad. The King refuses to see
her; Ginevra, like her compatriot Lucia di Lammermoor, has a
'mad scene', ending the act with a song which looks comparatively
simple for such a position, but could be made extremely touching
and pathetic if well sung.

In Act III Dalinda is rescued by Ariodante from two murderers
who have been hired by Polinesso to make away with her, and she
reveals the plot to him. In Ariosto's original story it is not Ariodante,
but Rinaldo, who rescues Dalinda and takes her to the best hotel in
St. Andrews;[1] Salvi compresses the action very adroitly, eliminating
Rinaldo altogether and making Ariodante appear instead—and much
more appropriately—as Ginevra's champion. Ginevra, according to
Scots law at that period, is to be burnt at the stake for unchastity,
unless some knight will prove her innocence in single combat.
(In Ariosto's version Rinaldo hears one true story from Dalinda,
who tells him quite openly that she herself had been Polinesso's
mistress, and Rinaldo at once sets off to champion Ginevra, because
he—or Ariosto—takes the view that it does not matter whether she
is chaste or not, so long as she is not found out; he asks in effect,
should there be one law for men and another for women? Leichtentritt, in his analysis of this opera, seizes, as one might foresee, on the
obvious resemblance to *Lohengrin*; but one may wonder whether
Lohengrin would have been as modernly tolerant and broadminded
as Rinaldo.)

The ordeal is set out with all ceremony. Lurcanio, who honestly
believes Ginevra to be guilty, appears as her accuser against Polinesso
as her defender, Polinesso hoping thereby to secure Ginevra in
marriage against her will and thus become heir to the throne.
Lurcanio kills Polinesso, who is carried out; he then offers to fight
another champion, and the old King says that if no other comes
forward he will fight himself. Ariodante, with vizor down, presents

[1] *Orlando Furioso*, canto V, stanzas 76, 79.

himself, but says he will not defend innocence with crime (i.e. fratricide). He raises his vizor and is recognized, to the great astonishment of everybody, as he was supposed to have been drowned. Here follow general explanations and rejoicings, but this is not the end of the opera. Dalinda and Lurcanio have to come to an understanding in considerable haste and not without some sense of humour; their duet has a delightful touch of comedy about it. Meanwhile, Ginevra is still in prison, where the rest bring her the good news and then leave her to a showy but very attractive duet with Ariodante. Finally, the scene changes again to a grand saloon, with a band of oboes and bassoons in a minstrels' gallery, and the opera concludes with an elaborate chorus and ballet.

Apart from one or two very conventional *castrato* arias of the type written for Senesino, the music is all on a distinguished level, and few operas of Handel exhibit so complete a unity of music and drama.

Alcina (1735) is based on a libretto by Antonio Marchi, set by Albinoni for Venice in 1725, but it must have been considerably altered, as some new characters are introduced. The story is derived from Ariosto, but, unlike *Ariodante*, it is a fantastic story of magic, more in the manner of *Orlando*, with the same sort of anticipation of Gozzi. It makes copious use of the ballet and the chorus, and is full of elaborate scenic effects. The dramatist seems to assume that his audience will be familiar with Ariosto, but he has much compressed the plot, and Rolli made further alterations. Thus he changes Melissa, the kindly enchantress who restores Ruggiero to sanity by means of a magic ring, into Melisso, described as the tutor of Bradamante; and both Melisso and Bradamante (in male attire) invade Alcina's palace to find Ruggiero and give him the ring. The modern English student may well find himself confused if he has not read Ariosto, and if he turns to Ariosto for a clue, he will only find himself still worse entangled. For all that, *Alcina* is one of Handel's dramatic masterpieces. It is all so utterly unreal that we cease to expect any sort of logical coherence, and at the same time the individual characters are so clearly drawn that we can never be in any doubt about them. Alcina is the enchantress who, like Circe, transforms her lovers into trees, beasts, and monsters, and finally, like a temptress in a medieval morality, is exposed as a hideous old hag. Bradamante, the former beloved of Ruggiero, is the heroic young woman in male attire, already familiar to us in several earlier operas, and Morgana, the sister of Alcina, is the sprightly and utterly irresponsible coquette.

The decorative scenes of chorus and ballet are always ravishing, and Alcina's great passionate outbursts are among the finest of Handel's creations. Ruggiero's air, 'Verdi prati', is one of his best-known songs, but Streatfeild, with his invariably subtle and penetrating insight, points out that apart from its context it loses all its psychological force. 'It is the knight's farewell to Alcina's enchanted garden, and Handel, with his unrivalled knowledge of the human heart, has contrived to suggest a touch of that regret, which, so long as men are what they are, can hardly fail to make itself felt at such a time.'

Atalanta (1736) was written for the marriage of the Prince of Wales. The author of the libretto is unknown. It is an Arcadian pastoral, obviously imitated from Guarini's *Il Pastor Fido*, full of light and charming songs and choruses. The songs are mostly short and easy to sing,[1] but wonderfully typical of this late period of Handel's style, in which he throws off trivialities with astonishing originality and genius.

Handel's health at this time was steadily deteriorating, and he was approaching that serious attack of paralysis which eventually sent him to the baths of Aix-la-Chapelle. This no doubt accounts for the deplorable feebleness of *Arminio* (1737), which is a return to the old-fashioned heroic type of libretto, an adaptation of one by Salvi, first set by Scarlatti for Ferdinand de' Medici's private theatre at Pratolino in 1703. The music is for the most part quite unworthy of Handel, and it can only be passed over in silence. *Giustino*, produced a month later, is not much better. The libretto was originally written by Count Nicolò Beregani for Legrenzi (Venice, 1683); it is in the heroic tradition, but contains curious supernatural effects. There is a vision of Fortune with her wheel, which may perhaps be classed as a dream scene, but also a sea-monster, anticipating *Idomeneo*, although the story of the Byzantine Emperor Justin (518–27) is historical and may be found in Gibbon (*Decline and Fall*, chs. 39–40). Gibbon, however, makes no mention of the monster, though most of the other characters of Handel's opera are named in his pages.

The libretto has evidently been cut down to the barest possible limits, and the sequence of events is sometimes difficult to follow. The airs are mostly short and simple; it looks as if Handel had a poor cast of singers and thought that his only chance was to avoid coloratura and make an obviously popular appeal. The story is filled out with work for a real chorus, which from a modern point of view is an

---

[1] A number of them are reprinted separately in Whittaker's series.

advantage. There are no ballets, though one or two could easily be
introduced. The opera reads like a last crazy and despairing effort
to make the best of a bad job and save a desperate situation.

Berenice (1737) is another drama of Salvi, set by Ruggeri for
Venice in 1711 under the title of *Le gare di politica e dell' amore*, a
title which would serve equally well for almost every Italian opera
of the period. It is the usual type of old Venetian libretto, with
even more than the usual jumble of operatic motives—politics, love
at first sight, self-sacrifice, and ladies who are constitutionally incap-
able of ever speaking the truth. A relic of the past is the old councillor,
Aristobulo, who soliloquizes on the evils of politics rather like Panta-
lone—always the honest old Venetian—in some of Gozzi's plays:

> Tiranna degli affetti, politica malnata,
> Ch' al giusto altrui voler sempre s' oppone,
> Sei di stato ragion senza ragione!

Such a comment on authority would be quite unthinkable to
Metastasio.

The overture is unusually good, and the minuet one of the loveliest movements ever written by Handel, or indeed by anyone
else; it is followed by a remarkably good gigue. Both gigue and
minuet are masterly examples of three-part writing. The rest of the
opera is mostly mediocre, but Seleuce, the sister of Berenice, has a
very characteristic contralto song, full of broken dramatic phrases
demanding a great voice and great emotional power. In the second
act Alessandro has a short but singularly beautiful air with a quite
astonishing phrase at the end:

Ex. 16

a - do-rar_____ con-vie-ne a me

The *coro* at the end is a minuet in D minor, which produces a
curiously melancholy effect.

Faramondo is another opera written for an inadequate cast. The
libretto is based on that of Apostolo Zeno, written for Pollarolo
(Venice, 1699) and is of the heroic type, like *Berenice*. It was so much
reduced for Handel as to be almost unintelligible. The hero, Faramondo, is even more persistently magnanimous than Metastasio's
Alexander the Great in *Poro*. The overture is one of Handel's best.
The introductory larghetto seems to describe some sort of emotional
contrast; the *fugato* has a grandly Handelian theme, and an even more

grandly Handelian end, followed by a minuet, obviously modelled on that in *Berenice*, but with a far ampler range and surprising unconventional effects. It is scored only for strings and oboes, but utilizes these modest means, often in three parts only, with a marvellous variety of colour. None of the songs are outstanding, but some are decidedly attractive, all the more so as they are generally sparing of conventional coloratura. There are 'act-tunes' to the second and third acts, and the opera ends with a *coro* of considerable length and dignity. It is noticeable in these later operas of Handel that the finale is generally much more extended than in those of the middle period. We may guess that Senesino, Faustina and Cuzzoni had no intention of wasting their energies on anything which did not show them off individually.

Burney was a good deal puzzled by Handel's next opera, *Serse* (1738), and was quite unable to trace the source of its libretto, which he calls one of the worst that Handel ever set to music; 'for besides feeble writing, there is a mixture of tragi-comedy and buffoonery in it, which Apostolo Zeno and Metastasio had banished from the serious opera'. Dr. Loewenberg, however, has shown it to be based on the *Xerse* of Nicolo Minato, set by Cavalli for Venice as far back as 1654, which at once accounts for its mixture of styles. But Dr. Loewenberg seems to have overlooked the fact that *Xerse* was remodelled in 1694 by Stampiglia and set by Giovanni Bononcini for Rome; and we may suspect that Rolli discovered it through his own connexion with Bononcini. *Serse* has often been called Handel's one incursion into comic opera, but it must be remembered that *Serse* is not an *opera buffa* of the Neapolitan type, still less of the later Venetian type; as Handel set it, it has much more affinity with the comedy operas of Scarlatti and others, written during the last quarter of the seventeenth century, generally for performances in private houses. We have already seen something of this comedy spirit in *Partenope*, though *Serse* is the first opera in which Handel brings in the old Venetian type of comic servant. It may be noted that there is a similar comic servant, with a song, 'O che bestia è la fortuna', in a style strongly resembling some of the comic songs in *Serse*, in Bononcini's *Camilla* (Naples, 1694), for which Stampiglia had provided the words, and *Camilla*, in an English translation, had been enormously popular in London from 1706 to 1728.[1]

---

[1] Dr. Loewenberg attributes *Camilla* to Marco Antonio Bononcini, but admits that there is considerable evidence for its being the composition of his brother Giovanni.

Xerxes is a purely imaginary King of Persia, and the opera is mainly concerned with his love-affairs. There are three young ladies, Rosmilda, tender and sincere, her sister Atalanta, amusingly unscrupulous, and Amastre, a princess from another country, disguised as a man and pursuing Xerxes, who has deserted her. The types are already familiar to us. Elviro is the comic servant of Xerxes' brother, Arsamene, who is in love with Rosmilda. 'The first act opens with a short recitative, and a charming slow cavatina, for Caffarelli, "Ombra mai fù", in a clear and majestic style, out of the reach of time and fashion' (Burney). This famous song does not seem to have been known as 'Handel's Largo' until the serious days of Queen Victoria. Its modern associations have become so sanctimonious that it is difficult to think of it simply as the thoughts of a lazy and sensual man lying in the shade of a tree, a situation not unlike that of Brahms's song 'Feldeinsamkeit'. *Serse* is full of light and charming airs, a large number of them short and without a *da capo*;[1] the two sisters anticipate Mozart's Fiordiligi and Dorabella. Even the 'act-tune' at the beginning of Act III has a quite unusual melodiousness and charm, exquisitely written in three parts, with suggestions of both Scarlatti and Purcell. The final chorus is also most attractive.

Stampiglia was again responsible, at least originally, for *Imeneo*, first set by Porpora for Venice in 1726, and adapted for Handel in 1738; but Handel's opera, although dated in the autograph September 1738, was not performed until 1740, and the final chorus there is dated 10 October 1740. In 1739 a 'dramatic composition' by Handel, *Jupiter in Argos*, was advertised for performance, but never saw the stage. From the manuscripts in the Fitzwilliam Museum it is evident that it was a mythological piece, more like a serenata, made up from songs taken from other operas. *Imeneo* is a sort of classical pastoral; the libretto was drastically reduced and the whole score is in much confusion owing to alterations. Its general atmosphere is light-hearted and artificial. There is a very amusing scene in which the heroine, Rosmene, pretends to go raving mad, to the consternation of the other characters. There is a good deal of chorus and ballet. One or two songs approach the style of the younger generation, Vinci, Leo and the rest, and in Act II there is an aria quite unlike Handel, yet hardly fluent enough for Vinci, though it has his type of melody and his commonplace basses in repeated quavers.

[1] Several are reprinted in Whittaker's series.

Ex. 17

Sor - ge nell' al - ma mi - a qual va sor-gen-do in cie - lo

pic - co - la nu - vo - let - ta

Half-way through the first part we come to the following cadence,

Ex. 18

la ter - rae il ma - rean - cor

which is the almost invariable cadence in Vinci and his contemporaries—from whom Mozart adopted it in his concertos—but there is
no other instance of it at all in any of Handel's operas.

Burney, whose sense of style in music of this period was far more
acute than that of any modern critic can be, points out many other
and earlier songs of Handel which he finds 'modern', and no doubt
Handel's lifelong allegiance to the tradition of Scarlatti must have
made him often seem antediluvian to the admirers of 'contemporary'
music. Burney says of this particular song that it has 'great spirit,
in a style that was then new, and which was long after continued on
the stage'. *Imeneo* is shorter than most of Handel's operas, and
Burney calls it an *operetta*. It ends with a pleasant minuet in E
minor, to which the chorus sing the following curious but doubtless
wise moral:

> Se consulta il suo dover
>   nobil alma o nobil cor,
>   non mai piega ai suoi voler,
> ma ragion seguendo va.
>
> E se nutre un qualche amor
>   ch' a ragion non si convien,
>   quell' amor scaccia dal sen
> e ad un altro amor si da.

The libretto of *Deidamia*, Handel's last opera (1741) is ascribed to
Rolli, and there seems to be no earlier opera known on the subject
which could have served him as a source, not even the very amusing
Achilles of John Gay, a ballad opera (1733), though that might con-
ceivably have suggested to Rolli a humorous treatment of the
subject in Italian. Rolli, however, treats the story rather differently

as regards lay-out; neither Thetis nor the consort of Lycomedes appear in his play. Metastasio wrote a libretto on the same subject, set first by Caldara (Vienna, 1736) for the marriage of Maria Theresa, but his version, as the circumstances demanded, is highly heroic and rigidly free from any sense of humour. A much earlier version of the story had been made by Ippolito Bentivoglio in 1663, which was set by Legrenzi for Ferrara and repeated the following year at Venice, but Rolli is hardly likely to have seen a copy of that. Rolli's drama is extremely well written and tells the story clearly with the minimum of literary affectations.

The overture is unexpectedly severe, and leads into a very effective march, rather in the style of 'See the conquering hero', during which Ulysses, Fenice, King of Argos, and Nestor (who has no singing part in the opera) arrive by ship and present themselves to Lycomedes, King of Scyros. Ulysses, as one might expect in a Handelian opera, introduces himself under another name, Antilochus. He tells Lycomedes that he has been sent by Agamemnon to ask the help of Lycomedes in the Trojan War. The King says he has already sent sixty ships; Ulysses asks for Achilles, who is supposed to be hidden in Scyros, but the King denies it. Ulysses replies in a short, heroic song, almost a caricature of Handel, but solid music. Lycomedes still denies the presence of Achilles, and says they may search the palace. Fenice now takes up the heroics with a fine bass song which needs intense concentration from both singer and orchestra. As the singers are obliged by operatic etiquette to quit the stage directly after their songs, Lycomedes is conveniently left alone to inform the audience confidentially that Achilles has been entrusted to his care; he has the feelings of a father, and of a friend to Achilles' father, and he is determined not to give him up. His aria is very dignified, with a touch of Purcell about it. The scene changes to a garden, where Deidamia, daughter of Lycomedes, talks to her friend Nerea about 'Pyrrha', as Achilles is called in the palace. This is a most charmingly schoolgirlish scene. Nerea has an air which is found in two versions; one is simple and rather Scarlattian, the other, composed on the same themes, much more showy and evidently written for a highly accomplished singer. Needless to say, the simpler version is much the better and the more appropriate of the two. Deidamia now has an amusingly juvenile conversation with Achilles, who is very boyish and energetic. As in Gay's version, she knows all about him; she does not say, as Gay does, that they share a bedroom, but she certainly mentions their 'occulti amori', though not

quite so plainly as in Gay. In fact, Rolli's Achilles does not seem to
have gone quite far enough for her desires; it is the girl who takes
the lead. One wonders if Handel ever came across Purcell's 'Dear
pretty youth' and 'Celemene'; he can hardly have failed to know
Orpheus Britannicus. But Deidamia keeps her secret, and she knows
how to trade on Nerea's schoolgirl adoration of her. Nerea's next
song, 'Si, che desio quel che tu brami', also appears in two versions;
one simple and rather gushing, the other, in quite a different style,
more severe, and with far greater depth of feeling—a most beautiful
aria, but much too mature for the character of Nerea. Ulysses tries
to talk to Deidamia, but she is not much interested in the war. She
is determined to conceal Achilles, and ends the act with a 'simile'
song about the nightingale hiding her nest in the topmost branches,
which gives her an opportunity for charming vocal effects which are
not at all difficult.

Act II starts with a very Purcellian act-tune. Ulysses returns
to his flirtation with Deidamia and tells her that if Paris had only
seen her first, Helen would never have had the smallest chance.
Deidamia is flattered, but not in a hurry. Ulysses makes his exit on
an obviously insincere declaration of love. Achilles meanwhile has
overheard it, and now becomes violently jealous. He repeats some
of Deidamia's remarks to Ulysses, putting a completely wrong
interpretation on them, and casts her off indignantly. Nerea now
comes in to say that Lycomedes has ordered a hunt to entertain
Fenice and Ulysses. The girls are to take part in it, and Deidamia
is terrified that Achilles will give himself away. (She has already told
Nerea the secret, in spite of all her good resolutions.) Nerea in
return tells her that Fenice has been making advances to her, and
suggests that if she and Deidamia respond more encouragingly to
their two admirers, they will be able to keep Achilles out of danger
by distracting the men's attention. Nerea shows how grown-up she
is by singing an aria rather in what Dr. Burney would have called
the 'modern' style. Deidamia is timid and anxious; her aria is a good
piece of character-drawing.

After Lycomedes has told Ulysses that he is too old to go out
hunting himself, the 'meet' begins with a long chorus in a quite
'beefy' English style, led by Ulysses, whose remarks on the similarity
of hunting and war anticipate those of Mr. Jorrocks. The hunt
begins, and a mysterious nymph has shot the stag and vanished
into the forest. Ulysses asks Fenice if he thinks Deidamia has a
love-affair; Fenice agrees that her air of innocence is too good to be

true. Can she be in love with either of themselves? Ulysses draws the conclusion that it must be Achilles, and that Achilles must have been the nymph who shot the stag. The nymph appears, and Ulysses starts paying her compliments and telling her that she is far lovelier than Deidamia. Achilles is not at all responsive, and when Ulysses displays yet more exaggerated ardour in a very effective coloratura aria, he points out that Deidamia is listening behind a tree. Ulysses, of course, makes his obligatory exit and Deidamia reproves Achilles for his indiscretion. He merely thinks it a very good joke, like Octavian with Baron Ochs. Deidamia does not, and has a tremendous outburst of schoolgirlish rage and grief. Fenice now tries the same game on Achilles, with similar results. The act ends with the return of the hunt and a shortened repetition of the chorus.

In Act III Fenice returns to the pursuit of Nerea, who simply laughs at him. He replies in a most curious air, a sort of Purcellian hornpipe in two repeated sections, to which the violins play a counterpoint in gigue rhythm. Nerea makes some cynical remarks about heroes and sings a very bright little aria in Handel's best comedy style. The scene changes to a gallery. Ulysses and Fenice have prepared their plot of displaying gifts for the girls; Lycomedes has gone to sleep after a heavy dinner. The drama proceeds according to the classical story. Achilles tries on the helmet, looks at himself in the shield as a mirror and, like Fiordiligi, finds it very becoming. There is a sudden blast of trumpets (*suono di trombe per assalto ex D♯*); Achilles is startled, and Ulysses says that a band of pirates is attacking the palace. Achilles at once cries out that he will defend it. Ulysses makes a long speech about the heroes going to the war and Achilles admits his identity. He sings a fine heroic song of quite boyish ardour and rushes off. Deidamia is miserable. Her aria, a much bigger one than she has hitherto had, is in a new form, a *largo* in 3/4 alternating in sonata form with a furious *allegro* in common time, calling on the storms to drown Ulysses and his ships. There is no *da capo*; the largo appears first in G minor, followed by the allegro in B flat major, and then the largo is repeated in G minor, leading into the allegro in the same key. Ulysses is highly pleased with himself and sings a big coloratura song to the effect that brains are needed in war as well as muscle. It is not heroic in style, but gives a powerful sense of security and assurance.

Lycomedes has a short scene with Deidamia. He is sleepy and platitudinous, very much the kind father making the best of a bad job. He approves of her love-affair, but only until Achilles goes to Troy. Metastasio in the same situation has the young people solemnly married by a priest at the back of the stage. Lycomedes warns Deidamia that it has been foretold that Achilles will be killed at Troy. Achilles now enters 'in heroic costume' and says he has obtained Lycomedes' permission to marry Deidamia before he goes to war. She is very angry and says she only pretended to love him in order to betray him, and that she really wants to marry 'Antilochus'. Achilles warns Ulysses against her, saying that if she marries him she will only be unfaithful to him as soon as he is gone. Ulysses tells him that he already has a wife at home and leaves Deidamia to Achilles, advising them to enjoy love if only for the moment. Achilles tries to console Deidamia, but she says it is useless, as he is predestined to fall before Troy. Achilles replies with a comment which would have horrified Metastasio, though it might have amused Offenbach:

> L'oracol parla quel che vuol Calcante.
> Ignoto è l'avvenir. Godersi importa
> Quel ben che la presente ora ti porta.
> Fian l'amor e la gloria le gioie mie:
> Da te dipende l'una, l'altra da me.
> Son nomi immaginati sol Fato e Fortuna.

After Deidamia has accepted his consolations in a song with very simple coloratura, typically Handelian, Nerea makes it up with Fenice. Again her song is found in two versions, one simple and pleasant, the other long and conventional, requiring a highly accomplished singer, and dramatically quite unsuitable. Lycomedes makes a little speech regretting that he is too old to go to Troy, and somewhat surprisingly invites Ulysses to join the hands of Achilles and Deidamia. Ulysses sings a very long duet with Deidamia, both addressing their words to Achilles, who does not sing at all. One would have expected a duet for the two young lovers, or at least a trio, with Ulysses in the rôle of the Marschallin, but no doubt the demands of the particular singers had to be taken into consideration. The opera ends with a gay and cheerful finale in *da capo* form.

There were only two performances of *Imeneo* and three of *Deidamia*; it is curious that both operas should have had so many alterations made in the music. None of them are dated in the autographs, and we have no record as to which versions were actually sung.

Deidamia was Handel's last opera, and we may well share Fitz-gerald's regret that he deserted the stage for ever afterwards, since *Deidamia* and a few of the other operas of Handel's late period show us a Handel turning his back on the grand heroic manner and advancing towards a new style of musical comedy. The analogy with Verdi makes one regret that the composer of *Acis and Galatea* never had the chance of collaborating in later life with his youthful partner. Gay in fact died before the production of his own *Achilles*. Had he only lived longer, would we not have gladly sacrificed all the oratorios for an English opera on that character of all characters whom the creator of Polyphemus could have envisaged in music more completely than anyone else—Falstaff?

In 1920, Dr. Oskar Hagen, not a musician, but a professor of fine art at the University of Göttingen, initiated a revival of Handel's operas on the stage, and since that date more than twenty of them have been performed in Germany (in new German translations), mostly at Göttingen, but also in other places. A few, notably *Rode-linda* and *Julius Caesar*, had widespread success in the course of the ordinary repertory, but most of them were given only at special festivals of more or less academic character. *Rodelinda* and a few others have had academic revivals in England, but so far Handel has not established himself in the professional repertory. Conductors who do get as far as considering Handel generally approach him from the wrong end. The managerial attitude is: 'I hear *Julius Caesar* was a great success in Cologne. Why not buy the scenery, costumes, &c., and import the whole thing just as they did it?' The conductor looks at a full score, but only reads the overture and the airs with full orchestra; the producer goes for a well-known name, such as Caesar, Admetus, or Xerxes, and is surprised to find that the plots bear no resemblance to what he remembers of classical history.

The only way to understand Handel's operas is the logical one: to begin with the librettos and read them word for word from beginning to end, and to do the same with the full scores, never allowing oneself to skip a note of the recitative, however 'dry' it may appear to be. It is fatal to regard a Handel opera (or indeed any opera) as no more than a string of famous arias; it is a drama, inseparable from its action and stage setting, and any concert performance is a sacrilege. The practical difficulties of Handel do not lie in the great *da capo* songs, except that those composed for *castrati* are sometimes impracticable for natural voices, either male or female, owing to the *tessitura*. A contralto song such as Handel wrote for Senesino will be full of coloratura which lies too low to be effective for a bass (as we can see by comparison with the songs written for Boschi and Montagnana), and an ordinary contralto or mezzo-soprano is not trained to make coloratura sound brilliant within that range. If we are ever to revive Handel in this country, we must start with those operas of his later period which were written for less accomplished singers. The plots have a sense of comedy familiar to us through Shakespeare; the songs are shorter, simpler, more varied in form and often much more directly appealing to the heart; the recitative can be made clear and dramatic, sometimes even pointed and witty. There is the further advantage of the chorus and ballet.

Handel's orchestra is an embarrassing problem for the modern conductor accustomed to the Mozartian orchestra as a normal standard. Handel's basis is the harpsichord, normally joined to the string bass; to this he adds such single instruments as he chooses for different effects, and the complete string band is used only for the greater occasions; it is only quite exceptionally that he adds to that flutes or oboes, trumpets or horns. The harpsichord is thus indispensable throughout; it is only very rarely indeed that Handel indicates *senza cembalo*, and the manuscripts make it quite clear that as a rule two harpsichords were employed. Handel's idea of an orchestra is in fact that of the *concerto grosso*—a group of two solo violins and solo violoncello, with harpsichord or theorbo, and a body of *ripieno* strings with a separate harpsichord. This presents great difficulties in a modern opera-house, even if the orchestra pit is large enough for Wagner and Strauss. Two harpsichords take up a great deal of space; good ones are difficult to obtain, and few pianists know how to play them properly. Modern harpsichords are built for solo recitals, and are completely ineffective for normal continuo work. At present it is doubtful whether there is sufficient demand to induce modern English makers to build powerful and resonant instruments suitable for theatres. Conductors hate the harpsichord; they are not accustomed to playing it, and they think that its jangling sound ruins the tone of fine string playing, all the more since the instrument which may sound adequate, or even inadequate, to the audience makes so much noise under their own noses as to give them the impression that it drowns the whole orchestra. On the other hand, it is impossible to re-orchestrate Handel and fill up the gaps with other instruments, as we ought to know by this time from our experience of Mozart's and Mendelssohn's 'additional accompaniments'. Pergolesi can be re-orchestrated because he is in the direct line leading to Cimarosa and Rossini, but Alessandro Scarlatti and Handel have an entirely different outlook.

If any director of opera thinks seriously of reviving a Handel opera today, he must start from the drama and begin by choosing the one which he thinks has the best story and plot, the clearest and most dramatic libretto; and he must then make sure of a translation which will do it justice and if possible more. The conventions of Handel's theatre must be accepted, and they must be respected too; from a modern audience we must be prepared to accept occasional laughter in the wrong place, but we must not deliberately ask for it. What is absurd and false in some of Handel's heroic operas is not the exaggeration of virtue, which great music can always make convincing, but the exaggeration of virtuosity. There is the same exaggeration of virtue—and of villainy too—in Wagner and Verdi; but Wagner made no concessions to the vanity of singers. Handel at any rate made no concessions to the vanity of conductors; in that golden age of opera they did not exist.

CHAPTER III

THE ORATORIOS

By JULIAN HERBAGE

ORATORIO and opera are nowadays considered as separate forms of musico-dramatic art. This is not only because oratorio has abandoned the theatrical trappings of stage performance, but also because secular and religious activities have tended to become confined into separate compartments of our lives. An audience of today would probably be surprised at witnessing festivities that combined 'the story of the Minotaur, the tragedy of Iphigenia, the Nativity and the Ascension', but the citizens of Perugia saw nothing incongruous in thus paying homage to Eugenius IV in the year 1444. The prototypes of oratorio and opera differed, not in treatment, but merely in subject. Poliziano's *Favola d'Orfeo* (perhaps as early as 1472) was based on the technique of the *sacre rappresentazioni* of the same era, though as it was written for a cultured princely court it far surpasses its model in literary and artistic merit. A century later Galilei set forth the principles of the monodic style in his *Dialogo della musica antica e della moderna* (1581) and both secular and sacred art were equally swift to realize the dramatic potentialities of the new medium. The same year, indeed, saw the production of the earliest surviving opera and what has been (perhaps not quite accurately) labelled the first oratorio.

If, in the year 1600, we had attended the performances of Peri's *Euridice* at Florence and of Cavalieri's *La Rappresentazione di anima e di corpo* at Rome, we should probably have been struck, not by any essential difference in the musical treatment, but by the stylistic simplicity of the operatic production and the variety and sumptuous staging of the oratorio. Fundamentally both works were based on the *stile rappresentativo* or recitative, by means of which the narrative part of the drama was musically declaimed by a single voice, instead of being spoken by an actor or sung by a chorus. Cavalieri's sacred piece had alternative endings, one with a dance, during the instrumental *ritornelli* of which the four principal dancers executed *un ballo saltato con caprioli*—in other words, leaps and capers. This use of stage effect in oratorio survived as late as

1818, when Rossini produced his *Mosè in Egitto* with its grand scenic device depicting the crossing of the Red Sea, a piece of machinery that went sadly astray at the first production. Certainly during the greater part of the seventeenth century opera and oratorio followed much the same course, except for the Latin oratorios of Carissimi, in which the choruses took on an importance unknown to opera, but later not unknown to Handel. The *oratorio volgare* was, almost more than the opera itself, an aristocratic entertainment that under the cloak of a sacred story exploited the glamour of the *bel canto* style.

In Germany the new operatic principles were slow in gaining a foothold. The chaos caused by the Thirty Years' War may have been partly responsible, though so far as oratorio was concerned, the Lutheran Church, while subscribing to a full liturgical use of music, was at first hostile to this new form of musico-dramatic expression. In the field of religious music the dramatic setting of the Passion story continued to be cultivated, but right up to the time of Schütz there was a marked differentiation between the style of true, liturgical Passion music and that of oratorio even on the subject of the Passion. In his 'history' of *Die Auferstehung Christi* (1623), Schütz accompanies the Evangelist's narration with four viole da gamba and continuo; his *Christmas Oratorio* (1664) employs a considerable orchestra and dramatic recitative; in his Passions proper (late 1650's to early 1660's), however, Schütz preserves a plainsong-like treatment of the Evangelist's part and declines—in the true Passion tradition—to introduce instruments of any kind. Composers of the next generation, notably Johann Sebastiani and Johann Theile, added instrumental accompaniments, the interpolated chorale and the soliloquizing aria or chorus on a poetic, non-Biblical text, and set the Biblical narrative in recitative style. Theile also wrote the scriptural opera *Adam und Eva* for the inauguration in 1678 of the Hamburg opera-house, the first public opera-house in Germany. Wherever opera went, oratorio flourished beside it—often as a Lenten substitute for it—but in Hamburg the taste for oratorio was at first satisfied by these 'scriptural operas' and by the introduction of oratorio-like interpolations into the Passion settings. In 1704 Reinhard Keiser, the leading composer at the Opera, went even further by dispensing altogether with the Biblical narrative and setting a completely rhymed Passion text by C. F. Hunold ('Menantes'): *Der blutige und sterbende Jesus.*

The eighteen-year-old Handel had arrived in Hamburg the year

before. Like many other young German musicians, he was attracted
by the city's flourishing musical reputation: with not only an opera-
house at the height of its glory but also a magnificent tradition of
church music. He at once embarked on a rivalry with Keiser, in
Passion-oratorio even earlier than in opera; apparently in the same
week as *Der blutige und sterbende Jesus* (Holy Week 1704), he produced a *St. John Passion*, preserving the Gospel narrative—the
omission of which in Keiser's work aroused the indignation of the
clergy—but with many interpolated verses by one of the opera-
librettists, Christian Postel.

Apart from the Evangelist, traditionally allotted to a tenor voice,
the only characters are Pilate (alto) and Jesus (bass). The chorus,
representing the crowd, sings in five parts, and, as in Keiser's work,
no use is made of chorales. The arias and duets, which form the
meditative commentary, are given to two sopranos, alto, two tenors,
and bass. The music displays not only an accomplished technique,
but also a strong feeling for dramatic expression. It is certainly
Germanic in its fullness of harmony and accompaniment, but its
melody owes much to such Italian influences as Cesti and Stradella.
As an example, Pilate's arioso 'Nehmet ihr' (Ex. 19*a*) shows a great
family likeness to the melody sung by the Consigliero in Stradella's
San Giovanni Battista (Ex. 19*b*). There are, however, many moments
that are unquestionably Handelian in style, and the whole score
possesses maturity and sureness of construction.

Postel's text is in the traditional two parts, sung before and after
the sermon. The first part deals with the events from the scourging
of Jesus to the dividing of the raiment. Apart from the Scriptural
passages, seven *soliloquiae* in the form of arias and duets are

introduced, always at dramatically apt moments. The chorus, throughout this part, is allotted only the exclamations of the crowd, and takes no part in the meditative comment, so a sense of dramatic consistency is maintained. Handel enhances the dramatic scheme by setting the Evangelist's narrative to a recitative which follows the cadences established by the Italian school. The two characters, Pilate and Jesus, sing in arioso throughout, and the short choruses, at first homophonic, later become fugal as though expressing the increased turbulence of the crowd.

A brief but impressive sinfonia precedes the opening recitative of the Evangelist, in which the florid passage on the word 'geisselte' (scourged) is typical of the word-painting so frequently used in settings of the Passion. The phrase 'Klag' o Mensch' from the following soprano aria also forms the motive of the final chorus, thus providing a unifying motive to the whole design. The duet for two sopranos, 'Schauet mein Jesus', begins in free canon in Italian style, but ends with a typically Handelian use of a repeated phrase, and the following chorus, 'Kreuzige', is based on the opening phrase of this duet. In the arioso of Jesus, 'Du hättest keine Macht', two flutes, in octaves with the strings, are introduced for the first and only time, and in the following soprano aria the contrast between the words 'Gefängniss' and 'Freiheit' is made by the wide intervals and slow common-time of the first section and the florid runs and quick triple measure of the second.

The first fugal chorus is the setting of 'Lässest du diesen los' and the fugal entries in the following 'Weg, weg mit den' lead to a homophonic adagio at the word 'Kreuzige'. The fugal passage is repeated at presto speed, and the repetition of 'Kreuzige', slowly and solemnly delivered, marks one of the dramatic climaxes of the whole work. There is no elaborate word-painting here: Handel, as usual, makes his greatest effect by the simplest means, and then changes from drama to soliloquy with an elaborate and vigorous *da capo* aria for the bass, to the words 'Erschüttere mit Krachen' (loud thundering, crashing). The tension of the previous scene could only have been resolved by this *aria d'agilità*, the prototype of many of Handel's later thundering bass songs. The casting of lots for our Lord's raiment produces some beautiful music, particularly the Italianate duet 'Welche sind', for two tenors, with which the first part ends.

The second part begins with the scene at the foot of the Cross. and carries on the narrative to the laying of Jesus in the Sepulchre,

The chorus is silent until the conclusion, when, in an elaborately conceived and deeply meditative movement, it sums up the Christian attitude to the Crucifixion. Five *soliloquiae* for solo and duet are introduced into this part, and Postel has skilfully made use of them to split up the lengthier portions of narration. Handel has perhaps failed to rise to the quiet, solemn dignity of these scenes, but his score still contains many beauties. The words of Jesus on the Cross are set with impressive simplicity to a slow, pulsing accompaniment from the strings, and at the exclamation 'Mich dürstet' Handel writes a remarkable vocal phrase, in which the mounting repetitions and the use of accidentals produce a truly baroque expression of agony and final exhaustion (Ex. 20). Another stroke of genius is the ending of the bass aria, 'O grosses werk', with Jesus's words, 'Es is vollbracht', set to the same music as when they were previously heard.[1]

Ex. 20

Taken in all, Postel's arrangement of the text and Handel's setting of it show an admirable blend of traditional and original treatment. Narration, characters, and commentary are clearly defined both in the disposition of the words and in their musical setting. This was an age of experiment in the setting of the Passion story, yet both

[1] Friedrich Smend (*Bach in Köthen*, Berlin, 1952, pp. 127–32) has shown that Postel's text for this great aria served as the model for the text of the aria 'Es ist vollbracht!' in Bach's *John Passion*. The relationship between the two Passions was noted by Percy Robinson in his article 'Handel's Influence on Bach' (*Musical Times*, July 1906).—*Ed.*

Postel and Handel seem to have avoided the errors of experimentalism, and created a balanced work equally moving and equally proportioned in its drama and its meditation. In this respect, the *St. John Passion* foreshadows an important aspect of Handel's later oratorio style. His Italian and operatic experiences were to give him a more flowing vocal line and a greater power of dramatic characterization. His choruses were to become more elaborate, and often more impersonal spectators of the story, as in Greek drama, but already, working in the restricted field of the German Passion, he had produced a work in which narration and commentary were perfectly blended.

The young Handel had naturally gravitated towards Hamburg. The Opera had principally attracted him, and during his four years' stay he had graduated from the post of second ripieno violin in the opera orchestra to the coveted position at the harpsichord. At the end of four years, however, he realized that Germany had nothing further to teach him, and the peculiar clashes of Hamburg's artistic and religious life had probably shown him the insecurity of any official position there. In any case Italy was still the Mecca of any aspiring young German musician. It was the land where poetry, painting and music had achieved their highest forms of expression but, above all, it was the land where the cultivation of the human voice had reached its peak of perfection. To a young man of Handel's consuming ambition, a pilgrimage to this Mecca of art and culture became a spiritual necessity.

Of all the cities of Italy, Rome was the centre of religious music. Opera had been temporarily banned by papal decree, but the Romans, whose love of dramatic music could not be so easily suppressed, evaded the issue by the cultivation of oratorio, which in Italy simply amounted to the substitution of a biblical in place of a classical plot. The veto on opera had also the effect of encouraging the performance of chamber music, and the palaces of the most illustrious families became the musical centres of the city. In Cardinal Pietro Ottoboni the arts possessed their most generous and enlightened patron. One of the wealthiest men in Europe, he had collected round him a circle of poets, painters, and men of letters pledged to serve the highest ideals in art. At his Monday evening meetings the best music in Rome was to be heard, the orchestra being led by the renowned Arcangelo Corelli.

The effect on Handel of this change in artistic surroundings is immediately noticeable in his creative output. In his Latin Church music, which dates from this period, the beginnings of a pure Italian style become evident. The occasionally crabbed melodic outline and stiff counterpoint of his German works give place to a smoothness and simplicity of melody. It was on Handel's second visit to Rome that he became the guest of the Marchese di Ruspoli, a figure almost as remarkable as Ottoboni himself. The Marchese was the Cardinal's chief rival as a patron of the arts. He was a leading figure of the Rome Academy known as Arcadia. The Arcadians numbered among their members the principal families, not only of Rome, but of Florence and other Italian cities, as well as the chief dignitaries of the Church and men of learning throughout Europe. For the Easter festivities in 1708 Ruspoli commissioned Handel to write an oratorio on the subject of the Resurrection. No expense was spared on the production. A temporary theatre was erected in the Bonelli palace, and the musical arrangements, under the direction of Corelli, were on a sumptuous scale, the orchestra consisting of over forty players.

The libretto of *La Resurrezione*, written by Carlo Sigismondo Capece, is no more than an average production. It is, of course, operatic in style, and introduces five characters: Lucifer (bass), an Angel (soprano), Magdalene (soprano), Cleophas (alto), and St. John (tenor). There are no choruses, except for the traditional choral conclusion to each of the two acts. The plot is of the simplest, and almost completely devoid of incident, and the only variety obtained is by an alternation of the scenes between Lucifer and the Angel, and of those devoted to the three mortal characters. Both libretto and score were probably written in haste, which may explain the reason for Handel's introducing (as Chrysander asserted)[1] some airs from his opera *Agrippina*, though most authorities agree that *Agrippina* was not composed—it was certainly not produced—until a year later. Whichever production was actually written first, the borrowings have some interest. One air, 'Hò un non sò che nel cor', occurs in both works without alteration to either words or music,[2] while 'Cade il mondo' from *Agrippina* is 'Caddi, è ver' in *La Resurrezione*.[3] But perhaps the most interesting example is the aria

[1] Chrysander's arguments for the priority of *Agrippina* are purely stylistic: cf. his *G. F. Händel*, Vol. I, pp. 201–4.

[2] Schering has drawn attention (*Zeitschrift der internationalen Musikgesellschaft*, Jg. IX, Heft 7, p. 247) to the close parallel of this song to the well-known gavotte from Corelli's Op. 5, No. 10, published in 1700. Since Corelli himself directed *La Resurrezione*, this 'borrowing' at least was made openly enough.—*Ed.*

[3] See also p. 152.

'Col raggio placido' from *Agrippina*, the character of which is quite different from that of Lucifer's great aria 'O voi dell' Erebo'. The rushing string passages (Ex. 21) make all the difference between the placid rays and daemonic lightnings. Incidentally, the melody of this song, too, can hardly be claimed as Handel's, as he borrowed it from the bass of the aria 'Costante ognor' in Keiser's opera *Octavia*,[1] of which Handel had been studying a manuscript score on his journey to Italy.

Ex. 21

In *La Resurrezione* Handel for the first time achieves a truly Italian melodic freedom. Not only the vocal line itself, but the instrumental parts are freed from any sense of laboured contrivance. Here is essentially an art that conceals art; its simplicity is deceptive, and is based on Handel's unique understanding of the function of melody. It is an incredible fact that after only a year's residence in Italy he had developed a fluent cantabile style that, combined with his contrapuntal learning, placed him at the age of twenty-three in the forefront of the composers of his time.

In addition, Handel's use of his orchestral resources has a variety and aptness which he rarely surpassed. The trumpets are used to brilliant effect in 'Disserratevi, o porte d'Averno', while solo flute, gamba and theorbo exquisitely paint the *alla siciliana* atmosphere of 'Così la tortorella'. Gamba and solo violin are allotted important parts throughout, and two of St. John's airs are accompanied by violoncello or gamba without harpsichord. The sombre, sustained tones of two flutes set the scene for Magdalene's accompanied recitative, 'Notte, notte funesta', and make a perfect foil to the vigorous

[1] See Sedley Taylor, *The Indebtedness of Handel*, p. 170.

F

string passages of the preceding 'O voi dell' Erebo'. A further contrast of tone-colour is provided by the airs for Magdalene and Cleopas accompanied in unison by violins alone. By means of these changing orchestral resources, from the power of the full orchestra to the delicate playing of solo instruments, Handel provides a constant sense of variety in his score, invariably enhancing the effect through his instinctive feeling for the appropriate instrumentation.

Handel's stay in Italy was undoubtedly the most formative period of his career. He enjoyed the hospitality of the most enlightened patrons that music has ever known, and lived in an atmosphere of cultured splendour that has rarely been surpassed. He came into contact with the leading musicians of his age, Corelli and the two Scarlattis among them, and absorbed the experience of the finest singers and instrumentalists to be found in Europe. He had arrived in Italy as a German; he left accepted by the Italians as one who spoke their own musical language. This Italian influence remained with him for the rest of his life, and through it his musical genius was later to achieve its fullest expression.

La Resurrezione and the *St. John Passion* were the important early factors in laying the foundation of Handel's oratorio style. To these German and Italian forms he was later to add the English tradition of choral singing before completing the basic elements of his oratorio design. But in 1711 the London success of his opera *Rinaldo* confirmed him in his operatic ambitions, and oratorio lay neglected for many years to come.

The years following the successful production of *Rinaldo* form a curious interlude in Handel's life. He lived in London as the guest of the Earl of Burlington, though still officially appointed to the Court of Hanover. He must already have formed his ambition to obtain artistic control of the Italian Opera in London, but seemed strangely uncertain as to his line of action, or else strangely cautious in consolidating his position. His setting, in 1713, of a *Birthday Ode* for Queen Anne and a *Te Deum* and *Jubilate* for the Peace of Utrecht showed his desire to ingratiate himself with the English, and at any rate secured him a pension from the Queen. More important, however, was the fact that the *Birthday Ode* caused him to consider the problem of setting English words to music. With his poor knowledge of the language, he must have had to study English models of choral composition, and the very opening bars of the *Ode* show his familiarity with the works of Purcell (Ex. 22). A few years later he gained even more valuable experience of setting the

English language in the anthems which he wrote for the Duke of Chandos.

Ex. 22

Meanwhile, Handel had made a last essay in the German oratorio style by his setting in 1716, of the famous Passion text by Barthold Heinrich Brockes of Hamburg: *Der für die Sünden der Welt ermarterte und sterbende Jesus*. This composition was probably produced during a period of leisure in Germany, and does not appear to have been written for any specific occasion. Brockes' poem, which was in rhymed metrical verse throughout, had aroused great interest, and had already been set by Keiser (in 1712) and Telemann (earlier in 1716)[1], so Handel may have had the secret ambition to eclipse their settings. In Brockes' poem the narration is confided to the usual Evangelist, though the Biblical words are paraphrased. There is a long list of characters, including Mary, Judas, John, James, Peter, Jesus, Caiaphas, and Pilate. There are plentiful *soliloquiae*, introduced on the slightest of pretexts, and sung by a soprano 'Daughter of Zion' and soprano, alto, tenor, and bass 'Believers'. The chorus, in addition to their taking the part of the Crowd, are allotted several 'Chorales of the Christian Church'.

It will be realized, from this large list of miscellaneous ingredients, that Brockes' libretto was muddled in its artistic aims and purpose. By paraphrasing the gospel text it confused the traditional division between the narration and the actual sayings of the characters. The

[1] Telemann's setting was performed at Darmstadt on 2 April 1716, two or three months before Handel's visit to Germany.—*Ed.*

too frequent *soliloquiae* interrupted the dramatic action, and the use of the chorus, sometimes realistically and sometimes meditatively, became hard to follow. Brockes and 'Menantes', in attempting to infuse new ideas into a traditional form, seem to have adopted the most unconvincing elements of both. But their librettos suffered also from another defect—namely, an almost masochistic enthusiasm for describing and prolonging the sufferings of our Lord with a wealth of detail that is, at its best, merely nauseating, though typical of the spirit of Lutheranism at this period. How it was that so many distinguished composers[1] were attracted to Brockes' text remains a mystery, as even its poetry is forced and drearily repetitive in sentiment. In dramatic and epic qualities it is almost completely deficient.

Handel's score is technically more mature than that of his earlier *St. John Passion*, the vocal line is more flowing, and the counterpoint moves with greater ease. But, though it is difficult to find a movement unworthy of its place in the score, the complete effect is less spiritually moving than the simpler and more artistically coherent *St. John Passion*. There are many airs of real beauty, such as Jesus' agonized 'Mein Vater! schau, wie ich mich quäle' or the typically Handelian 'Durch die Marter'. Handel considered 'Eilt, ihr angefocht'nen Seelen' attractive enough to include in his second version of *Acis and Galatea*. Bach, too, who made a copy of part of Handel's score, used the basic idea of this number, with its questioning choral exclamations of 'Wohin', in his *St. Matthew Passion*. The chorales, though simply harmonized, are effectively laid out and the setting of 'Schmücke dich, O liebe Seele' (to the words 'Ach, wie hungert mein Gemüte') is outstanding. But there seems little inward inspiration, little spiritual driving force, behind the setting of the text. The music itself is beautiful enough, and much of it was later incorporated in *Esther* and *Deborah*. But the impression remains that Handel was writing music to a text that did not move him, and he certainly took no interest in the performance of this oratorio. What is more, it seems to have convinced him that the German Passion was developing along the wrong lines, and could never become the oratorio form of the future. He never set a German text again, and it was left to Bach, with his deep religious feeling and reverence for tradition, to produce the swan-song of Passion music.

Handel's association with the Duke of Chandos at Cannons

[1] Including J. S. Bach who adapted most of the non-scriptural texts of his *St. John Passion* from Brockes.

produced a strange experiment that was to have even more important results than the Chandos Anthems. It was at Cannons in 1720 that Handel wrote what was later to become his first English oratorio. Though described as a masque, it was anything but dramatic in form, and, though performed privately with full scenery and costume, it possessed but little stage action. The idea of *Haman and Mordecai: a Masque*, based on the first five chapters of the Book of Esther, is supposed to have been conceived by Arbuthnot and executed by Pope. The libretto is divided into six scenes, and, while it offered Handel a conventional musical canvas, it made little use of the dramatic possibilities of the Biblical story. Pope, indeed, must have assumed that the tale was fully familiar to his audience. In the first scene Haman swears vengeance on the Jewish people, though the reason, Mordecai's refusal to do him homage, is never made clear. Then follows a scene in which the Israelites, unconscious of Haman's proposed vengeance, rejoice that their persecution is ended, now that Esther is Queen. An Israelite enters in the third scene bearing the tidings of Haman's plan to exterminate them, on hearing which rejoicing is turned to lamentation. In the fourth scene Esther learns from Mordecai the fate that is to overtake the Jews, and agrees to intercede with the King, though entering his presence uninvited may cause her death, according to the laws. The fifth scene opens with Esther in the presence of King Ahasuerus, who with his sceptre gives the sign of pardon for her intrusion. He grants her request that Haman and he shall attend her feast, and the scene ends with an Israelite rejoicing that Jehovah 'comes to end our woes, and pours his vengeance on our foes'.

The final scene is the most important and extended, and takes place at the feast. Ahasuerus offers Esther any gift up to half his kingdom, and Esther asks him to prevent Haman's proposed massacre of the Jews. Ahasuerus realizes that Haman's vengeance is directed towards Mordecai, who has previously saved the King's life, and, in spite of his pleas, orders Haman's execution—not, however, as in the Biblical story, on that very gibbet which Haman had prepared for his enemy. The masque ends with one of those extended songs of praise and thanksgiving that were to become a feature of Handel's oratorios.

Pope's poem contains few really dramatic situations, and its lack of characterization must have been an embarrassment to Handel, but it was not far removed from the generalized emotions, the re-joicings, lamentations, and so forth, which he had set to music in his

Chandos Anthems, or even from the meditative moments in the
Brockes *Passion*. Much of the *Passion* music was called into use, the
chorus 'Wir wollen alle eh' erblassen' becoming 'Shall we of servitude
complain', 'Erwachet doch' being worked into a new form in 'O
Jordan, sacred tide', and 'Brich, mein Herz' is 'Dread not, righteous
Queen', 'Meine Laster' appearing almost note for note as 'Tears
assist me' and 'Was Wunder, dass der Sonnen Pracht' as 'O beauteous
Queen, unclose those eyes'. In each case the music is more or less
appropriate in its new context; indeed, in the case of Haman's
opening and vengeful aria, 'Pluck root and branch', his use of the
accompaniment figure of Judas's aria, 'Lasst diese That' seems more
convincing than in the original version. The chorus which follows
consists of a typically Handelian homophonic introduction, leading
into a fugue containing as a counter-subject Haman's phrase,
'Pluck root and branch'.

The scene of the rejoicing Israelites contains some beautiful
music, particularly the air 'Tune your harps', with its sustained
oboe solo in dialogue with the voice, against which violins and bass
provide a figure in pizzicato quavers. The air 'Praise the Lord with
cheerful voice', an anticipation of 'Sacred raptures' from *Solomon*,
has an important obbligato part for harp, and the first use of accompanied recitative is dramatically reserved for the entrance of the
third Israelite with the news of impending persecution. The chorus
of lamentation which follows is in siciliana style, and the isolated
exclamations of the word 'Mourn' are a device that Handel was also
to use in many later works. The scene between Esther and Mordecai
is good Handel, but nothing more; both poet and composer have left
Mordecai a somewhat dim figure. An inspired moment in the next
scene is Esther's duet with Ahasuerus, where her pleading and his
reply are dovetailed together in a manner both dramatically natural,
yet vocally clear and melodious (Ex. 23). This duet, perfectly suited
to its situation in the masque, was one of the borrowings from the
Brockes *Passion*, as, with alterations, was the following chorus,
'Tyrants may awhile presume', which provides a typical example of
Handel's fugal treatment of a four-line stanza. Three fugal subjects
are used in succession, the first based on the opening couplet, the
second and third on the two following lines. An instrumental
introduction provides a separate orchestral figure, characterized
by triplets, which acts as a ritornello linking the three fugal
sections.

The following air and chorus are a prophecy of the Israelites'

Ex. 23

triumph of the last scene. To make this dramatically clear, the introduction to the air is an *entrée* in Lully's style. Horns are here used for the first time, and come into their own in the *concertante* prelude of the chorus 'He comes to end our woes'. This chorus, with a second section in which the words 'Earth trembles' are set to an ostinato orchestral accompaniment, is a foretaste of 'Glory to God' from *Joshua*.

The last scene opens with a long *recitativo secco* which leads into Haman's pleading air, 'Turn not, O Queen'. Despite its beauty, its characterization scarcely rings true, nor is Esther's answering 'Flattering tongue' interesting, except for its elaborate obbligato allotted to the violins and its typically operatic opening with a 'motto' phrase for the voice which then remains silent for eleven bars. Indeed, the solo music in this scene is completely eclipsed by the elaborate final chorus, consisting of over three hundred bars. In form this mighty chorus is held together by the repetitions of the lines 'The Lord our enemy has slain', and, later, but more important, 'For ever blessed be Thy holy name'. Between the repetitions of this song of praise occur, first, two fugal episodes by the chorus, then a Purcellian duet for alto voice and trumpet, 'Let Israel songs of joy repeat', next a short duet for Esther and Mordecai, and lastly a duet in canon for two bass voices.

From a dramatic point of view, this final chorus completely overshadows the rest of the work. Taking into account the fine and elaborate overture in three movements[1] with which the masque began, *Haman and Mordecai* resembles nothing so much as a Chandos Anthem extended into an evening's entertainment by the insertion of some not very dramatic scenes after its orchestral prelude. Its instrumental beginning and choral ending are both magnificent, but the rest is comparatively slight, and, though containing some lovely moments, is strangely lacking in characterization for the composer who ten years earlier had written *Rinaldo*. Handel himself completely forgot the work for a dozen years, and probably would not have revived it, had not Bernard Gates of the Chapel Royal arranged a performance on Handel's birthday in 1732. At this performance, and at a further one at the Crown and Anchor Tavern sponsored by the Academy of Ancient Music, the singers appeared dressed in character, as at the first performance at Cannons. The success was so great that Handel considered putting his masque on the public stage, but the Bishop of London intervened, forbidding the representation of a Biblical story in costume. Handel's reply to this arbitrary edict marks the true beginning of his oratorio enterprises. He was also spurred to action by a pirate performance of his masque at York Buildings. This was on 20 April, 1732 and on 2 May he announced his own production. The wording of his advertisement is significant:

N.B. There will be no acting on the stage, but the house will be fitted up in a decent manner for the audience. The Musick to be disposed after the manner of the Coronation Service.

'After the manner of the Coronation Service' is indeed the operative phrase, for Handel realized that his greatest successes with the public had been those works which he had written for ceremonial occasions, particularly the anthems which he had composed for the Coronation of George II. This was the ingredient which would take the place of costume and scenery, and it was this epic choral element which was to become a basis of his English oratorio style. *Esther* was hastily adapted to fit this new conception. Samuel Humphreys, a poet who had sought the patronage of the Duke of

---

[1] The second and third of which are substantially identical with the third and second movements of the Trio Sonata, Op. 2, No. 4.—*Ed.*

Chandos, was given the task of revising the original text. His additions greatly improved both the dramatic aspect and the epic quality of the original masque. An opening scene for Esther was introduced, as Esther's part, originally written for a boy soprano, had to be elaborated to display the vocal accomplishments of Signora Strada. It begins with the pastoral air 'Breathe soft, ye gales' elaborately scored for flutes, oboes, violins in five parts, bassoons, and theorbo. Then follows 'Watchful angels', borrowed from 'Ferma l'ali' in *La Resurrezione*, and an 'Alleluja' from the Latin motet, *Silete venti*. Mordecai, now an alto, is given the florid air 'So much beauty', and the scene ends with the Coronation Anthem, *My heart is inditing*. A second scene, between Ahasuerus and Haman, explains the plot in a manner that Pope's libretto had failed to achieve, and ends with Ahasuerus's bravura air 'Endless fame'. Incidentally, Ahasuerus, originally a tenor, is translated into a male soprano, thus conforming to the normal operatic casting of the time, and providing an opportunity for vocal display by the celebrated Senesino. The third and fourth scenes follow the two opening scenes of Pope's masque, except for an additional air for Esther, 'No more disconsolate', taken from the Chandos Anthem, *O praise the Lord*.

The second act opens with an interesting transposition, the chorus 'Virtue, truth and innocence' from the fifth scene of *Haman and Mordecai* being now reset to the words 'Tyrants may a while presume'. Dramatically this is a far better placing for this chorus, which now attains a prophetic character that keeps the action alive. Then follows, as before, the scene between Esther and Mordecai which is somewhat incongruously capped by the anthem *As pants the Hart*, an *alla siciliana* duet, 'Blessings discard', and Mordecai's 'Hope a pure and lasting treasure'. The scene of Esther and Ahasuerus wisely remains unaltered, for, in spite of its borrowed music, it was the best part of the original masque, but at its conclusion the act is rounded off by the interpolation of the Coronation Anthem, *Zadok the Priest*, to the words 'Blessed are all they'. The only alteration is the omission of the 3/4 section, 'And all the people', from the original anthem.

In the third act, the air 'Jehovah crowned' and chorus 'He comes', corresponding to the end of the fifth scene of the masque, makes an excellent introduction to the scene at the feast, which is unaltered except for the interpolation of Ahasuerus's song on a ground bass 'Through the Nation', which has a choral ending. The final chorus is an equally spacious setting to that of the masque version, but now each line is set homophonically, and all are joined together by a florid 'Alleluja'. Later, Handel rewrote this chorus, bringing it back nearer to its original form, but he still discarded the somewhat Purcellian 'verses' of the original setting.

Esther, in its final version, certainly approaches Handel's mature oratorio style in its blend of epic choruses and dramatic scenes. Taken as a whole, though, the work shows signs of being a pasticcio of former successes. It contains such disparate elements as the Italian *La Resurrezione*, the German *Passion* according to Brockes, together with the Chandos and Coronation Anthems. The result was bound to be hotchpotch, and, though Humphreys had made a fairly creditable dramatic libretto, Handel had not conceived enough original music in *Esther* to make the characterization convincing. Nevertheless, *Esther* was a success and Handel was not slow to learn its lesson. By the most fortuitous circumstances, it had become the first English oratorio, and at least it was good enough to show Handel the direction in which English oratorio might eventually develop.

The success of *Esther* encouraged Handel to embark on a similar work for the following Lent (1733). He entrusted Samuel Humphreys with the libretto, which was based on the story of Deborah, as related in the fourth chapter of Judges. Humphreys' libretto is arranged to give Handel full scope for a number of large choral scenes, between which the principal characters are allotted the usual operatic variety of arias expressing the usual hackneyed and bombastic sentiments. From this point of view his book provides plenty of contrast and suitable climaxes. But, apart from its indifferent verse, it is totally undramatic and lacking in characterization. This absence of dramatic element is reflected in the fact that there are only two meagre accompanied recitatives in the whole oratorio; even the principal incident, the slaying of the sleeping Sisera by Jael, being related after the event in a conventional *recitativo secco*.

This lack of drama and characterization seems to indicate that Handel was as yet unaware of the full potentialities of the new medium he was creating. He was still attempting merely to combine his successful ceremonial choruses with solos of operatic cast calculated to display the technique and virtuosity of his Italian singers. Much of the music was borrowed from earlier works, including the Brockes *Passion*, the Chandos and Coronation Anthems. Thus, while *Deborah* was the first oratorio that Handel wrote for public performance in a theatre, it would have been only a comparative advance on *Esther*, were it not for the grandeur of its double choruses, performed, as the *Daily Journal* announced, 'by a great number of the best voices and instruments'.

The overture to *Deborah* is unique in that two of its four movements consist of literal orchestral transcriptions of two choruses from the oratorio itself. As these are the famous Baal Chorus and the answering prayer of the Israelites, one might imagine that some dramatic purpose was intended, except that the choruses occur in reverse order, and between them comes an orchestral transcription of the chorus 'O Praise the Lord' from the Chandos Anthem, *The Lord is my light*. Since a programmatic overture would have been something of an innovation to Handelian audiences, they would scarcely have recognized the impropriety of giving the cheerful Baal-worshippers the last word.

The first scene, on Mount Ephraim, offers splendid opportunities for large-scale choruses, allotted to the Israelitish Priests and People. The extended double-chorus, 'Immortal Lord of earth and skies', makes use of two subjects from the ninth Chandos Anthem, *O praise the Lord*. The treatment of the opening and close is massively homophonic, while the words 'To swift perdition' and 'O grant a leader to our host' gain urgency by fugal treatment. The following duet between Barak and Deborah is a charming siciliana, though hardly suited to the words 'Where do my ardours raise me?' The short answering chorus 'Forbear thy doubts' is a new working of a subject that had already been used by Handel in both the Brockes *Passion* and the second Chandos Anthem. Its warlike atmosphere provides an admirable foil to the following brief chorus, 'For ever to the voice of pray'r.' Like many of Handel's prayer choruses, this begins quietly and fugally, building up to a homophonic utterance with the theme allotted to the basses. The use of the double chorus in 'O hear Thy lowly servants' pray'r' provides a sonorous climax to this scene of supplication, while the rushing orchestral accompaniment in 'O blast with Thy tremendous brow' makes a vigorous conclusion to the choral sequence. This excellent, mainly choral, scene might well have ended here, and it is a significant commentary on mid-eighteenth-century taste that Barak has to conclude it with a graceful but irrelevant siciliana to the words 'How lovely is the blooming fair'.

The scene then changes to Kedesh Napthali, in order to introduce the character of Jael, and provide both her and Deborah with their conventional quota of arias. To Deborah is allotted the typically

Handelian 'Choirs of Angels', borrowed from 'Heil, der Welt' in the Brockes *Passion*. Jael's air is a less happy setting, the words being forced to fit the music.[1] In the following scene the Israelite army has encamped at Kedesh, where Abinoam urges his son Barak to be valorous in the coming battle. His air 'Awake the ardour of thy breast' has some affinity with 'That God is great' from the ninth Chandos Anthem, *O praise the Lord*. Barak's answering 'All danger disdaining' is a conventional *aria di bravura*, and the scene ends with the chorus 'Let thy deeds be glorious', adapted to the music of the Coronation Anthem, *Let thy hand be strengthened*.

The final scene of the first act opens with the entry of a herald who proposes a parley, haughtily reminding the Israelites of their captivity. Here, as in all the recitatives, there is little drama or character in the music. Handel was obviously not yet sufficiently conversant with the English language to set it as effectively as he did Italian. The following chorus uses the music of 'Let justice and judgement' from the Coronation Anthem, *Let thy hand be strengthened* and Humphreys' new words, 'Despair all around them', are well suited to Handel's notes. But a complete dramatic anti-climax is provided by finishing this part with an 'Alleluja', for no other apparent reason than that it concluded the Coronation Anthem, and Handel did not wish to waste this excellent piece of occasional music.

The whole of the second act takes place on Mount Tabor, and, though it is over-long, it contains the most dramatically effective part both of Humphreys' book and Handel's score. The fine opening chorus, 'See the proud chief', has something of the anticipation and suspense of the entry of Polyphemus in *Acis and Galatea*. Particularly striking are the accented minims to the words 'With sullen march' and the cries of 'Jacob, arise'. Sisera's music, though, has little character, his first aria being merely designed to show off his special brand of vocal technique. The three following airs are all taken from the Brockes *Passion*, and fit their new situation more or less effectively. The last of them, 'Impious mortal', is somewhat learned in contrivance, but forms the perfect preparation to the highly effective chorus 'O Baal! Monarch of the skies', built mainly on a two-bar ground-bass in gigue rhythm. 'Handel', wrote Edward Fitzgerald, 'was a good old Pagan at heart', and he certainly excelled in the simple and vigorous portrayal of idolatrous song and dance. The answering invocation of the Israelites again introduces the double

[1] There is an alternative setting of the text, in 3/4 time.

chorus in massive homophony, and is succeeded by the fine contrapuntal chorus 'Plead thy just cause'.

The climax of this act, and indeed of the whole oratorio, is the
quartet with double chorus 'All your boast', based on a quartet
from the early *Il Trionfo del Tempo*. The forces are equally divided
between the Israelites and the Canaanites; Deborah, Barak, and the
First Chorus represent the former, while Sisera, Baal's Priest, and
the Second Chorus oppose them. Handel, with sure dramatic
instinct, has reserved the antiphonal use of his choruses for this
moment, and their defiant challenges are hurled at one another with
a broad and masterly touch. After this choral sequence comes a
succession of four solos for the principal Israelitish characters.
Three are from earlier works: Abinoam's is taken from *Aci, Galatea
e Polifemo* ('Precipitoso nel mar'), Deborah's from *Esther*, and Jael's
from *Il Trionfo del Tempo*. After the duet 'Smiling freedom', in
Handel's popular minuet style, the act closes with the chorus 'The
great King of Kings', taken from the Coronation Anthem, *The King
shall rejoice*.[1]

According to the libretto, the third act should begin with a
'Military Symphony' to usher in the victorious Israelites. It does
not appear in the score, and was probably borrowed from an earlier
opera. However, the triumph of Israel is duly suggested in the
broad intervals of the chorus 'Now the proud insulting foe', as is the
discomfiture of Baal in the minor chromatics of 'Doleful tidings'.
The following three airs scarcely live up to their important position
in the oratorio,[2] but the final choral sequence, which includes two
movements from *The King shall rejoice*, provides a fittingly impressive conclusion. Taken in all, *Deborah* is a very effective pasticcio,
though it possesses most of the faults of this type of production.
Its greatest moments lie in its contrast of the worshippers of Jehovah
and Baal, a dramatic device that Handel exploited in varying forms
in his later oratorios.

It is perhaps necessary to place *Athaliah* in a class apart from
Handel's other oratorios, as it was composed for a special occasion.
The Vice-Chancellor of Oxford had invited Handel to give some
performances at the University Theatre in connexion with the
'Publick Act' in 1733, and thus *Athaliah* was designed for a univer-
sity audience rather than a London theatre. Samuel Humphreys

[1] From 1744 onward Handel substituted 'The mighty power' from *Athaliah*
for this chorus.
[2] In 1744 Handel cut the songs of the Israelitish women.

again supplied the libretto, and wisely modelled it on Racine's tragedy. He thus achieved a book that had considerably more inherent drama than any that Handel had previously set. The incidents are taken from the twenty-second and twenty-third chapters of the Second Book of Chronicles, but their dramatic presentation owes everything to Racine. Pope, in writing *Haman and Mordecai*, was basically influenced by the great French dramatist, though he failed to assimilate Racine's characterization and psychology. In *Athaliah*, Humphreys follows Racine as closely as possible, and thus his libretto, though poetically turgid, gave Handel opportunities of characterization of which he fully availed himself. The opening chorus of maidens, Athaliah's foreboding dream, and the attempt to bring Joas within her power are all Racine's additions to the Bible story. Humphreys made use of them all, though he omitted the final tragedy of Athaliah's death.

Handel's score is far lighter and more Italianate than *Deborah*, and it is significant that he was later able to transfer most of the music to the Italian serenata, *Parnasso in Festa*, produced in the following year. It has great dramatic and musical coherence, solos often leading into choruses, and much dramatic use being made of accompanied recitative. But perhaps the most important feature of *Athaliah* is that for the first time in Handel's oratorios the principal characters are treated as dramatic personalities. Athaliah's entrance is particularly effective, and her opening accompanied recitative with its sinister semiquaver figure is masterly. The choruses here are far more subtle in characterization than those in *Deborah*, particularly the fugal 'Cheer her, O Baal', while Athaliah's 'Softest sounds no more can ease me', with its flute accompaniment, presages the coming tragedy. Only at the end of this act is a false note struck, once more with a redundant 'Hallelujah' chorus.

The second act opens with a fine double chorus, 'The mighty pow'r', with solo interpolations by Joad. The following airs, Josabeth's 'Through this land' and Abner's 'Ah, canst thou but prove me', are characteristic and melodious Handel, and the portrayal of Athaliah grows in stature with her 'My vengeance awakes me'. The solo and duet 'Cease thy anguish', given to Joad, Josabeth, and Joas, is a pretty tune obviously aimed at the groundlings, but the final chorus, allotted first to the maidens, next to the priests and lastly to the full ensemble to the words 'Rejoice, O Judah', makes a fine conclusion to the act.

The third act begins with Joad's accompanied recitative 'What sacred horrors', towards the end of which the strings foreshadow the arpeggio accompaniment of the air and chorus 'Jerusalem', in which Joad prophesies Athaliah's doom. The antiphonal treatment of the solo voice in prophecy and the chorus in prayer is majestically effective. The short double chorus 'With firm united hearts' which follows the revelation of Joas as the rightful king provides more than a foretaste of the passage 'King of Kings, for ever, Hallelujah!' from *Messiah*, and the scene ends with the ceremonially festive double chorus 'Around let acclamations ring', in which trumpets and timpani are added to the score. More, perhaps, could have been made of the following entrance of Athaliah, but a cut in the libretto here may explain her rather tame appearance to a short *recitativo secco*. Amends are later made by Mathan's dramatically descriptive 'Hark, his thunders round me roll' and Athaliah's 'To darkness eternal', somewhat reminiscent of Lucifer's music in *La Resurrezione*. The duet of Joad and Josabeth, 'Joys in gentle trains appearing', is charming Handel in his lightweight Italianate style, and in the final double chorus, 'Give glory', trumpets, horns, and timpani fanfare over vigorous string passages, as the voices, in massive homophony or broad counterpoint, deliver their concluding paean of praise.

In the five years that followed the production of *Athaliah*, Handel wrote no further sacred oratorios. He was fully occupied with his partnership with John Rich at the newly opened Covent Garden Theatre and with his battle with the Opera of the Nobility. It is therefore convenient to look on *Esther*, *Deborah*, and *Athaliah* as representing Handel's nonage in the new art form. Each work had taught him a lesson. From *Esther* he had learnt the epic power of the chorus; from *Deborah* he had perceived the value of using his chorus to contrast two conflicting ideas or ideologies; from *Athaliah* he had discovered that oratorio, as much as opera, provided possibilities of dramatic characterization. It was that much-maligned figure Charles Jennens who brought Handel back to the field of oratorio. Jennens had offered Handel an oratorio book as early as 1735, though whether this was *Saul* has not been discovered. But three more years were to elapse before Handel's interest in oratorio composition was to be fully rekindled.

In 1732 Handel, quite unprepared, had been forced into oratorio almost in self-defence. In 1738 he resolved, of his own accord, to put all his energies into oratorio, though it was not until a few years later that he finally abandoned his operatic ventures and made oratorio his exclusive sphere of composition. Meanwhile, he prepared his plans with his usual thoroughness, and even had an organ built which would give him greater visual command over his performers.[1] In Charles Jennens he had a librettist who, if poetically inclined to bathos, at least had a strong sense of drama and characterization. The libretto of *Saul*, taken as a whole, is vivid and powerful from beginning to end. The only exception is the character of the High Priest, whose moralizings, while worthy in sentiment, tend to hold up the action. Handel subsequently realized this, and cut out the character completely. Otherwise the incidents and climaxes are excellently disposed, and the principal characters grow in stature and psychological interest. Jennens was an ardent student of Shakespeare, of the tragedies especially and of *Lear* in particular. Saul is no mere victim of insane jealousy; he is a tragic kingly figure stalking inevitably to his doom. His daughters, Merab and Michal, are admirably contrasted, the elder proud and scornful, the younger loyal and loving. His son Jonathan is torn between filial duty and his love of David, and David himself achieves his full stature in his final elegy on the death of his friend and his enemy.

Handel's music is unique in its barbaric splendour, its crude human passion and its evocation of atmosphere. It is the only score in which he uses trombones, though how he obtained them is something of a mystery, as the only players in England were the Royal musicians. The overture, designed on a large scale, is in four movements, of which the third is virtually a concerto for Handel's newly-built organ.[2] The following 'Epinicion, or Song of Triumph, for the victory over Goliath and the Philistines' is a broad choral sequence ending with a magnificent Hallelujah. The airs are not the strongest part of the oratorio, and interest is revived only with the entry of the maidens singing of David's triumph. Their dance, accompanied by carillon, may be an early example of Handel's borrowing from other composers, but Saul's interpolated recitatives are highly dramatic in their suppressed jealousy, which bursts out in his magnificent airs, 'With rage I shall burst', and the equally effective 'A serpent in my bosom warm'd'. The latter ends unconventionally without a final symphony, but with a rapid, descending scale passage, as Saul hurls his javelin at David. Jonathan's accompanied recitative

[1] On this £500 organ and the 'carillon' also used in *Saul*, see Jennens' letter of 19 September 1738, to the Earl of Guernsey, printed by Sir Newman Flower in *George Frideric Handel: His Personality and His Times* (revised edition, London, 1947), pp. 271-2.—*Ed.*

[2] Cf. Chrysander, 'Händels Orgelbegleitung zu *Saul*' in *Jahrbücher für Musikalische Wissenschaft* (Leipzig, 1863), p. 411.—*Ed.*

'O filial piety' finely portrays his inner conflict between his father and his friend, though his following aria is somewhat conventional. The first act ends with a chorus in strict fugue, 'Preserve him for the glory of thy name', which demonstrates how well Handel knew the dramatic value of fugal structure.

The second act begins with the famous chorus 'Envy! eldest born of Hell', on a one-bar ground-bass consisting of a descending scale. Those choruses in Handel which form a commentary on the action are often given their dramatic character by such formal devices, but generally there is a surprise in store, in this case the chromatic passage to the words 'Hide thee from the blackest night'. The following scene between David and Jonathan is pedestrian Handel, but on the entry of Saul the music again attains dramatic power. Particularly effective is the two-bassoon accompaniment to Jonathan's 'Sin not, O King'. The duet between Michal and David, and its accompanying chorus, is no more than a pretty air, after which a formal *sinfonia* in two movements marks the passage of time. The remainder of the act contains no exceptional music, except for the dramatic conclusion to the duet 'At persecution I can laugh', and the final chorus, 'O fatal consequence of rage', with its strange canonic subject (Ex. 24) and its later impressive accentuation of the word 'blindly'.

Ex. 24

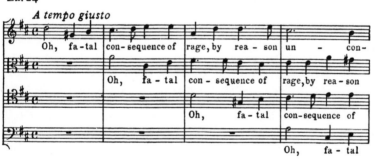

The dramatic climax of the oratorio is reserved for the third act, which opens with the superb scene at Endor. Saul's finely characterized accompanied recitative 'Wretch that I am' is followed by the witch's orchestrated invocation, 'Infernal spirits', and, as a culminating piece of orchestral tone-painting, the ghost of Samuel appears to the hollow, sombre tones of two bassoons. No romantic composer of the nineteenth century could have painted more effectively the unearthly horror of this scene, which inevitably presages Saul's final tragedy. A formal military symphony, another of Handel's borrowings, suggests the battle in which Saul and Jonathan are slain, and the news is brought to David by an Amalekite. Towards the end of David's air, 'Impious wretch', we have a foretaste of his lament, and the music, at first vigorous, slows down into the strains of the 'Dead March'. Here the antiphonal tones of trombones and flutes suggest the slowly passing cortège, and, in the chorus 'Mourn, Israel', with its flowing bass, Handel has written one of his most poignant laments.[1] The elegiac mood reaches its climax in the beautiful air and chorus, 'In sweetest harmony they liv'd', which has the simplicity, and the major mode, of all Handel's deeply-felt utterances, and subtly recalls the melodic shape of the 'Dead March'. The final chorus, 'Gird on thy sword', might easily have produced an anticlimax, had not Handel designed it on such a bold and extended scale. It is in three sections, the first mainly homophonic, with brilliant orchestral figuration, while the sudden modulation from C major to A major at the words 'Go on' produces a striking effect. In the second, fugal, section, the phrase 'Go on, pursue' is used as a counter-subject, while in the third section homophony, fugal writing, and brilliant orchestration provide a powerful conclusion to the most dramatic of Handel's oratorios.

On 1 October 1738, only four days after he had completed *Saul*, Handel set to work on *Israel in Egypt*, beginning with 'Moses and the Children of Israel'. It is probable that Jennens was at least partly responsible for the selection of the words, taken from Exodus and the Psalms, with a single recitative from Isaiah. The work was originally to have been called *Exodus*, and the present second part, a mighty song of praise similar to the 'Epinicion' at the beginning of *Saul*, though on a grander and more extended scale, was conceived

---

[1] For the 'Elegy on the Death of Saul and Jonathan' Handel originally intended to adapt his Funeral Anthem for Queen Caroline, interspersing the choruses with recitatives for David (printed by Chrysander in his biography, Vol. III, p. 41.)— *Ed.*

as an independent composition. Then came the idea of preceding it with Israel's tribulations: using the Funeral Anthem—which had failed to find a home in *Saul*—as a lament for Joseph (Part I) and composing 'Part ye 2 of Exodus' which we now know as Part One.

Israel in Egypt is the most baffling of Handel's oratorios, particularly since it raises in acute form the problem of Handel's borrowings from other composers.[1] Even if we dismiss the semi-fabulous Erba and Urio, shadows who have left no other mark in musical history, we cannot evade the fully authenticated achievements of Stradella and Kerll. Handel's borrowings in *Israel in Egypt* can be placed in proper perspective only when it is realized that sixteen out of the thirty-five airs, duets, and choruses may owe something, and occasionally practically everything, to the work of other composers. This fact is staggering but it is useless to argue for or against moral justification. The borrowings must be accepted, and it is only profitable to assess the use that Handel made of them.

---

[1] A letter of Samuel Wesley's shows it was no secret as early as 1808—and it became publicly known in 1831, with the publication of Crotch's *Lectures*—that Handel had not only, like every other eminent composer, reused his own music freely in later compositions and drawn on the common stock of period mannerisms, but freely borrowed and adapted material—ranging from mere themes to complete movements—from the work of other composers. The matter was fully investigated by Chrysander in his three-volume life of Handel (Leipzig, 1858, 1860, and 1867); Chrysander also published some of these 'Handel sources' as supplements to the great edition of the Händel-Gesellschaft. The nineteenth century had forgotten the earlier practice of 'parody' and judged these Handelian borrowings with unjustifiable moral rancour, though it is clear that Handel cannot have tried to conceal them and although Chrysander made it clear that Handel vastly improved most of the things he borrowed. Further allegations of borrowing, not always fully substantiated, have been made, notably by Prout (in *Monthly Musical Record*, May and June 1894), Schering (*Zeitschrift der internationalen Musikgesellschaft*, April 1908), and Seiffert (in *Kirchenmusikalisches Jahrbuch* for 1903, and *Bulletin de la Société 'Union Musicologique'*, 4ième année, 1924). The bulk of the evidence was admirably summed up for the English reader, with copious musical illustrations, by Sedley Taylor in *The Indebtedness of Handel to Works by Other Composers* (Cambridge, 1906). On the other hand, Percy Robinson in his book, *Handel and His Orbit* (London, 1908), and in various articles (notably 'Handel, or Urio, Stradella and Erba' in *Music and Letters*, October 1935) brought forward very strong evidence that at least two of the works published by Chrysander in the Händel-Gesellschaft supplements are really early compositions by Handel himself: that the *Te Deum* alleged to be by Francesco Antonio Urio was written by Handel himself at the Castello di Urio, on Lake Como, in 1709, and that the *Magnificat* attributed to Dionigi Erba was composed by Handel at the house of Monsignore Benedetto Erba, afterwards Archbishop of Milan and Cardinal. Robinson's further argument for the Handelian authorship of the Serenata which Chrysander published as Stradella's is less convincing; it shows, on grounds of style, that the work is probably not Stradella's but fails to prove any more than the possibility that it is Handel's.—*Ed.*

He also borrowed, in a smaller way, from his own earlier works, though his stock-in-trade in this direction had already been well-nigh exhausted by *Esther* and *Deborah*. *Israel in Egypt*, therefore, remains a baffling work to assess at its true value. It is unique in that its complete epic and dramatic force lies in its choruses, and of these nearly half contain the work of other hands. Yet Handel's additions to these choruses provide the clearest demonstration of the manner in which a work of talent can be converted by a touch of the pen into a work of genius.[1]

Israel in Egypt has no overture, though for the first performance Handel prefaced the 'Lamentation of the Israelites for the Death of Joseph' with the G minor introduction now printed with the original form of the music, the Funeral Anthem.[2] It opens, after the recitative 'Now there arose a new king', with the double-chorus 'And the children of Israel sigh'd', in the depths of despair and bondage. The impersonal tones of the alto voices are allotted the opening subject, and the basses enter only when the main material of the chorus has been stated.[3] The fugal writing proceeds sombrely towards the massive lamentation of the concluding bars. In 'They loathed to drink of the waters', derived from an earlier organ fugue (No. 5 of the *Six Fugues*)[4], Handel produces an effect of horror and desolation by the severity of his contrapuntal writing. The air 'Their land brought forth frogs' is eminently unsuccessful in evoking the right atmosphere, but the double chorus 'He spake the word', borrowed from the much-discussed Serenata by Stradella, is fully evocative of the plague of flies in its buzzing orchestral accompaniment. It is typical of Handel's genius that such a simple device could convert a conventional piece of music into a unique example of descriptive writing. The 'hailstone' chorus also owes much to Stradella, though here again its greatest strokes of genius, the shouts

[1] The borrowings in *Israel* are described, with copious parallel examples, in Sedley Taylor, op. cit., pp. 47–163.

[2] *Israel* was never popular in Handel's lifetime. Even for the second performance (11 April 1739) he made cuts and insertions (detailed by Chrysander, Vol. III, p. 91, of his biography), and when the work was revived in 1756 he withdrew the 'Lamentation' and substituted a substantial part of the First Act of *Solomon*. But we should recognize that *Israel*, as posthumously published, consists of the second and third parts of a work for which Handel never provided a satisfactory first part.—*Ed.*

[3] Arnold Schering ('Händel und der protestantische Choral', in the *Händel-Jahrbuch* for 1928, pp. 34–5) has drawn attention to the appearance of the first line of 'Christ lag in Todesbanden'—probably evoked by the word 'bondage'—in connexion with 'And their cry came up to God', especially at bar 38 et seq.—*Ed.*

[4] Cf. pp. 235 and 247.

of 'Fire' and the rushing orchestral accompaniment, are Handel's
additions. But the greatest of the plague choruses is undoubtedly
'He sent a thick darkness', which, with its freely modulating, recita-
tive-like phrases, uncannily suggests the groping of the blind in a
'darkness that might be felt'.

'He smote all the firstborn' is based on themes adapted from
another organ fugue, with two subjects (No. 1 of the same set), and
displays once more Handel's power of evoking nemesis by contrapuntal means. The orchestral accompaniment, relentlessly
emphasizing the accented beats, suggests that Handel here inter-
preted the word 'smote' literally rather than figuratively. The
chorus 'But as for his people' borrows from Stradella the much-
criticized sheep motive, but perhaps more remarkable is its completely Purcellian ending. Much of this oratorio must have seemed
antiquated to the audiences of 1739, utilizing, as it did, the styles and
even the music of a previous century. The sequence of choruses
dealing with the Exodus is a further example of Handel's adopting
the methods of an earlier age. Of these choruses, 'Egypt was glad'
is based with the barest minimum of adaptation, on an organ
canzona by Johann Kaspar Kerll, from the *Modulatio Organica
super Magnificat* published in 1686, 'He led them through the
deep' from Handel's own *Dixit Dominus*, composed at Rome,[1]
'But the waters' from the Chandos Anthem, *The Lord is my
light*,[2] and, lastly, 'And believed the Lord' from the Serenata by
Stradella.

The whole of the second part—really the third—is, in effect, a
gigantic song of praise and triumph. The orchestral opening immediately sets the scene with a fanfare-like phrase which is repeated
through a brilliant succession of keys, returning to the tonic for the
entry of the massive double chorus 'Moses and the children of
Israel', based on a similar succession of modulations. The following
double chorus, 'I will sing unto the Lord', is one of the finest Handel
ever wrote. The first line is set to a broad theme (see Ex. 59 *b*) and
the setting of the second line, with its semiquaver divisions on the
word 'gloriously', provides a brilliant contrast. The final line, 'The
horse and his rider' is given a rhythmically vigorous subject, and in
the elaborate working out of these three subjects the choruses are
used at first antiphonally and finally combine in massive syllabic
counterpoint. The duet in canon, 'The Lord is my strength', has a
pleasing, if unoriginal, subject which is worked with Handel's

[1] See p. 157–9.   [2] See p. 174.

usual skill. It is, indeed, instructive to compare Handel's working with the more primitive original version, for the same voices, in the 'Erba' *Magnificat*.[1] The start 'He is my God' derives from the same source, but the chorus 'And I will exalt him' with its ingenious use of two fugal subjects, both set to the opening line of the text, appears to be a fresh composition. One regrets to admit that the duet 'The Lord is a man of war' was not original, too, but it is at least an extremely ingenious pastiche, involving the reworking of several thematic fragments both from the *Magnificat* and from the 'Urio' *Te Deum*. The whole of the next choral sequence is derived, to a greater or lesser extent, from the *Magnificat*, though its finest touches, such as the conclusion of 'Thy right hand, O Lord', are fresh inspirations. The epic atmosphere of this part is well sustained by the two bravura airs 'The enemy said' and 'Thou didst blow', the latter with a descriptive orchestral accompaniment. The double chorus 'The earth swallow'd them' is again taken almost note for note from the *Magnificat*, which explains the false accentuation of the first word (the original text is 'Sicut erat in principio') and the following duet, 'Thou in thy mercy', also comes from the same source (the section 'Esurientes implevit bonis').

The double-chorus 'The people shall hear' has been described as 'probably the greatest of all Handel's polyphonic compositions'.[2] Its opening motive owes something to the chorus 'Doleful tidings' in *Deborah*, but the treatment of the material is so broad and extended that it reaches a completely new plane. The setting of the words 'shall melt away' is one of Handel's most inspired examples of word-painting, as is the unison 'they shall be as still as a stone' with its octave drop. The suggestion of the actual Passover by a theme of smoothly rising and falling thirds is equally apt, and culminates in a rising scale passage in the bass which majestically spans an interval of an octave and a half. The suitably pastoral 'Thou shalt bring them in' leads to the final choral sequence, beginning with the double chorus 'The Lord shall reign', set to a broad quasi-liturgical motive. It is delivered first in unison over a moving quaver bass, and then repeated twice with different harmonies to a brilliant orchestral counterpoint. The repetition of this chorus after a brief recitative has a most impressive effect, and, after a further short recitative, the final chorus 'Sing ye to the Lord' opens in similar manner, the unison subject 'The horse and his rider' being interpolated between

[1] Quoted at length in parallel by Sedley Taylor, op. cit., pp. 93–113.
[2] Sedley Taylor, op. cit., p. 162.

the two harmonized versions of the motive. After this point the music is a note-for-note repetition of the chorus 'I will sing unto the Lord', thus providing a musical coherence to the whole second part of the oratorio.

Israel in Egypt is unique among Handel's oratories in that the chorus is the protagonist throughout. This is, of course, mainly due to the choice of text, which deals, not with persons, but with the destinies of a people. To sustain such an epic conception, particularly in view of the unavoidable textual repetitions, would seem almost beyond human power. Had Handel been able to rely solely on his own creative genius, he might have achieved the miracle, but for a reason unknown to us today he felt forced to fall back on older or borrowed material, so that much of his score is remarkable more for its science and craftsmanship than for its inspiration. When he relied on himself, or when he made instinctive and unerring dramatic additions to his borrowings, he created perhaps the finest choruses he ever wrote. But, taken in all, *Israel in Egypt* must be described as his most superbly triumphant failure, and he never attempted to set another text on similar lines.

The failure of *Israel in Egypt*, a failure which Handel first tried to mitigate by producing a version 'shortened, and intermixed with songs' mostly in Italian for the soprano, La Francesina,[1] deflected Handel from oratorio once again. But three years later his operatic ventures suffered their final collapse. In 1741 he produced his last opera, *Deidamia*, a failure which ran for only three nights, and he turned his back on opera for good and all. The decision must have been a bitter blow for a man of his pride and obstinacy, but characteristically it proved to be right. Within a few months of the closing of the opera-house doors, Handel was at work on *Messiah*, to a text that had been supplied to him by Charles Jennens.

The selection of the words of *Messiah* is a remarkable achievement, reflecting the humanistic spirit of the age rather than conventional religious dogma. Though its Scriptural text deals with the prophecy, birth, crucifixion, and teachings of our Lord, it possesses a universal spirit that raises it above the letter of doctrine. Its message is summarized in the words which Jennens sent to Handel as an introduction to the first printed word-book of the oratorio:

And without controversy, great is the mystery of Godliness; God was manifested in the Flesh, justified by the Spirit, seen of Angels, preached

[1] See footnote 2 on p. 92.

among the Gentiles, believed on in the World, received up in glory. In whom are hid all the treasures of wisdom and knowledge.

Thus the Gospel story is related, not by a theatrical narrative, as in the Passion oratorios,[1] but on a metaphysical plane. For some, this places it outside the category of a truly religious work; for others, it possesses the universal essence of true religious aspiration. For Handel, it provided an epic canvas on which to paint the hope, suffering, faith, and brotherhood of his own spiritual world. If his music occasionally presents us with the pomp of kings rather than a visionary mysticism, he was merely expressing the attitude of his age towards the eternal truths of religious belief.

Handel's score is remarkable for the simplicity with which it obtains its greatest effects. The overture consists of two movements only, both in the minor, and Handelian audiences would have expected a concluding air in dance measure. 'But how exquisitely', wrote Dr. Burney, 'are judicious ears disappointed!' A transition to the major brings the serenely beautiful accompanied recitative 'Comfort ye'.[2] The following air, 'Ev'ry valley', is at least interesting in demonstrating how much instrumental sonata-form owes to the vocal aria, while the chorus 'And the glory of the Lord' provides a typically Handelian climax to the tale of prophecy. The next section of the oratorio contains darker thoughts, and is dominated by the bass soloist. His air 'But who may abide' in its original form, with its questioning bars of silence, is already impressive, but in its revision, with its dramatically descriptive *prestissimo* to the words 'For he is like a refiner's fire'—it exists in no fewer than three forms altogether—has a unique intensity of expression, even for Handel. The chorus 'And he shall purify' begins austerely, each voice in turn announcing the fugal subject,[3] which is elaborated until the final words gain force by being uttered in syllabic counterpoint. The prophetic strain is continued in the air and choruses 'O thou that tellest', written by Handel for the impersonal tones of the male alto rather than the vibrant warmth of the female voice. 'The people that walked in darkness', if performed as Handel wrote it and

---

[1] Though Schering has pointed out (*Geschichte des Oratoriums*, p. 278) that certain numbers—'He was despised', 'All they that see him', 'Thy rebuke hath broken his heart', and 'He trusted in God'—'might well have a place in a German Passion'. —*Ed.*

[2] Of which the orchestral theme derives from an idea of Handel's youth.—*Ed.*

[3] Based on Handel's own Italian duet, No. 15, *L'occaso ha nell'aurora* (cf. Sedley Taylor, op. cit. pp. 36–7); the coloratura on 'purify' is explained by the original word 'prima*vera*' and the shortage of syllables in the English text.—*Ed.*

without Mozart's luscious clarinets,[1] presents a vivid picture of the indeterminate wanderings of unbelief.

The story now approaches the Nativity with the chorus 'For unto us a child is born'. Except for the great cries, 'Wonderful! Counsellor!' its lighthearted music was originally written by Handel to Italian words about the deceitfulness of the blind god of love (*Nò, di voi non vo' fidarmi*', Chamber Duet No. 16), which explains the false accent on the first word. But by a sublime stroke of genius the inserted 'Wonderful, Counsellor' raises both the chorus and the oratorio to a completely new plane. The Nativity itself is described, not as an actual event, but by means of the shepherds who were vouchsafed a vision of the Heavenly Host.[2] Here, in the chorus 'Glory to God', in which trumpets are introduced for the first time, the heavens are revealed in Miltonic splendour—though Handel's own direction, *da lontano e un poco piano* ('softly, from a distance') is generally ignored. 'There is more *claire obscure* in this short chorus', wrote Burney, 'than perhaps had ever been attempted at the time it was composed'. The bravura air 'Rejoice greatly' and the pastoral 'He shall feed his flock' provide first a spontaneous, and then a meditative, comment on the Nativity. Both offer examples of Handel's numerous changes of mind in *Messiah*; the familiar form of 'Rejoice greatly' is a rewriting of the original version in 12/8 time:

Ex. 25

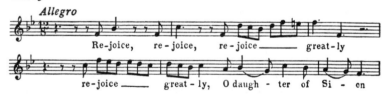

evidently recast because of the proximity of 'He shall feed his flock'; while the familiar form of the latter was superseded in a later autograph by a duet version, for alto and soprano.

[1] The baroque orchestra was already obsolete in the 1780's when German musicians began to cultivate the Handel oratorios. First Joseph Starzer (*Judas Maccabaeus*, 1779), then J. A. Hiller (*Messiah*, 1786) and Mozart (*Acis and Galatea*, 1788; *Messiah*, 1789; *Alexander's Feast* and the *Ode for St. Cecilia's Day*, both 1790) were constrained to re-score the works for the completely different 'classical' orchestra and, with far less justification, made various cuts. See Abert, *W. A. Mozart* (Leipzig, 1924), Vol. II, pp. 617–23; Köchel, *Mozart-Verzeichnis* (third edition, ed. A. Einstein, Ann Arbor, 1947), pp. 715, 721, 755 and 1032; and *Händel-Jahrbuch*, 1933, pp. 124–5, for fuller bibliography.—*Ed.*

[2] The little arioso, 'And lo! the angel of the Lord' gave Handel a great deal of trouble; there are no fewer than three settings even in the original autograph score.—*Ed.*

If the final chorus in this part, 'His yoke is easy', adapted from the same Italian duet already plundered for 'And He shall purify' again affords an example of strange coloratura—'easy' set to a flourish that originally illustrated the word 'ride' (laughs)—its subject is so graceful and its working is so smooth that Handel may be forgiven for falling back on early material.

The second part of the oratorio covers a wide scope, from the Passion and the Resurrection to the spreading and acceptance of the Gospel. The subtle differentiation between the solemnity of the opening chorus, 'Behold the Lamb of God', and the poignancy of 'Surely He hath borne our griefs', is a masterly stroke. Between these two choruses, both in the minor, comes Handel's most pathetically expressive air, 'He was despised', in the major key and with the simplest melodic outline—though it was of course intended that this outline should be ornamented in the *da capo*.[1] Our emotions of grief have been extended to the full, and the following chorus 'And with His stripes' appeals to the intellect with its clear and regular fugal writing in *a cappella* style, the instruments merely doubling the voices. The apparently descriptive theme in 'All we like sheep' is in reality borrowed from the same chamber duet (No. 16) as had been used in 'For unto us', but its adagio ending, in which the voices enter in canon to the words 'and the Lord hath laid' is an awe-inspiring stroke of original genius. The mocking of Jesus and the Passion of our Lord are notable for their tragic nobility of treatment. Particularly remarkable is the accompanied recitative 'Thy rebuke' which achieves a sense of utter desolation by its modulations, through remote keys, from A flat to B major.

The scene of the Ascension is set by the chorus 'Lift up your heads', the only five-part chorus in the work, opening in antiphonal dialogue and ending in a climax of counterpoint. In the brilliant 'Let all the angels', the fugue subject is accompanied by its diminution in half note-values. The air 'Thou art gone up' seems insufficiently expressive of its sentiment and Handel appears to have been dissatisfied with it, as he made four separate workings of the same musical material. The chorus 'The Lord gave the word' ushers in the sequence dealing with the spreading of the Gospel, and its opening unison admirably contrasts with the activity of the

---

[1] This is one of the arias for which we have contemporary ornamentations probably sanctioned by Handel himself: cf. Seiffert, 'Die Verzierung der Sologesänge in Händels *Messias*', in *Sammelbände der internationalen Musikgesellschaft*, Vol. VIII, p. 581, where the ornamented version is given in full.—*Ed.*

part-writing which follows. 'How beautiful are the feet' was set by Handel in a number of different ways:

A: a *da capo* aria for soprano with middle section on 'Their sound is gone out'.

B: the first part only of A, with 'Their sound is gone out' set as a chorus in E flat. Apparently Handel's favourite version, and the one in general use.

C: transposed to C minor for alto; 'Their sound is gone out' set as a tenor solo in F.

D: duet for soprano and alto, with chorus (extended text) (D minor).

E: an earlier form of D, with the duet for two altos (D minor).

F: a version similar to D and E (Fitzwilliam Museum, Cambridge) for alto solo and chorus.

G: also similar to D and E, but with an orchestral introduction from one of the Chandos Anthems (H.-G., Vol. 34, p. 239) converting it into an independent piece.[1]

The bravura air 'Why do the nations' is typically vigorous, and leads, without *da capo*,[2] into the chorus 'Let us break their bonds asunder', which, if taken at the same tempo, produces an overwhelming effect. But the climax of everything that Handel wrote for chorus is to be found in the 'Hallelujah'. Its opening subject is essentially Handelian, and the words 'For the Lord God omnipotent reigneth' are set to Handel's favourite 'Non nobis Domine' theme. The subject of 'And He shall reign' has superb dignity, while 'King of Kings', set to a single note, gives opportunities for the most triumphant background of 'Hallelujahs'.

Perhaps the greatest inspiration of *Messiah* is to be found in the beginning of the third part. It would seem that no musical utterance could cap the 'Hallelujah' chorus, but Handel was also a master of simplicity. In the air 'I know that my Redeemer liveth', accompanied only by violin and bass, we reach the most spiritually intense

[1] Versions F and G are not in H.-G. On G see Barclay Squire, *Catalogue of the King's Music Library* (London, 1927), Part I, p. 95; this is presumably the version composed for the Chapel Royal which Seiffert (Preface to *Messiah*, H.-G., Vol. 45) took to be E.—*Ed.*

[2] Bukofzer's supposition (*Music in the Baroque Era*, p. 338, footnote) is certainly erroneous. Not only are the autographs unanimous in omitting the *da capo* but one of them expressly directs that 'Let us break' is to follow the second part.—*Ed.*

moment in the oratorio,[1] which leads naturally into the choral sequence, 'Since by man came death'. Here is a statement of the
essence of Christian belief, and the alternation of unaccompanied
voices with brilliant instrumentally accompanied choruses admirably
suggests the antithesis of 'For as in Adam all die, Even so in Christ
shall all be made alive'. The air 'The trumpet shall sound' is
Purcellian in cast, and the quavers should probably be performed in
'dotted rhythm' throughout. The following duet, 'O death, where is
thy sting', is taken from an earlier chamber duet (No. 14, *Se tu
non lasci amore*),[2] and the music fails to rise to the poetry of the
words, though some amends are made in the working of the chorus
'But thanks be to God', partly based on the same material. The final
air, 'If God be for us', again has the most marvellous text, but
Handel has set it in merely a formal manner. The concluding
choruses, however, are Handel at his finest. Of these, 'Blessing and
honour', unless Handel's instruction of larghetto is strictly followed,
is liable to sound jaunty through too fast a pace, while the final
'Amen' is usually taken at too slow a speed. This last movement is
indeed an amazing example of Handel's contrapuntal skill. In the
course of it, as Burney writes, 'the subject is divided, subdivided,
inverted, enriched with counter-subjects, and made subservient to
many ingenious and latent purposes of harmony, melody, and
imitation'. Some bars of the score seem almost impossible of
realization, except by a celestial choir. One is tempted to say that to
interpret this amazing contrapuntal conception Handel demands
singers with as great a musicianship as he himself possessed.

Messiah stands apart from all Handel's other oratorios. Its text
alone places it in a category by itself. But its setting also is more

---

[1] This is one of the numbers for which contemporary or nearly contemporary
ornaments have been preserved (Ex. 26); they are printed at length by Seiffert
(*Sammelbände der internationalen Musikgesellschaft*, Vol. VIII, pp. 594–5). But
Beyschlag and others have contended that Handel tolerated only a bare minimum
of ornamentation.—*Ed*.

Ex. 26

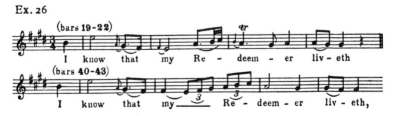

[2] Cf. Sedley Taylor, op. cit., pp. 45–6.

continuously inspired than anything else that Handel ever wrote.
It is a spiritual epic that could have been conceived only by a composer with an instinctive sense for the dramatic in music. Its key-
note is simplicity and directness of statement, but it is a simplicity
in which are 'hid all the treasures of wisdom and knowledge'. As
Tolstoy once wrote, 'Art is not a pleasure, a solace, or an amusement; art is a great matter. Art is an organ of human life trans-
mitting man's reasonable perception into feeling. In our age the
common religious perception of men is the consciousness of the
brotherhood of man—we know that the well-being of man lies in
union with his fellow-men.' Handel surprisingly achieved this
ideal in an age in which Dr. Johnson could declare that music was
'the only sensual pleasure without vice'.

Within a few days of completing *Messiah*, in September, 1741,
Handel was at work on the oratorio of *Samson*, adapted by Newburgh Hamilton from the *Samson Agonistes* of Milton. Hamilton's
libretto follows Milton closely in general outline, and makes use of
much of his verse. But he was faced with the impossible task of
condensing a 1,750-line dramatic poem into the limits of an oratorio
libretto, and his scissors-and-paste technique, though often highly
ingenious, dealt death to Milton's poetry. Though Milton's
sentiments are preserved, his language suffers a strange bowdler-
ization. A single example must suffice. Where Milton wrote:

> Therefore God's universal law
> Gave to the man despotic power
> Over his female in due awe,

Hamilton could only translate it into the banal couplet:

> To man God's universal law
> Gave pow'r to keep his wife in awe.

The whole of *Samson* suffers from this mixture of the sublime and
the ridiculous, yet, even so, it is the sublime that triumphs. *Samson*
provided Handel with perhaps his best oratorio text, and certainly
with the one which became the archetype of his future oratorio
productions.

Milton's list of *dramatis personae* is small, and Samson himself
dominates the stage until the final catastrophe, which, as in Greek
tragedy, is narrated by a messenger. Hamilton follows roughly the
same procedure, except that he has invented the rather dim character
of Micah to voice the more personal sentiments of the Israelitish

Chorus. He has, however, economized on Milton in making the giant Harapha summon Samson to the feast of Dagon. He has also added an effective opening scene of Philistine festivity. This gave Handel the opportunity of writing one of the most brilliant of his oratorio overtures. It is in three movements, the second of which is a spirited fugue[1] and the last a sprightly minuet (borrowed from Keiser's *Claudius*) in which the horns—always associated in Handel with paganism—are effectively used. The opening chorus, 'Awake the trumpet's lofty sound' has much of the spirit of Purcellian Druids junketing, an impression that is increased by the triple-time air of the Philistine woman, 'Ye men of Gaza'. The opening chorus acts as a ritornello, binding the scene together. Handel later added two more arias—'Loud as the thunder's awful voice' (tenor) and 'Then free from sorrow' (soprano)—with a further return of the choral ritornello.

Samson's music throughout has a dignity of suffering. He is the first, and greatest, of Handel's heroic oratorio tenors, and his two airs, 'Torments alas' and 'Total eclipse', set the scene of his bondage and misfortune. The latter is followed by the inspired chorus 'O first created beam' in which homophony, fugue, and orchestral counterpoint are used to telling effect; Manoah is one of Handel's grand old men, and his scene with Samson is marred only by the interpolations of the conscientious Micah. There is, however, the consolation of such superb music as Samson's bravura air 'Why does the God of Israel sleep?' and the chorus 'Then round about the starry throne'. It is perhaps a pity that this act could not have been curtailed, so as to include Micah's lovely 'Return, O God of hosts' and the chorus 'To dust his glory they would tread', into which Micah's melody is skilfully woven. As the score stands, the arbitrary act division tends to spoil the effectiveness of Dalila's entrance.

Dalila's first air, 'With plaintive notes', sets her character at once. She is a rococo seductress, and, though her streamers wave in the wind, she never 'sails like a stately ship' (as Micah says she does). Her duet with Samson, 'My faith and truth', is Purcell-Watteau also, and the addition of a chorus of virgins completes the charming scene. But she is capable of showing her claws, as the duet 'Traitor to love' amply shows. More platitudes follow from Micah, but the chorus 'To man God's universal law' is a fine example of

[1] Incorporating material from a fantasy in Gottlieb Muffat's *Componimenti musicali*: cf. Sedley Taylor, op. cit., p. 14.

Handel's fugal writing, despite the absurd weakening of Milton's text.

Handel excelled in the portrayal of giants; Goliath, the 'monster atheist' of *Saul*, the 'monster Polypheme' and the braggart Harapha are all subtly differentiated, despite their common bulk. Harapha's 'Honour and arms' and the duet 'Go, baffled coward' are both admirably characterized, and the solemn chorus 'Hear, Jacob's God', modelled on Carissimi's 'Plorate filii Israel' in his *Jephte*, makes an impressive conclusion to the scene. The act ends with the contrasting of Pagan and Christian choruses that so delighted Handel and his audiences. 'To song and dance' again brings the horns into their own, while the grand battle between Dagon and Jehovah is joined in 'Fix'd in his everlasting seat', in which trumpets and timpani assure us that Jehovah will be the victor.

The third act opens with Harapha summoning Samson to attend the festivities of Dagon. His air is an excellent piece of characterization, and most dramatic are the pauses after the unaccompanied exhortation, 'Consider! presuming slave!' The chorus 'With thunder arm'd' displays the drama that can be obtained from *da capo* form, and if Samson's air 'Thus when the sun' is not one of his finest, it at least keeps the action alive, as does Micah's air and chorus, 'The Holy One of Israel'. Dagon, however, is not so fortunate, and his worshippers have been allotted some very trite music. As a contrast comes the simple beauty of Manoah's 'How willing my paternal love', which forms an admirable point of repose before the catastrophe, vividly portrayed in the 'Symphony of horror and confusion' which interrupts Micah's recitative so dramatically and is then woven into the Philistines' chorus, 'Hear us, our God!', its rushing orchestral figuration alternating with the traditional descending chromatics of tragedy.

Micah's air and the following chorus are hardly as fine as the similar passages in *Saul*, and Handel wisely transferred the immortal 'Dead March' from his earlier work after the second performance of *Samson*. The scene of mourning is completed by the chorus, with recitative and arioso solos, 'Glorious hero', suitably coloured at the opening by the tones of the bassoons. Its strophic construction, its semi-chorus of virgins and its unaccompanied solo for the Israelitish woman form a most impressive picture of the funeral cortège. Whether Handel originally intended the oratorio to finish at this point is not clear. Certainly the two concluding numbers are later additions, the bravura air 'Let the bright Seraphim' being composed

for Signora Avolio, who had sung in *Messiah* at Dublin. But triumphant endings are a feature of Handelian oratorio, and only in one case
did he end on anything approaching a tragic note. The final chorus
'Let their celestial concerts' certainly concludes *Samson* in a blaze
of glory, trumpets and timpani adding their fanfares to the broad
choral themes.

Samson was in many ways a turning-point in Handel's oratorio
career. Not only was it a continued success from its first production,
it was also the first of his dramatic oratorios in which English
singers came fully into their own. The exquisite Horace Walpole
may have written of 'a man with one note in his voice, and a girl
without ever an one', but the days of the Italian male soprano in
oratorio were numbered. Henceforth Handel's heroes were mainly
to be tenors, and their parts were to be written to display the capabilities of the theatre singers John Beard and Thomas Lowe. While
in Italian opera the tenor and bass voices were still used to portray
villains and comic characters, in oratorio Handel made them heroes
and patriarchs. His Hebrew leaders thus attained a virility unknown
to the more effeminately cultured emperors and princes of the operatic stage. Though Senesino was a great and even dignified actor,
it is doubtful whether Handel would ever have created such parts
as Joshua and Jephtha for him. Even if Walpoles rallied Handel
for deserting the Italian convention, and even if he still employed
the alto voice for those characters, like Solomon, who were not
primarily men of action, he anticipated and prophesied, in many of
his later oratorios, the vocal revolution that was only completed half
a century later in opera.

If Handel, like Gluck, had found a Calzabigi for his librettist, he
might have founded a school of oratorio, instead of leaving some
supreme examples of the triumph of music over indifferent texts.
His librettists were indeed oddly chosen. Most of them were at
least twenty-five years his junior, and few of them had any real
dramatic experience. Samuel Humphreys admittedly wrote one
opera libretto, but was mainly known for his translations of Italian
operas. Jennens was an amateur whose Shakespeare editions evoked
the sarcasm of scholars. Newburgh Hamilton's only recorded
dramatic achievements are the two comedies, *The Doating Lovers*
and *The Petticoat Plotter*. Only James Miller, who wrote the libretto
of *Joseph*, achieved any status as a dramatist, and unfortunately his
work is that of a theatrical craftsman rather than of a creative artist.

The libretto of *Joseph* runs on well-oiled wheels, but displays little understanding of either the scope or the limitations of the oratorio form. With its countless 'asides' and its artificial construction, it is redolent of the worst period of eighteenth-century drama. The story of *Joseph* comes from the Book of Genesis, where it is related, with much incident, in chapters xxxix to xlv. Miller, like Pope in *Esther*, seems to have left out all the incidents which motivate the action. The plot is certainly unfolded with skill, but the absence of reason for every development gives the composer little chance of truly dramatic characterization and climax. The original text was far too long, particularly in its recitatives, and Handel curtailed it greatly. His original score was completed on 12 September 1743, but numerous changes were made for later performances.

Joseph is therefore inclined to be an uneven work. Handel could make little of the sketchy characters of Phanor and Asenath, but rose to his full stature in the dramatic figure of Simeon, the majestic music of Pharaoh and the youthful innocence of Benjamin. After an overture in four movements, which seems to have been originally conceived as a *sonata a tre*, the first act opens with Joseph in prison, presumably through the machinations of Potiphar's wife. His opening air, 'Be firm, my soul', in *da capo* form with an accompanied recitative replacing the middle section, paints the scene in traditional operatic manner. The following numbers are in no way remarkable, and it is only when Joseph is taken to Pharaoh to interpret his dream that dramatic interest rekindles. The accompanied recitative in which he reveals its meaning is preceded by a short orchestral introduction in two sections, the first based on the vigorous figure associated with the fat cattle, and the second on the slowly-moving theme of the lean kine. The chorus 'Joyful sounds' is an example of how Handel could obtain broad effects by the simplest means. The march-like opening phrase is announced by the sopranos alone and then repeated in full harmony with the theme in the bass, while the vigorous quaver accompaniment later introduced by the violins and the florid runs of basses and sopranos which momentarily break up the homophonic texture all add to the vigour of the chorus.

Asenath's music in this scene is unlucky in its clumsy verse and awkward accentuation, though her duet with Joseph, 'Celestial virgin', is a pleasing air in minuet rhythm. The entry of the trumpets is reserved for the sprightly processional march, but the first big climax comes at the chorus 'Immortal pleasures'. It opens in full harmony, and in the following fugal section the broadly descending crotchet subject on 'May those below' is answered by a rising

H

counter-subject to the words 'and be as blest as great'. Pharaoh's
majestic bravura air 'Since the race of time begun' gains brilliance
from its trumpet passages and leads into the chorus 'Swift our
numbers', based on the same material and including in its score both
trumpets and timpani.

The second act, opening with the chorus 'Hail, thou youth', is
preceded by a florid *sinfonia* for violins and bass, and the cries of
'Hail' punctuate its later fugal developments. A second section, to
the words 'Zaphnath Egypt's fate foresaw', is an elaborate fugue in
which, towards the end, three subjects are ingeniously combined.
Equally fine is the chorus 'Blest be the man', with its ostinato
accompaniment resembling the pealing of bells. The chorus enters
homophonically with the opening line, which acts as a ritornello
between which the remaining lines are treated in a succession of
fugal episodes, the entry of the trumpets and timpani being delayed
till the final bars. As a contrast to these choruses of rejoicing comes
Simeon's prison scene, again distinguished by its fine accompanied
recitative, but, whereas the music of Joseph's captivity was essentially noble in character, here the music suggests the suppressed
agitation which bursts to the surface in the air 'Remorse, confusion,
horror', with its rushing orchestral accompaniment that at moments
sinks to an even more sinister *tremolando pianissimo*.

Joseph's air 'The peasant tastes the sweets of life' is an effectively
simple siciliana with the suggestion of a drone bass throughout, over
which the upper strings play mainly in thirds and octaves with the
voice. In the middle section, in common time, the contrasting idea
of 'grandeur' is suggested by florid divisions, while the concluding
bars admirably yet simply portray the words 'we die thus while we
live' (Ex. 27). Simeon's air 'Impostor! Ah! my foul offence' is again

Ex. 27

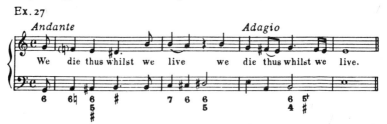

dramatic, with its agitated bass figure and chain of suspensions on the
bassoons. At last Asenath has a charming and delightful air in 'The
silver stream', with its descriptively purling melody and accompaniment, one of the numbers re-cast at a later period. The chorus of

brethren is a pleasing little fugue with two subjects, and the youth and innocence of Benjamin is admirably portrayed in the air 'Thou deign'st to call'. The act ends finely with the chorus 'O God, who in Thy heav'nly hand' in *a cappella* style; it opens and closes with slow sections in full harmony, between which a fugal allegro treats three expressive and contrasted fugal subjects in combination with powerful effect.

Act III opens with a *sinfonia* which appears to serve no other purpose than to mitigate the tedium of the somewhat uninteresting string of airs which follow. Poor Asenath is again badly served in having to sing of 'O Jealousy, thou pelican' and avoid the rhythmic accent on the last syllable of the bird. Benjamin's air 'O pity', with asides from Joseph, preserves the youthful freshness of his character, and the chorus 'Eternal monarch of the skies' would be impressive, were it not for the banality of the words of its fugal subject, 'And grant us aid we don't deserve'. The scene of Simeon's pleading with Joseph is most expressive, and Handel has taken the unusual course of writing the following dynamics in his score: '(*forte*) Thou had'st my lord (*dolce*) a father once (*un poco forte*) perhaps hast now (*pianissimo*) O feel, feel then for us'. After his final accompanied recitative 'Lay all on me', Joseph's revelation of himself to his brethren falls a little flat, and the duet between Joseph and Asenath 'What's sweeter than the new-blown rose', later set as a solo, seems merely the conventional happy ending. Equally haphazard seems the choice of the final chorus from the Dettingen Anthem, written the same year[1], to conclude the oratorio.

For *Belshazzar* (1744) Handel returned to Charles Jennens for his libretto. It is possible that the composer had received some financial assistance from the wealthy dilettante, as he writes of his anxiety to get to work on the new oratorio 'in order to answer in some measure the great obligation I lay under'. Handel evidently appreciated the dramatic possibilities of the text, but, alarmed at the excessive length of the first act, begged Jennens to keep the remaining acts short. 'It is a very Noble Piece', he wrote on receiving the second act, 'very grand and uncommon; it has furnished me with expressions, and has given me opportunity to some very particular Ideas, besides so many great Chorus.' But the enthusiastic Jennens could not be dissuaded from over-writing, with the result that his libretto was a top-heavy piece of work. Handel curtailed it considerably before setting it, and later made even further excisions.

[1] See p. 178.

The principal characters in *Belshazzar* are delineated with equal subtlety to those of *Saul*. Belshazzar, the dissipated tyrant, is matched by the matronly, almost matriarchal, figure of his mother, Nitocris. Cyrus, though cast for a mezzo-soprano, has great dignity, while his companion general Gobrias ranks with Handel's most sympathetic and expressive bass parts. Daniel, without so many dramatic opportunities as David in *Saul*, nevertheless eclipses his prototype from the earlier oratorio. But dramatically the greatest advance is in the characterization of the choruses, particularly those of the Babylonians. The elaborate stage instructions show that Jennens conceived his libretto in theatrical terms, and a living stage action must also have been in Handel's mind when he composed the music.[1]

The opening scene, in the Palace of Babylon, is remarkable for the accompanied recitative of Nitocris, 'Vain, fluctuating state', and her following air 'Thou God most high', both of which, using the most original musical language, provide a prologue to the story of the Babylonians' downfall. Daniel's aria, 'Lament not thus, O Queen', is notable for its modification and variation of the *da capo*. The second scene is described as 'The Camp of Cyrus before Babylon. A view of the city, with the River Euphrates running through it.' The Babylonians are 'upon the walls, deriding Cyrus, as engaged in an impracticable undertaking' and their chorus is graphically descriptive of their boredom at the siege, which they relieve by derisive shouts of 'Cyrus, hark!' Gobrias's air 'Oppressed with never-ceasing grief' is an excellent musical combination of the motives of sorrow and revenge, while Cyrus's vision of the fall of Babylon is set to a most dramatic accompanied recitative. The scene ends with the finely-conceived chorus of Persians 'All empires upon God depend' which, starting in massive homophony, develops into an elaborate fugue in which the lengthy subject is later split up and each component phrase developed.

The third scene takes place in the house of Daniel, who is seated 'with the prophecies of Isaiah and Jeremiah open before him'. His music has great dignity of utterance, especially the air 'Thus saith the Lord', freely constructed on a three-bar ground-bass. This leads to the broad chorus 'Sing, O ye Heav'ns', marred in its fugal section through the false accentuation of the word 'Jacob', but ending in a

---

[1] Leichtentritt (*Händel*, Stuttgart and Berlin, 1924, p. 440) detects programmatic traits in the overture: soft chords, suggesting the writing on the wall, thrice interrupting the festive *allegro*.

powerful 'Hallelujah, Amen'. The last scene in the act takes place
in Belshazzar's palace to the strains of conventional bacchanalian
music. More interesting is Handel's increased expressiveness in
setting *recitativo secco*, and the lifelike dialogue in the duet between
Nitocris and Belshazzar, 'O dearer than my life, forbear'. The
chorus 'By slow degrees', with its slow introduction and two fugal
sections, inevitably recalls both in sentiment and treatment the earlier
'O fatal consequence of rage' from *Saul*, and again achieves remarkable word painting with the fugue subject, 'And ev'ry step' (Ex. 28).

Ex. 28

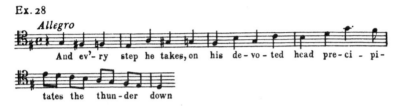

The second act begins with the stage direction, 'Without the City,
the River almost dry'. The chorus 'See from his post' is in three
movements[1] of which the middle one, set for two contrasted semi-
choruses, makes effective use of Purcellian verse-anthem technique.
A somewhat Purcellian touch is also noticeable in the brief chorus
'To arms, to arms', in which trumpets and timpani are introduced
for the first time. Belshazzar's feast, which follows, rightly provides
the dramatic climax of the oratorio. Some suitably cheerful and
robust bacchanalian music opens the scene, but Handel reserves his
powers for the incident of the writing on the wall. In the recitative
and chorus 'Where is the God', the sinister appearance of the moving
hand, Belshazzar's terror-stricken cry, the confusion of the guests
which turns to anxious muttering as they perceive the writing, all
are graphically described in a movement less than forty bars in
length. The journey of the wise men summoned to Belshazzar's
court is charmingly, if inaptly, depicted in a symphony marked
'Allegro Postillions', its main motive being unmistakably reminiscent
of an English coaching horn.[2] The remainder of the scene, including
Daniel's interpretation of the writing, fails to maintain the same

---

[1] In the first of these, Handel borrows again from his Italian duets: No. 19,
Fronda leggiera e mobile.—Ed.

[2] Though Schering (*Zeitschrift der internationalen Musikgesellschaft*, Vol. IX,
p. 247) and Seiffert (*Bulletin de la Société 'Union Musicologique'* 4ième Année,
p. 22) regard it as an echo of the 'Postillons' movement in the B flat Suite in the
third series of Telemann's *Musique de table*. See also the *sinfonia* to Act II of
Semele, composed the year before.—*Ed.*

standard, and indeed the wise men's confession of ignorance is almost
ludicrously brief and banal. But Handel rarely nods for long, and the
final chorus in praise of Cyrus, 'O glorious prince', is a fine example
of vigorous choral writing backed by brilliant orchestral colour.

In the third act, Jennens' over-writing produced its inevitable
consequence; Handel was forced practically to abandon his choruses
in order to allot the customary airs to each of the principal soloists,
and thus the whole balance of his oratorio scheme was hopelessly
disturbed. Despite the fact that Nitocris's opening air 'Alternate
hopes and fears'[1] is one of the most inspired and dramatic that
Handel ever wrote, and that Cyrus's bravura air 'Destructive war'
brilliantly employs the full strength of the orchestra, a main ingredient of Handel's oratorio pattern is almost completely lacking.
The choral element is confined to the brief but effective 'Bel boweth
down' and two final choruses adapted from the fifth Chandos
anthem, *I will magnify Thee.* Under such handicaps Jennens'
dramatic resourcefulness seems to have deserted him, and one has
to scan the libretto to learn that Belshazzar is killed off during a short
and conventional 'Martial Symphony'. Handel did his best to
retrieve the situation, but in vain. *Belshazzar*, though it contains
many fine moments and much of Handel's most dramatic music,
ends more inconclusively than any other of his oratorios, with the
possible exception of *Alexander Balus.*

The year 1745 must have been a critical period for Handel. His
Lenten oratorio performances had been unsuccessful, and he was
forced to close his doors without fulfilling his obligations to his
subscribers. In the summer came the rebellion of the Young
Pretender, and Handel, Protestant by religion and Hanoverian by
allegiance, must have fully shared the anxieties of most Londoners
in the months that followed. By the end of the year, however, the
danger was over, and Charles Edward Stuart had retreated to Scotland. Handel had every reason to celebrate this deliverance; not
only as a loyal citizen, but also to keep faith with his disappointed
subscribers of the previous season. In the *Occasional Oratorio* he
fulfilled this double obligation more than handsomely. Rarely has
an occasion of national rejoicing been celebrated in so massive a
musical manner.

The author of the libretto is unknown, though it is conjectured to
have been Dr. Thomas Morell. The words of the first two acts are

---

[1] Like a number of the arias in this act it exists in two versions, one of which,
the second, makes fresh use of material from his first aria in Act I.—*Ed.*

adapted from Milton's verse translations of the Psalms, while the
third act draws largely on suitable extracts from *Israel in Egypt*.
It is, in effect, hardly so much an oratorio as a gigantically extended
anthem. Handel throughout adopts the pomp and circumstance of
his most grandiose style, of which the overture, in four movements
ending with a march, is a classic example, though its third movement, a lovely oboe solo, offers momentary relief from the flood of
musical rhetoric. The opening air 'Why do the gentiles tumult'
and the chorus 'Let us break off' are based on Biblical words that
Handel had already set in *Messiah*, and it is interesting to compare
their treatment. Again Handel allots the solo to the bass, but here
it assumes the nature of an accompanied recitative. The words
'uplift with pow'r' are set to a phrase that Arne had made famous in
'Rule, Britannia', and this same phrase is also to be found later in
the air 'Prophetic visions' to the words 'War shall cease, welcome
peace'. The chorus 'Let us break off' is based on two simple subjects, the second being a free inversion of the first, and each lending
itself to canonic imitation both separately and together. This
chorus acts as a ritornello, linking together the following airs. Of
these, the tenor solo 'O Lord, how many are Thy foes' has a skilfully
worked oboe obbligato, while 'Jehovah, to my words give ear' is
accompanied only by a solo violoncello.

The soprano's 'Fly from the threat'ning vengeance' is an effective
aria d'agilità, but it is eclipsed by the bass's accompanied recitative,
'Humbled with fear', with its awe-inspiring setting of the words
'throw thyself down' (Ex. 29). His air 'His sceptre is the rod' suffers,

Ex. 29

like so much of the oratorio, from excessive length, and its excellent theme becomes tedious after 170 bars. The soprano solo and chorus 'Be wise' seems to have been originally conceived as a chamber duet, but in the second part of the chorus the words 'Scattered like sheep' has a singularly happy fugal subject. The tenor's 'Jehovah is my shield' demands the limit of endurance, lasting for 220 bars, but amends are made in the fine concluding chorus 'God found them guilty', where, as usual, the horns are invoked to depict the enemies of righteousness.

While the first act had dealt with the disasters of war and of the Divine displeasure it incurred, the second anticipates the blessings of peace. The simple melodiousness of the opening air 'O liberty', accompanied only by continuo, appealed to Handelian audiences to such an extent that it later found a more permanent home in *Judas Maccabaeus*. The victory of Protestantism and the Hanoverian dynasty is magnificently celebrated in the chorus 'May God from whom all blessings spring', expanded from 'Around let acclamations ring' in *Athaliah*, and the bass air 'To God our strength', with oboe and trumpet obbligato, provides the material for the chorus 'Prepare the hymn'.[1] But all these choruses of thanksgiving serve merely as a prelude to the mighty 'Hallelujah', one of Handel's most masterly pieces of contrapuntal writing, in which at least five subjects and counter-subjects are used in combination.

The third act is a triumphant paean of victory. Its introductory symphony is taken from the First and Sixth of Handel's *Concerti grossi*, Op. 6, after which follows a series of extracts from *Israel in Egypt*, consisting of the chorus 'I will sing', the air 'Thou shalt bring them in' and the choruses 'Who is like unto Thee' and 'He gave them hailstones'. The following air 'When warlike ensigns' transfers the scene from Egypt to Scotland with its sly dig at the skirl of the bagpipes (Ex. 30). The remainder of the oratorio, including the famous air 'The enemy said' from *Israel in Egypt*, builds up

Ex. 30

Allegro

---

[1] In which German critics (Leichtentritt, op. cit., p. 466, and Schering in *Händel Jahrbuch*, I, pp. 36–7) have found what they consider a deliberate quotation of the last phrase of 'Ein feste Burg'.—*Ed.*

surely to the final climax, the choruses 'Blessed are they' and 'God save the King', the music of which is taken from the Coronation Anthem, *Zadok the priest*. The breadth and majesty of the *Occasional Oratorio* are unique. On account of its borrowings it has been labelled as a pastiche. Such criticism is completely superficial; the *Occasional Oratorio*, despite its longueurs, is one of Handel's most majestic conceptions, and its present neglect is to be deplored.

Handel's association with the Rev. Thomas Morell began with *Judas Maccabaeus* (1746) and lasted the rest of his life. Handelian biographers have pilloried Morell, just as they have pilloried Jennens: everything the composer did was right, everything the librettist did was wrong. Actually, Morell was extremely well-read, particularly in the classics. He was a most accomplished amateur musician and witty conversationalist. As a poet he often descended into bathos, but more often coined a happy phrase. He was certainly not a born dramatist, but he realized that Handel's oratorios were based on the principles of Greek drama, which he was well able to imitate, albeit in somewhat sterile fashion. If he produced no masterpiece, he certainly created a number of more or less workmanlike texts. He made allowances for Handel's quickness of temper, and possibly gave in too much to Handel's 'haughty disposition', but it must be remembered that there are only too few examples of a poet and musician of equal standing being able to find common ground, or temperamental equilibrium, in a musico-dramatic production. Morell was about as good a librettist as Handel could hope to find, particularly in the mid-eighteenth century, and Handel was wise in remaining faithful to Morell throughout most of the remainder of his career.

The warlike story of *Judas Maccabaeus* was intensely topical. It was, indeed, a thinly disguised song of praise to England's deliverer, 'Butcher' Cumberland. Its composition coincided with the trials of the rebels held throughout the country, and with the executions which were taking place from London to Carlisle. Handel, attentive to the mood of his audience, sketched his music in crude, vigorous outline. The *Occasional Oratorio* had possessed majesty; it was a noble paean of thanksgiving for deliverance. *Judas* pandered to the triumphant militarism of the public, and Handel seems deliberately to have written down to this larger audience. Gluck was in London at the time, and had attempted to honour Cumberland's victory in his opera, *La Caduta dei Giganti*. It was a dismal failure, and the story goes that the unfortunate composer brought his score to Handel, begging him to name the reason for its lack of success.

'You have taken far too much trouble over your opera,' Handel
cynically remarked. 'Here in England that is a waste of time. What
the English like is something they can beat time to, something that
hits them straight on the drum of the ear.'

The plot of *Judas Maccabaeus* is epic rather than dramatic. It
opens with the Israelites mourning the death of their leader, Mattathias, father of Judas Maccabaeus. Simon, Judas's brother, exhorts
them to take heart and trust in the Lord of Hosts, who will appoint
their new leader. As all pray, the word of the Lord is revealed to
Simon who prophesies that Judas will now lead them to battle, and
after a call to arms from their new captain the Israelites sally forth
against their foes. In the second act they return victorious after
having routed Apollonius and the forces of Samaria. While the
praises of Judas are being extolled, a messenger enters with the news
that the armies of Antiochus are marching against Israel. Again all
is lamentation, and again Simon and Judas rally the Israelites to
arms, and lead them to victory. The third act is a long drawn out
paean of praise in honour of the conquering hero, Judas.

Handel realized at once that such a repetitive libretto could only
be set on the simplest lines as a gigantic pageant. There would be
no chance for real characterization, and the prevailing emotions must
be expressed in the simplest and most conventional terms. The
opening chorus, 'Mourn, ye afflicted children' conforms to this
pattern, as does the following duet, 'From this dread scene'. The
chorus 'For Sion lamentation make' is effective in its use of bassoons,
and the air 'Pious orgies', originally conceived as a 'Dead March'
for Mattathias, has the dignity of simplicity.[1] But the culmination
of this scene, the air 'Arm, arm, ye brave' and the chorus 'We come
in bright array' are obviously aimed at the groundlings. The songs
in praise of liberty are charming and melodious, particularly the
version of 'Come, ever smiling liberty' as a duet in canon. But as air
succeeds chorus and chorus succeeds air one becomes increasingly
aware of Handelian technique and Handelian gift of melody, and
increasingly less conscious of Handelian genius and dramatic
power. The final chorus of the first act, 'Hear us, O Lord' provides
the perfect example of technical facility combined with musical
cliché.

So the oratorio continues, with many fine numbers such as 'Fall'n
is the foe', and the pretty duet and chorus 'Sion now her head shall

[1] The Händel-Gesellschaft edition also gives an alternative version in E flat for
bass.—*Ed.*

raise', added in 1756 or 1757 and based on material from Bononcini's aria 'Peno e l'alma fedele'. There are also airs such as 'The
Lord worketh wonders' and 'Sound an alarm', the latter introducing
three trumpets and timpani for the first time, which only Handel
could have written. The interest rarely flags, for there are few *da
capo* arias, and a great many single numbers lead into choruses.
The choruses themselves are mainly built on the most conventional
themes, but their treatment displays all Handel's supreme mastery
of effect. Nothing could be more immediately impressive than
'Sing unto God', with its massive homophony, its running semiquaver passages, and its brilliant orchestration. Yet it is all too easy
on the ear, and one can almost hear Handel saying, as he is reputed
to have done, 'To be sure, you have picked out the best songs, but
you take no notice of that which is to get me all my money'. Indeed,
not content with the popularity of his score, Handel later interpolated successes from other works, including the air 'Wise men.
flatt'ring', accompanied by flutes and horns, from the opera
Agrippina of 1709,[1] and 'See, the conq'ring hero comes' from the
oratorio *Joshua*. When Dr. Johnson wrote the prologue to his
tragedy, *Irene*, he admitted he was 'Studious to please, yet not
asham'd to fail'. Handel, in *Judas Maccabaeus*, is both studious and
shameless in his effort to avoid failure. He did not waste his time:
he hit the English straight on the drum of the ear. The unique
popularity of the oratorio—it was played more often in Handel's
lifetime than *Messiah* or *Samson*—proves that the composer knew
what his public really wanted. Luckily for posterity, Handel was
not often so cynical in his objectives.

The success of *Judas Maccabaeus* encouraged Morell to search
the First Book of Maccabees for a further oratorio plot. He chose,
perhaps unwisely as it turned out, the story of *Alexander Balus*
(composed in 1747 and performed in March of the following year).
On the face of it there seemed plenty of dramatic possibilities in this
tale of the Syrian King's marriage to Cleopatra, daughter to Ptolomee
of Egypt, and of Ptolomee's treacherous attack on his son-in-law's
kingdom. The plot could also be nicely balanced by the character
of Jonathan, the Chief of the Jews, whose nobility could act as a
foil to Ptolomee's villainy. Musical colour could be provided by
the contrasting choruses of Israelites and 'Asiates'. Unfortunately,
the tale, from a dramatic point of view, ends inconclusively with the

---

[1] Agrippina's last aria 'Se vuoi pace'. The revised version of this youthful piece,
in *Judas*, must have been one of Handel's last works.

deaths of both Alexander and Ptolomee. Cleopatra is left to mourn
the loss of husband and father, while all that Jonathan can do is to
meditate on the mysterious workings of Providence, a sentiment
which the chorus of Israelites echoes with a perfunctory 'Allelujah,
Amen'.

Handel's score, like Morell's libretto, is strangely unequal. Up to
half-way through the second act it contains many fine and colourful
pages, but as Morell's drama becomes increasingly feeble in construction and execution, so Handel's music becomes less inspired
and increasingly mechanical. The opening chorus, 'Flush'd with
conquest', is most attractive. It consists of a triumphal march, begun
by oboes and bassoons, with trumpets and horns soon added to the
score. Its simple but unusual theme is evidently meant to set the
Asiatic atmosphere, and it is certainly one of the most original of
Handel's pagan choruses. Jonathan's air 'Great author of this
harmony' immediately stamps him with nobility of character, while
the flourish of trumpets which precedes the entry of Ptolomee,
together with his over-fulsome bravura air, 'Thrice happy the
monarch', clearly proclaims him the villain of the piece. Even more
subtly drawn is the youthful, fresh, yet exotic character of Cleopatra.
Her exquisite opening air 'Hark, he strikes the golden lyre' is notable
for the passages in which two flutes play antiphonally with two solo
'cellos, harp, and mandoline. Alexander's first air 'Fair virtue shall
charm me' is based on 'D'amor fù consiglio' from *La Resurrezione*,
and shows that he is to be the royal lover rather than the successful
soldier. This brilliant scene ends with the chorus 'Ye happy nations
round', of effectively festal character.

The next scene provides two charming airs for Cleopatra, 'Subtle
love', with its flowing arpeggio accompaniment of triplets, and
'How happy should we mortals prove', with its attractive and original
rhythm. The music of her confidante Aspasia is equally delightful,
but subtly lighter in character. The following airs for Alexander are
both excellent, the instrumental introduction of the second of them,
'Mighty love now calls to arms', again being borrowed from *La
Resurrezione* ('Disserratevi o porte d'Averno'). The act ends impressively with the song and chorus of Jonathan and the Israelites,
'Great God, from whom all blessings spring'. Jonathan's melody[1]
has a noble dignity, enhanced by the repeated entries of the chorus
to the words 'These are thy gifts, O King'. A silent pause bar leads

[1] Its first phrase practically identical with 'Shall we of servitude complain' in
Esther, and hence looking right back to the Brockes *Passion.—Ed.*

to the chorus 'To thee let grateful Judah sing', a finely worked fugue with two subjects.

The second act includes the magnificent chorus 'O Calumny!', obviously a successor to 'Envy, eldest born of hell' from *Saul*, but constructed on a far more powerful and extended bass, which is announced at the outset in unison and octaves (Ex. 31). Cleopatra's 'Tost from thought to thought' is finely descriptive, and Ptolomee's 'Virtue, thou ideal name' adds to his villainous stature. The wedding music, however, is a disappointment, and, like Morell's text, rarely rises above conventional mediocrity. Two of its numbers, 'Ye happy people' and 'Triumph Hymn' were transferred from the incidental music to Smollett's *Alceste*.[1]

Ex. 31

Largo, e staccato

A *sinfonia* precedes the third act, which opens in the Palace Gardens. Cleopatra's air 'Here amid the shady woods' is delightfully accompanied by muted strings and pizzicato 'cellos, but the sudden intrusion of a chorus of 'ruffians' sent by Ptolomee to abduct her, comes perilously near the comic. Their repeated assertions of 'Mistaken Queen, the gods and Ptolomee have otherwise ordained', interrupted by Cleopatra's cries for help, belong more rightly to Gilbert and Sullivan, and the situation might have been treated more effectively in accompanied recitative. Alexander's two following airs are marred by the artificiality of the lyrics, and far more impressive is Aspasia's 'Strange reverse of human fate'. Jonathan is given another fine and dignified air in 'To God, who made the radiant sun', and the chorus 'Sun, moon and stars' has a powerful fugal ending. The scene in which Cleopatra learns of the deaths of both her husband and her father is Handel at his best, and her two airs 'O take me from this hateful light' and 'Convey me to some peaceful shore' are exquisitely contrasted expressions of grief. Unfortunately, an anti-climax is provided by Jonathan's air with chorus 'Ye servants

[1] See p. 149.

of th' eternal King', and the perfunctory choral 'Allelujah, Amen' in a minor key makes probably the least satisfactory of all Handel's oratorio conclusions.

Alexander Balus is indeed the strangest of Handel's oratorio failures. He began it with enthusiasm, and the first act is given an orchestral colour only rivalled by such works as the opera *Giulio Cesare*. Then gradually both Handel and Morell sink into banality. Can it have been that the composer was driving his librettist too fast? Morell, in his memoirs, admits that he could never keep pace with Handel's inspiration. Handel, exhilarated by the success of *Judas Maccabaeus*, may well have pushed ahead at too great a speed. Even so, the inequality of *Alexander Balus* remains a puzzling phenomenon, and seems to indicate that Handel worked far more through the inspiration of words than most critics are inclined to admit.

Whenever Handel found the time, he made it his practice to compose two new oratorios for his following season. Having finished *Alexander Balus* in July 1747, he immediately started work on *Joshua*. Here was a subject more nearly related to *Judas Maccabaeus*, with another successful Jewish leader as its hero. The plot of *Joshua* has all the warlike glamour of the earlier work, but, in addition, Morell has provided a love interest and considerably more characterization. Again his four principal characters are clearly drawn. Joshua himself is the man of action, the heroic tenor which the singing of John Beard on the one hand, and the support of the London Jews on the other, had made an essential ingredient of his oratorio scheme. Balanced against him is the youthful figure of Othniel, with his love for the charming Achsah, and to complete the picture there is the patriarchal Caleb, one of Handel's grandest old men. Though the libretto is based on a succession of incidents rather than a series of dramatic situations, the epic nature of these incidents are sufficient motivation for the plot. *Joshua*, indeed, deserves to take a high place among Handel's oratorios.

Handel's choral writing in *Joshua* is considerably more subtle than in his earlier works. Only a brief orchestral introduction precedes the opening chorus, 'Ye sons of Israel'. The second subject of this chorus, to the words 'Ev'ry tribe attend', already foreshadows the theme of 'See, the conq'ring hero comes'. Joshua himself introduces the chorus 'To long posterity' with its graphic description of the passage over Jordan, and his fine bravura air 'Haste, Israel, haste' leads into the ingeniously-worked choral fugue of two subjects 'The Lord commands'. A charming pastoral scene follows between Othniel and Achsah, culminating in the air, with flute obbligato, 'Hark, 'tis the linnet' and the melodious duet 'Our limpid streams'. The act ends with the majestic chorus 'May all the host of Heav'n', the single subject of which is announced unaccompanied at the outset by the sopranos.

The March at the beginning of the second act is borrowed from a harpsichord rigaudon by Muffat,[1] and the magnificent chorus 'Glory to God', so much admired by Haydn, owes much to the *Laudate pueri*, written in Rome in 1707, though its descriptive middle section, to the words 'The nations tremble', is new even if its basic idea comes from Purcell's Frost Scene or Lully's 'Chœur des Trembleurs'. Caleb's 'See the raging flames arise' is a fine bravura air, but even more impressive is the choral prayer, on a ground bass, 'Almighty ruler of the skies', in which the entry of horns and trumpets at the words 'His glory did on Sinai shine' provides an unforgettable moment. The despondency of the chorus of defeated Israelites is excellently contrasted with Joshua's inspiring 'With redoubled rage return', and Othniel's gavotte 'Heroes, when with glory burning' was well worth reviving from *Agrippina*, where it had figured as the aria 'L'alma mia frà le tempeste'. Achsah's beautiful siciliana 'As cheers the sun' provides the needed moment of repose before the dramatic incident of the sun standing still, graphically described in the solo and chorus 'O thou bright orb'. The diminuendo conclusion of this chorus, to the words 'they yield, they fall, they die', is an example of descriptive simplicity paralleled only by such choruses as 'Glory to God' in *Messiah*.

The opening chorus of the third act, 'Hail, mighty Joshua', is a further proof of Handel's increasingly subtle choral writing, and the unexpected modulations of its orchestral introduction (Ex. 32) are skilfully worked into the choral texture. Rarely has Handel achieved such a noble blend of humility and dignity as in Caleb's air and chorus 'Shall I in Mamre's fertile plain'. It embodies the whole spirit of the Old Testament in its patriarchal faith in Jehovah's mercy. The solemn prayer 'Father of mercy' is offset by the somewhat Roman rejoicings of 'See, the conq'ring hero comes', which transforms the celebration to a scene of earthly pomp and pageantry. But Achsah, in 'Oh! had I Jubal's lyre' (the original idea of which again came from the *Laudate pueri*) transfers the rejoicing to a celestial plane, which is admirably sustained by the final chorus 'The great Jehovah'.

[1] The pieces are printed in parallel by Sedley Taylor, op. cit., pp. 12–13.

Ex. 32

If *Joshua* has not taken its place among Handel's most popular oratorios, it is certainly neither the fault of the music nor that of the libretto. It abounds in fine airs and noble choruses; its dramatic action is full of contrast. Perhaps it falls between drama and pageant, perhaps the love-scene between Othniel, an alto, and Achsah is artificial to modern ears. Perhaps the choruses are too subtly wrought, and perhaps too great a stature is demanded from Joshua himself. Whatever the cause, it is rarely heard today, and lovers of Handel are unacquainted with what might have been one of his most popular and inspiring oratorios.

After the comparative failures of *Joshua* and *Alexander Balus* Handel set to work earlier than usual in preparing his two new oratorios for the following season. He also experimented in his choice of libretti. He decided that the craze for warrior heroes had ended, and, indeed, he seemed temporarily to lose faith in the tenor voice for his leading rôle. It is not certain who produced the libretti for *Solomon* and *Susanna* (both 1748), though the former is attributed to Morell. Certainly there could be no greater contrast than between these two works, and it would seem that Handel, again unsure of himself, was endeavouring to feel the pulse of the public. *Solomon* is a large-scale, highly-coloured pageant with practically no dramatic action, while *Susanna* is the most intimate and operatic of Handel's sacred oratorios.

There is no attempt to weld the plot of *Solomon* into a coherent whole. The three acts, based on the Books of Kings and Chronicles, set forth three separate aspects of Solomon's greatness. The first deals with the piety of Solomon, the dedication of the temple, and Solomon's conjugal happiness. In the second act the wisdom of Solomon is displayed in his famous judgement between the two harlots. The third act is devoted to the visit of the Queen of Sheba, and glorifies the riches and splendour of Solomon's court. Handel fully realized that such a triptych would have to be painted upon the most gigantic canvas, and he therefore made use of a double chorus (accompanied, it seems, by two organs) and at times an elaborate subdivision of his string orchestra. *Solomon* is unique in its complex balance of orchestral forces, though somewhat surprisingly there is not an equal complexity in the use of orchestral colour. *Saul* and *Alexander Balus* have vividly coloured scores; *Solomon* has by far the richest orchestral texture of any of the sacred oratorios.

The first act contains some of the most impressive and elaborately wrought choruses which Handel ever wrote. The opening double chorus 'Your harps and cymbals sound' is a masterpiece of antiphonal writing in which the various subjects are combined with the utmost contrapuntal skill. Equally effective are the dramatic exclamations on the word 'sound'. Considering also the brilliant orchestral background, this certainly represents the acme of Handel's choral style. The solo of the Levite, 'Praise ye the Lord', is an impressively worked canon, and the double chorus 'With pious heart' opens with remarkably bold harmonies which form an introduction to a most expressive and dramatic fugal section. The breadth and dignity of the music continues in Solomon's accompanied recitative 'Almighty power', in which the scoring for two violas and two bassoons gives great character to the scene. Zadok's 'Sacred raptures' is an excellent example of Handel's achieving majesty by the simplest means, and only in the somewhat archaic *alla breve* chorus 'Throughout the land' is the splendour of the scene relaxed, though the final pedal-point and modulation on the word 'power' retrieve the situation.

As a contrast to the pomp and majesty of the opening, the remainder of the act stresses the pastoral. The mood is begun in Solomon's air 'What though I trace each herb and flower', which leads naturally into the scene between Solomon and his Queen. Strangely enough, neither Handel nor his librettist attempted to

I

characterize the daughter of Pharaoh, and her most characteristic air, 'With thee th'unshelter'd moor I'd tread', is no more than a pretty ballad tune. But never has Handel written more exquisitely sensuous music than the chorus 'May no rash intruder' which concludes the act with soft-breathing zephyrs and sleep-lulling nightingales.

The second act again begins with a song of praise, embellished with the orchestral splendour of trumpets, horns, timpani and divided violas. Yet the music of this opening double chorus 'From the censer curling rise' is conventional rather than inspired, and only comes fully to life at the fugal episode 'Live for ever, pious David's son', which makes most happy use of a theme from an early violin sonata.[1] On the contrary, the scene of judgement between the two harlots is admirably characterized. Particularly effective is the air and trio 'Words are weak to paint my fears'. The first harlot sings in sustained, dignified phrases which are interrupted by the garrulous quavers of the second harlot, while ever and anon Solomon interposes magisterially with the same theme, 'Justice holds the lifted scale'. The characters of the two women become even clearer in their following airs, the excitedly vengeful 'Thy justice, great King' of the second harlot with its climax, 'I shall tear the lov'd infant from thee', and the renunciatory 'Can I see my infant gor'd' of the first harlot, which even the banality of the words cannot spoil. In the five-part chorus 'From the east unto the west' the wisdom of Solomon is praised in a gavotte-like measure which gains dignity through its simple and effective points of imitation and its use of the strings in *concerto grosso* fashion. After Zadok's dignified, if conventional, 'See the tall palm' and a pastoral air allotted to the first harlot the act is concluded with the chorus, in *da capo* form, 'Swell the full chorus', in which the solid four-part choral writing and the bright orchestral colouring of trumpets and timpani produce a massive and brilliant effect.

The visit of the Queen of Sheba, which occupies the whole of the third act, is treated after the manner of Dryden's *Alexander's Feast* in that Solomon displays his glory in a musical banquet to his royal guest. The music, taken as a whole, is effective in a conventional way, but Handel has reserved no surprises for the occasion, and the character of the Queen herself is dimly drawn. The opening *sinfonia* is rightly one of the most popular of Handel's orchestral movements, though the transcriptions of it generally heard do little

[1] H.–G., Vol. 27, p. 47.

justice to its masterly instrumental balance and counterpoint. The
Queen's first air 'Ev'ry sight these eyes behold' is a melodious
gavotte, while Solomon's air and chorus 'Music, spread thy voice
around' adopts a minuet rhythm. The use of the double chorus is
reserved for the vigorous and martial 'Shake the dome', with its
powerful antiphonal effects and insistent orchestral rhythms. Contrasting moods are provided by the choruses 'Draw the tear from
hopeless love', again with important parts for divided violas and
bassoons, and 'Thus rolling surges rise'. Handel's musical banquet
lacks nothing in variety; the chef has provided an excellently contrasted series of dishes, and the two final and elaborately-scored
choruses 'Praise the Lord with harp and tongue' and 'The name of
the wicked'—the latter with a rhythmic echo of 'May no rash
intruder'—make an admirable conclusion to any *table d'hôte* musical
meal. But one secretly wishes that Handel had for one moment
thrown aside his recipe book and allowed his inventiveness full rein.
Solomon's riches and splendour are shown off just a little too obviously and ostentatiously to the credulous Queen of Sheba. Maybe
this is historically correct, or maybe the opening scene of the oratorio
sets a standard impossible to maintain. Of the three panels of this
musical triptych this last should have been the greatest, but it is
merely a workmanlike anthology of Handel the technician.

The history of Susanna in the Apocrypha is 'set apart from the
beginning of *Daniel*, because it is not in the Hebrew'. It is a little
masterpiece of dramatic storytelling, perfectly suited to musical
treatment. The complete tale is told in sixty-four verses, and a
librettist would be wise not to extend this miniature domestic drama
beyond its natural length. Handel's librettist, however, was faced
with the task of extending the tale to cover the usual three lengthy
acts. He accomplished his task as well as could be expected, and his
dramatic climaxes are carefully spaced. Inevitably, though, he had
to indulge in padding, particularly in his opening scenes, and
thus *Susanna*, despite many moments of charm and inspiration,
remains a somewhat attenuated evening's entertainment—as Handel
acknowledged by the cuts he made in 1759.

The faults of the libretto are reflected in Handel's music, but the
score also possesses a strangely intimate quality which is unique
among his oratorios. The overture, in the French style, is a charming
composition with a particularly attractive fugal subject. The opening
chorus, 'How long, O Lord', has little to do with the tale, and is
possibly a piece of music salvaged from an abandoned oratorio.

It is set to the classic chromatically descending ground-bass, and ingeniously inverts the ground both in the middle section and at the conclusion. The characters of Joachim, Susanna, and her father Chelsias are then drawn with Handel's usual skill in a succession of well-contrasted airs of which the most attractive are Joachim's pastoral 'When first I saw my lovely maid', Susanna's answering 'Would custom bid the melting fair' and Chelsias' 'Peace crown'd with roses'. This scene of domestic bliss, however, is extended beyond the endurance of any but a sentimental audience of the mid-eighteenth century, and even the excellently-contrived chorus 'Virtue shall never long' suffers from the genteel propriety of its text. Interest is rekindled with the appearance of the two Elders, the first a high, hypocritical tenor and the second a deep, extrovert bass. The accompanied recitative 'Tyrannic love' is a gem of characterization, and the following ballad air 'Ye verdant hills' fully establishes the canting emotions of the first elderly satyr. His companion's passion is more forthright, and admirably portrayed in his vigorous 'The oak, that for a thousand years', an extremely fine bravura air. The act ends with an elaborate chorus 'Righteous Heav'n', consisting of two fugal sections linked by a repetition of the homophonic introduction.

In the second act Handel has more pictorial and dramatic material to build upon. Susanna's 'Crystal streams', which begins with an anticipation of Wagner's *Waldweben*, is an exquisite pastoral evocation, while the two contrasted airs of her attendant, 'Ask if yon damask rose' and 'Beneath the cypress' gloomy shade', are two of Handel's most delightful miniatures in song. The characters of the two Elders are enhanced by their following airs, but the climax of the act is the trio between Susanna and the Elders, in which the vigorous and clear-cut delineation of the characterization anticipates the ensembles of a Verdi opera. There is a most dramatic touch in Susanna's dignified 'If guilty blood' when, in the middle section, the second Elder interrupts in recitative with the words 'Quick to her fate the loose adultress bear', and the chorus 'Let justice reign' is sufficiently non-committal to enhance this dramatic action. Joachim's bravura 'On the rapid whirlwind's wing' brings the virtuous husband on the scene again, and provides the chorus with the cue for the concluding 'O Joachim, thy wedded troth', an excellent fugal movement, again in two sections.

The third act opens with the chorus 'The cause is decided' in which Handel skilfully dovetails the individual utterances of the voices and builds them up to the massive shout of 'Susanna is guilty'. Susanna's air 'Faith displays her rosy wing' both rises to musical heights and sinks to textual bathos, but the first Elder's 'Round thy urn my tears shall flow' is a perfect portrayal of musical hypocrisy with its overstressed chords of the diminished seventh. Daniel's music, however, is something of a disappointment, though perhaps little else could be expected when he has to sing about 'Chastity, thou bright Cherub'. Chelsias, hitherto a rather heavy father, is given a vigorous and effective air with chorus in 'Rouse your voice', the trumpets being here introduced for the first time. Susanna's bravura 'Guilt trembling' and her duet with Joachim are merely conventional pieces, but the final chorus, a march in honour of connubial virtue, makes a welcome and exhilarating change from the usual 'Hallelujah, Amen', and ends the oratorio on the domestic and intimate note in which it has been most successful.

The year 1749 was a busy one for Handel. The Peace of Aix-la-Chapelle demanded celebration, and the *Fireworks Music* was the result. In addition, Handel became connected with the Foundling Hospital in this year, so only one new oratorio was composed in preparation for the following Lent. Morell's libretto for *Theodora* was derived from the writings of Robert Boyle (1627–1691), whose complete works had been published as recently as 1744, and the Preface to the libretto also acknowledges a French drama as a further source. The story deals with a noble Christian lady of Antioch, who is cast into prison for refusing to attend a pagan feast in honour of Venus. Didimus, a Roman officer and a secret convert to Christianity, resolves to rescue her at the hazard of his life, and is aided by his friend Septimius, the officer in charge of Theodora's guards. He effects Theodora's escape by exchanging clothes with her, but is himself brought to trial. Theodora gives herself up in an attempt to save Didimus, but he will not accept her sacrifice, and both decide to die together for the sake of their faith.

> Yet deem us not unhappy, gentle friend,
> Nor rash; for life we neither hate nor scorn:
> But think it a cheap purchase for the price
> Reserv'd in heaven for purity and faith.

This is one of the best of Morell's libretti; the plot is well managed, the character of Theodora is powerfully drawn, and the language is, on the whole, noble without being stilted. Handel has fully risen to every situation, yet *Theodora*, possibly because of its

tragic ending, was a failure. Its lack of success hurt the composer
deeply, and he is said to have remarked that 'The Jews will not come
to it, as they did to *Judas Maccabaeus*, because it is a Christian
story, and the ladies will not, because it is a virtuous one'. Yet
it is no exaggeration to say that in *Theodora* Handel composed the
noblest and most finely-characterized soprano role of his whole
career.

The first act[1] opens with a recitative in which the Roman Governor
Valens proclaims a feast in honour of Dioclesian's natal day, and his
'Go, my faithful soldier, go' is a fine air in *pomposo* style, which is
continued in the chorus 'And draw a blessing down'. Valens' ruth-
less character is displayed in the vigorous 'Racks, gibbets, sword and
fire', while the following chorus 'For ever thus stands fix'd the
doom' has the 12/8 swing and the instrumental parts for horns so
often used by Handel to express pagan sentiments. Much of the
music of Didimus, written for a male contralto, is florid to modern
ears, but Septimius' air 'Descend, kind pity' is a charming melody
in which the *fioriture* arise naturally from the words. Theodora's
first air, 'Fond, flatt'ring world, adieu!' has a most striking theme
(Ex. 33) which Handel was later to use in a chorus in *Jephtha* to the
words 'Whatever is, is right'. It immediately sets her character as
fervently devout, yet resigned to the sufferings which her faith
draws down upon her. The chorus 'Come, mighty Father' is adapted
from a chamber duet by Clari,[2] but its flowing theme is admirably
adapted to the words. The charming 'As with rosy steps' sung by
Theodora's confidante Irene, provides a moment of relaxation which
is dispelled by the severe fugal chorus 'All pow'r in heav'n above'.
Theodora's pious devotion is then epitomized in the immortal
'Angels ever bright and fair', which is carefully placed to form both
the emotional and the dramatic climax of the first act.

Ex. 33

[1] For the third movement of the fine overture, Handel again borrowed a complete
movement from Gottlieb Muffat's *Componimenti* (cf. Sedley Taylor, op. cit., pp.
10–12). This explains the title 'Trio' which has puzzled more than one commenta-
tor; Muffat's movement was really a trio.—*Ed.*

[2] Cf. Sedley Taylor, op. cit., p. 29.

The second act opens with the pagan rites in honour of Venus, admirably depicted in the choruses 'Queen of Summer' and 'Venus, laughing from the skies', the orchestral colour of the latter again being dominated by the horns and oboes. Handel's pagans always have an ear for a catchy tune, and an almost complete ignorance of counterpoint. These hearty festivities throw into even greater relief the poignancy of Theodora's prison scene. Her two contrasted airs, 'With darkness deep' and 'Oh that I on wings could rise' are each preceded by a short symphony in which repeated chords on the strings are answered by a single held note on the flutes. Nothing could be more simple, nor more effective, particularly since the tone-colour of the flutes has been held in reserve for this one occasion. This whole scene is so striking that the following airs of Didimus, Septimius and Irene seem commonplace by comparison, and even Didimus' charming minuet-like tune 'Sweet rose and lily' would appear to have strayed from some lighter entertainment. Theodora's 'The pilgrim's home' is a lovely siciliana, spoilt by a plethora of verbal similes, but her duet with Didimus 'To thee, thou glorious son of worth' again raises the music to the sphere of tragedy, and this mood is nobly sustained in the chorus 'He saw the lovely youth'.[1]

Morell's management of the last act is hampered by having to provide each of the soloists with the necessary number of airs. Theodora's 'When sunk in anguish' maintains the noble dignity of her music and is also most original in its formal construction. The devotional mood is maintained in the chorus 'Blest be the hand', written mainly in canon and imitation. In the middle of this chorus Theodora enters with a lengthy unaccompanied subject which is later woven into the choral texture as a *canto fermo*, and the whole scene most movingly suggests Theodora's prayer as she resolves to surrender herself to death. This resolution is finely portrayed in the duet 'Whither, princess, do you fly', in which Irene's pleadings are answered by Theodora's gentle determination. The following airs are conventional, though Valens' 'Cease, ye slaves' has some effective bravura passages. The chorus 'How strange their ends' is given a remarkably expressive subject (Ex. 34)[2] which acts as an emotional preparation for the air and duet 'Streams of pleasure ever flowing', in which Didimus and Theodora serenely await their martyrdom. Their tranquil resignation is reflected in the quietly-flowing final

---

[1] Which Handel himself is said to have considered 'far beyond' the 'Hallelujah' chorus in *Messiah.—Ed.*

[2] Another borrowing from Clari: see Supplement 4 to H.-G. (Leipzig, 1892), p. 37.

chorus 'O love divine',[1] of which the minor key suggests a solemn
ecstasy. Macfarren regrets that Morell did not make this final
chorus an opportunity for exultation, but others will feel that the
whole character of Theodora's music artistically demands a quiet
conclusion.

Ex. 34

The failure of *Theodora* caused Morell to return to the Old
Testament for his next oratorio libretto. In the story of Jephtha,
related in the eleventh chapter of the Book of Judges, he felt he had
discovered his best oratorio plot, and he certainly attempted to fill it
with every ingredient for success, including battle choruses, a chorus
of virgins to welcome the victorious Jephtha, and a happy ending,
complete with the conventional 'Hallelujah, Amen'. But though
Jephtha (1751) is well laid out dramatically, its poetry is more than
usually forced and turgid, and, apart from the central incident in
the tale, it gave the ageing composer little chance of doing more than
travelling once more over the same ground that he had covered in
so many previous productions. Handel, faced with approaching
blindness, had frequently to interrupt work on his score, and this
may account for the several borrowings from the Masses of Franz
Johann Habermann.[2] Yet despite every handicap, *Jephtha* maintains a high musical level, the characters are well developed, many of
the melodies are remarkably fresh, and the dramatic situations are
vigorously exploited.

The opening scene, consisting of an air by Zebul, one of Handel's
less interesting basses, and two choruses, is borrowed from Habermann, and is remarkable only for the fact that Handel considered
the music worth borrowing. Jephtha's first air 'Virtue my soul shall
still embrace', though eminently melodious, is hardly characteristic,
and the same might be said of Storge's 'In gentle murmurs' and

---

[1] Partly based on the aria, 'Cease, ruler of the day' in *Hercules*: see p. 271.—*Ed.*

[2] Cf. Sedley Taylor, op. cit., pp. 15–27, where a number of passages are quoted
at length in parallel.

Hamor's 'Dull delay and piercing anguish'. But this melodiousness well suits the character and sentiments of Iphis, whose air 'Take the heart you fondly gave' is charmingly simple and simply charming. The chorus 'O God, behold our sore distress' is again partially borrowed from Habermann, and leads to the dramatic air 'Scenes of horror' in which Storge's character is powerfully delineated. As a contrast, Iphis's 'The smiling dawn of happy days' is a sprightly and tuneful bourrée, and the act ends with the finely descriptive chorus 'When his loud voice in thunder spoke' in which the verbal accentuation is happily wedded to the vigorous fugal subjects.

At the opening of the second act Morell's verbal infelicities cause Handel some difficulty, and the 'Cherub and Seraphim, unbodied forms' come fully to life only when 'They ride on whirlwinds, directing the storms' to two of Handel's most happily illustrative themes. Of the airs which follow, the most attractive is Iphis's 'Tune the soft melodious lute', with its engaging 3/2 rhythm, and Iphis is again well served in the gavotte 'Welcome as the cheerful light',[1] which is taken up by the chorus of virgins. This air forms the climax of the drama, for in welcoming home the victorious Jephtha, Iphis falls a sacrifice to his vow. Jephtha's consternation finds dramatic expression in the powerful 'Open thy marble jaws, O tomb' and the scene builds up to the magnificent quartet 'O spare your daughter', an impressive example of Handel's ensemble writing. But still Handel's dramatic genius is not exhausted. The simple pathos of Iphis's 'Happy they' is followed by the poignant desolation of the accompanied recitative 'Deeper and deeper still', and then comes the final chorus which, beginning sombrely with 'How dark O Lord, are thy decrees', gradually works round to its inscrutable ending, 'Whatever is, is right'—curiously adapted from the introduction to 'Fond flatt'ring world' in *Theodora*. There is, perhaps, more unrelieved tragedy in the four sections of this chorus than in anything else Handel wrote. It was composed under great physical difficulty, and approaching blindness forced Handel to lay the score aside just as he had set the words 'All hid from mortal sight'. The whole music thus reflects the composer's own fortitude and resignation in face of the greatest personal adversity.

The third act begins with two airs for Jephtha which set in contrast his paternal anguish and his pious submission. In the first,

[1] Zebul's 'Freedom now once more possessing' is resurrected from *Agrippina* (Pallante's 'La mia sorte fortunata') and Jephtha's 'His mighty arm' borrows its introduction from a Habermann Mass (see Sedley Taylor, op. cit., pp. 20–1).

'Hide thou thy hated beams', the opening symphony is borrowed, effectively this time, from Habermann.[1] The second air is the immortal 'Waft her, angels', one of the most nobly beautiful of Handel's melodies. Iphis follows with 'Farewell, ye limpid springs', a siciliana of simple pathos, and the chorus 'Doubtful fear', notable for its fine fugal writing, makes impressive use of a chromatically descending subject to the words 'Hear our pray'r in this distress'. After this powerfully-moving scene the Angel's 'Happy, Iphis, shalt thou live' is somewhat too sprightly and long-drawn-out;[2] more effective is Jephtha's arioso 'For ever blessed be thy holy name'. The opening of the chorus 'Theme sublime' is again a borrowing from Habermann,[3] but admirably sets the scene of joyful thanksgiving. There is a happy piece of word-painting at its conclusion when, after a passage of running quavers, the basses intone in minims the words 'and thy mercies shall endure', sustaining the last syllable over five bars. Convention then demands that each of the principal characters should be given an air of rejoicing, and that Iphis and Hamor should be given a duet, but a welcome surprise is in store when Handel ends the conventional duet as a quintet for all the principals. The final chorus is particularly joyous and tuneful in its themes, and the 'Hallelujah, Amen' appears as a lively countersubject to its closing line 'So are they blest who fear the Lord'.

Jephtha has been described as being in many respects one of the most perfect oratorios that Handel ever produced. It certainly typifies the oratorio pattern of Handel's later years. All the characters, with the exception of Zebul, are well drawn and the dramatic scenes are handled with a wealth of musical expressiveness. If it has a fault, it is that many of the airs are a little too conventionally pleasing. Handel seems determined to avoid another failure like *Theodora*, and though the dramatic moments brought from him some of his finest music, there is the feeling that at other times his eye was rather too attentive to his audience. The rhythms of gavotte, bourrée, and minuet peep out a little too obtrusively in his melodious score and contrast a little too obviously with the scenes of real dramatic power and inspiration.

If Lord Kinnoul had spoken of *Jephtha*, rather than of *Messiah*, when he complimented Handel on 'providing the Town with so fine

[1] Cf. Sedley Taylor, op. cit., pp. 24–5.

[2] The *sinfonia* heralding the Angel's appearance is the finale of the early Violin Sonata in D, already drawn on in *Solomon* (see p. 122).—*Ed.*

[3] Cf. Sedley Taylor, op. cit., p. 23.

an entertainment', he would probably have drawn no rebuke upon his head. Handel's sacred oratorios were primarily designed for entertainment, and their composer regarded himself first and foremost as an impresario and craftsman. He turned from opera to oratorio because the latter was a medium which appealed to the respectability of the increasingly well-to-do English middle class. Compared with opera, it was inexpensive to produce, whereas opera, to which Handel had devoted all his earlier energies, was a fashionable foreign importation which too often proved itself a costly financial gamble. Handel was a craftsman, writing for a public whose every reaction he attempted to calculate. His art came naturally and incidentally through craftsmanship, and, if it led him to create works of genius, it was not through any desire to write for posterity. Handel's sacred oratorios must be judged primarily as entertainments against the social and artistic background of his age. If we do this, we shall see more clearly where they transcend their immediate objective, and appreciate those qualities which place many of them among the immortal works of artistic creation.

CHAPTER IV

THE SECULAR ORATORIOS AND CANTATAS

By JULIAN HERBAGE

DURING his visit to Italy, Handel composed two semi-dramatic works, the subjects of which were later to be moulded into his first and last English secular entertainments. These were the serenata *Aci, Galatea e Polifemo*, hastily composed for the wedding of the Duca d'Alvito at Naples in 1708, and the more substantial *Il Trionfo del Tempo e del Disinganno*, written at Rome earlier the same year to a text by Cardinal Panfili. In both works the subject is potentially more important than its treatment, as Handel was later to realize. The mythological subject of *Aci, Galatea e Polifemo* was later to be enlarged into *Acis and Galatea*, and opened the way for other works on mythological subjects, such as *Semele* and *Hercules*. *Il Trionfo del Tempo*, on the other hand, derived its subject from the medieval moralities, and can be seen as the precursor of *L'Allegro, il Pensieroso ed il Moderato* and *The Triumph of Time and Truth*.

This miscellaneous body of secular works is far more difficult to classify than the sacred oratorios, since its artistic ancestry is far more varied. Generally speaking, each work contains a different combination of the ingredients of cantata, masque, ode, opera, and oratorio, as dictated by the poetic basis of the text. In these secular works Handel was often setting the best poets of the English language, including Milton, Dryden, Congreve, and Gay, and in general their libretti were far more fresh and original than the stilted and conventionally sentimentalized texts of the majority of sacred oratorios. Handel, on whom fine language always acted as a powerful inspiration, captures with rare sensitiveness the poetic spirit of his texts, and thus the best of his secular works contain a peculiar spontaneity and Englishness which is often absent from his sacred oratorios. It was perhaps this quality in Handel's secular music which caused Holst to exclaim, 'Why didn't the old chap write more of that sort of thing?' for in this music Handel's genius has evoked the powerful rhetoric of a Dryden, the polished wit of a Congreve, or the pastoral geniality of a Gay. Even when his imperfect knowledge of the English language causes him to make an awkward setting of the noble

cadences of Milton's classic verse, he can still recreate the essential
spirit of its poetry.

Aci, Galatea e Polifemo is little more than an extended cantata
for three solo voices. The text contains the minimum of dramatic
plot or incident, and even though, at the climax, Polifemo kills Acis
by hurling a rock at him, the work ends with the conventional finale
alla gavotta in which all three characters unite to sing the praises
of constancy in love. The interest of the music lies mainly in the
characterization of Polifemo, written for a bass voice with a compass
of two-and-a-half octaves. The extraordinarily wide intervals,
including leaps of two octaves, humorously convey the stature of the
giant, and the contrast with Aci is even more marked through the
latter being allotted to a high soprano voice. Polifemo also has the
most striking of the solo airs, the bravura 'Sibilar l'angui d'Aletto',[1]
with its brilliant trumpet parts and rushing scale passages, effectively
contrasting with the dramatic 'Fra l'ombre e gl'orrori' with its
enormous range from A natural above middle C to D natural below
the bass stave (Ex. 35). Galatea's part is written in the alto clef, and
of her airs the most effective are 'Sforzano a piangere', with obbligato
parts for oboe and 'cello in dialogue, and 'Se m'ami, oh caro!'[2]
accompanied by two 'cellos and bass. Aci's airs are also notable for
their instrumentation, the lovely siciliana 'Qui l'augel da pianta'

Ex. 35

he spe-ra pia-cer, ne spe-ra pia-cer_____ non

tro - va mai pa - - ce, ne spe - ra pia-cer

---

[1] Three years later transferred, almost unchanged, to *Rinaldo* (see p. 23).
[2] Later used in *Il Pastor Fido*; another of her airs, 'Benchè tuoni', was borrowed
for *Teseo*.—*Ed.*

containing long passages accompanied only by a solo oboe and violin, while the moving death song 'Verso già l'alma' has a throbbing quaver accompaniment for strings which dramatically breaks into detached staccato chords at the words 'Lento palpita il mio cor'.

The ensembles are even more interesting. In the trio 'Proverà lo sdegno' the characters of the three principals are subtly differentiated, while in the later 'Dolce, caro' the two lovers sing a serene duet, between the phrases of which Polifemo fulminates in vigorous recitative, a foretaste of 'The flocks shall leave their mountains', which provides a similar climax in the English *Acis and Galatea*. Handel, with his genius for vocal characterization and subtle variations of instrumental colour, has succeeded in making a vivid and dramatic miniature out of a completely nondescript libretto. Twelve years later he was to reset the same fable, but this time to a libretto conceived by a poet and dramatist admirably equipped to do full justice to its pastoral and dramatic qualities. The result was a work that some consider Handel never surpassed in the perfection of its form and spontaneity of its music.

Handel's visit to Italy had been of the utmost importance in developing his musical style. Equally important was his residence with the Duke of Chandos in adapting that style to the inflections of the English language. At Cannons he came into contact with a circle of poets and men of letters which included Pope, Hughes, Arbuthnot, and Gay, and he responded to their influence just as he had absorbed the ideals of the Arcadians in Rome. In England the traditional musico-dramatic form was the masque, of which the poetic and literary basis dated back to the court entertainments of Ben Jonson. Though in the time of Purcell it had been absorbed into that peculiarly English creation, the semi-opera, it had still maintained its individuality, and had emerged in a more concise poetic and dramatic form in such works as Congreve's *The Judgement of Paris*.

Gay's libretto of *Acis and Galatea* adopts the Congreve masque as a model, though there is an increased use of the chorus to compensate for the lack of 'scenes and machines'. It is the chorus who at the opening set the pastoral atmosphere, who warn the lovers of the approach of 'the monster Polypheme', who lament the death of Acis, and who comfort Galatea in the final apotheosis. The text provides a perfect vehicle for musical treatment, and Handel has not only absorbed the essential spirit of the English masque style, but has also brought to his score a truly Mediterranean sparkle. This is immediately reflected in the *presto* overture in Italian concerto style, while the drone-bass of the chorus 'O the pleasure of the plains' carries the echo of Calabrian shepherds' pipes. As in the Chandos Anthems, the choruses are in five parts throughout, the tenors being divided, while the string orchestra contains no part for violas. Galatea is introduced with one of Handel's most charming bird-songs ('Hush, ye pretty warbling choir') while the tender passion of Acis is revealed in the yearning 'Where shall I seek the charming fair?' and the blissfully ecstatic 'Love in her eyes sits playing'. The character of Damon, with his cynical advice about the cares of love, provides relief from the almost too blissful scene, which concludes with the duet and chorus in gigue rhythm 'Happy we'.

Gay has dramatically reserved the entrance of Polyphemus until the second part of the masque, and the approach of the giant is vividly portrayed in the opening chorus 'Wretched lovers'. It begins severely in *a cappella* style, warning the lovers of the fate that must surely overtake them. Then come the excited semiquavers of 'Behold the monster Polypheme', against which the phrase 'Wretched lovers' is still continued as a *canto fermo*. The appearance of Polyphemus is signalized by the abandonment of this contrapuntal treatment, and detached chords on a descending bass depict his 'ample strides', while his 'gyant roars' produce running semiquaver passages from the bass voices, supported by the strings in unison and octaves. After this powerful chorus, Polyphemus's amorous confession strikes the right preposterous note, enhanced in the air 'O ruddier than the cherry' by the wide interval between his bass voice and the high, sprightly counter-melody on flute (recorder) and violins. Damon, always ready with advice, is given the lovely air 'Would you gain the tender creature', curiously prophetic of the type of melody which Arne was later to make so much his own. Acis responds with the brilliant 'Love sounds th' alarm', which both completes the delineation of his character and also vocally provides an admirable contrast to his earlier airs.

The trio 'The flocks shall leave the mountains' forms the dramatic climax of the masque, as did the trio 'Dolce, caro' in the Italian serenata. The treatment in the later work is more subtle and musically close-knit, the steadily-flowing rhythm being maintained through Polyphemus's interjections of 'torture, fury, rage'. The death of Acis is condensed into eight most effective bars of *recitativo-arioso* which lead into the chorus 'Mourn, all ye Muses', the style of which owes much to Purcell, and suggests Handel's familiarity with *Dido and Aeneas*. Galatea's air with chorus 'Must I my Acis still bemoan' gains in effectiveness through the absence of soprano voices in the chorus. The transformation of Acis into a fountain is described in Galatea's 'Heart the seat of soft delight' with its rippling, dotted-note accompaniment in which the flutes double the violins in the upper octave. The final chorus 'Galatea, dry thy tears' is a flowing minuet in which the homophonic treatment of the chorus is admirably contrasted with an elaborate violin obbligato.

In addition to the completely separate Italian and English versions of *Acis and Galatea*, Handel produced in 1732 a curious bi-lingual entertainment, which combined the music of both previous productions, and also included some new numbers and adaptations from earlier works. This strange *pasticcio*, reminiscent of the early days of Italian opera in England, was given as a counterblast to the performance of the Cannons version which the Arnes, father and son, were presenting at the Little Theatre in the Haymarket. Handel, with expensive Italian operatic singers on his pay-roll, obviously had to retaliate with an entertainment for his operatic patrons, in which their favourite singers would be given the principal roles. His text was therefore based on an enlargement of the Italian version, of which he retained some eight of the original numbers, while transposing and rewriting others to suit the capabilities of Strada and Senesino, who played Galatea and Acis respectively. From the English version he took half a dozen numbers, including the opening and final choruses, and translated the words of 'Where shall I seek' into 'Lontan' da te'. Two further choruses were borrowed from the *Birthday Ode* and the Brockes *Passion*, and two more, including the charming minuet 'Smiling Venus' (with the alternative Italian words 'Care selve') were specially written for the occasion, as were a handful of arias and much of the recitative.

The resulting full evening's entertainment is little more than a curiosity, but is at least interesting in that it shows how Handel, until he abandoned opera for oratorio, still relied entirely on his operatic singers and audience. Though the King's Theatre and the Little Theatre stood opposite each other in the Haymarket, there was, musically speaking, an unbridgeable gulf between them. Even ten years later, when Handel courageously introduced English singers into his oratorios, Horace Walpole scathingly referred to them as 'the goddesses from the farces, and the singers of roast-beef from between the acts of both the theatres'.

The Anglo-Italian version of *Acis and Galatea* was certainly not an idea of Handel's choosing. It had been forced on him by the challenge of the Arnes' pirated production of the Cannons masque. During the next few years Handel was too busy fighting the 'Opera of the Nobility' to compose any new works in oratorio style. But as this operatic war of attrition gradually reduced both sides to near-bankruptcy, Handel increasingly realized the value of his Lenten performances in recouping some of his operatic losses. He could neither obtain nor afford any singer to compete with the 'Nobility's' redoubtable Farinelli, while the loss of Carestini from his own company and the departure of Princess Anne, who had married the Prince of Orange, deprived him of the two chief supports of his operatic schemes. In July 1735 he wrote to his newly-found friend and patron Charles Jennens: 'There is no certainty of any scheme for next Season', but added, 'it is probable that something or other may be done'.

The most important 'something or other' turned out to be a setting of Dryden's Cecilian ode *Alexander's Feast* (1736). This ode had been originally set by Jeremiah Clark in 1697, and in 1711 Thomas Clayton had produced a new version, which was apparently a complete failure.[1] The task of adjusting the words 'necessary to render them fit to receive modern composition' was allotted to Newburgh Hamilton, who, in his own words, confined himself 'to a plain division of it into airs, recitatives, or choruses, looking upon the words in general so sacred as scarcely to violate one in the order of its first place'. Newburgh Hamilton certainly undertook his task with due reverence, and made several improvements, such as altering the words 'The Prince, unable to conceal his pain' from a chorus to a solo. Unfortunately, as a concession to the tastes of the times, he felt constrained to add some final lines of his own, so that the ode could end with the usual sprightly chorus in minuet time that convention demanded. Handel, of course, accepted the compromise, though at later performances he was persuaded to realize its artistic error, just he later removed Jennens' *Moderato* from Milton's *L'Allegro ed il Pensieroso*.

As *Alexander's Feast* is one of the few works in which Chrysander, the editor of the Händel Gesellschaft edition, followed the printed score rather than Handel's manuscript, it is of interest to note the composer's original idea in setting the ode. In the first part he intended the chorus 'The list'ning crowd' to be repeated after the

---

[1] Marcello's *Timoteo* is a setting of an Italian translation of Dryden by Antonio Conti: cf. Chrysander, *G. F. Händel*, Vol. II, pp. 424–6, and A. d'Angeli, *Benedetto Marcello* (Milan, 1946), pp. 88–9 and facsimile 12.—*Ed.*

air 'With ravish'd ears'. There is also the instruction 'Concerto per
la Harpa, ex B' after the recitative 'Timotheus plac'd on high'.
The recitative 'The praise of Bacchus' was originally written for a
bass (Mr. Erard), and after the air 'He sung Darius' is the crossed-
out instruction 'Coro dal segno'. In the second part, in the recitative
'Thus long ago' there are two blank lines left for 'Harpa', but most
interesting of all is the completely different ending of the ode. The
chorus 'Let old Timotheus yield the prize' is followed by the words
'segue il Concerto per Organo', and then comes a recitative, of which
the words—

> Tune ev'ry string, your voices raise
> Joy dwell on each melodious tongue
> Of bright Cecilia be your song
> In smoothest lines, in softest lays.

are neither in the contemporary printed version nor in the Händel
Gesellschaft edition. This is followed by the aria 'Your voices raise'
(set as a recitative in the printed version and that of the Händel
Gesellschaft), while the duet 'Let's imitate her notes above'[1] finds no
place in the original manuscript.

Dryden's poem is without doubt the finest of all Cecilian odes,
not only on account of its vigorous and picturesque verse, but also
in respect of its varied and well-regulated incident. It offers the
composer an occasion for the musical expression of every emotion
and passion, and its climaxes are admirably disposed. Handel seized
on every opportunity provided by the text, and his score is vivid and
vigorous throughout. Dryden's terse, epigrammatic style is immediately captured in the march-like song and chorus 'Happy pair'
with its broad melody and sprightly passages in dotted rhythm on
the violins. A sense of spaciousness is provided by the opening
symphony of 'The list'ning crowd', and the orchestral figuration is
amply developed to form a background to the massive homophonic
writing of the song and chorus 'Bacchus ever fair and young', while
bassoons and violas bring a darker colour to the air and chorus which
tell of the fate of the dead Darius. The song 'Softly sweet in Lydian
measure' is an exquisite air with 'cello obbligato, and in the chorus
'The many rend the skies', built on a five-bar ground-bass, Handel
makes use of remarkable effects of chiaroscuro, thus matching it to
the earlier chorus 'The list'ning crowd'.

The second part is even more remarkable. Handel has reserved

---

[1] Based on an Italian cantata: see p. 194.

the trumpets and drums for the chorus 'Break his bands of sleep asunder'[1] in which the two-bar ostinato on the timpani, combined with brilliant trumpet and string passages and the broadly vigorous treatment of the chorus brings to mind Mozart's remark of Handel, that 'when he chooses he can strike like a thunderbolt'. The famous 'Revenge, Timotheus cries' is notable as being the only *da capo* aria in the final version of the work, and in its middle section the 'ghastly band, each a torch in his hand' are vividly portrayed by the sombre tones of three bassoons, doubled by *divisi* violas and 'cello, the organ playing the bass *tasto solo* throughout. The song and chorus 'Thais led the way' adopts the Purcellian idiom, and its simple, minuet-like refrain makes an admirable foil to the following choruses in praise of Cecilia, in which Handel for the first time exerts all his contrapuntal skill. Fine as is the chorus 'At last divine Cecilia came', with its homophonic introduction and fugal continuation,[2] it is eclipsed by 'Let old Timotheus yield the prize'. Here four soloists announce in turn a suitably descriptive vocal subject to each of the four lines of the text[3], and these four subjects are combined by the chorus into a majestic fugal pattern. After this unique piece of writing the final chorus, both in text and in music, comes as an anti-climax, though its sprightly rhythm, reminiscent of the conventional operatic finales of the times, doubtless sent the eighteenth-century audiences away well satisfied by Mr. Handel's fine entertainment.

The success of *Alexander's Feast* doubtless encouraged Handel to search for a further Cecilian Ode to set to music. Dryden's Ode for the celebration of 1697 is more conventional in its material and pattern, but its verse is still powerful and evocative. In accordance with custom the trumpet, flute, violin and organ are successively praised, but an original touch is provided at the conclusion of the poem, when the Last Judgement is suggested in the lines:

> So when the last and dreadful hour,
> This crumbling pageant shall devour;
> The Trumpet shall be heard on high,—
> The dead shall live, the living die,
> And Music shall untune the sky.

[1] The accompaniment to the preceding recitative, 'Now strike the golden lyre again' is based on the keyboard Capriccio in G minor.—*Ed.*

[2] The fugue-subject seems to have been adapted from one by Graun: cf. Sedley Taylor, op. cit., p. 35.

[3] Three of them derived from a trio of 1708: see p. 198.

Though the Ode is a comparatively minor work, the music is none the less inspired. The use of diminished sevenths is most effectively employed in describing 'Nature underneath a heap of jarring atoms', and though the original idea for this accompanied recitative came from two newly-published harpsichord pieces by Muffat,[1] Handel's improvements are equally remarkable for their dramatic force and technical skill. In the chorus 'From harmony' (again indebted to Muffat) the words 'through all the compass of the notes' is aptly illustrated by a scale passage, at first ascending and later descending, while 'the diapason' is characterized by a pedal note, emphasized by the suspensions in the orchestral parts. The air 'What passion cannot Music raise and quell' has an elaborate 'cello obbligato, while the song and chorus 'The trumpet's loud clangour' pays the sincerest form of flattery to Purcell's 'Come if you dare', particularly in 'the double, double, double beat of the thundering drum'. The air 'The soft complaining flute' is accompanied by *traverso*, lute, and organ, and the 'sharp violins' employ their very bottom note at the words 'depth of pain'. It is interesting that the air in praise of the organ (yet again derived from Muffat) includes a part marked 'Organ Diapasons', as the eighteenth-century instrument was often weak in this fundamental tone-colour. The powers of Orpheus are described in a movement with an elaborate introduction, marked 'Alla Hornpipe', and the final chorus is on an extended scale. The opening takes the form of a chorale of which each line is introduced by the solo soprano, unaccompanied, and repeated by the chorus with orchestral figuration: this is followed by an elaborate fugue dominated by the two subjects 'The dead shall live' and 'Music shall untune the sky'.

The comparatively small scale of the *Ode for St. Cecilia's Day* is no doubt the reason why it is rarely performed today. But it is a work which displays both Handel's technical accomplishment and also his instinctive self-association with the spirit of the poem which he is setting. Perhaps more important is the essentially English character of the whole conception. Handel here carries forward the torch of Purcell, who himself once described music as 'a forward child, which gives hope of what it may be hereafter in England when the masters of it shall find more encouragement'. Handel has been

[1] From the *Componimenti* (probably published in the first half of 1739: see *Zeitschrift der internationalen Musikgesellschaft*, Vol. IX, pp. 188–9): cf. Sedley Taylor, op. cit., pp. 6–8. All three movements of the overture—later expanded into the Concerto Grosso, Op. 6, No. 5—and other passages in the Ode, are indebted to Muffat.—*Ed.*

accused of destroying the English musical tradition. Actually, despite his foreign origin and early training, he did more than any other composer to fulfil the tradition of Purcell. It is the tragedy of English music that over a century and a half had to elapse before a native composer arose who was within measurable distance of the greatness, technical and inspirational, of Handel.

The success of *Alexander's Feast* and the *Ode for St. Cecilia's Day* no doubt encouraged Handel to search among the English poets for a further oratorio libretto, while the failure of *Israel in Egypt* caused him temporarily to favour a secular rather than a sacred subject. Another incentive in this direction may have been the successful production in 1738 of Dalton's adaptation of Milton's *Comus*, with music by the twenty-eight-year-old Thomas Arne. Handel could scarcely have resisted such a challenge, remembering that it was the Arnes who, six years earlier, had pirated his own *Acis and Galatea*. Accordingly, he accepted from Charles Jennens a libretto of which the first two acts were based on alternate stanzas of Milton's poems *L'Allegro* and *Il Pensieroso*, while the third act consisted of Jennens' own lines in Miltonic style praising the virtue of Moderation.

L'Allegro (composed between 19 January and 4 February, 1740) is, in effect, an allegorical oratorio on somewhat similar lines to *Il Trionfo del Tempo* (which Handel had revived in 1737), with Mirth, Melancholy, and Moderation as its principal characters. While it offered Handel great scope for his powers of descriptive writing, it had the disadvantage that Milton's metre was insufficiently varied for setting in the eighteenth-century style, particularly by one who was still comparatively unfamiliar with the cadences and inflexions of English speech. Furthermore, Jennens' concluding act could not fail to be merely a pale imitation of what had gone before, and Handel wisely discarded it in later performances as soon as he was decently able to do so without giving offence to his friend and patron. Thus, while the oratorio contains several of Handel's freshest and most delightful airs, the patchwork construction of its libretto, its almost complete lack of dramatic interest and the diminuendo of its conclusion, all tend to make it a somewhat unsatisfactory entertainment.

The interest of *L'Allegro*, indeed, lies entirely in the picturesque charm and contrast of its individual airs and choruses. There is no overture,[1] and the oratorio opens with Mirth and Melancholy each

---

[1] Both in London and Dublin Handel used existing concertos as overtures to Parts I and II, and an organ concerto as overture to Part III.—*Ed.*

inveighing against the other in short accompanied recitatives, the orchestra in each case impersonating the opposite character. The melody of Mirth's first song, 'Come, thou goddess fair and free' owes much to Purcell's 'Nymphs and shepherds', while in his next air and chorus the words 'laughter holding both his sides' are effectively illustrated by staccato runs on the syllable 'ho' of 'holding'. The air and chorus 'Come and trip it as you go' adopts a sprightly minuet style, and contrast is provided by Melancholy's following scene consisting of accompanied recitative, solo, duet, and chorus, the three latter being constructed on the same two-bar ground-bass. The air 'Sweet bird, that shun'st the noise of folly' is both the most elaborate and the most exquisite of all Handel's bird-songs, and affords an exacting test for both solo flute and coloratura soprano. The jovial song and chorus 'Mirth, admit me of thy crew' introduces horns to describe the sounds of the chase, but most lovely of all Mirth's airs is the brief siciliana 'Let me wander not unseen', a perfect musical evocation of Milton's beautiful lines. Indeed, this whole final scene, including the descriptive accompanied recitative 'Mountains, on whose barren breast', the pealing chimes of 'Or let the merry bells ring round', the dancelike chorus 'and young and old come forth to play', leading to the quiet conclusion 'Then past the day to bed they creep,' forms a pastoral cantata unsurpassed, both in words and music, in its description of the English rural scene.

The second act shifts the action from country to town, and neither Milton nor Handel is so successful in capturing its atmosphere. The air 'But oh! sad virgin' is elaborately conceived with a highly ornamental 'cello obbligato, but the music scarcely comes to life. More successful is the solo-and-chorus 'Populous cities please me more', with its descriptive semiquavers to the words 'busy, busy hum', and its trumpets and drums suggesting the 'high triumphs' of the text. Throughout this act Handel is hampered by Milton's verse which, though it makes good reading, is epigrammatic rather than lyric or descriptive. It is little wonder that Handel could make no more than a superficial setting of such lines as:

> I'll to the well-trod stage anon,
> If Jonson's learned sock be on;
> Or sweetest Shakespeare, Fancy's child,
> Warble his native wood-notes wild.

The first line produces a good, broad tune, while the last breaks into the inevitable ornamental triplets, but the whole verse resists and resents musical treatment. More successful is a comparatively banal couplet such as:

> These delights, if thou can'st give,
> Mirth, with thee I mean to live.

which at least provides the opportunity for a vigorous air and chorus characterized by a brilliant trumpet obbligato. At the end of the act, however, Handel saves the situation by a purely musical device, based on his unique powers of improvisation. The short homophonic chorus 'Then let the pealing organ blow' contains three silent pause bars marked 'organo ad libitum', and after a short soprano recitative comes the instruction 'Organo ad libitum il soggetto della fuga seguente'. The fugue in question is the final chorus of the act, 'These pleasures, Melancholy, give',[1] and the elaborate treatment of its two subjects shows that Handel must have been a master of extemporization on its themes. Would that he had recorded for posterity what must have been a unique musical experience, for nowhere else in his oratorios has he allowed himself such happy scope for improvisation at the organ.

Of the last act of *L'Allegro* it is only necessary to record that Handel's music is no more inspiring than Jennens' text. Though Handel's courtesy to his friend and patron may have prompted him to write from Dublin, 'I assure you that the words of the *Moderato* are vastly admired', it is significant that as early as April 1741 he had announced '*L'Allegro ed il Pensieroso* with Dryden's *Ode*'. Thenceforth, apart from the Dublin performances, the work was always given in this form on the few occasions on which it was produced in London.

If, as has been suggested, Arne's production of Milton's *Comus* caused Handel to turn to Milton's poems for an oratorio libretto, it is also likely that Arne's setting of Congreve's *The Judgement of Paris*, given at Drury Lane in 1740, was equally responsible for Handel's interest in Congreve's opera *Semele*. It was the custom of rival operatic composers to compete with each other by setting the same libretto, and, though Handel would obviously not demean himself by entering into rivalry with a young theatre composer such as Arne, he could at least endeavour to show the upstart Englishman how to set an English poet to music. *Semele* was written by Congreve in 1707, the year in which Addison had entered the operatic

---

[1] It is based on the last part of the trio setting of *Quel fior che all' alba ride* (1708). —*Ed.*

field with his ill-fated *Rosamond*. Congreve, however, was wiser
than Addison, both because he did not attempt to put his opera on
the stage, though John Eccles apparently wrote music for it, and also
because he followed the form of the English masque rather than that
of the newly-imported Italian opera. Handel's instinct and intuition
are nowhere more clearly displayed than in his realization that
Congreve's 'English Opera' had to be set in the style of Purcell
rather than in the Italianate idiom to which he was accustomed.

Congreve's preface to *Semele* shows his indebtedness to Dryden.
He describes recitative as 'a kind of prose in Musick; its beauty
consists of coming near Nature, and in improving the natural
accents of Words by more Pathetick or Emphatical Tones'. Like
Dryden, too, he concentrates on the supernatural, his mortals
generally being engaged in temple scenes and sacrifices, while his
immortals airily descend in clouds, rainbows, and machines drawn
by peacocks. Congreve, indeed, accepted the Italian conventions
only in so far as they were acceptable to English audiences, and his
libretto is therefore in the tradition of such works as *Venus and
Adonis* and *Dido and Aeneas*. It might have been a prototype of
English operatic entertainment, in spite of the fact that modern
critics of Congreve have dismissed it as an insipid affair of no
consequence.

Handel, in *Semele* (1743), has displayed a dramatic instinct as sure
as Purcell's. His score is totally unlike his Italian operas, and
shows a unique understanding of both the English masque and the
Purcell-Dryden semi-opera. Its greatest music, apart from one or
two immortal airs, is contained in its accompanied recitatives and,
although not intended for the stage, the whole work is remarkable for
its essentially dramatic approach.

The first act is charmingly summarized by Congreve: 'Semele
is on the point of Marriage with Athamas; which Marriage is about
to be solemniz'd in the Temple of Juno, Goddess of Marriages, when
Jupiter by ill Omens interrupts the Ceremony; and afterwards
transports Semele to a private Abode prepar'd for her.' Handel's
music for this act owes much to the sacrificial scenes of Purcell,
but in such numbers as the quartet 'Why dost thou thus untimely
grieve' he brings in his operatic experience of characterization.
Again in the accompanied recitative 'Wing'd with our fear' he
describes with dramatic power Jupiter's descent in the shape of
an eagle, and his abduction of Semele. The indecision of Semele
throughout this act has been admirably portrayed, particularly in

the beautiful air 'O Jove! in pity teach me', while the final air and chorus, 'Endless pleasure, endless love', shows decisively where her feelings really lay, and is a perfect setting in gavotte style of Congreve's polished verse.

The second act opens with a scene between Juno and her attendant Iris, which is again a masterpiece of characterization, particularly Juno's accompanied recitative 'Awake, Saturnia', with its vengeful expressiveness, and her air 'Hence Iris, hence away', with its vigorous rhythm. 'O sleep, why dost thou leave me?' with its lovely 'cello obbligato, changes the scene to the atmosphere of Loves and Zephyrs which surround Semele and Jupiter in their amour. The whole act from now on assumes the character of a Purcellian masque, particularly in the choruses 'How engaging, how endearing' and the *alla hornpipe* 'Now Love, that everlasting boy'. But if these choruses and the final scene between Ino and Semele owe a debt to Purcell, Jupiter's air 'Where'er you walk' is an individual creation which no one except Handel could have achieved.

In the last act the opening scene between Somnus and Juno produces one of the finest airs in 'Leave me, loathsome light', and the opening symphony, characterized by bassoons and organ *tasto solo*, achieves an atmosphere as evocative as the Witch of Endor's scene in *Saul*. The dramatic continuity of this act is remarkable, and is effected through the extensive use of accompanied recitative and the omission of the chorus. The action is carried forward in dialogue, first between Semele and Juno, the latter disguised as Ino, and singing only in recitative as, with 'artful Insinuations', she prevails on Semele to make the fatal request to Jupiter. The following scene, between Jupiter and Semele, provides the dramatic climax of the whole opera. Its culmination is reached with the two final accompanied recitatives, and never in his whole output has Handel surpassed Jupiter's 'Ah, whither has she gone?' or Semele's 'Ah me! too late I now repent' (Ex. 36). The catastrophe is powerfully evoked in the chorus 'Oh, terror and astonishment', with its remarkable chromatically-descending final phrase, started by the sopranos over a pedal bass, and finally descending to the bass part itself. Even Congreve's happy ending is matched by Handel's vigorous 'Happy, happy shall we be', with its most original fugal subject.

Semele is a work which, if given stage presentation, would probably appeal more to modern audiences than any of Handel's operas. Never has Handel captured more successfully the spirit of a poem, and never has he sustained more successfully dramatic atmosphere.

Ex. 36

Larghetto assai e piano

for pi-ty I im-plore   I   faint   for pi-ty I im-plore, oh help, oh

help!   I can no more

One marvels how anyone except an English musician could have matched the subtle style of Congreve, yet there can be no doubt that in *Semele* Handel has created the prototype of what might have become a truly English opera. The English operatic composer of today would be well advised to study Handel's score, and study it carefully, for Handel's genius in this work consists in the most subtle touches, which produce their effect both through their dramatic sense of timing and also by their varied and economical use of resources.

Among Handelian anecdotes is one of Dr. Morell's complaint to the composer that his setting of an air in *Judas Maccabaeus* was not worthy of the words. Handel was rightly indignant. 'Mein musick is good musick', he exclaimed. 'It is your words that is bad.' Only too often the words which Handel set were bad or mediocre. His greatest strokes of inspiration were due to texts by such poets as Gay, Dryden, Milton, and Congreve, and, of course, the immortal prose of the Bible. It is no accident that *Messiah, Samson, Alexander's Feast, Acis and Galatea*, and *Semele* are among his greatest and most sustained achievements. In his other oratorios he may succeed in spite of his text, but is too often defeated by it. Thomas Broughton, who wrote the libretto of *Hercules* after Sophocles' drama, was certainly an eminent scholar, but he unfortunately happened to live in an age which regarded Rowe's *Fair Penitent* as the pinnacle of tragedy. His libretto is eminently worthy, but it lacks true dramatic characterization and a sense of the theatre. Congreve, in *Semele*, may be criticized for his lighthearted treatment of the fable, but at least his characters are drawn with the same polished ease and truth to nature which distinguishes *The Way of the World*. Broughton's are merely puppets that adopt the conventional postures of the eighteenth-century tragic stage.

It is through Broughton's shortcomings, rather than the composer's, that *Hercules* (composed in 1744 at the same time as *Belshazzar*) is not the greatest of Handel's oratorios. Certainly it is one of the most remarkable of Handel's scores. The musical characterization of Dejanira alone makes it unique. She is not, like Juno, merely a vengefully jealous wife, but is a psychological study in the destructive power of jealousy. Handel suggests this dominating trait in her character in her very first air, 'The world, when day's career is run', which, in its tortured chromatic phrase (Ex. 37), expresses a more complex emotion than mere sorrow at the absence of Hercules. Her son Hyllus is little more than a stock character, but Handel manages to invest his accompanied recitative 'I feel the God' with great dignity and power. The chorus, as in Greek drama, acts as a commentary throughout, and, though sometimes holding up the action, its music is always carefully wrought, as in the elaborate fugue ('immortal fame') of 'Oh, filial piety'. Indeed, the score too often shows Handel's obsession with technical contrivance, and many of the airs seem mechanical as a result. Only with the entry of Iole does Handel bring a warmth of lyrical emotion into the music, in particular in her impassioned air 'My father', with its serene continuation 'Peaceful rest'.[1] Hercules himself is merely sketched as a bluff, vigorous character, in his air 'The God of battle', while the final chorus of the first act, 'Crown with festal pomp', employs conventional Handelian methods of musical rejoicing.

Ex. 37

[1] As Leichtentritt remarks (op. cit., p. 456), 'the new, so-called Gluck style is here already fully developed'.—*Ed.*

The second act is notable for Iole's expressive air 'Ah! think what ills', and Dejanira's consuming passion is strikingly portrayed in the chorus 'Jealousy', in which the voices enter arrestingly on a chord of the diminished seventh. The fugal continuation, to the words 'Trifles light as floating air', has a most descriptive subject, and on the return of the 'Jealousy' music the diminished seventh gains extra pungency through its tonic pedal-bass; this is the most striking of Handel's choruses descriptive of the baser passions. Contrast is provided by the voluptuous chorus 'Wanton god of am'rous fires', with its ascending scale-passages of triplets, but the drama is resumed with Dejanira's vigorously scornful 'Resign thy club', in the middle section of which the chromatically-descending phrase on 'Venus and her whining boy' displays once more her vindictive passions. Unfortunately, Broughton has here had to make his characters act like puppets, and the duet between Dejanira and Iole, followed by the chorus 'Love and Hymen', in gavotte style, ends the act on a false note of joyful reconciliation.

The prelude to the third act once more reiterates the note of tragedy with its alternate passages marked *largo* and *furioso*. Lichas describes in dignified manner the mortal accident to Hercules in the air 'Oh, scene of unexampl'd woe', but the opening of the chorus 'Tyrants now no more shall dread' has a banal theme, and only comes to life at the words 'the world's avenger is no more'. The tortured death of Hercules is magnificently realized in the *concitato* air 'Oh Jove! what land is this', but the climax of the oratorio comes with Dejanira's 'Where shall I fly?' in which, her mind unhinged by the catastrophe, she alternately imagines herself scourged by snakes and scorpions, and pleads to be hidden from the hateful sight. This extended vocal scena is dramatic and poignant beyond anything else that Handel ever wrote. In it, and in Hercules' death scene, Handel exploits to the utmost every dramatic musical effect known to the eighteenth century. The harmony is amazingly bold, modulations are completely unprepared and shattering in their effect (Ex. 38). The scene is dominated by a chromatic phrase which had been implicit in Dejanira's first air, and thus her loss of reason seems the inevitable result of her fatal jealousy. *Hercules* should have finished on this note and its happy ending suits it ill. Congreve, master dramatist that he was, could toy with his characters in *Semele*, and by artifice make everyone live happily ever after. Broughton had no such dramatic ability to retrieve himself from the tragic situation, and all Handel could do was to write a conventional ending which,

Ex. 38

your keen-est mal-ice   yield to De-jan-i-ra's   mis-
-tak-en   cru-el   treach-er-ous De-jan-i-ra.

charming as it is, fails to sound convincing after such immensely powerful music.

The history of another Handel work connected with Hercules is rather curious; it links his name with two other eminent figures. Though Tobias Smollett was later to achieve fame as a novelist, his early ambition had been to become a writer of tragedies. He came to London in 1739 with the tragedy *The Regicide* in his pocket, but failed to get it produced. Ten years later, shortly after the publication of his first novel, *Roderick Random*, he offered to John Rich of Covent Garden an *Alceste* based on the tragedy by Euripides. Rich accepted the play, and decided on a spectacular production. He engaged Servandoni to paint the scenery, and asked Handel, 'in liquidation of a debt too heavy for Handel to pay in money', to write the music. The score was completed early in 1750, but for some reason the tragedy was never staged. The music, however, was too good to waste, and accordingly a month or two later Handel fitted it with a new libretto based on the story of Hercules' choice of Virtue in preference to Pleasure as related by Xenophon. The resulting work, *The Choice of Hercules*, described as a 'Musical Interlude' and containing a few additional numbers, was in March 1751 introduced as 'an additional new act' to *Alexander's Feast*.

The adaptation of the music to its new text was most skilfully achieved, and only on rare occasions is it at all out of keeping with its new situation. The characters are Pleasure, a high soprano who, like Rowland Hill's Devil, has all the best tunes, Virtue, a

mezzo-soprano who is musically less well served, Hercules, an alto, who
has very little to do for the central character, and an Attendant on
Pleasure (tenor) whose single song 'Enjoy the sweet Elysian grove' is
one of the most charming airs in the whole piece. The opening is
given over to Pleasure, suitably characterized in an orchestral introduction by a rippling, dotted-note rhythm and ornamental scale-
passages on flutes, bassoon, and strings. Her first air, 'Come,
blooming boy', is a voluptuous melody in a triple-time minor, and
its sprightly violin counter-subject is later woven into the vocal
texture of the chorus 'Seize these blessings', based on the same
musical material. Pleasure's next air, 'Then the brisk sparkling
nectar', has a suitably vigorous and syncopated rhythm, and its
Bacchanalian atmosphere is enhanced by an obbligato part for horns.
Virtue's entrance is not so fortunate, as her song, originally set to
the words 'Gentle Morpheus', with ornamental solo passages for
flute and violin, is scarcely apposite to her exhortations about 'manly
youth'. She is better served in the following 'Go assert thy heav'nly
race' with its vigorous *tutti unisoni* accompaniment, and the air and
chorus 'So shalt thou gain', in the stately measure of a Lully *entrée*,
achieves strength and brilliance through the introduction of the
trumpets. Pleasure replies with a ravishing song and chorus in
gavotte style, 'Turn thee, youth', but Hercules' first air, 'Yet can I
hear that dulcet lay', suffers from the fact that it was again originally
an invocation to Morpheus: indeed, an alternative setting of 'Gentle
Morpheus'.

The climax is reached with the trio 'Where shall I go?' The
smooth, voluptuous curves of Pleasure's vocal line contrast with the
more formally-shaped ornamentation of Virtue's phrases, and towards the conclusion the two contestants answer each other in free
inversion, while Hercules' final 'Where shall I go?' ends indecisively
on a half-close. From now on Virtue is better served. Her air
'Mount, mount the steep ascent' has a broad melodic line and
vigorous treatment. The chorus 'Arise, arise!' is laid out with
orchestral brilliance, and its massive vocal homophony alternates
with close fugal writing at the words 'claim thy native skies'. Even
finer is the final chorus 'Virtue will place' which, beginning on an
ostinato ground-bass, concludes with an elaborately worked fugue
with two subjects, that provides a magnificent apotheosis.

Before considering Handel's last oratorio, *The Triumph of Time
and Truth* (1757), we must turn back nearly half a century to consider the youthful work in which it is rooted: *Il Trionfo del Tempo*

e del Disinganno (1708). After the success of Handel's oratorio
La Resurrezione in Rome, the Cardinal Ottoboni had naturally been
anxious for the young Saxon composer to return to his patronage.
Among Ottoboni's circle was Cardinal Panfili, known by the pseu-
donym of 'Fenizio' among the Arcadians, who was a prolific dramatic
poet of some talent.   Panfili wrote for Handel an allegorical poem in
which Beauty, at first tempted by the seductive delights of Pleasure,
is eventually won over to a higher aim by the reasoning of Time and
Truth.   Panfili's text, though it gave Handel little dramatic scope,
at least provided him with the opportunity of composing a succession
of contrasted arias and ensembles in which he could also exploit the
virtuosity of the players in Corelli's orchestra.   His score displays
throughout both his consummate technical accomplishment and also
his thorough absorption of the Italianate style.

The chief interest of *Il Trionfo del Tempo* lies in its variety of
treatment, both vocal and orchestral.   There are only four characters,
Bellezza (Beauty) and Piacere (Pleasure), both sopranos, Disinganno
(Truth), an alto, and Tempo (Time), a tenor, and the work, strangely
enough, appears to end with an air for Bellezza, rather than with the
conventional chorus of the principal characters.   The individual
numbers maintain a high standard of excellence, and the whole work
is scarcely less important than *La Resurrezione*.   Particularly effective
use is made of chromatics in Piacere's air 'Fosca genio' and Tempo's
answering 'Urne voi', with its dramatic alternations of repeated
quavers and semiquavers in the accompaniment.[1]   In the duet
between Bellezza and Piacere there are florid obbligato passages for
oboes and violins, while Bellezza's 'Un pensiero nemico' is admirably
characterized by its *moto perpetuo* violin figure in vigorous semiquavers.   Tempo's 'Nasce l'uomo', answered to the same music by
Disinganno's 'L'uomo sempre', has a charming minuet refrain, and
the following instrumental sonata is a brilliant miniature concerto
with solos for organ, violin, viola, 'cello, and oboes.   The organ again
has an important solo part in Piacere's 'Un leggiardo giovinetto', and
Bellezza's 'Venga il Tempo' has a gigue-like accompaniment for
continuo which lends itself to brilliant extemporization.   The first
part ends with the quartet 'Se non sei più', mainly accompanied by
the upper strings in unison.

[1] Arnold Schering (*Zeitschrift der internationalen Musikgesellschaft*, Vol. IX,
pp. 244–6) suggested that Handel had modelled this on a *recitativo accompagnato*
in Giacomo Perti's *Nerone* (1693), but the parallel is only general and not very
close.—*Ed.*

Ex. 39

The second part opens with one of Piacere's loveliest airs 'Chiudi, chiudi', beginning on a dominant chord with aery oboe trills echoed by the violins (Ex. 39). The quartet 'Voglio Tempo' is characterized by the high, sustained notes of Bellezza's vocal line and the transparent part-writing for the other voices. Most beautiful of all is Piacere's 'Lascia la spina', originally a sarabande in the opera *Almira*, and later to achieve immortality as 'Lascia ch'io pianga' in *Rinaldo*. Disinganno's 'Chi già fu' is based on the same material as Lucifer's 'Caddi, è ver' from *La Resurrezione*, and must have been a favourite theme with Handel and his audiences, as it occurs elsewhere in his works.[1] Piacere's last air, 'Come nembo che fugge', is aptly illustrated by rapid obbligato passages for oboes and 'cellos and the final apotheosis of Bellezza is achieved with serene dramatic beauty in her song 'Tu, del ciel ministro'. Here detached chords in the strings provide a steady, throbbing pulse, over which the voice and solo violin soar in celestial dialogue.

Nearly thirty years passed. The year 1737 was probably the most hectic and catastrophic in Handel's life. His operatic plans had suffered a collapse, and a stroke of apoplexy forced him to take the cure at Aix-la-Chapelle. At such periods of crisis his creative powers were apt to fail him, and he would borrow either from his own or from other composers' stock-in-trade. In *Il Trionfo del Tempo* he possessed a work unknown to English audiences and well suited to the Italian singers which he had at his disposal. Certain alterations were necessary, since the Roman version was now thirty years old, and musical styles had changed. Of the ten new numbers which Handel wrote for the 1737 revival,[2] many seem to be in no way an improvement on the originals, but Handel, at the time he wrote them, had doubtless every reason for making his revisions in order to accommodate the singers and instrumentalists which he had at

[1] E.g. as 'Cade il mondo' in *Agrippina*.
[2] On the other changes in the 1737 version, unknown to Chrysander and omitted from the Händel-Gesellschaft edition, see Streatfeild's article, 'The Granville Collection of Handel Manuscripts' in *The Musical Antiquary* for July, 1911, pp. 218–20.—*Ed.*

his command. If the 1737 production had remained the final version of this allegorical oratorio, a detailed comment on these changes might be profitable, but it seems evident that the performance was hastily produced, and the fact that, twenty years later still, Handel made a final version of his score, seems to indicate that he regarded the 1737 production as merely a stopgap. But if this revival did nothing else, it kept the oratorio alive in his mind, and caused him to return, in the last years of his life, to the theme which he had first set to music fifty years earlier.

As the frontispiece to an eighteenth-century publication of the Chandos Anthems, there is an engraving entitled 'The Apotheosis of Handel'. This title might equally serve to describe the final version of *The Triumph of Time and Truth*, for this, Handel's last oratorio, dictated in blindness, includes music composed throughout his whole career. There are roughly a dozen airs from the original Roman oratorio, while other airs and choruses are taken from a Chandos Anthem, *Parnasso in Festa*, *Il Pastor Fido*, *Terpsicore*, and the Foundling Hospital Anthem. Yet the oratorio can in no way be described as a *pasticcio*, except in the narrowest sense. It is a testament of Handel's art, a serene document which at one and the same time records his youth, his maturity, and the mellowness of his age.

The English libretto, which is said to have been written by Morell, is in part a close translation of Panfili's poem, but an extra character, Deceit, has been added, and a Chorus provides a commentary to the allegorical tale. Morell, relieved of the necessity of providing pious sentiments for a Biblical story, shows himself to be a quite capable poet. The opening chorus, 'Time is supreme', is borrowed from the Prince of Wales' Wedding Anthem, *Sing unto God*, and its continuation is notable for the alto solos accompanied by trumpet. Beauty's 'Faithful mirror' is a transcription of the 1708 'Fido specchio', but the resetting of 'Fosco genio' as 'Pensive sorrow' loses greatly in effectiveness, and one wishes that the eighteenth century had not been so dominated by musical fashion. The later setting would undoubtedly have been commended by Burney, but the earlier one possesses a greater depth of emotion to modern ears. Pleasure's air and chorus 'Come live with pleasure' repeats the successful formula of such airs as 'See, the conq'ring hero comes' in its semi-chorus of boys' voices followed by the full choir, and Counsel's 'The beauty, smiling' is interesting in that the original continuo part of the earlier version ('Se la bellezza') is now provided with a violin counterpoint, an excellent example to students of how

L

Handel might have realized a figured bass. The next two airs, by
Beauty and Truth, are given simpler settings than in the original
version, and the chorus 'Strengthen us, O Time',[1] after its homophonic introduction, develops into an interesting fugue on two subjects, of which the second also appears in foreshortened form.
Deceit's 'Happy Beauty' and 'Happy, if still they reign' are both
characterized by elaborate parts for the horns, and Time's 'Like
the shadow', originally 'Nasce l'uomo', is followed by a chorus in
which again the altos are given the most important part.

The opening of the second act is in the pastoral atmosphere of
Parnasso in Festa and *Pastor Fido*, and borrows from the music of
these pieces. The chorus 'O! How great the glory' is the hunting
chorus 'Oh, oh questa', and Pleasure's air 'Dryads, Sylvans', a graceful musette, was originally 'Non tardate' in *Parnasso*. Indeed, the
remaining airs in this act are either taken from the original *Il Trionfo*
or from *Parnasso* and *Pastor Fido*, and include some of the most
delightful of Handel's arcadian music. 'Pleasure's gentle zephyrs'
is the final form of one of Handel's loveliest idyllic pieces, previously
introduced in the cantata *Lungi da me* and in *Agrippina* ('Volo pronto').
In strong contrast 'Fain would I' ('Io vorrei due cori' of the 1708
version), like 'Sorrow darkens every feature' in the first act, is
almost Bachian. The final chorus, 'Ere to dust is chang'd that
beauty', borrowed from Graun's Brunswick Passion, returns to a
more serious note.

In the third act it must be regretted that Handel did not make use
of the lovely melody 'Lascia la spina' for 'Sharp thorns despising'.
Presumably the tune had become too well known in *Rinaldo*, and so
he substituted the lighthearted 'Hai tanto rapido' from *Terpsicore*,
cleverly adapting it to suit the new words. A strange interpolation
is the chorus 'Comfort them, O Lord' from the Foundling Anthem.[2]
The words of this movement, quite inapposite to the context, must
have been very near Handel's heart, and he must have felt impelled
to include them in his last oratorio. The final airs, 'Like clouds,
stormy winds' and 'Guardian angels' are both from the 1708 version,
and the oratorio ends with an 'Allelujah' which is as textually point-
less as it is musically effective; it is thematically related to the finale
of the Organ Concerto, Op. 4, No. 4.

It would be gratifying, for sentimental reasons, to acclaim *The*

---

[1] Borrowed from the third Chandos Anthem.
[2] Cf. p. 178. The music is based on a chorus from a Mass by Lotti: cf. Sedley
Taylor, op. cit., pp. 179–82.

Triumph of Time and Truth as 'the most remarkable of all Handel's oratorios'.   Certainly it is a remarkable anthology of Handel's music, and also a typical example of his methods of utilizing and improving on earlier material.   But it lacks the unity of conception which stamps his finest works: the sunlit scene of *Acis and Galatea* with its pastoral charm, the descriptive power of *Alexander's Feast*, the intensity of atmosphere in *Saul* and *Belshazzar*, the heroic character of *Samson*, uniquely portrayed, and rivalled only by *Jephtha*.   There is *Semele*, remarkable for its dramatic continuity, *Solomon* for its voluptuous, and *Israel in Egypt* for its austere but magnificent, choruses.   And then, completely apart, stands *Messiah*, perhaps the most remarkable work ever created by human mind.

CHAPTER V

THE CHURCH MUSIC

By Basil Lam

T H R O U G H O U T his life Handel was an occasional composer, always writing for some practical purpose and adapting his style to circumstances with a magnificent unawareness of the later belief that an artist should be moved only by his own inner conflicts. When he was in Rome in 1707 he followed the proverb and set Latin psalms; when a decade later James Brydges, Duke of Chandos, crowned a successful career of peculation as Paymaster-General by building a private chapel for his mansion at Edgware, Handel turned to English words and produced a set of anthems impeccably Anglican in tone. Four Coronation Anthems (1727), the famous Dettingen Anthem, and *Te Deum* (1743) were his chief contributions to the Church of England apart from the Chandos Anthems, together with a couple of Royal Wedding Anthems (1734 and 1736) and the Funeral Anthem for Queen Caroline (1737), which is a masterpiece in its own right.

Thus, compared with Bach, Handel put little of his creative energy into church music, for the oratorios are historical dramas and have acquired an adventitious sanctity for which they were not designed. If Handel had remained in Germany he would doubtless have produced many cantatas in the style he must have learned from Zachow, but the Church of England in the eighteenth century was, if not Laodicean, at least no warmer than was necessary for comfort, and knew better uses for its wealth than the maintenance of musical resources of a kind to appeal to Handel. The Chandos Anthems remain therefore an isolated group, the only representatives of the Protestant cantata in Handel's output, for the Coronation music belongs to a class of composition not designed to promote meditation or reflection, activities usually inappropriate at such functions.

Let us consider first the early church works in Latin. The setting, for soprano with two violins and continuo, of Psalm 113 (*Laudate pueri*) is, according to Chrysander, the earliest Handel autograph extant, dating from the period 1701–3. It is a diffuse, rambling composition, one of those 'interminable cantatas' which his friend

Mattheson criticized, but already a leaning towards the Italian style is evident; it would be difficult to find any German characteristics here and the influence of his Italian travels on Handel's style, though very great, must not be overestimated in view of this proof that he wrote *all' Italiana* while still a provincial student at Halle. Some five years later Handel made a new setting of the text, completing his work at Rome on 8 July 1707. This is a far more elaborate composition, with full strings, oboes, and a five-part chorus in addition to the soprano solo. A certain amount of material from the earlier setting is used, and direct comparison, where it is possible, reveals the great progress made by the young composer in this period. For example, the recitative 'Quis sicut Dominus' appears thus in the Halle version:

Ex. 40

In the later setting Handel replaces this conventional passage by the first of his choral recitatives (Ex. 41). The grandeur of these bars is prophetic of later sublimities, and he surely remembered his youthful inspiration when more than thirty years later he set the same words in English for *Israel in Egypt* ('Who is like unto Thee').[1]

Remarkable also is the return for the final Amen to the music of the opening, a device which gives some unity to a form otherwise somewhat inconsequent. Another product of the Italian journey was the ambitious setting of Psalm 110 (*Dixit Dominus*), a work on the grand scale, of which certain portions, e.g. the opening chorus, are worthy of the mature Handel. The orchestral introduction is finely

---

[1] Passages from the 'Gloria' of this work were introduced almost unchanged, forty years later, in 'Glory to God' in *Joshua*.—*Ed.*

Ex. 41

spacious with bold though unidiomatic string-writing; Corelli might well have complained of such things as this which is merely keyboard figuration transferred to the violin.

Ex. 42

The five-part chorus is declamatory in Carissimi's manner but acquires solidity from a plainsong theme. The total impression is imposing and the piece must have contributed to the astonishing success Handel gained in Italy. So must the few bars of choral recitative to the words 'Juravit Dominus' in which the northern composer offered the Italians a touch of baroque harshness. There was of course plenty of chromatic writing in Carissimi, Legrenzi and other Italian masters, but smoothness ruled and Handel's abrupt transitions belong rather to Bach's world.

Ex.43

Remarkable also is the 'die-away' end of this section with its directions in successive bars: *piano, piano piano più piano, pianiss pianississ.*

Baroque declamation at its most extravagant is displayed in the setting of the word 'conquassabit' ('He shall wound the heads over many countries'); Handel drastically expresses this idea in a five-part chorus with this strange device:

Ex. 44

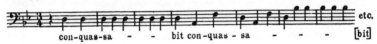

con-quas-sa - - - bit con-quas - sa - - - [bit]

The final 'Gloria' shows perhaps for the first time Handel's immense power of rhythmic expansion in a loosely constructed fugue on three subjects, one of which is the plainsong theme heard earlier in the work. With the evidence of such achievements as this chorus we can understand better why he made such a deep impression on the musical world of Italy. Northern science is here united with the fiery energy of the Italian baroque and the same combination of qualities was still valid for Handel when years later he wrote the triumphant double fugue, 'The horse and his rider', for *Israel in Egypt*. It would be hard to overpraise this magnificent piece in which for the first time Handel revealed his full power of movement. The final section 'Et in secula', built on a single theme with repeated notes and a conventional sequence, develops a momentum far beyond the scope of any other baroque master, Bach only excepted. For anything comparable we must look to the next century and to Beethoven's Ninth Symphony, a work sustained by the same complete confidence of a composer in his ability to handle any material, however vast, in terms of controlled energy.

Handel's Italian journey produced no other achievement of such splendour as this *Dixit Dominus*, though the opening of the setting of Psalm 127, *Nisi Dominus*[1] is grand enough in conception to have suggested the imposing introduction to the first Coronation Anthem, *Zadok the Priest*. In the Psalm this device, persistent violin arpeggios over a quaver bass, is used unrhetorically to produce music of Corellian sweetness and transparency. The bass gives the effect of an ostinato but is in fact varied with a deftness worthy of Mozart; these early works show that Handel's technique, though less intellectually impressive than Bach's, was based on a no less wonderful innate understanding of the very nature of musical language. His supreme mastery of composition has been underrated merely because

---

[1] Of which H.–G. prints only five numbers. The Novello edition adds a 'Gloria Patri' for double chorus, double orchestra and two organs. See T. W. Bourne, 'Handel's Double *Gloria Patri*', in *Monthly Musical Record*, Vol. XXVII (1897).

it is less readily analysable in terms comprehensible to scientific
and non-musical minds than is the profound logic of Bach's *ars
combinatoria*. Handel rarely develops his thesis to a rigorous proof,
but his variety in detail is that of Nature itself. Bach's wood may
be more profound but the trees in it tend to be all alike.

To the same Italian period Chrysander assigns without certainty a
Salve Regina for soprano with violins and continuo. It contains an
interesting written-out organ solo, but is chiefly remarkable for the
romantic sentiment of its conclusion—one of Handel's rare lapses
from classical propriety. Perhaps he was momentarily influenced by
the more sentimental aspects of Mediterranean Catholicism.
Mozart's adolescent religious compositions have the same ambiguou
sensibility as Ex. 45.

Ex. 45

Elsewhere in the piece Handel explores expressive possibilities in
harmonic detail which in maturity he resorted to but rarely. Like
Beethoven he developed a vast and spacious manner in which the
kind of harmony that draws attention to a single chord or progression
would detract from the grandeur of the whole design. Connoisseurs
of 'remarkable' or 'interesting' harmony frequently forget this truth
and in consequence vastly overpraise otherwise inferior music for its
moments of imagination which ought really to be anthologized to
spare musicians the tedium of listening *in extenso* to the works in
which they occur. One such moment in the *Salve Regina* demands
quotation (see Ex. 46). Handel's Italian period is rich in these
bold touches; others may be found in the serenata *Aci Galatea e
Polifemo*, and in the solo cantata *Nel dolce del oblio* occurs an
enharmonic change to which a parallel could be found only in Mozart
at his most disconcerting. Another striking detail in the *Salve Regina*
is the treatment of the word 'suspiramus' exactly like Monteverdi's
in his setting of the same text for two tenors. Is it possible that this
was still performed in Italy in the eighteenth century?

To a somewhat later period (1715–20) belongs the elaborate

Ex. 46

motet for soprano solo with oboe and strings *Silete venti*. This has
a *symphonia* in two movements of which the first was later used as
opening of the well-known Organ Concerto, Op. 4, No. 2, in the
same key of B flat; the allegro occurs in the fourth Chandos Anthem.
At the entry of the voice Handel uses a dramatic and effective device
already employed in the cantata *Aminta e Fillide*, where the overture
is interrupted in full course by the words 'Arresta i passi'. In the
motet a passage of running semiquavers is similarly brought to an
abrupt end by the words 'Silete venti, nolite murmurare frondes'.
The text is of the erotic-religious kind for which the Song of Songs
provided a respectable precedent, and one wonders for what occasion
Handel set words so remote from his usual taste in such matters;
mysticism is a quality rarely attributed to him but here he joins
company with Crashaw or the Spanish poet saints and sets to music
of great beauty such things as

> Dulcis amor, Jesu care
> Quis non cupit te amare,
> Veni transfige me.

Reminiscent of the elder Scarlatti at his finest is the andante, 'Date
serta, date flores'. The work ends with a long and refreshingly
secular 'Alleluia' in the form of a gigue.[1] It is a remarkable instance
of Handel's versatility that he should have written this intensely
'continental' work to a Latin text in the period when, in the Chandos

---

[1] Used again in *Esther* (see p. 81).

Anthems, he was providing the Anglican Church with some of its most durable and characteristic music.

For public or royal occasions Handel was the ideal Laureate, perhaps the only great artist to rise unfailingly to the needs of great events, or rather to rise above them, for the grandeur with which our imaginations invest the English eighteenth century is largely a consequence of Handel's magnificent tributes to such events as the Peace of Aix-la-Chapelle or the coronation of George II. Handel was perhaps no classical scholar but in these popular works (using the epithet in its original sense) he seems to evoke 'the long glories of imperial Rome' and the idea or image of public rejoicing or mourning inspires him to nobility and grandeur as the Augustan age inspired Virgil, and the Latin hexameter, 'stateliest measure ever moulded by the lips of man', is not more splendid than Handel's spacious polyphony and massive diatonic harmony in his anthems for State occasions.

For the coronation of George II in 1727 Handel set four texts of which only one, *My heart is inditing*, had been used by Purcell for James II. The first, *Zadok the Priest*, is perhaps, the most splendid of all such compositions. Its orchestral opening, derived in essence from the early *Nisi Dominus* (q.v. *supra*), is comparable only with certain of Beethoven's magnificent yet simple devices. Lower strings and wind maintain an unbroken flow of repeated quavers for no fewer than 22 bars of moderate time, while the violins in thirds or sixths build up a series of arpeggio figures, all on the most elementary progressions, until the chorus in seven parts with trumpets and drums enter with the opening words. Nothing could be more magnificent than this choral harmony, with its simple diatonic discords.

Ex. 47

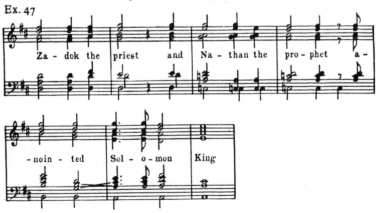

The rest is more conventional, as it ought to be; great moments are not for repetition and the ceremonial rejoicings that follow are exactly suited to an occasion of which convention is the essence.

The second anthem *The King shall rejoice* is no less jubilant but does not exclude a lyrical note in its second movement 'exceeding glad shall he be' where the trumpets are silent, to return with great effect with the words 'Glory and great worship hast thou laid upon him'. The concluding 'Alleluia' though of great length succeeds in evading monotony though tied to its key by the natural trumpets. Such peaks of technique are so frequent in Handel that it is easy to overlook the inability of any other composer of the time, Bach excepted, to achieve them.

In the two other anthems the most notable section is the grave and expressive larghetto for the words 'Let justice and judgement be the preparation of thy seat'; ready as Handel was to express the more external pomp of the occasion he emphasized in this section the deeper thoughts implicit in the coronation service though his acquaintance with the Hanoverians would not have made him unduly hopeful of the fulfilment of this pious aspiration.

At the end of 1737 Handel returned to London from Aix-la-Chapelle, where he had been recovering from a paralytic stroke, brought on perhaps by the accumulated worries and distress of his operatic failures. His first composition after this grave illness was the Funeral Anthem *The ways of Zion do mourn*, which was occasioned by the death of Queen Caroline, his patron in former years. (He had written duets for her as early as 1711). There could be no more convincing evidence of Handel's magnanimity than this noble work in which, without sacrificing anything of his own style, he fulfils the tradition of English church music so that we are reminded of Byrd, and, more closely, of Gibbons. Burney remarked on this evocation of past styles, evident not only in the details of harmony mentioned by him, but in the severely diatonic writing as a whole. It is astonishing that the atmosphere of grief should be established without frequent recourse to the standby of every composer in such circumstances: chromatic descents and poignant appoggiaturas. The introduction, written two years later when Handel used the anthem as a prologue to *Israel in Egypt*, is comparable for noble restraint and dignity with nothing outside his own work until Mozart's *Masonic Funeral Music* and the slow movement of the *Eroica*. As in so many of Handel's greatest things, there is nothing original anywhere, yet the total effect is unmistakable.

Thematic development of a high and subtle order is shown by
the first chorus. Strings and oboes outline in staccato chords
what is to be the *canto fermo* of the whole movement (a theme
closely resembling the chorale 'Nun komm der Heiden Heiland').
This is sung by altos and then by tenors with, at the second entry,
two unobtrusive figures in the strings. The basses and finally the
sopranos have the *canto fermo*, each voice appearing separately.
Now with a series of fugal entries the chorus take up the two accompanying figures which are in fact principal counter-subjects to the
main theme. This impressive movement repays the closest study as
an example of Handel's technique.

The deliberate archaism of 'Their bodies are buried in peace' has
often been quoted though it has not always been noted that the
following section 'But their name liveth evermore' is no less in the
old style of English church music. It would be a superficial judgement to ascribe this to Handel's opportunism. As has been suggested
earlier, he seems to have been profoundly moved by the sense of
public events and assumes in the Funeral Anthem the style appropriate to the Roman *gravitas* so wonderfully evoked by this work.
'Man is a noble animal, splendid in ashes and pompous in the
grave.'

Although the twelve Chandos Anthems, written for the most part
in 1716–18, form only a small proportion of Handel's output they
have a special importance in that they are the only examples of their
kind to survive.

English church music, after the splendours of Byrd and Tallis,
prolonged by Gibbons, had finally declined into the respectable but
fatally provincial specimens so numerous in Tudway's collection,
could provide no works comparable with the wealth of German
examples available to Bach. Purcell, equal in genius to Buxtehude,
was divided, in his anthems, between a nostalgic attraction towards
the old contrapuntal style, and the practical composer's realization of
the need to meet the royal taste with the latest imported fashions.
The finest things in English church compositions before Handel
were, on the whole, motets and full anthems in the archaic style.
Blow's *Salvator mundi*, Purcell's early *Burial Service*, attained profundity in daring harmony which Handel was not inclined to imitate,
doubtless to the great relief of Burney, whose vigorous denunciation of
such 'crudities' would have been impaired in conviction had such
things appeared in his revered Handel.

For the Chandos Anthems, then, Handel could find no model in

England and these cantatas are basically in the German style taught to him by Zachow, though Italian influences are never absent, especially in the arias. Despite their lyrical freshness and youthful energy these anthems should not be compared with Bach's cantatas. To Handel the production of church music was an episode in a life devoted to a non-dogmatic humanism whereas for Bach, the cantata, firmly based on the chorale, was the centre of his creative work. The true comparison is between Bach's cantatas and Handel's oratorios and to seek in the Chandos Anthems the unequalled depth and inventive richness of Bach's far more numerous cantatas is to miss the genuine merits of Handel's works of which the subtle Anglicanism, if sometimes of the kind so affectionately derided by John Betjeman, is equally capable of the profound statements in T. S. Eliot's later poems. What is entirely absent, and by its absence gives perhaps the most genuinely English feature of this music is the mystical intensity, not always free from morbidity, so often present in Bach.

The first anthem, a setting of Psalm 100, is practically identical with the Utrecht *Jubilate* written in 1713 and is therefore, with the *Birthday Ode* for Queen Anne, Handel's earliest English composition. Owing to the modest resources of the chapel at Cannons Handel was forced to reduce the four- and five-part choruses of the *Jubilate* to a mere three voices and the oboes have to serve for the trumpets of the earlier version. Both works draw on the *Laudate Pueri* in D major, a product of the Italian journey of 1707. For the anthem Handel added a prelude for oboe and strings. There are no violas and the introduction, like so many others in the Chandos set, is a trio sonata. As such, these instrumental pieces do not reveal their best qualities when performed by large string orchestras. This first anthem, with the thematic connexion between its prelude and other related compositions, is dealt with under the heading Utrecht *Te Deum* and *Jubilate*.[1]

The second anthem, *In the Lord put I my trust*, on a text compiled from four Psalms (Nos. 9, 11, 12, and 13), is preceded by a two-movement introduction—borrowed from the Sonata, Op. 3, No. 5, and famous (it ought to be notorious) in the inflated arrangement by Elgar who, with misguided application of his superb orchestral technique, turned a pair of unassuming trio pieces into something rich and strange. The fugue also appears in F sharp minor, in a suite for harpsichord. The anthem itself is not remarkable, though its

[1] See pp. 175–6.

first chorus has a pastoral quality rarely allowed to appear in the rough and unready choral singing generally associated with performances of Handel. The Bach-like air for tenor, 'But God who hears the suff'ring pow'r', is expressive in an obvious way but the best thing in the whole work is the D major chorus, where Handel revels in the prospect of the Almighty showering on the heads of the wicked 'snares, fire, and brimstone' a Snark-like assemblage of penalties which the text aptly describes as 'this dreadful mixture'.

Much finer is the opening of the third anthem, *Have mercy on me, O God*, where Handel achieves without effort the pathos and chromatic intensity of Purcell or Humphrey. Here surely English influence must be allowed, not only in the chromaticism of the vocal lines but in the whole texture with its three voices and persistent quaver accompaniment. Distinctly un-English, however, is the clumsy declamation which mars nearly everything in these Chandos works though it is surprisingly absent from *Acis and Galatea*. On this very point Burney most justly observed, having declared Handel superior to Purcell in nearly all respects, 'Yet in the accent, passion and expression of English words, the vocal music of Purcell is some-times, to my feelings, as superior to Handel's as an original poem to a translation'. This point neglected, nothing could be more convinc-ing in Purcell's manner than the opening of the movement quoted:

Ex. 48

As it proceeds, the impressive piece gains in power and intensity with all Handel's typical breadth and this movement, unlike much in the anthems, may be compared with Bach without detriment.

No less fine is the tenor recitative 'For I acknowledge my faults'. Here again Handel shows that he can match the Passion recitative of Bach when he chooses. In the choruses the limitation to three voices does not prevent Handel from constructing spacious and dignified movements. This in part is achieved by giving independent lines to oboe and violins, sometimes as in the fine 'Thou shalt make me hear of joy and gladness' producing a complexity of texture often lacking in his later choral style. It could indeed be argued that the restrictions imposed on him by the slender resources available at Edgware helped to create in these Chandos choruses a style admirable in itself and possessing the qualities of lucidity and grace. Most of these choruses are, in Handel's sense, double fugues though generally this means only that two subjects alternate or that the main theme and countersubject are presented simultaneously from the opening. The final chorus of this third anthem is a fine example of impressive music constructed on the most conventional material. Less conventional and characteristic of Handel's technique is the way in which the free instrumental parts double the voices sometimes for only a few notes in bland disregard of academic principles. As always, his aim is to produce an effect on the hearer, rather than a correct specimen of a well-made fugue in so many parts. In modern times so much music is read and not heard that it is easy to forget that the reality of a composition is what can be heard. What the eye does not see the ear will not grieve at and the analysts who have developed an eye for fifths, octaves and other venial sins have perhaps caused the alternative organ for musical reception to lose its powers. How many 'irregularities' so gleefully revealed would ever have been found by the *ears* of their discoverers?

The introduction to the fourth anthem, *O sing unto the Lord a new song* (Psalm 96), is even more trio-like than others in the set and suggests a chamber-music performance for the work as a whole which is marked by charm and smoothness rather than by any obvious grandeur. The allegro, much modified, appeared later in the motet *Silete venti*.[1] Nothing could be more different from Bach's treatment of the same text than the long-breathed opening with its oboe solo. The harmony is of the greatest possible simplicity and the part given to the soprano is completely Italian; these sequences and tied-over phrases might appear in almost any trio or solo sonata

[1] See p. 161.

of Corelli. But this enchanting piece is not as simple as it looks. When the chorus enters, the oboe solo and not the soprano provides its material:

Ex. 49

The idyllic mood of this opening is scarcely maintained in the stiff, even prim, little fugue that follows. Perhaps it is not by Handel, for though he could on occasion rival even Vivaldi in dullness he rarely indulges in full closes at every entry in a fugue. This chorus is strangely similar in this respect to one of Bach's equally rare instances of the same weakness ('Sicut locutus est' in the *Magnificat*). The fine tenor solo, 'The waves of the sea rage horribly', is more characteristic though the waves have a lifelike monotony in the persistence of the semiquavers in which they are depicted. The rest of the anthem is not especially noteworthy.

The fifth anthem *I will magnify Thee* exists in two versions, both related to the trio sonata in the same key, A major (Op. 5, No. 1). In the first version two movements of the sonata are used as introduction (the trio was published nearly twenty years later but is almost certainly an early work) and other portions are converted into vocal pieces, an interesting example of Handel's methods of adaptation. The opening chorus is not remarkable, but the tenor aria 'Every day will I give thanks' is not only beautiful in itself but seems to contain the latent ideas of two more precious things, 'Thou wilt bring them in' from *Israel in Egypt* and 'I know that my Redeemer liveth'. It is regrettable that another tenor aria in very similar style should occur later in the work, especially as it is by no means as good. Such occurrences suggest that Handel was not always or even generally conscious of the effect made by a long work as a whole. In the second version of this anthem the same opening andante is used but the allegro is suppressed and instead the latter part of the andante is turned into an alto solo on the text used for a chorus in the first setting. This is followed by the duet, from the fourth anthem, to the words 'O worship the Lord in the beauty of holiness' given here to alto and bass (really a high baritone part). This is followed by a splendid chorus from the eighth anthem, *O come let us sing unto the Lord*. The words in both are 'Glory and worship are before him'. The original (if it be so, for there is no means of telling) is for four-part chorus, but the present version is laid out for solo quartet and *ripieni* alto, tenor, and bass. The words 'glory, worship, power' are declaimed in a style almost reaching back to Carissimi both in its simplicity and in its surprisingly splendid effect. Still drawing on the eighth anthem, Handel continues with the next chorus 'Tell it out among the heathen' (cf. Ex. 52). It is not surprising that he should have made a second use of this piece which is worthy to stand beside the greatest oratorio choruses of his later years.[1] The rest of the fifth anthem is by comparison with the splendid chorus somewhat of an anticlimax though the final 'Amen' with its alto solo is brilliant and effective. It is often the misfortune of Handel's greatest things to dwarf their surroundings.

The sixth anthem, *As pants the hart* (Psalm 42), exists in no fewer than four versions. It contains in one version one of Handel's very few examples of a chorale used as *canto fermo*. So inappropriate is the original text of the melody to Handel's purpose here that it seems reasonable to suppose that this movement, based on 'Christ lag in Todesbanden' may be an early effort written as an exercise possibly for Zachow and adapted here to an English text. The introductory sonata is also immature in style, consisting of a movement in triple time, evidently andante (there is no indication of tempo) and a closely knit allegro with no special appropriateness in mood to what follows. This allegro is present only in version A. The work as a whole presents a series of fascinating problems, for the various movements are extensively recomposed, some are omitted, others completely reset to different music. The severe opening chorus for three voices with other entries in orchestral parts in A is replaced in B by a motet-like piece for six-part chorus (it is rarely if ever in six real parts). In C this six-part chorus has only organ accompaniment. Yet another version (H.-G., Vol. 36) gives substantially the same piece but four bars shorter.

[1] It appears a third time—with the second, alto solo, version of the opening number—at the end of *Belshazzar*.—Ed.

M

The aria 'Tears are my daily food' exists in a bewildering diversity difficult to make clear without extensive quotation, but giving valuable evidence of Handel's unaccountable methods in adapting material. The ingenuity shown in this one example should dispel the idea that his motive was to save trouble. A, B, and D are all variants of the same motive but while A and B have each a ritornello widely differing though on vaguely similar basses, D takes the melody of A and puts it on a ground bass. B has a new melody but retains the essentials of A. C is an entirely fresh setting with a chromatic bass of chaconne type closely related to that used in the Brockes *Passion*. It is surely evident that whatever reason Handel may have had for these remarkable changes the impartial critic must allow that we have here not indolence or indifference, but something not far from Beethoven's tireless search after the perfect expression of an idea. The *canto fermo* movement appears only in B and is sung by tenors and basses with strings and oboes. The strings include violas in this version and though the works written at Cannons omit violas, this fact does not really help in dating the different versions of the anthem as it could have been written earlier as well as later, for violas seem to have been readily available in London where they were used by Handel in the Utrecht *Te Deum* and *Jubilate* of 1713. (When the *Jubilate* was used at Cannons as the first Chandos Anthem, the violas were omitted.)

The pathetic duet 'Why so full of grief' must surely have provided Bach with a famous theme[1] in the *St. Matthew Passion*; if this be so, it is one of the very rare connections between the two masters.

Ex. 50

Why so full of   grief O my soul?

Other movements show no less surprising changes in length and texture, but the whole question is too obscure and complex for cursory treatment. What makes it especially hard to understand is the fact that, as in the best-known of Handel's revisions, the dozen versions of the 'generally omitted' 'Thou art gone up on high' (*Messiah*), the music itself is not what posterity has selected as particularly inspired.

The seventh anthem *My song shall be alway* contains nothing of

[1] Cf. also the theme of the allegro finale of Handel's Trio Sonata, Op. 2, No. 1.—*Ed.*

special value or interest though a brief 'Hallelujah' chorus which forms its conclusion is perhaps prophetic in its rapid reiterations. The 'sonata' became the first movement of Op. 3, No. 3.

No. 8, however, *O come let us sing unto the Lord* is one of the very finest of the whole set.[1] The overture is bold and spirited though the little fugue[2] is somewhat obvious in its conventional episodes but the opening chorus is splendid in its very plainness, contrasting rapid declamation with an intonation of elemental simplicity.

Ex. 51

O come let us sing un - to the Lord

It is followed by a tenor aria, in which the words 'we are the people of His pasture and the sheep of His hand' prompt Handel to write for two recorders with his easy but inimitable evocation of the pastoral. The spacious work, as large as Bach's most extensive cantatas, continues with the two magnificent choruses already mentioned in connexion with the fifth anthem. The first, 'Glory and worship are before him', is declamatory, in common time, and leads (with a change to A major and triple time) to one of Handel's noblest inventions, 'Tell it out among the heathen'. The words are declaimed with immense vigour by a series of solo voices (not so indicated here but marked 'soli' in the fifth anthem). For once Handel achieves in this period a masterly piece of English declamation. Nothing could be more apt to the text than:

Ex. 52

Tell it. Tell it out a-mong the hea - then that the Lord is King.

This material is worked up to a conclusion in the dominant and with the change of text comes a new and splendid idea in Handel's chorus: 'And that he made the world so fast it can't be moved'.

A very striking theme built on a sequence of fourths is combined with a monotone to which with naïve but immensely convincing pictorialism the idea contained in 'so fast it can't be moved' is declaimed:

<hr />

[1] Nos. 8 and 9 are confusingly published separately by Novello as 'Fifth' and 'Sixth'.—*Ed.*

[2] Another version of which appears in the Trio Sonata, Op. 2, No. 5.—*Ed.*

Ex. 53

As these two ideas expand, the first theme re-enters in great triumph to its own text until the basses settle on a dominant pedal to which after a few bars they return reinforced by the tenors, and the orchestra adds a final triumphant statement of the main themes. After this, relief and contrast are provided by three arias in succession, all good Handel and the last, 'For look, as high as the Heaven is', something more. This F sharp minor adagio with its long phrases in a broad 12/8 is not unlike some of Bach's profound sayings in the same tempo and metre. The last chorus, 'Rejoice in the Lord ye righteous', would be outstanding in a work less notably provided in choruses. This anthem is one of the finest in its entirety and if the inevitable comparison with Bach's cantatas is made, such a composition as this need not fear the issue.

The ninth anthem, 'O praise the Lord with one consent', is also distinguished in its choruses of which the first is one of Handel's large designs, with a ritornello stating the familiar melody to be heard later and then proceeding to a spacious yet expressive setting out of the other material which, curiously enough, alternates with the *canto fermo*.

Typical appearances of both themes are:

Ex. 54

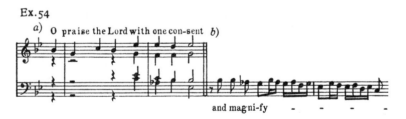

No further portions of the hymn are used in this first section which leads without break into a fugue containing dangerously pompous sequences especially in the bass. The music is fine in itself but parodists of Handel generally fasten on this kind of thing:

Ex. 55

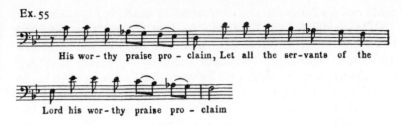

His wor-thy praise pro-claim, Let all the ser-vants of the

Lord his wor-thy praise pro-claim

More worth notice is a moment of delicate beauty heard twice in the chorus 'With cheerful notes'. Such Mozartean touches are far less rare in Handel than is yet generally conceded.

Ex. 56

With the return to common time, majestic use is made of the hymn melody which, first stated in plain harmony then becomes a *canto fermo* in Handel's unsystematic but always effective manner. In such things, though he uses far less science than Bach, the result is sometimes more satisfactory for if Handel's constructions are sometimes ramshackle Bach's are occasionally too rigorously designed according to a pattern imposed by the material, e.g. certain chorale preludes which relentlessly and at excessive length apply the prescribed treatment to line after line of the melody used. In this anthem, fine as the remaining movements are, it is matter for regret that Handel did not end with the noble chorus mentioned. All facility has its dangers and Handel, the supreme rhetorician, could not always resist the temptation to multiply his perorations.

Of the tenth anthem, *The Lord is my light*, the aria 'One thing have I desired' with its two recorders, is in its quiet way, the finest part. The naïve realism of 'The earth trembled' with bass rumblings for thunder, staccato chords for lightning, and so on, may in its day have been more impressive than it is now, when it seems a pale foreshadowing of *Israel in Egypt*. Far more impressive is the searching chromaticism of the short chorus 'They are brought down and fallen' with its subject anticipating the great fugue of the Concerto grosso, Op. 5, No. 4.

Ex. 57

They are brought down and fall'n but we are ris-en we are ris-en

How close Handel's language is to that of Corelli and the other Italians may be seen in the subject of the last chorus in this anthem.

Ex. 58

a) Handel

b) Corelli (Trio Sonata, Op. 3, No. 9)

The two versions of the eleventh anthem, *Let God arise*, show puzzling features. The second version in Arnold's edition evidently contains alternative versions not intended for successive inclusion in a single performance. From the presence of violas and the more elaborate choral setting (in five parts) in the A major version, it seems that this is probably a revision and that the Chandos form of the anthem is the one in B flat. If this be so, it is still puzzling that Handel should have omitted the splendid quartet gigue 'O sing

Ex. 59

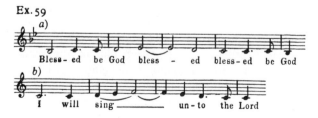

a)

Bless-ed   be God   bless - ed   bless-ed   be God

b)

I   will   sing ————   un-to   the Lord

unto God'. (This surely cannot be a chorus with its difficult and brilliant vocal figuration.) It is notable that the chorus 'O God, at Thy rebuke both the chariot and horse are fallen' with its obvious anticipation (though in text only) of *Israel*, is followed by a triumphant chorus with 'Hallelujah' of which the musical connexion with the oratorio is unmistakable (see Ex. 59).

The same ancient subject is used for the finest section of the twelfth anthem, *O praise the Lord ye angels of his*. This work with the trumpets and oboes clearly belongs, in its present form, to a period either earlier or later than the Chandos set as a whole and may have been written in 1713, the year of Handel's first works for the English church. The chorus in question 'My mouth shall speak the praise of the Lord' is for all its simplicity a truly magnificent specimen of Handel's festive style. Bell-like descending scales with declamatory four-part choral harmony alternate with solo passages until a climax is built up with trumpets and oboes in unison, a striking tone-colour neglected by later masters.

Considered as a set, the Chandos Anthems represent almost every aspect of Handel's work, and his greatness in its various aspects of power, charm and pathos could be measured here, were all his other works lost. Incidentally, modern research which undermines the originality of so many of his compositions has yet to question the provenance of these anthems, though Handel himself made considerable use of them in his own later work. Not comparable in depth or range of religious experience with Bach's cantatas, these anthems represent in its noblest aspect the 'religion of all sensible men'.

It remains to consider Handel's other service music: the Utrecht *Jubilate* and *Te Deum*, three other *Te Deums*, the Dettingen Anthem and *Te Deum*, and the Foundling Hospital Anthem. When Handel first established himself in London he seems rapidly to have discovered friends at Court, for presumably the *Te Deum* and *Jubilate*, written in 1713, must have been commissioned works; it is unlikely that the Peace of Utrecht stirred him to such a degree that he spontaneously produced music to celebrate it. Chrysander points out that Handel, always sensitive to his audience, closely followed the setting made by Purcell in 1694, which he doubtless heard during his frequent visits to St. Paul's as it remained the favourite work of its kind.

Handel, contrary to his custom in later works, produced in the *Te Deum* a single entity in more than a dozen sections but without the discontinuity of the cantata style. Curiously enough, Bach's cantatas show a similar change in outlook. An early work of Bach's such as *Gottes Zeit* (No. 106) has a unity lacking in the typical cantata form of his maturity. From this point of view, the later formal developments of the baroque period were retrograde.

Handel's unusual brevity in the Utrecht *Te Deum* does not prevent impressive expansions at such passages as 'Thou sittest at the right hand of God'. The final chorus draws on the immemorial theme quoted earlier (Ex. 59*a*). In this work as a whole, Handel appears as a kind of musical architect using conventional material for a purpose to which originality would be not only inappropriate but even offensive. To demand original ideas in work of this kind would be as unreasonable as to have asked a Palladian architect to devise new orders for every building he designed. Neglect of this fact is the fatal weakness of the criticism which assesses merit according to originality in dealing with eighteenth-century music.

The *Jubilate* (or first Chandos Anthem) is similarly conventional in the right way and many of its finest features owe their effect to their placing in the work (another architectural device). For example, the words of the final 'Gloria' are set to the simplest chords long held by an eight-part chorus (reduced to three parts for the Chandos version) accompanied by the most obvious figuration in the strings. Anything more striking or personal would be as inapt here as would a new version of the Latin text. The duet 'Be ye sure that the Lord he is God' has canonic dialogue for solo violin and oboe and brings a note of Corelli-like sweetness and gravity into a work which could scarcely be other than festive.

Handel made three other settings of the *Te Deum* for various occasions, of which two (those in B flat and A) are closely related. The first setting, in D,[1] was, according to Chrysander, written soon after the Utrecht composition and was intended for the Chapel Royal. Its introduction, in which the voices participate, became the instrumental opening of the Utrecht *Jubilate* when the latter was used as the first Chandos Anthem. The allegro in the same overture is the same as the opening of the Utrecht *Te Deum*, another curious instance of Handel's use of material in different works. The solo 'When thou tookest upon Thee' in this D major *Te Deum* appears later in the seventh Chandos Anthem.

The two other settings, in B flat and A, are more extended and contain at least one first-rate piece of Handel, the tender and profound setting of 'When thou tookest upon Thee':

---

[1] Sometimes called the 'Queen Caroline' *Te Deum* from its performance in 1737.

Ex. 60

In the second version, in the A major setting, with flute and
bassoon, this shows even more striking a resemblance to the equally
beautiful 'He led them forth like sheep' (*Israel in Egypt*). Perhaps
Handel remembered this earlier invention of his own and was led
by the recollection to adopt for the later composition Stradella's
similar theme. The B flat version contains one of Handel's extremely
rare uses of unaccompanied voices, for 'When Thou hadst overcome
the sharpness of death' is set in archaic style for treble, two tenors
and bass solo, without continuo. While it is doubtful whether these
Te Deums are likely to be heard, the occasion for their use rarely
arising in the twentieth century, such movements as the one quoted
from should not be forgotten.

This kind of solemn and popular music in the true sense of the
term finds its apotheosis in the Dettingen *Te Deum* of 1743, written
to celebrate the victory at which, as everyone knows, George II led
his troops in person. Handel seems to have accepted readily the
convention by which the Almighty was assumed to have special
responsibility for national victories and it would be rash to attribute
his recourse to a *Te Deum* by Urio to any scruples about the appropriateness of the occasion. Here, it must be admitted, plagiarism
goes beyond mere indebtedness for themes which in any case were
generally common property, invented by the *Zeitgeist* rather than by
any composer. Handel's work is really an expansion and arrangement and in modern times would have been described as by 'Urio,

transcribed Handel'.[1] Its conventional splendours of D major trumpets have not lost their power to stir the breast but the grandeur is heavily material, a matter of instruments rather than of ideas and imagination. Curiously enough, the setting of 'When thou tookest upon Thee' is adapted from the earlier *Te Deum* in B flat (Ex. 60) and in its new version acquires a vague though unmistakable resemblance to 'Et in Spiritum sanctum' in Bach's B minor Mass. It is certainly the most genuinely beautiful thing in the work and should be performed separately as it must be hoped that no further occasions for the use of the whole *Te Deum* will arise.

The anthem *The King shall rejoice* (H.–G., Vol. 36) was written for the same occasion as the Dettingen *Te Deum*. Some of its material occurs in *Joseph* and it is not outstanding as music, being merely a typical laureate composition in the official key of D major.

It is well known that Handel was deeply charitable in an age when welfare was generally neglected and that he used to direct a yearly performance of *Messiah* for the Foundling Hospital. For the same institution, of which he became a governor, he compiled in 1749 the Foundling Hospital Anthem which, no doubt to meet an obvious demand, he concluded with the 'Hallelujah'. chorus. The work includes one notable piece presumably written for it (unless it be an earlier piece revived for its appropriateness), an intensely Bach-like setting of the chorale 'Aus tiefer Not'. This fine chorus is worth examination as an example of Handel's ability in a kind of music rarely associated with him but in which he had a skill that, in different circumstances, would have enabled him to continue the German tradition which in the bulk of his work is submerged by his allegiance to Italy.

Many of these occasional church compositions have fallen into oblivion with their occasions but music has never had such a laureate, unofficial though he was, able to give to events of which the glory was ambiguous and even spurious the ideal nobility and easy grandeur of classical Rome at its height.

[1] If 'Urio' was not in this case, the young Handel himself: see footnote on p. 91.—*Ed.*

CHAPTER VI

THE SONGS AND CHAMBER CANTATAS

By ANTHONY LEWIS

WHEN Handel left Germany in 1706 he was, by the scale of his later development, still a comparatively raw young craftsman—despite the fact that he had already several operas (all lost except *Almira*), a Passion, and a substantial quantity of chamber music to his credit. By the end of three years in Italy he had acquired the ease and confidence of the mature composer who knows what he wants to say and how best to say it. After this period the stream of Handel's inspiration was to grow both wider and deeper, but it was in Florence, Rome, and Naples that its course was settled. Without excluding himself from drawing on other sources, he decided during this impressionable time that the main flow of his creative impulse should derive from Italy and, with similar reservations, that his guiding channel of expression should be the human voice. Handel's Italian stay, therefore, occupied a critical position in his creative life, and the works it produced demand and repay close examination.

Prior to his Italian tour, Handel's most important experience had been gained in the field of opera, and it was no doubt in that medium that he hoped to make his reputation in Italy, its natural home. Yet on arrival in Rome Handel found all opera suppressed by papal edict. This situation might well have discouraged him had the ban been respected in the spirit as well as in the letter. But the Italian aristocracy had developed far too abiding a taste for opera to allow themselves to be denied its pleasures entirely. As a substitute, they gave musical parties at which the main entertainment was the performance of chamber cantatas. These cantatas contained, on a smaller scale, much the same ingredients as the operas that had been suppressed, while the singers taking part in them had simply transferred themselves from the stage to the salon. Handel wrote a large number of such cantatas for performance at the houses of wealthy patrons like Cardinal Ottoboni and Prince Ruspoli, and it is with these works that we shall be principally concerned in this chapter.

In the hands of Carissimi the Italian chamber cantata was firmly

established as a popular musical form, and after his time its development was closely linked with that of opera. In both fields the name
of Alessandro Scarlatti featured largely. He was an even more prolific composer of chamber cantatas than of operas, and may be said
to have standardized the type which Handel took as a model. In its
simplest form this consisted of the alternation of two or more recitatives and arias describing the situation and emotions of a single
character, after the manner of a short operatic excerpt. The arias
were contrasted in style within the limits of the recognized cate-
gories, and the recitatives, generally *secco*, were occasionally *stromen-
tato* if an orchestra were available. The use of obbligato instruments
was another source of variety, while additional characters and even
some sort of vocal ensemble might be introduced. With larger forces
and an expanded libretto, the cantata often developed into a serenata.

Handel left examples of chamber cantatas of every type from the
least pretentious to the more elaborate, and managed to extract an
astonishing amount of variety out of the narrow range of subjects—
generally dealing with the pangs of unrequited love—offered by his
librettists. It did not take him long to master the conventional
pattern, and he then took great delight in departing from it, with
many lively experiments in form, style, and orchestration. He made
the chamber cantata his training ground in Italian operatic technique,
and emerged from this exercise of his skill soundly equipped for his
London ventures. For in the meantime he had acquired not only an
efficient technical apparatus, but also a rich store of material upon
which he was able to draw to good purpose for the rest of his life.
For one of the most remarkable features of the cantatas is the way
in which thematic fragments, reshaped melodies, and complete
movements from them are to be found constantly recurring in
Handel's works at every stage of his career. So, in addition to
deciding the future course of his main creative stream, the Italian
tour provided many of its perennial springs as well.

Of the Italian cantatas for solo voice and continuo, those for
soprano are by far the most numerous. One of the first points of
interest that attracts attention in this collection occurs in the cantata
Ah! che pur troppo è vero (No. 1),[1] where in the second aria Handel
has left what at first sight appears to be a realization of the continuo,
i.e. the completion of the harpsichord part by the addition of a treble
line to the bass. The upper, or right hand, part in the autograph is in
a different coloured ink from the rest and looks like a later insertion,

---

[1] The numbering is that adopted in H.–G., Vols. 50 and 51.

and it has been conjectured that Handel filled out the bass at the request of a singer who wished to accompany herself at the keyboard. If this were so we should have a valuable indication of Handel's methods of accompaniment from a thorough bass. But closer examination does not support this assumption. The upper line consists of a single part except at the close, where chords are given, and although the resulting two-part harmony is admirably self-sufficient, it is not continued throughout and there are passages left with the bass unharmonized. Furthermore, the indications of phrasing in the added part suggest a bowed instrument rather than the harpsichord, and the gaps in the treble line occur where one would expect an obbligato instrument to be silent. Join to this the fact that the whole aria is clearly an earlier study for the beautiful 'Come rosa e su la spina' in *Apollo e Dafne*, where a richer and more lyrical form of the added part is given to the violins in unison, while the broken semiquaver figure in the bass is transferred to a solo 'cello, and it becomes evident that we must regard Handel's interpolation as a sketch for a violin obbligato part and not as a guide to the harpsichord player.

Aure soavi e liete (No. 3) is a delightful example of the shorter cantata and shows incidentally that its ingredients are by no means stereotyped. In the first aria, 'Care luci' there is no conventional *da capo*, but the effect of recapitulation is obtained by ending with part of the music of the first section adapted to the second couplet of the words—a skilful and telling device. After a second short recitative, an arietta in the French manner completes this unusual scheme.

Although both the arias in *Care selve, aure grate* (No. 4) follow the usual form, they have other features that are uncommon. 'Ridite a Clori' has an opening phrase that looks square and unpromising, but after some facile imitation between voice and bass that does not augur too well, Handel lifts the aria on to a new plane with a striking progression such as he often seems to have had in reserve to redeem similar situations elsewhere:

Ex. 61

ri - di - te a Clo -ri, er - bet - tee fior - i, s'al-tro mai sen - to

'Non ha forza' is in the very rarely found 2/4 measure, and the melody with its dotted rhythm sounds like a jaunty popular dance tune, from which indeed it may well have been derived.

Quite different in mood is the opening of *Chi rapi la pace al core?* (No. 5), where the questioning appeal of the disconsolate lover is conveyed in an expressive adagio, whose sequences of falling thirds seem to characterize his dejection. This is one of the cantatas where a stringed instrument can add much to the expressiveness of the continuo. The florid bass line of the second aria is almost in the nature of an obbligato part, and calls for sustaining power beyond the normal capacity of the harpsichord.

The vocal style of these cantatas is highly exacting for the singer—indeed, rather more so than in the majority of the operas and oratorios. However, many of the elaborate ornamental figures and bravura passages, though demanding considerable agility, lie quite comfortably for the voice and can readily be made to sound effective. Such *fioriture* were the stock-in-trade of the prima donnas of the day and the composers that served them, but Handel was by no means content to build up his vocabulary from a conventional idiom, however successful it might be. As with everything else that he absorbed into his style, and in the Italian period he was assimilating rapidly, the vocal clichés of Rome and Naples were not admitted without receiving the imprint of his personality, and were given just that extra turn of phrase that was needed to give them new meaning and distinction. Nor, as might be expected, was he satisfied to rely on outside sources for his materials—not that they would have sufficed in any case to cover the wide emotional range of these cantatas—and he showed the resourcefulness of his invention in devising a terminology of his own which gave the singer opportunities for display without robbing the composer of his individuality. This was not achieved without a measure of compromise, since beauty of vocal sound was not Handel's only criterion, as was the case with some of his contemporaries. He was sufficient of a German to insist upon the importance of the purely musical element, if need be occasionally at the expense of the voice—a very grave heresy in this period. Closely allied as were the chamber cantatas with operatic forms and methods, there was a perceptible tendency towards greater intimacy of expression than was normal in the theatre, and this aroused in Handel a more intense and penetrating quality in declamation, to which in any event he would have been inclined, by virtue of his early training. The result was that smoothness was often sacrificed in favour of a rugged independence of outline, sharper in impact, and richer in content, but appreciably less grateful to sing.

A passage such as the following, from *Da sete ardente afflitto* (No. 9), makes few concessions to the conventional view of what constitutes a vocal contour, but for that very reason would have stood more forcefully out of its context as indicating an emotional climax.

This may seem to have been a rather primitive and uncouth method of securing an effect, but it was at least likely to make more impression on a contemporary listener than the polished urbanity with which such sentiments were usually delivered. The later version of this melody in *Susanna* ('the parent bird in search of food') in which this passage is eliminated, has greater refinement, but considerably less pungency.

Lest it should be thought that these melodic asperities should be more frankly attributed to inherent defects in Handel's technique, one has only to turn to such cantatas as *Del bell' idolo mio* (No. 11) and *Filli adorata e cara* (No. 20), both of which contain beautiful examples of a smooth yet expressive cantilena—in the first an andante aria ('Formidabil gondoliero') which has a line of unusual pliancy, and in the latter a tender little siciliana ('Lungi da te'). Handel learnt the true art of the siciliana at Naples, and it is in these early chamber cantatas that it first becomes fully incorporated in his style. He found it particularly well suited to certain moods, and always handled it with great sympathy and lyrical power. In his

music other types of aria may sometimes disappoint us; those founded
on this graceful measure very rarely do so.

Turning from the voice to its only partner in this intimate ensemble, the instrumental bass, one discovers there also splendid
richness and vitality. In Handel's larger works the bass, often only
a unit in an orchestral group, though a constant source of power,
has not the same individuality that it enjoys in these cantatas. Here
it constantly rises above the humble role of being a mere support or
foil—the good listener in a one-sided conversation who knows how
to start a subject going, to maintain it by appropriate remarks at
judicious intervals and to round it off by a well-balanced observation
at the end. Frequently the importance of its contribution promotes
its status to a level with that of the voice, so that the mutual relationship is more that of a duet than a solo with accompaniment. One
could not view in any other light the noble 'Se al pensier dar mai
potrò' from *Sarei troppo felice* (No. 53)[1] where the bass almost
outvies the upper line in expressive content, nor indeed the two fine
arias in *Non sospirar, non piangere* (No. 43), in which the voice first
spans tremendous chasms down which the bass plunges with stirring
abandon, and then leads its partner in a close canon productive of
most fruitful consequences.

The bass is, naturally, the main source of harmonic energy, and it
is usually through some uncommon feature in the shape of its principal figure that Handel is incited to his more adventurous excursions. In 'Troppo caro' from *Occhi miei che faceste?* (No. 44) it is
the chromatic steps and leaps in the opening continuo phrase that
induce him to follow strange paths later, while a similar mode of
progression in the second recitative in *Lungi n'ando Fileno* (No. 29)
leads to such a harmonic labyrinth that he finds some difficulty in
extricating himself in time for the succeeding aria.

Thus, in a sense, does the character of Handel's bass influence the
course of his melody, while the general relationship between the two
components is fundamental to the structure of the cantata as a whole.
By subtle adjustments of this relationship Handel is able to secure
an added degree of variety in a pattern that otherwise might become
too stereotyped. One of the advantages of a comparatively rigid
convention is that the smallest departure from it obtains a dis-
proportionately striking effect. So that when the introductory

[1] This cantata is printed by Chrysander in an incomplete form; the manuscript
in the Granville collection has three more movements (cf. *The Musical Antiquary*,
July 1911, p. 221).—*Ed.*

ritornelli are omitted in both arias in *Nella stagion che, di viole e rose* (No. 37) this is felt to affect the entire balance of the cantata, so carefully regulated is the normal mechanism, and the delicate charm of the work receives an extra distinction thereby. Similarly, the antiphonal treatment of voice and continuo in 'Lascia di più sperar', from *Menzognere speranze* (No. 32) suggests a kind of declamation that belongs more to a recitative than to an aria and the effect of the customary alternation is thereby disturbed. *Nice che fa?* (No. 39) besides possessing another example of an aria starting with the entry of the voice, includes also the type in which the second section is in a different tempo from the opening—in this instance a sorrowful adagio to which a recitative cadence seems the natural ending before the return to the initial allegro. In the entrancing *Zeffiretto* (No. 71) this order is reversed, a lyrical adagio taking the place of the habitual opening recitative and having a fleet allegro as intermediate contrast. A more revolutionary scheme than any of these is pursued in *Udite il mio consiglio* (No. 67), which begins with a noteworthy piece of declamation (during the course of which one encounters a double sharp in the bass figuring) that is succeeded by a sort of canzona in which the two parts are as equally balanced as in a duet. The voice ends before the full close—a device more typical of Wolf than of Handel—and a more or less conventional aria follows. The cantata then proceeds on familiar lines until just before the end, where a brief return is made to the canzona movement, and finally—a brilliant stroke this—the earlier refrain 'Fuggite, ah! si fuggite, que' suoi furtivi sguardi!' is repeated in a concluding recitative.

Many such means of obtaining added flexibility and power are combined in the finest of these soprano solo cantatas *O Numi eterni!* (No. 46). The conflicting moods of the outraged Lucretia are most vividly represented in music that not only rises, as one might expect, to a peak of almost savage emotion, but has also a dignity that gives the passionate outburst real tragic force. The rich ornamentation of the melodic line has an intimate poignancy that suggests the idiom of Leipzig rather than that of Florence. The recitatives have a special freshness and vigour in the brief respite these give from the endless complaints of dejected lovers. The subject provides little scope for the usual tepid languishing, and Handel is stirred by this exhilarating change of atmosphere to produce declamation highly varied in style and of surpassing intensity.

An interesting curiosity that deserves mention here is the cantata Handel wrote in praise of himself. This unique piece of

self-advertisement originated at one of the meetings of the highly exclusive Arcadian Academy at which Cardinal Panfili improvised
a poem in honour of Handel and asked the composer to set it to
music himself. Though it was known that this incident had taken
place, it was not till 1911 that Streatfeild found a copy in the Granville Collection and described it in his *Musical Antiquary* article on
the Collection; in 1935 Professor Dent, who had found another copy
of *Hendel, non può mia musa*, in the University Library at Münster,
brought about its first modern performance in the Handel Festival
at Cambridge in 1935. However, Handel—unlike Proust and others
—does not appear to have found his own character a very absorbing
subject; even the comparison with Orpheus, in his own favour,
does not stir him to any very elaborate demonstration. Nevertheless
his contemporaries were probably much amused by the application
of the current formulas to this unusual theme.

Of the cantatas for alto, *Figlio del mesto cor* (No. 19) contains a
spacious largo of impressive breadth and nobility, 'Son pur le
lacrime', built over a bass of the kind that seemed to hold a special
interest for him at this time:

Ex. 63

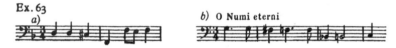

a)   b) O Numi eterni

Lungi da voi (No. 28) is also notable for a slow aria of solemn,
pensive beauty; in a sustained movement of this nature Handel will
maintain a long, unbroken line of extreme plasticity that demands
expert control and phrasing from the performer. The second aria,
'Chi sa? vi rivedrò', claims some attention too for the delicate
charm of its dialogue between voice and continuo. *Vedendo amor*
(No. 69) is another cantata that possesses many good things, amongst
them an early study for the lovely 'Va tacito' in *Giulio Cesare*.[1]

The bass voice makes but a rare appearance in works of this type.
It then occupied a rather lowly place in the Italian operatic hierarchy,
being mainly associated with minor *buffo* parts, which was scarcely
calculated to make it the romantic ideal of the fashionable salon.
The few examples that remain of its use in the present connexion
make it clear that they were written for a special purpose, and
probably for a particular singer—Boschi. *Dalla guerra amorosa*
(No. 8) is an ironical warning against the perils of love, and obviously
requires a singer with a lively stage personality to do full justice to

[1] See p. 30.

its malicious humour. The light-hearted simplicity of its style and
its burlesque of the more solemn conventions make one think of
La Serva Padrona, and indeed it might well be Uberto who delivers
the final sentiments: 'He who is a slave to love lives in chains;
doubtful is his reward, but certain his suffering . . .'. In contrast to
the majority of the cantatas, this may be regarded as the representative, on the smaller domestic scale, of the *opera buffa*.

Nell' Africane selve (No. 36) does not merely exploit the possibilities of the register, it stretches it to extremes of height and profundity
and demands that the voice bridge the gap by a series of formidable
leaps. A quotation of two bars will suffice to indicate the nature of
the singer's problem:

Ex. 64

(inciam - - - pa)

It is difficult for us today to believe that such gymnastics were
intended to be taken relatively seriously. The piece seems to become
perilously near an entertaining circus turn, introducing an imposing
menagerie most realistically in the opening recitative, and calling
for some daring trapeze work in the succeeding aria. Perhaps what
Tovey called 'the Great Bass(oon) Joke' added its extra syllable only
in Haydn's day.

A number of the solo cantatas exist in two or more versions.
Sometimes these versions are substantially the same, except for the
transpositions necessary to bring them within the range of different
voices. But such transposition can rarely be exact, having regard to
the limitations of the accompanying instruments, and in the course
of adaptation more often than not Handel will take the opportunity
of making some small but significant changes. In *Dolce pur d'amor
l'affanno* (Nos. 15 and 16), apart from some slight extra embellish-
ments, the soprano version of the first aria does not differ greatly
from the alto original, but the recitative that follows is drastically
altered, producing a much smoother effect. Of the concluding aria
there is yet a third version to be found in *Stanco di più soffrire*
(No. 64), which would seem to be also the earliest, since much of
the slack that weakens its construction is taken up in the tautened
line of the other two examples. A glimpse of Handel's care over
details of workmanship is provided by a comparison of the *da capo*

bar in the three versions. First of all he makes a definite break, but
this is rather halting rhythmically, so he amends this to enable the
opening phrase of the ritornello to follow directly after the cadence
of the second section. This now sounds too abrupt a transition
harmonically, and when he adapts the aria for soprano he inserts a
bar of modulation to serve as a bridge. These are scarcely the signs
of the slapdash craftsman that some might expect to find in so rapid
a worker.

It is not always easy to choose between the alternatives. In the
two settings of the following passage from *Sento là che ristretto*
(Nos. 56 and 57), one recognizes the clearer declamation of the
second, but at the same time regrets the loss of the more expressive
cadence in the first.

Ex. 65

One is faced by a similar predicament in *E partirai, mia vita?*
(Nos. 17 and 18), where one is in general agreement with the extra
refinement secured by revision, while wondering occasionally
whether it is quite worth the cost.

Ex. 66

Dimmi, O mio cor (No. 12) and the other version of the same setting that forms the greater part of *Mi palpita il cor* (No. 34) also cause some perplexity, but on the whole the decision must be in favour of the latter, if only by a short margin. In neither case does Handel seem quite to have solved the movement problem set by the static, repetitive nature of the main subject of the first aria, but he achieves a more convincing statement in the second by the omission of a clause in the opening phrase of the solo and by the alternation of the rhythm in the bass.

The introductory arioso to *Mi palpita il cor*, which gives it its alias, is a link with another story that will be told later. The insertion or omission of such movements was, however, not an uncommon feature of the recasting of these cantatas. The tempestuous middle aria in *Lungi dal mio bel nume* (No. 25), describing the fate of a skiff in a storm at sea, is thus discarded at the order, one suspects, of some singer who could not endure the rivalry of the virtuoso part for the continuo. In *Se pari è la tua fè* (Nos. 58 and 59) it is the proportion of recitative that is changed; certainly it is unusually slender in the first version, consisting of only one line of music. In the revision it is much more extensive—having the last word in fact. Here, too, we see the human instrument at work, exacting longer cadenzas from the composer and, more laudably, insisting on improved verbal accentuation. In this instance Handel has skilfully managed to satisfy the vanity of the singer without undue damage to the musical fabric, but more delicate material cannot so easily sustain such treatment. The charming little allegro, in triple measure, that ends *Ninfe e pastori* (Nos. 40, 41 and 42) is made to sound rather ridiculous by the addition of much vocal prancing and curvetting. On the other hand, the exclusion of the initial arietta is no great loss; for some reason Handel appears to have written out the *da capo* of this movement *in full* in the first version—surely an alarming symptom for an inquiring psychologist. More reassuringly normal is his behaviour in connexion with *Sei pur bella* (No. 54). The likelihood is that for this cantata the work of a contemporary (No. 55) was raided, albeit with a nice discrimination, to the extent of a pleasant, if slightly restless aria. Chrysander is cautious, but I think we may pay Handel the compliment of not saddling him with the responsibility for the rest of the rifled cantata, which is singularly dreary and undistinguished. As with all his 'borrowings', Handel made excellent use of his selected item, introducing therein many subtle improvements in the process of incorporation, and placing it in the company of original work of his own with which it had every reason to be proud to be associated.

Before dealing with the cantatas with obbligato instruments, some reference must be made to the solo songs with continuo in other languages. While in Italy Handel set a small number of French *chansons*, presumably for the enjoyment of a distinguished visitor, or possibly some noble patron exiled by marriage, such as the Spanish Princess at Naples for whom he wrote *No se emendera jamas*. These *chansons* tell us little new about Handel, but confirm his capacity for adapting himself, chameleon-like, to match the prevailing complexion of any given style. They are as distinctively French as the cantatas are Italian, his lack of familiarity with the language being no more conspicuous in one case than in the other: he attains the useful working average of the eighteenth-century cosmopolitan that served him throughout his career. There are examples of the typical French air with two balanced strains and of the kind of arioso declamation favoured by Rameau, while in *Nos plaisirs seront peu durables* there is the additional interest of a melody written over a chaconne-like recurring bass, an uncommon feature in Handelian solo song.

Handel's contributions to the English domestic repertoire were not very weighty, consisting chiefly of the lighter type of love song and ephemeral patriotic ditties, nor do those responsible for the words appear to have given him much cause for encouragement.

A foreigner confronted with lines of doubtful syntax that do not scan may perhaps be forgiven for unwittingly adding to the confusion. Certainly in one of the more lucid and regular passages from *Yes, I'm in love*, his choice of repetitions seems a little unfelicitous:

> 'Tis not her Face that Love creates
> For there no Graces revel,
> 'Tis not her shape, for there the Fates (*repeat*)
> Have (*repeat*) rather been uncivil.

Most of these are simple strophic songs, in which the same melody had to serve for a number of verses. Consequently, to a composer trying to cultivate the bluff English manner, the exuberant imagery and abrupt changes of mood of political versifiers must have created some troublesome problems. Here is a sample from *A Song on the Victory over the Rebels by his Royal Highness the Duke of Cumberland* (1745), set to a hearty, swinging tune:

> In his Train see sweet Peace, fairest Offspring of Sky,
> Ev'ry bliss in her Smiles, ev'ry Charm in her Eye,
> Whilst that worst Foe to Man, that dread Fiend, Civil War,
> Gnashing horid [*sic*] her Teeth fast bound to his Car.
> *Chorus:* Your glasses charge high, &c.

It is therefore with some relief that one returns to the refined sufferings of Italian lovers, expressed in those cantatas in which Handel occasionally added to the basic ensemble of voice and continuo an obbligato instrument or an orchestral group. Handel was apt to be careless about naming his instruments in the score, and this might be disconcerting did not the range and character of the parts leave little room for ambiguity. *Nel dolce dell'oblio* (No. XVII)[1] is, however, expressly styled *cantata a voce sola con flauto*, and is as clearly designed for the colour of that instrument, whose fickle, caressing tones provide an appropriate commentary to the 'Night thoughts of Phillis'. It is laid out very simply and is content to make its appeal by its unaffected and adroitly balanced dialogue between soprano voice and flute. A slight affair, perhaps, but possessing winning charm that cannot be disregarded.

There is another cantata with flute obbligato of a more substantial type. *Mi palpita il cor* (No. 33) is a title that has been mentioned before in connexion with a cantata with continuo accompaniment

---

[1] The Roman figures refer to the numbering of the Italian cantatas with instruments in H.–G., Vols. 52 and 53.

only (No. 34)—itself a later version of yet a third cantata (*Dimmi, O mio cor* (No. 12)). The link between Nos. 33 and 34 consists only of the introduction, an alternation of recitative and arioso. After that point both music and text are entirely different and in the case of the former at any rate, there is a notable advance in quality. With a strange confusion of thought Chrysander includes what is virtually a new work together with its earlier namesake amongst the continuo cantatas, though it is patently in the obbligato category, and yet gives the transposition for soprano and oboe (No. XXVII) its correct classification, which makes an already complicated situation even more involved. There can certainly be no question of the obbligato part having been an afterthought, as he suggests; the interdependence of the two upper lines is too close for them to have originated separately. The flute weaves itself enchantingly round the voice, in quietly elegiac mood in the largo aria, then with a sprightly gaiety at the more cheerful prospect foreseen in the allegro. Altogether this must be rated one of the most delightful of the solo cantatas, and one that deserves to be better known. That it was a popular favourite at the time is suggested by the existence of an alternative version a minor third higher. Only part of this is given in the Händel-Gesellschaft edition (No. XXVII), but it is all extant and may be found in the King's Music Library (R.M. 20.e.4). Allowing for the necessary adaptation to a different voice and instrument, Handel makes few substantial alterations, except to prolong the cadence at the end of the second part of the final aria. This translation into new terms is admirably successful.

While he was at Naples Handel wrote an odd little cantata to Spanish words—the native tongue of a princess who was a member of the Academy there. This has a guitar as obbligato instrument; it probably supplied the continuo as well, since the bass parts in the arias are practically identical, and it has an independent melodic line only when the voice is silent. In response to some caprice, the music is written out with the intention of giving it an archaic appearance, in notes of twice or four times their normal value expressed, by no means consistently, in obsolete symbols. The purpose of all this is somewhat mystifying; it might have been a misguided affectation of classicism, but was more probably a private *jeu d'esprit* whose savour is lost on posterity. Apart from one or two attempts at producing an unfamiliar lilt in the rhythm, the musical substance lacks any hint of appropriate local colour. The phrases are short winded and beyond a certain mild sophistication, create no very solid impression.

More significant musically are the delicate *Pastorella, vagha bella*[1] which has an elaborate *cembalo concertato* part, and *Un' alma inna-morata* (No. XXIII) for soprano with what is presumably violin obbligato. In the latter, which one would place early on internal evidence, the ritornelli are abnormally long. The violin has no fewer than thirty-three bars of solo in the first aria before the entry of the voice, whose opening phrase lasts only two bars, and even those are shared with the violin! Handel must indeed have had a complaisant singer on this occasion. The other two arias are not equal in interest with the first, which contains some florid and eloquent three-part writing that recalls the composer's Hamburg origin.

Reference must be made here to the German songs[2] that were the fruit of Handel's short visit to the Continent in 1729. The words are by B. H. Brockes, whose *Passion* Handel had set in 1716, and the unspecified obbligato instrument was most likely intended to be the violin, though there are cases where the oboe or flute would be equally effective. As befits their character, these songs incline towards the type of subjective emotion so strongly marked in the church cantatas of Bach, and there are moments when the customary cleavage of style and temperament between the two great con-temporaries almost seems to disappear. Nor in terms of quality is the comparison unfitting, for Handel's splendid lyrical gift is worthily displayed by such examples as *Meine Seele hört im Sehen* and *Flammende Rose*, while *In den angenehmen Büschen* is a resource-ful study in subtle tone-painting which the Leipzig master might well have been pleased to claim as his own.

When the number of additional instrumental parts in these cantatas is increased to two or more, certain changes can be detected in the relationship between the voice and its companion ensemble. First of all, the number of independent lines is seldom more than three (as in the obbligato aria), however many instruments are involved, but if counterpoint is maintained against the solo, it will be either all played in unison or distributed piecemeal amongst the group. The intricate polyphony of Bach's cantatas would be quite out of keeping here. There is also a greater sense of perspective between solo and ritornello; the intimate atmosphere recedes as the musical image grows in depth, until eventually we feel we have left

[1] Not in H.–G.; published in the series 'Organum' edited by Seiffert (Kistner & Siegel).

[2] Not in H.–G. Published by Hermann Roth (Drei Masken Verlag, Munich), in 1921, republished (Breitkopf & Härtel) in 1931; separate numbers in 'Organum' (Kistner & Siegel).

the salon for the Great Hall. More scope is given for including new elements in the general plan; a self-sufficient consort is now possible that can supply introductory *sinfonie* and accompany recitative. Purely harmonic support to the voice is often provided, aiding or replacing the continuo, and lending added emphasis at suitable points. Naturally there were also greater opportunities for variety of colour, of which Handel was not slow to take advantage.

A convenient link between the obbligato and orchestral styles is provided by *Tu fedel? tu costante?* (No. XXII). This opens with a three-part instrumental sonata of modest pretensions that serves as an overture. After a passage of recitative, which is throughout the cantata accompanied only by the continuo, the violins combine for the aria 'Cento belle'. Except that the style in some places suggests tutti rather than solo, this could as well be an aria with obbligato, to judge by the close contrapuntal writing, which gives it the appearance of a chamber music trio. More advantage is taken of the extra resources in the second aria, where for long stretches the voice is supported only by the violins, the second violin providing the bass. This is a welcome change in a class of music where the background colour of the harpsichord in the continuo could become monotonous. The authentic orchestral technique is resumed in 'Se non ti piace amarmi', from which was later derived 'Let's imitate her notes above' in *Alexander's Feast*. Both the accompaniment and the ritornelli are strictly harmonic in character, and are designed to contrast, rather than in any way to compete, with the voice. In the brief arietta which ends the cantata the violins double the vocal line throughout, quite a common procedure in such cases, but one that seems to us now rather inartistic. Perhaps it was an attempt on the composer's part to ensure that what was actually sung had some connexion with what he had written.

Both *Clori, mia bella Clori* (No. IX) and *Figlio d'alte speranze* (No. XV) contain arias in which the continuo regains its original status as principal factotum to the voice, the upper strings being allowed only some valedictory remarks when the latter has left the scene. Elsewhere, however, the violins have some pregnant contributions to make, imparting great delicacy by their gentle broken chords in 'Chiari lumi', discreetly sighing in thirds in 'Mie pupille', and expatiating in tender lyrical strain in 'Troppo costa ad un alma'. The cantatas for bass make use of the orchestra in recitative, *Cuopre tal volta* (No. XI) at the beginning, *Spande ancor* (No. XX) after the first aria. *Cuopre tal volta*, which is probably one of the earliest of

the cantatas and may even have been partly written before the
Italian visit, has a spirited D major aria which Handel afterwards
completely transformed by turning it into the minor and altering
its character to represent the restless anguish of the deserted Armida;
in the process something is lost of the energy and impetus of the
original.

The two soprano scenas, of which *Armida abbandonata* (No. XIII)
is one, show, as one would expect, the strings in a more dramatic
role. Energetic triple stopping in open semiquaver movement takes
the place of the continuo during the introductory recitative of
Armida abbandonata, while frenzied scale passages punctuate the
desperate appeal of the sorceress to the elements. In *Agrippina
condotta a morire* (No. XIV) the fall of Jove's thunderbolt is graphically represented thus:

and similarly characteristic and expressive phrases accompany the
voice throughout the long expostulation in which Agrippina's turmoil
of emotions is skilfully conveyed by means of brief strains of arioso
interrupted by recitative. In the course of the usual Handelian
metamorphosis of themes, the first of these two tragic characters was
later to borrow from the other, since one of the violin figures associated here with Agrippina becomes in *Rinaldo* the subject of the
richly scored lament of Armida.

Many of these cantatas are uneven in quality, but *Crudel tiranno
Amor* (No. X) maintains a consistently high level in three well
contrasted arias. The second, 'O dolce mia speranza', is a particularly
fine example of the delicate pathos that Handel can extract from his
favoured slow 12/8 measure. *Delirio amoroso* (No. XII) cannot
challenge this musical standard, but the addition of an oboe and a
flute to the orchestra lends it an extra piquancy of colour that is
specially noticeable in the delicious introduction, where the oboe has
an unusually independent part, and in the aria 'Lascia omai le brune
vele', which opens with the statement by the flute of a bar in lively
dotted rhythm that was to reappear with greater prominence in the
D major Violin Sonata and *Jephtha*. In *Ah! crudel, nel pianto mio*
(No. 1) the flute is replaced by a second oboe, but not for the purpose of enabling the pair of oboes to dog the footsteps of the violins,

as so often in early eighteenth-century music. It is in fact the woodwind that take the lead, announcing at the very start one of the most
persistent of Handel's motto-themes (*cf. Agrippina, La Resurrezione,
Rinaldo, L'Allegro, Joshua*, etc.):

Ex. 68

and in the second section of the final aria the first oboe has even an
elaborate solo obbligato role. As well as oboes and flutes *Tra le
fiamme* (No. XXI) assigns the viola da gamba a place in the score
distinct from the continuo, but seems to derive little material benefit
from this relative extravagance except to produce, rather paradoxically, an attractively diaphanous texture in 'Voli per l'aria' (a distant
connexion, in the minor, of the popular 'Come rosa' in *Apollo e
Dafne*).

The main interest of the music in honour of St. Cecilia (Nos.
V, VI, VII and VIII) is the opportunity it gives for comparing the
various modifications and rearrangements of the different versions,
though the aria 'Sei cara' in No. VI (used in the English ode, *Look
down, harmonious Saint*, No. VIII, to the words 'Sweet accents')
has a certain mellifluous charm. The hymn to the Virgin *Ah! che
troppo ineguali* (No. XXVI) is couched in far more sincere and convincing terms.

At this point we now leave the solo songs and cantatas and turn
to those chamber works in which two or more voices are engaged.
These form a less homogenous group and are more widely dispersed
over Handel's life, not only the Italian period being represented but
also the years in Hanover and quite a late stage of his London career
as well.   In the case of the duets and trios we are moreover concerned with a fundamentally different type of composition, no
longer founded on the contrast between a dominant solo and a subservient ripieno, but growing out of the continuous interplay of
equal partners. The ritornello disappears and interest is concentrated
on the dialogue between the voices, usually carried on in close
imitation. This has much in common with certain types of the
contemporary instrumental music, and the *da capo* aria is largely
abandoned for the linked series of contrasted movements found in
the *sonata da chiesa*.

The first important duets are those which Handel wrote for the
Hanoverian court between 1710 and 1712. They are based on the

chamber duets of Steffani, his immediate predecessor in the Elector's service, who brought the form to a high pitch of refinement. No artistic secret was long proof against Handel's penetrating insight, and to judge by the fluent assurance of his style, he might have been the actual possessor of Steffani's unrivalled experience, instead of its very recent legatee. But he was aware of the dangers as well as the advantages of the conventional technique. In a closely wrought piece of this type, where the equality of the participants is accepted as axiomatic, there is a danger of proceeding from one facile antithesis to another, begetting either weariness or irritation in the hearer. Handel shows great skill in the variation and contrast of his phrase-lengths, as witness *Troppo cruda, troppo fiera* and especially *Amor*, where in the last section a short diatonic phrase is tellingly introduced against a long chromatic melody. In *Va, speme infida* the first section is resumed at the end to round off the design, while elsewhere one notes gratefully, as a departure from routine custom, the voices answering instead of imitating one another at the beginning of a movement. The delicacy and pathos of *Tanti strali* and the intimate expressiveness of *Se tu non lasci amore* show what an impressive level was attained in this group of duets.[1]

The other main collection dates from thirty years later (1741-5) and reveals the composer in his full maturity. Handel seems to have recognized that this music was of a quality too fine to be restricted to such a limited sphere, and much of it was used again in the choruses of the great oratorios he was then writing. Some of the transformations are indeed rather startling, *Quel fior che all' alba ride* (The flower that blooms at dawn), as Mr. Herbage has already pointed out, becomes 'His yoke is easy', and *Nò, di voi non vo' fidarmi, cieco Amor, crudel beltà* (No, I will trust you no longer, love is blind and beauty cruel) is better known as 'For unto us a Child is born'; but he would indeed be churlish that complains at having both versions. Perhaps anticipating some such sour-minded comment, Handel reset the original Italian words of two of the *Messiah* choruses. *Beato in ver chi può* and *Ahi, nelle sorte umane* are well worthy of this distinguished company; that *Fronda leggiera* falls short is due to an andante larghetto that is rather unduly pedestrian after the mercurial brilliance of the opening.

[1] The last section, 'Non havran mai', of *Sono liete* was fused with a theme from Telemann's *Musique de Table*, Prod. II, No. 3, to form the allegro subject of the *Judas Maccabeus* overture: see Winton Dean, 'Handel Reconsidered', *The Score* (September, 1954), p. 49.—*Ed.*

The two remarkable trios, composed in Italy, also had a choral sequel, both main sections of the second, an earlier setting of *Quel fior che all' alba ride*, being converted into choruses in *Alexander's Feast* and *L'Allegro*[1] respectively. The first of these is a regular *tour de force*, being a fugue on three subjects, 'Quel fior che all' alba ride' ('Let old Timotheus yield the prize'), 'E tomba ha nella sera' ('Or both divide the crown') and 'Il sole poi l'uccede' ('She drew an angel down'), to which with daring virtuosity he added yet a fourth ('He rais'd a mortal to the skies') in the cantata, inserting it between the last two entries without leaving a trace of joinery. If anyone should doubt whether Handel himself knew more about counterpoint than his cook, let him examine these pages.

Such ensemble pieces as there are in the cantatas for two or more voices are based on the form of the solo aria, yet they nevertheless find opportunity for a fair amount of imitation. But the cantatas (some of them are elaborate enough to be termed serenatas) are too overshadowed by operatic convention to allow of much emphasis on vocal ensemble (one duet per evening was the ration in the theatre), and one must look elsewhere for their real wealth. This is usually to be discovered in detached fragments such as 'O! come chiare e bello' from the cantata of that title (No. XIX), which is not only intrinsically interesting but has the added distinction of being assigned to a character called Olinto, which was the name by which Prince Ruspoli was known in the Academy. The incomplete cantata *Conosco che mi piaci* (No. XXIV) is tantalizing since it begins in the middle of what seems to be its most expressive aria. It contains others, though, well worthy of attention, including 'Son come quel nocchiero' (scored for violas divisi with flutes at the octave), the delicate 'Un sospiretto' and the piquant little duet between Cloris and Thyrsis at the beginning of the second part.

In general these larger scale cantatas are apt to be unequal, but there are two notable exceptions. The first of these is *Arresta' il passo* (No. III), whose French overture is dramatically interrupted by the first line of recitative. The arias have great charm and contain much delicately poised coloratura.[2] The engagingly repeated rhetorical questions in Fillide's 'E un foco' and Aminta's delightful romance are characteristic of the spirit of the work, which is rounded off with a brilliant final duet.

---

[1] See footnote on p. 143.

[2] Three of them were used again in *Agrippina*, and one—with the beginning of the overture—in *Rinaldo.—Ed.*

Even finer quality is shown in the superb *Apollo e Dafne* (*La terra è liberata*) (No. XVI). So consistently rich is Handel's invention in this score that it is hard to discriminate between Apollo's vigorous 'Spezza l'arco e getta l'armi', with its interplay of woodwind and strings, the lively duet 'Una guerra ho dentro', the haunting lyricism, in solo and ritornello, of 'Come rosa in su la spina', and the precipitous 'pursuit' aria with violin and bassoon concertati, to say nothing of several others that would be outstanding in any other context. But if one were forced to make a selection, it must be the exquisite 'Felicissima quest' alma', in which soprano and oboe obbligato vie with one another in a contest of Olympian beauty over an ethereal accompaniment of pizzicato strings. When Handel wrote this peerless idyll, he had yet to write the great arias whose titles are now household words, yet he never achieved anything finer. It represents the peak in a work that itself crowns all his achievements in this field. It is evident that the crude young Saxon had taken to himself such lustre as Italy could lend him, while adding a brilliance of his own that far outshone his contemporary models. *Apollo e Dafne* is Handel's *Entführung*, possessing that inimitable freshness and spontaneity of youth that always gains a special place in our affections despite the later claims of more mature and imposing qualities. With it alone in his portfolio Handel would have had no cause to regret his Italian adventure.

CHAPTER VII

THE ORCHESTRAL MUSIC

By BASIL LAM

MEASURED by quantity alone, the instrumental music forms no more than a minor part of Handel's vast output. Yet certain concertos and sonatas contain evidence of his greatness no less convincing than may be found in the more obviously 'great' oratorios, though in neither case is it easy to account for the greatness, and the technique of his most valuable inspirations shows all the distinguishing features found equally in evidence in works marked otherwise only by a fatal dullness and facility.

Fortunately for the critic, his orchestral compositions seem to have been written for Handel's own pleasure and the level of interest is remarkably high for this most unequal of all great masters. Perhaps it was this lack of attention which led the late Ernest Walker in a moment of impatience to deny Handel his position among the half-dozen supreme composers on the grounds that a man who took so little trouble over his work could not really stand beside Bach, Mozart, and Beethoven, or at any rate did not deserve to, though Mozart and Beethoven would never have doubted that to be in Handel's company was an honour to be sought rather than a favour to be conferred. It is true that the twelve Concerti grossi, Op. 6, show less evidence of hard work than the six Brandenburg Concertos but it is a difficult choice, and perhaps a meaningless one, to select either group to represent the highest achievement of baroque orchestral music. Handel may sometimes have damned the age, but he did not write for posterity and it is by a strange irony that so much of his music, e.g. the organ concertos, has survived only in a distorted form with the result that his genuine grandeur and antique nobility of style have been obscured by the false grandeur of mere noise and physical size. Nowhere in his orchestral music is there a trace of grandiloquence, and the one composition intended for performance on a Berlioz-like scale, the *Fireworks Music*, is a masterpiece of pure composition which would bear transference to the medium of the trio sonata without losing its essential qualities. The twelve Concerti grossi are almost chamber music, as are the organ concertos, while

the only ambitiously scored works, the concertos for multiple orchestras, are by far the weakest, whereas, according to the popular
modern view of Handel, they should have inspired his greatest
thoughts. If we want richly scored Handel we must seek in the
operas, where he was a bold innovator; his orchestral works based
as they are on the string ensemble offer no original textures and have
nothing to commend them but magnificence of invention and the
rarely absent personality of their composer.

It has frequently been remarked that if the piano sonatas alone
had survived to represent Beethoven, little of his personality would
remain unknown in terms of music. This is a doubtful proposition
and a similar test might more convincingly be applied to Handel and
the Concerti grossi, Op. 6, though it is easier to exclaim at their
greatness than to analyse it. As in Handel's music generally, the
quality which makes imperishable stuff out of the common language
of the eighteenth century is sheer energy of mind. The originality
that is considered essential in the twentieth century was not sought
by the Augustans and many of the finest things in the concertos might
have been described, in terms of our contemporary canons somewhat thus: 'Mr. Handel is greatly indebted to Corelli, Vivaldi,
Steffani and other masters, both for his themes, his basses, and the
general form of his movements. There are a few original harmonic
devices in these compositions, but criticism seeks in vain for any
strikingly novel ideas'. All of such a criticism would be true,
though absurdly irrelevant to the real evaluation of these noble
works.

The opening of the First Concerto may serve for an example of
the plain grandeur with which Handel invests the most commonplace procedures:

Ex. 69

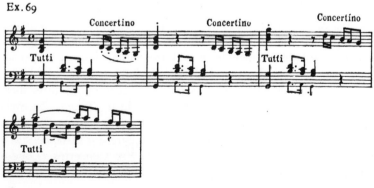

o

This statement of key may be paralleled in a hundred concertos by
lesser hands, but the rising position of the chord with the sonorous
descent to the open G string of the violins gives this conventional
opening that mysterious distinction which would cause any musician
to exclaim 'Handel!' after the first two or three bars. Even more
mysterious, incidentally, is the indubitable fact that a similar immediate response of recognition is evoked by passages borrowed by
Handel from other composers. Critics exigent of originality will find
more to admire in the profound harmonies at the end of the movement quoted above, yet the seemingly commonplace opening is no
less characteristic of Handelian grandeur. It is impossible for the
writer on Handel to avoid comparison with Bach, and such comparisons, by no means always to Bach's advantage, have their
utility in an age which tends to express its veneration for Bach by
derogatory estimates of Handel.

An obvious example is the treatment of a tonic chord opening in
the work mentioned and in the Sixth Brandenburg Concerto. Bach
sophisticates his B flat chord with a canon between the two violas,
but maintains a mechanical pulse of quavers in the bass, which per-
sists for some sixteen bars. It would be absurd to deny the wonderful beauty of sound produced in this way, but the effect, considered
rhythmically, is that of a logical reasoned discourse, whereas Handel's
opening resembles some powerful rhetorical speech. An age grown
rightly suspicious of noble sounding rhetoric naturally prefers
Bach's quieter attitude, though Handel's rhetoric is never false and
belongs to the Roman tradition, like so many traits which suggest
powerfully that Handel was perhaps the only complete classic, in the
antique sense, among the great composers. Certainly if literary
parallels were to be sought an examination of Pope would prove
unprofitable (though Dryden would be nearer the mark) and his
affinities must be pursued in Virgil or the ancient historians. Cowper's
often-quoted 'the more than Homer of his age' suggests that his
near-contemporaries may have had the same view; it is perhaps
more than coincidence that Italy should have transformed Handel
from a diffuse composer of 'interminable cantatas of little merit'
into the master of a concise yet brilliant style and though the twelve
Concertos under consideration belong to his late maturity (1735-40)
the Italian manner is never far away. Compare, for instance, Ex. 70
from the third of Alessandro Scarlatti's Six Concertos (London,
1750),

Ex. 70

Largo

with the fourth movement of Handel's Seventh Concerto:

Ex. 71

Adagio

etc.

Many such comparisons could be made, for Handel seems never to have forgotten the impression made on him by Italian music in his youth; there is profound symbolism in his return at the end of his life to the Italian oratorio *Il Trionfo del Tempo*.

So, in a sense, the twelve string Concertos are Italian music, deriving their sweetness from Corelli and their rhythmic life from Vivaldi, many of whose subjects would pass for Handel. No great music has been more derivative, yet none bears more firmly the impression of personality. In brief extracts much of Handel might be taken for the work of many a lesser composer, but his peculiar energy of mind is unmistakable when a movement is seen as a whole. In these Concertos, written in the astonishingly short period between the end of September and the last week of October 1739, there is a good deal of conventional writing and not every work is a masterpiece, but the set represents Handel at the very peak of invention, writing, it seems, for his own pleasure, for although the concertos were used in oratorio performances within a few weeks of their composition, he had an adequate reserve of orchestral music to meet this need.

An eighteenth-century view of the comparative merits of the twelve Concertos is given by the choice made, presumably by Burney, for the Commemoration of 1784, at which Nos. 1, 5, 6, and 11 were performed. Burney gives an enthusiastic, though not uncritical, commentary on each of these, and then remarks that Handel's contemporaries thought his concertos for strings inferior to those of Corelli or Geminiani. Admitting that they had more knowledge of string technique, Burney says very justly that Handel had far more fire and invention. It is not, however, altogether surprising that the admirers of Pope should have preferred Corelli, for his balanced periods are more akin to Pope's exquisite couplets than is the 'long majestic march' of Handel.

The First Concerto, of which the opening has already been cited,[1] is in fact more like Corelli than are most of the remainder of the set. Symmetry prevails in the allegros; the 6/8 last movement is strangely reminiscent, in a general way, of Domenico Scarlatti, and the 4/4 movement, vaguely fugued, that precedes it, is unusual for Handel in its four-bar rhythms and frequent full closes.

The next Concerto in F is more characteristic, and has a nobly spacious opening, no mere introduction but a full movement, long enough to establish the key before it is disturbed by the restless vigour of the D minor allegro. There is nothing of Corelli here; Beethoven is suggested by the persistence with which every bar (but one) is pervaded by the theme;

Ex. 72

A strange and original design follows with a twice-heard alternation of two distinct ideas in different tempi; the first, largo, is a dialogue in single bars between the full strings and the two solo violins; it is succeeded by a mysterious section with repeated quavers, marked *Larghetto andante e piano*. Orthodoxy seems to return in a sturdy three-voiced fugue, but a sudden *pp* (marked by Handel) brings a most unfugal episode with repeated chords and a phrase of great antiquity in solemn dotted minims above. The two ideas alternate several times and are heard in combination, a device which is not meant to display profound contrapuntal science.

Another grand gesture like that of the First Concerto opens the Third, in E minor. A strange feature is the insistence of the first theme which is given three times by the full strings, answered differently each time by the solo violins. The effect is almost that of the slow movement in Beethoven's Fourth Piano Concerto. Seriousness is maintained by the andante, with its Bach-like suspensions and boldly 'atonal' theme. Few composers would venture a subject with two ambiguous intervals:

Ex. 73

[1] The scores of Nos. 1 and 2 in the Granville Collection have additional parts for two oboes, which usually double the violins. In some passages, however, as in the opening of No. 1 (Ex. 69), the oboe parts are independent.—*Ed.*

This theme gives an emotional intensity which makes the movement not unworthy of comparison with the opening of Bach's *St. Matthew Passion*; the end is especially impressive with its startling bass entry. B, G, D sharp, C, G *sharp*. Handel rarely makes such a personal statement as this profoundly tragic piece. Abrupt changes of key are a feature of the following allegro with its stern unison ritornello. This abruptness may seem grim or humorous, or as in Beethoven's scherzos, both at once. Geniality returns in the delightful polonaise, where drone basses on the G and D strings of violas and 'cellos give a pastoral air to the aristocratic measure. As this device demands the relative major G, an E minor finale is necessary, a piece which otherwise adds little to the work.

It is surprising that Burney did not choose the Fourth Concerto, in A minor, for the Commemoration. Its first movement is surely one of Handel's finest with much of Bach's romantic warmth in its *affettuoso* paired semiquavers. It expresses an aspect of Handel too little regarded, the sensibility that elsewhere makes the Passion recitatives in *Messiah* as wonderful as anything of the kind in Bach. The following allegro is a splendid fugue, more extended than most of its kind and filled with unquenchable energy which is more than compensation enough for the looseness of its fugal construction. A similar triumph of imaginative technique appears in the next movement where the bass moves persistently in slurred pairs of crotchets with all the effect of a ground bass, though none is used. The last movement is again exceptionally full in development; it is almost completely homophonic and derives its power and coherence from rhythmic development in a manner scarcely found in other composers. This Fourth Concerto is one of Handel's rare examples of the orthodox four-movement form.

The Fifth Concerto has no fewer than six movements of which the first, second and last are taken from the smaller *Ode for St. Cecilia's Day*. Chrysander pointed out that the opening movement was derived from a harpsichord piece by Gottlieb Muffat, but it seems to have escaped notice that the theme of the fifth movement is modelled on one of Domenico Scarlatti's sonatas (*Essercizi per Gravicembalo*, No. 23):

Ex. 74

a) Handel

b) Scarlatti

Brilliant and charming though this Concerto is, it is hard to share Burney's enthusiasm for it though it would stand out among the productions of lesser masters.

The next work in the set, in G minor, has four splendid movements and a slight one, the last. According to Burney, Handel himself used to give the Concerto without either the fourth or the fifth movement. He also says that the musette was used by Handel as a separate piece to make an interlude during oratorios. The first movement is profoundly moving in its dramatic pathos, more alive now than much of the dramatic expression in Handel's operas. Once more it is breadth of development that reveals the stature of the composer. Corelli might have written the first four bars, but only Handel could expand this idea, with every variety of rhythm and harmony, to a long movement. A severe fugue, in four real parts, follows. It deserves Burney's praise, but is concise rather than expansive.

The crown of the work is the musette, a most original conception in which various episodes alternate in a kind of rondeau, with the gravely beautiful main theme, a *locus classicus* for Handel's unmatched sense of string tone. The pastoral drone basses of the traditional musette take on inexplicable depths of meaning here, much as the merely picturesque rustic convention is transformed in the hands of Virgil, or of Hardy for that matter. Such melodies as this owe nothing to anyone but their inventor and are more significant of Handel's mind than all the plagiarisms that industry may discover in his hundred volumes:

Ex. 75

It is not easy to see why Handel omitted the next movement, a fine spirited allegro somewhat in Vivaldi's manner. Another echo of Scarlatti is surely present in the last movement (bars 29–38).

Handel reduces criticism to silence by writing in the Seventh

Concerto a fugue, no less solid than his usual exercises in this style, on a theme consisting of a single note. Fortunately he does not use it to display skill in the treatment of stretto but instead shows convincingly that for his purposes the rhythm of a subject is its principal feature. After such wit, the largo comes with an effect of surprise for it is an emotional piece of work, the most Bach-like movement in all the concertos, profound in harmony and unusually close-woven in its four-part texture. The remaining movements are less serious, especially the final hornpipe.

As Chrysander remarks, these twelve Concertos show a bewildering variety of form, no two being quite alike, and this diversity is especially marked in the departure of the Eighth Concerto from all forms. It is a mixture of the suite and the sonata, having the scheme: Allemande—Grave—Andante allegro—Adagio—Siciliana—Allegro. (This last, though not so named, is in the style of a polonaise.) There are signs of keyboard origins, especially in the allemande, and this perhaps accounts for the experiment, too diverse to be successful, though all the movements are excellent in themselves, especially the siciliana which is reminiscent of a beautiful soprano-alto duet in *Giulio Cesare*.

A somewhat similar plan, if plan it be, is followed in No. 9 which has seven movements. The first two of these might belong to a normal four-movement concerto of an earlier period and are reminiscent of the *Water Music*. (Were they perhaps a part of the 1715 version?)[1] Next comes a larghetto in siciliana style, a loose fugue with a rambling subject, already written with the inscription 'Overture' in the previous year, a little minuet and finally a gigue which is so like Corelli that it might be included in a work of his without incongruity. In fact it is only the superb quality of the last two of the set which prevents the conclusion that Handel was losing interest in his plan to write twelve Grand Concertos.

No. 10, in D minor, opens with a kind of French overture. There follow an air and three allegros, of which the second is first-rate Handel, developed broadly with admirably planned alternations of soli and tutti. Formally, the scheme of the work is hard to justify.

Burney remarked on the freedom and waywardness of the first movement of the A major Concerto, No. 11, and the piece is certainly

---

[1] There seems to me to be a close spiritual affinity between this concerto and *Serse*, written the previous year: cf. the bars of the opening largo with that of 'Ombra mai fu', and points in both second movement and gigue with 'Dirà che amor per me.'—*Ed.*

hard to classify. It has the normal disposition of ritornello and episodes, but these are extremely diverse and include a repeated-note figure of a kind not found elsewhere. In this piece Handel seems to improvise with his orchestra, but the powerful rhythms of the main theme bind the whole movement together so that the final impression is of solidity. After a fugue and a few bars of largo we reach, in the andante, the centre of the work, with a theme ideally Handelian in its simplicity, which conceals a subtle phrasing, and in its unassuming strength. The old cliché of hemiola rhythm takes on a new significance, sounding like a new discovery:

Ex. 76

This splendid theme is built into a large design with gigue-like episodes for a solo violin and at every return the theme is changed while retaining its identity. Such music is essential Handel, owing nothing to his models and offering few points of comparison with his contemporaries. No less fine is the last movement with its terse subject and fantastic episodes. It has a form no less surprising than that of the first movement for, after a brief middle section still based on the main material of the whole piece, there is an extensive recapitulation. Burney says that some of the solo passages seem inspired by the keyboard rather than the violin. Taken as a whole this must be rated among the very best of the concertos: a monument of sanity and undemonstrative strength.

To complete the set Handel returns in the final Concerto, in B minor, to a more orthodox form, for if the short largo before the final gigue be regarded as introductory the work becomes a normal concerto grosso with alternating slow and quick movements. Dotted rhythms characterize the first movement, a fine example of the opera-overture gambit though the expected fugue does not materialize, Handel providing instead a homophonic piece owing much to its graceful theme. This is chamber music and suffers sadly in the usual heavy-footed bustle of a large orchestra which passes for Handelian style in most modern performances. Fine as this is, and the last movement shows no falling-off, the glory of this Concerto is its central movement, one of the greatest melodies ever written by

Handel or by anyone else. Here the permanent inspiration of Italy rises in all the freshness of his youth, with the added weight and gravity of years, to produce one of those tunes that speak to every degree and level of musical experience. There could be no more convincing testimony to Handel's greatness of mind and heart.

Although the Concerti grossi, Op. 6, are the crown of Handel's orchestral music, he had preceded this by a number of works some of which are still occasionally heard, while others by no means deserve to be forgotten. First of all come the three Oboe Concertos, published by Chrysander in H.–G., Vol. 21 (Nos. 8, 9, and 10 of Seiffert's practical edition). These agreeable little works are among Handel's earliest instrumental music, the third of them being ascribed to the year 1703 when the young composer was at Hamburg. Although the concertos each contain a fairly prominent oboe solo part, they are really concerti grossi in which the *concertino* is reduced to a single instrument, rather than solo concertos like those of Vivaldi who gives far more prominent and extensive passages to the oboe.

The first concerto, in B flat, is well known and is perhaps the best of the set, though its phrasing is square, and the first movement has a bass of extreme conventionality. Immaturity is chiefly detectable in the squareness, for Handel developed slowly, and was at first content to follow established models, though the trios for two oboes and bass, said to have been written when he was only twelve, show that he had no less grasp of the essentials of style than had Mozart at the same age. However the neat symmetry of the opening of this little concerto would be unlikely, if not impossible, in his mature work; the first phrase of tonic theme is repeated with a close in the dominant, and though larger rhythms develop, the bass remains confined to short formulas. The siciliana is a most beautiful piece of Italianate melody, more extended than is usual in such pieces; the subdominant colouring towards the end is especially attractive. Symmetry is evident again in the final vivace which adheres rigorously to its 4-bar phrases.

In the second concerto, also in B flat, the role of the oboe is far less clear, for although the score is headed 'oboe solo' with tutti and soli violins (there are no violas) the oboe has only three notes of solo in the whole of the first movement and in the lively fugue that follows it has none whatever, being occupied entirely with doublings of the two violins. This fugue is borrowed from the Trio Sonata, Op. 2, No. 4, with considerable alterations.[1] The two remaining

[1] It also figures in the overture to *Esther.—Ed.*

movements are also borrowed, in this case from another Trio Sonata, Op. 5, No. 1. That the adaptation was made in haste may be inferred from Handel's somewhat perfunctory handling in the andante of a problem that would surely have aroused the interest of Bach, to whom the adaptation of music from one medium to another was evidently a fascinating study in technique, as may be seen in many amazing instances such as the adding of a four-part chorus to the slow movement of the D minor Concerto. Handel's problem in the present instance was to convert a three-part texture into one of four, a transformation admitting of few satisfactory solutions, as the extra part will be redundant if the original texture has been well contrived. The oboe leads with the first phrase, to be answered by the violins in sixths and thirds. This transparent artifice takes Handel through half the movement with a few independent phrases, until a surely unmistakable sign of haste appears when for the remaining ten bars he shamelessly resorts to doubling whenever the independent part becomes difficult to manage. It is impossible to imagine Bach committing a similar breach of contract.

So clumsy, in fact, is this transcription that the question is bound to arise: did Handel make it himself? These two works in B flat, together with the Concerto grosso in C mentioned later, appeared in the fourth part of Walsh's *Select Harmony* as Concertos 1 to 3, only the first, the *Concerto in 'Alexander's Feast'*, bearing Handel's name. The remainder of the set comprises one work by Veracini, and two by Tartini of which the second again lacks the composer's name. Walsh displayed his notorious possession of what may be euphemistically described as a sense of business when, as Chrysander observes, he advertised in the *Daily Post* for 11 November 1741, these six concertos, of which only three are by Handel, in the following terms: 'This day is publ. Compos'd by Mr. Handel: 1. Twelve grand Concertos ... op. 6. 2. Twelve concertos ... op 3 & 4. 3. Select Harmony, 4th Collection to which is prefix'd that celebrated concerto in *Alexander's Feast*. . . . All Compos'd by Mr. Handel'. In other words, Walsh seems to have deliberately suggested that all six concertos were by Handel, who at the end of that year was in Dublin. Perhaps Walsh thought a certain amount of advertiser's license could be risked at a time when Handel was out of England and barely recovered from the financial disaster to which the failure of *Deidamia* in the previous January had been the prelude. This problem of transcription is further complicated by the existence of a so-called Sonata in B flat, with solo violin and orchestra of full strings with

oboes (H.–G., Vol. 21, p. 108; Seiffert's edition, No. 11) in which
the theme of the andante under consideration is treated in a quite
different manner after the opening bars.[1] Handel certainly makes a
finer thing out of it here, although Chrysander assigns it to the
earliest period, before 1710. The violin solo could have been transferred unaltered to the oboe, yet we must assume that if Handel himself fabricated the andante of the Oboe Concerto, he chose instead
the later Trio Sonata version, unsuitable though this was to his
purpose.

The third Oboe Concerto, in G minor (No. 10 in Seiffert's edition)[2]
is a pleasant little work, with a reasonable amount of genuine solo.
It has a squarely phrased sarabande for its second slow movement
and the theme of the final allegro was presumably in Handel's mind
when he wrote the Organ Concerto in the same key (Op. 4, No. 3,
second movement). What is interesting here is that the continuations
are totally different in the two movements and represent separate
treatments of a common idea.[3]

Ex. 77

a) Oboe Concerto
Allegro

b) Organ Concerto
Allegro

The *Concerto in 'Alexander's Feast'* (H.–G., Vol. 21, p. 63;
Seiffert, No. 7) has points of special interest. Handel completed the
first part of *Alexander's Feast* on 5 January 1736 and the whole
work was finished on the 17th, that is with Newburgh Hamilton's
added text, the Dryden Ode having been concluded on the 12th.
The Concerto in C, which was performed as an interlude, bears the

[1] For Handel's workings of a minor version of this theme, see p. 270.

[2] There is a manuscript of this concerto at Cambridge in which Handel has
arranged the first few bars 'per il viola da gamba', presumably intending to adapt
the whole work for that instrument. It has in modern times been adapted as a
'cello sonata.

[3] It is one of Handel's favourite 'generating themes' (see p. 266). Other early
forms of it will be found in the finale of the Trio Sonata, Op. 2, No. 2, and the
finale of the Flute Sonata, Op. 1, No. 4. The latter version in A minor, is also
worked out in No. 18 of the Aylesford pieces for harpsichord. Another treatment
of the form shown in Ex. 77 (*b*) will be found in the Trio Sonata, Op. 2, No. 6.
It is interesting that, except the two cases in A minor, this theme seems always
to occur in G minor.—*Ed.*

date 25 January 1736. Thus its composition must have been undertaken immediately after the Ode itself. Analysis of the music suggests however that the work is not an original composition but an arrangement or even a direct copy of some concerto by Vivaldi or another Italian.[1] Admittedly Handel's own style is often more Italian than that of the Italians themselves, but certain qualities are never absent even from his most perfunctory adumbrations of the art of composition and music which lacks harmonic cogency and rhythmic vitality alike should arouse immediate suspicion when it bears the name of one who did not feel that it was necessary to invent everything that appeared in his works.

The first movement has eighteen bars of ritornello of which the rhythmic scheme is this: 2+2 (repeat of first 2 bars) closing in the tonic, 4 bars consisting of one-bar phrases closing in the dominant, a further 2+2 to the subdominant. A further simple pattern of scarcely less obvious squareness ends the ritornello. The bass, devoid of rhythmic interest, follows the harmonic outline of the main part in plain crotchets as do the second violins and violas. The suggestion is advanced here that the original was a unison ritornello like that in Bach's D minor Concerto (itself perhaps not Bach's invention) and that Handel added the remaining parts which merely harmonize the theme. At no point in the course of this first movement do the basses escape from their purely harmonic servitude, a weakness nowhere found in Handel except in song-like slow movements for a solo instrument, and in these the very simplicity of the bass has its own cogency. A fragment from the second episode,

Ex.78

Violin I   Violin II

shows the un-Handelian poverty of the musical invention. The short largo which follows is not without beauty but it is unlike

[1] On the other hand, Seiffert's demonstration of parallels with Telemann's A major Concerto (*Musique de Table*, first set) in his study 'G. P. Telemann's *Musique de Table* als Quelle für Händel' (*Bulletin de la Société 'Union Musicologique'*, 4 ième Année, premier fascicule) supports the Handelian authorship—paradoxically —by the very fact of Handel's other leanings on the *Musique de Table.—Ed.*

Handel to have three cadences in the tonic in the first six bars with the chords of dominant and tonic providing the harmony for all but one of the first twenty crotchet beats. The next movement, allegro, again fails to show Handelian characteristics but has many features of the more routine part of Vivaldi's unequal and vast output. The episodes for the *concertino* are built, if the metaphor be admissible of such flimsy constructions, on the barest formulas with no variety of rhythm to redeem them from banality. Despite a certain vigour in the tutti passages at times, the music is flat and uninspired in a way not found in Handel's dullest pages. The Concerto ends with a kind of gavotte (not so marked in the score) which, agreeable enough in its main idea, displays a long middle section for the two violins alone each in turn providing for its companion a bass resembling those given as examples in elementary counterpoint manuals.

The six Concertos, Op. 3, have always been popularly known as 'the Oboe Concertos', perhaps to distinguish them from the Concerti grossi, Op. 6, and from the various sets of Organ Concertos. The title is not altogether appropriate, for although oboes appear in all six works (one only in No. 3 as alternative to a flute) they do not always, or even generally, take a leading part. Arnold in his edition assigns the composition of these concertos to 1720, saying they were written at Cannons and published about 1729. This second date should be some five years later, but the attribution of their composition to the years 1716–22 seems reasonable and is consistent with their style. Hawkins says that they were produced for the occasion of the wedding of the Princess Royal (1733), but this may well refer only to public performance or to certain public visits at that date.

In their variety of orchestration and form these are the nearest parallel in Handel's works to Bach's Brandenburg Concertos which were written in the same period, Bach's dedication bearing the date 1721.

Although the advantage in finish and studied perfection lies with Bach, Handel's concertos are not unworthy of the comparison, though his greatest achievement in the concerto form was to come nearly twenty years later in the Op. 6 set of 1739. Strangely enough, the earlier works are less in chamber music style than Op. 6 although the latter were styled 'Grand Concertos'. Burney noted this point, saying that the Op. 3 Concertos were admirably suited to performance on a large scale; they fall somewhere between the *al fresco* style of the *Water* and *Fireworks Music* and the more intimate manner of the concerti grossi or even the organ concertos. Consequently a certain plainness in harmony is noticeable with broad planning and due exploitation of contrasts in tone-colour rather than of subtlety in fine detail.

This point is illustrated by the opening of No. 1, where a bold unison ritornello alternates with passages for two oboes or for a solo violin which makes much of the conventional string formulas derived from Corelli and other Italians. Divided violas give a notable richness to the orchestra and the movement as a whole displays admirable vigour. This is the Handel of English tradition, bluff and hearty, writing music for plain men with no nonsense about them. Two recorders appear in the sarabande-like movement that follows; Handel shows the surprising variety possible in baroque orchestration by giving the bass to the bassoons. Later one oboe and a solo violin join in florid dialogue with every possible contrast between tutti and soli strings, bassoon and 'cello in the bass, and the divided violas. Scoring like this is far more 'modern' than is generally recognized and shows that Handel was by no means bound to the recent view, with which he was perhaps unacquainted, that his scoring was founded on the principle that a tone-colour, once adopted at the beginning of a movement, had to be retained until its end. Two *concertante* 'cellos appear in the third and final movement, which however is in G minor, is strangely brief and seems to have strayed from another work. It is hard to believe that Handel intended to write a three-movement concerto with its first movement in B flat, and two others both in the relative minor. As the Second Concerto, also in B flat, has five movements, the guess may be hazarded that one of these should belong to the previous work.

It is in the Second Concerto, of Op. 3 that the title 'Oboe Concerto' is seen to be far from correct, for the first movement gives most of its material to the violins. Handel's rhythmic vitality is shown in full power here, with the saraband-like movement of the main orchestra set against a constant flow of semiquavers in the solo violins. The bass, while never strictly repeated, gives something of the effect of a chaconne, an effect of which the grandeur would not be enhanced by a true ground bass. Handel never erred in calculating an effect, and it is typical of his methods that he should aim at, and triumphantly achieve, the inner content of a form without being over-concerned with contractual obligations to produce a text-book specimen. The same is true of his fugues. One of these follows, borrowed from the *sinfonia* to the Brockes *Passion*, and later extensively rewritten as a keyboard fugue in the same key (published as No. 3 of the set brought out by Walsh in 1735). The first entries may be quoted as showing Handel's indifference to an academically-inclined posterity:

Ex. 79

Quite apart from details of part-writing what is to be said of the viola entry with its conflation of the main theme and the figure that vaguely resembles a counter-subject? It is noteworthy that Handel removed this resemblance to the counter-subject in the keyboard version, though the entry still gave him trouble and he then had to let the part rest for a whole bar. The remaining movements of this excellent concerto are respectively in the manner of a minuet and of a gavotte. It is of some interest that Boyce in his Symphony in D minor (No. 8) seems to have modelled his first and last movements on those of the present work, for, although there is little thematic resemblance, comparison shows unmistakable affinities, e.g. in both finales, the gavotte melody is accompanied in a middle section by a running quaver bass and finally is given to the oboes with triplets in the violins.

Little need be said of Op. 3, No. 3,[1] in G, the finale of which is identical with No. 2 of the same set of keyboard fugues. Here the keyboard version seems to have been the original—Chrysander dates it as early as 1710; it is somewhat roughly conscripted into orchestral service with violas doubling the bass at the octave even when this takes them above the middle voice of the three. It would be rash to set such casual work as this against the fugal movements in the Brandenburg Concertos.

[1] The first allegro (which appears in the 'Sonata' of the seventh Chandos Anthem) is based on a favourite theme-combination which appears in the *Birthday Ode* for Queen Anne, the Brockes *Passion*, the first chorus of *Deborah* (at 'O grant a leader to our host') and elsewhere.—*Ed.*

Op. 3, No. 4, in F, was used for various purposes. It first appeared in 1716, as a fresh overture to the opera *Amadigi* on its revival, and was also played at an orchestral benefit concert, deriving from the latter appearance the name of 'The Orchestra Concerto'. It is a most attractive work, unusual in form in that its first three movements are like an orthodox French opera overture: a pomposo introduction with dotted rhythms, a loosely constructed fugue, and a kind of minuet, which also appears in a keyboard version in G as No. 34 of the Aylesford pieces. To this seemingly complete scheme are appended an allegro in the style of the *Water Music* and another minuet, this time with a regular trio. This minuet had originally appeared (in G) as the finale of the Flute Sonata, Op. 1, No. 5; it was then transcribed in F for harpsichord (Aylesford pieces, No. 9) and this version, with slight changes, was used in the Concerto; the final version, again for keyboard, is the second minuet of the *Courante e due minuetti* in the Third Collection of harpsichord pieces. The admirable subject of the first allegro may be quoted to show Handel's immense rhythmical vitality; wonderful as are Bach's fugue subjects, he could not express in a few bars the supple gay strength which never failed Handel through all his disappointments and failures:

Ex. 80

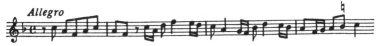

The expectations roused by this theme are not disappointed and the movement is one of the finest in all these concertos. If it were, say, by Telemann it would certainly be quoted as evidence of his superiority to Handel. The rest of the work is not quite on the same level, though the trio of the final minuet has a suggestion of Haydn with its doubling of violas, bassoon and second violins and witty suspension of judgement on the decision whether the middle part or that given to the first violins is really the tune.[1]

Neither No. 5 nor No. 6 is of especial merit and both have an air of hasty fabrication to complete a set of six. The first two movements of No. 5 belong to Cannons and were used as overture to the second Chandos Anthem. The fugue appears yet again in the Sixth Suite for harpsichord, in F sharp minor. This was the version known to Mattheson who in his *Der vollkommene Capellmeister* devotes an

[1] The keyboard version of the trio (Aylesford pieces, No. 62) makes it clear that the first-violin melody was an afterthought.—*Ed.*

analysis to it, praising the novelty of the scheme in which (he says) a subject is announced and immediately replaced by two others, as though it failed to please, only to reappear later combined with the themes that had supplanted it. Mattheson was evidently no pedant; his spirited defence of Handel's unorthodox fuguing suggests that pedants had objected to such freedom and he remarks trenchantly, 'Handel can beyond question sit in the first (i.e. the highest!) class in the school of counterpoint'. Less perceptive critics have made, and continue to make, the mistake of failing to understand that Handel's immense technique was never cultivated as an end in itself, but to serve the aims of living expression. The Kerll canzona used in *Israel in Egypt*[1] is far more ingenious in contrapuntal device than the loose double fugue which Handel wrote for 'I will sing unto the Lord' but it is not difficult to decide which is the better music.

The last work in this set would not satisfy a subscriber who insisted on the full interpretation of Walsh's promise to furnish six concertos. It has but two movements, an allegro in D major which appeared in *Ottone* in 1723, and a version of the well-known D minor piece in 3/8 time which was used elsewhere in the Third Suite for harpsichord, where it forms the finale to a set of variations, and again in the Organ Concerto, Op. 7, No. 4. It is odd that Handel should have been willing to detach this piece from its variations, and its quality is not such as to explain his fondness for it.[2] Certainly it makes small pretence to belong in its surroundings among the other concertos of Op. 3.

Taken as a whole, this set, while containing a considerable quantity of first-rate Handel, is not free from the perishable elements of *Gebrauchsmusik*. To say this is not to deny that much of the greatest music has been inspired by practical necessities, but when the occasion is one in which the conditions of a particular time and place do not merely provide the occasion for a work but have an effect on its design, the resulting masterpiece (as it often is) is not for all time. A dead convention has taken with it to the grave much of Handel's best work in the Italian operas, and the assembling of prefabricated units in these concertos robs them of architectural qualities. To find the same nobility of invention in less transient forms we must turn back to the string concertos of Op. 6.

The 'legend' according to which Handel wrote the *Water Music* to propitiate George I when that monarch followed his truant musician to London is now generally believed to be untrue. Queen Anne died

<hr>

[1] See p. 93.   [2] See also p. 267.

P

in 1714 and the *Water Music*, we are told, was not given until three years later. It is impossible to believe that Handel waited nearly three years before attempting to regain the royal favour and in fact he travelled to Hanover with the King in July 1716. If anyone hoped to gain favour by the production of the *Water Music* it must surely have been Kielmansegge who bore the expenses of the occasion, a generous, even magnanimous, gesture in the circumstances—for his wife was the King's mistress. However, despite the conclusive evidence of a royal water party, with music by Handel, on 17 July 1717, the matter is by no means beyond doubt for Chrysander[1] quotes Mainwaring's story of a similar water party on 22 August 1715, when Handel, prompted by the ultra-royalist and philharmonic Kielmansegge, is said to have provided music which was so well liked by the King that he restored the composer to his favour. Professor Abraham, however, has suggested an explanation which accounts for both stories.

Among the Handel manuscripts in the British Museum are two movements used with different scoring in the *Water Music* of 1717 but, according to Chrysander, written two or three years previously. The second of these pieces is the celebrated *Alla Hornpipe*. Chrysander, who tells the not unexciting story of their purchase by the Museum on his insistence,[2] published them as a 'concerto' in Vol. 47 of his great edition—they appear as No. 24 in Seiffert's 'practical edition'—and poured scorn on Rockstro[3] for asserting that they were part of the *Water Music*. Chrysander himself, in his *Vierteljahrsschrift* article, then goes on to compare these two movements—in F, scored for oboes, bassoons, horns and strings—with the versions in D (with trumpets and the whole lay-out of the scoring altered) which form an indubitable part of the *Water Music*, without realizing that he held in his hand what is probably the key to the whole mystery. The Barrett Lennard manuscript in the Fitzwilliam Museum at Cambridge,[4] Walsh's edition for harpsichord (*c.* 1743) and Arnold's edition in score all agree, despite minor differences of arrangement, in giving a series of pieces in F major and D minor, scored (in Barrett Lennard and Arnold) for oboes, bassoons, horns, and strings, followed by another

---

[1] *G. F. Händel*, Vol. I, p. 425.

[2] 'Händels Instrumentalkompositionen für grosses Orchester' in *Vierteljahrsschrift für Musikwissenschaft*, Vol. III, p. 1.

[3] *The Life of G. F. Handel* (London, 1883), p. 99.

[4] William C. Smith, 'The Earliest Editions of the *Water Music*' in *Concerning Handel* (London, 1948), p. 271.

series of pieces in D major and G major and minor, in which trumpets are introduced in all the main, D major, movements. The change of key-centre and change of instrumentation surely indicate as clearly as possible that we have to do with two separate works, of which the second opens with a revised version of two movements—Chrysander's 'concerto'—which belong in key and instrumentation to the first and perhaps originally closed it. The Brandenburg envoy's report of 19–30 July 1717,[1] correctly describes the instrumentation of the second series: 'des trompettes, des cors de chasse, des haut bois, des bassons, des flutes allemandes, des flutes françaises à bec, des violons et des basses' and, although he is perhaps exaggerating when he says the music lasted 'une heure chaque reprise', his statement[2] that the King insisted on the whole being played three times, twice before supper and once after[3], suggests that something less than the complete *Water Music* was performed. Is it not fairly clear that the *Water Music* of 1717 was that in D major, with trumpets? As for the F major *Water Music*, without trumpets, Chrysander's 'concerto' seems to show that it was earlier in date, so that it may well have been played (as the 'legend' says) in 1715.

That Handel executed the commission or commissions with enjoyment seems clear from the superb quality of much of the music. There is no sign of perfunctoriness and the writing is full of invention, not merely in broad outline but in the elaboration of inner parts and the carefully planned orchestration. Music like this does not need the occasion for which it was devised but retains permanent value. In any event the influence of the occasion here was not a musical one, but merely encouraged Handel to write for large and varied resources, with the happy result of inspiring, in the second series, some of his most splendid scoring in which a four-fold contrast is possible between trumpets, horns, oboes, and strings.

The F major overture is a modestly orchestrated piece with oboe solo and strings; Handel evidently preferred to build up his resources gradually as the royal party drifted towards Chelsea. Horns enter in the third movement, a strange design where a boldly simple allegro is played twice, enclosing a D minor andante between its repetitions which the horns restrict to F major with a persistence

---

[1] Printed by Wolfgang Michael in 'Die Entstehung der *Wassermusik* von Händel' in *Zeitschrift für Musikwissenschaft*, Jg. IV (August–September, 1922), p. 585.

[2] Confirmed by the report in the *Daily Courant* (reproduced in Chrysander's *Händel*, Vol. III, p. 147).—*Ed.*

[3] Not 'once before and once after supper', as Sir Newman Flower prints in all editions of his biography.—*Ed.*

that just escapes tedium. The D minor andante, however, has a
beauty far removed from Hanoverian George and his party who, it
may be ventured, did not shed their native earthiness even when they
were on the water. The elegiac gravity and noble calm expressed
here surprise in such surroundings much as Purcell's Trio Sonatas
must seem an odd product to have emerged from Restoration
society. Handel's unassuming grandeur shows itself in the F major
development of the opening melody:

Ex. 81

This pastoral melody[1] with its reminder of *Acis and Galatea* ('The
flocks shall leave the mountains') is expanded with echoes to sixteen
bars. On the cadence into F major the strings begin a broad development of the melody most cunningly interwoven with its original

Ex. 82

[1] It is developed from the opening phrase of the Oboe Sonata, Op. 1, No. 6.—
Ed.

version in the oboes. Such combining of imagination and technique is given only to the greatest; Handel's achievements of this kind are less analysable in terms of academic formulas than are those of Bach, and so escape notice.

Handel made the second of the two movements rescored from the 1715 series into one of his most splendid orchestral pieces. In its D major form, with trumpets, the rhythmic energy of the main theme[1] is especially stirring, though hornpipes no less eurhythmic were written by other hands, e.g. one by Gottlieb Muffat in a suite in B flat, but the middle section, based in a manner worthy of Beethoven on a short phrase near the beginning of the movement, is genuine Handel of a high order and shows the magnificence of his string writing in which again only Beethoven may be ranked his equal. None of the remaining movements reaches this level of excellence.

In April 1749 Handel was commissioned to provide music for a display of fireworks in the Green Park, to celebrate the Peace of Aix-la-Chapelle. Evidently vast resources were put at his disposal and for once he wrote music on a scale comparable with nineteenth and twentieth-century performances of his more normal works. His own note in the score gives the exact numbers of the original wind orchestra (to which strings were added for subsequent performances): 9 trumpets, 3 timpani, 9 horns, 24 oboes, 12 bassoons, and the new-constructed double-bassoon.

If the music had been lost, it could reasonably have been conjectured that Handel must have produced empty rhetorical stuff redolent of the 'pork and beer' which were all that Berlioz could see in him. What in fact he wrote was music of the purest classical grandeur and perfection, worthy of an ideal Rome rather than of the Hogarthian splendours and miseries of Georgian London. He was not to be expected to know that the Peace was merely a politicians' convenience and the historical occasion has no more to do with the music than has the fact that the fireworks set light to the pavilion. What indubitably inspired Handel to exercise the full power of his imagination was the sense of a great public rejoicing of which the theme was peace. It is gratifying that the music written in the *Occasional Oratorio* in honour of 'Cumberland the Butcher' is vastly inferior,[2] nor is much of *Judas Maccabaeus* really much better.

[1] A wonderful transformation of the B minor original form in the Flute Sonata, Op. 1, No. 9.—*Ed.*
[2] But compare the contrary opinion expressed by Mr. Herbage on p. 113.

A puzzle for musicologists is provided by the existence of two earlier versions[1] of the overture to the *Fireworks Music*, the first in F and the second, like the final version, in D. This last is by far the finest and shows that Handel could at times work almost as hard as Beethoven in refining an idea. One of the most splendid touches of eloquence in the opening bars appears only in this final version and must be quoted, for its simplicity is of the essence of Handelian grandeur. The overture begins with this:

Ex. 83

which was in the earlier versions only in two parts, given to horns in the first draft and to trumpets in the second. Handel seizes the opportunity to harmonize the theme in full so that when it is repeated the harmony can be changed. Not even Bach, the master-harmonist, could have done finer things within the strict diatonic limits imposed by natural brass:

Ex. 84

This opening is developed with the utmost breadth, and every elementary procedure (such as a move to the dominant) is invested with grandeur. The allegro begins with antiphonal flourishes, but here again sheer power of composition turns the most obvious material into music of unmistakable greatness, some new resource of rhythm or scoring being introduced with infallible judgement whenever banality might threaten. Only that very Handelian masterpiece, Beethoven's *Weihe des Hauses*, shows a comparable power in the working of conventional themes.

Of the remaining short movements it must be admitted that the 'Réjouissance' is not distinguished. The siciliana, however, entitled 'La Paix', expresses, by some miracle of style, an almost *Messiah*-like pastoral mood in terms of the full orchestra available, with all

[1] H.-G., Vol. 47, pp. 71 and 80. See also Chrysander's comparative study in *Vierteljahrsschrift für Musikwissenschaft*, Vol. III, pp. 157–70.—*Ed.*

its brass complete. The closing minuet revives the inspiration of Purcell's trumpet tunes, than which there could be no higher praise.

With the *Water Music* and *Fireworks Music* Chrysander published in H.–G., Vol. 47,[1] two other concertos for larger resources. These are not of especial interest and are mainly drawn from the oratorios, including *Messiah*, which provides the first allegro ('And the glory of the Lord') of the Concerto in B flat and the third movement ('Lift up your heads') of the one in F. Both these works are written for a triple orchestra consisting of strings with two 'choirs' of oboes and bassoons, to which horns are added in the second work. Little beyond curiosity and amusement would be served by their revival, and their original use remains uncertain. As the second concerto remains incomplete despite its nine movements, it seems that only some further Georgian water-party like those of 1715 and 1717 could have induced Handel to produce a work of such size and insignificance. Perhaps there were three barges for the orchestra.

One of the most familiar anecdotes concerning Handel's early years tells of his friendly contest with Domenico Scarlatti, whom he met at Venice, in the autumn of 1707. It is said that whereas Scarlatti was considered the finer harpsichord player, by a narrow margin, Handel was admitted his superior as organist. Five years previously Handel had been for a year organist of the Cathedral at Halle, and although he never attempted the Gothic complexity of Bach's writing for the organ, he was reckoned, by those who had never heard Bach, to be the greatest organist of his day.

The organ concertos thus occupy a special place in his work, and show him as the predecessor of Mozart and Beethoven: that is, as a great composer writing concertos for his own performance in public. Already in 1708 he had included a somewhat empty 'sonata' for organ and orchestra in *Il Trionfo del tempo*, but a further thirty years passed before the First Set of organ concertos was published as Op. 4 by Walsh. A second collection, mostly of transcriptions from other works, appeared in November, 1740. Far more important is the Third, posthumous Set, Op. 7, containing much new material and few arrangements, composed between 1740 and the end of Handel's life. A so-called Fourth Collection, published by Arnold in 1797, contains nothing of importance.

As occasional music designed for performance between the acts of the oratorios, these concertos display the inequalities, as well as

[1] Nos. 27 and 28 of Seiffert's 'practical edition'.

the splendid inspirations of Handel's improvisatory rhetoric. His unsurpassed vitality appears in the variety of form, never attempted by other prolific masters, Bach always excepted. The countless orchestral concertos of Vivaldi, for instance, show every possible type of instrumental sound, from the mandoline upwards, but are, for the most part, written in a highly efficient form standardized for rapid production. Such manufacturing processes were not suited to Handel's temperament, and though these organ concertos contain empty passages, conventional melodic phrases, and sometimes perfunctory arrangements from other works, they are all individuals, sustained by a never failing rhythmic energy which never lapses into the machine-like regularity of Bach's weaker inventions. Handel's inattention to detail does, however, produce especially in these concertos, one consequence especially dangerous to modern performance. This is his frequent omission of the music itself. Mozart did not, in most of his piano concertos, trouble to write out every note of the solo part, but Handel not infrequently leaves whole movements to the skill and invention of the performer.

For example, the splendid Concerto in D minor and major (Op. 7, No. 4) consists of three movements only—an adagio, followed by two allegros—but this seemingly anomalous scheme is not intended and the usual concerto grosso form of alternating slow and quick movements is preserved by the direction inserted between the two allegros—'organo ad libitum', that is, a whole movement is missing, and modern studies in Handel's style have so far produced as improvisations in such cases efforts which escape the commonplace only by diverging into the incongruous.

This difficulty, combined with a grossly magnified scale of performance in which the deplorable resources of the modern or Victorian organ are inserted to drown the orchestra unless it in turn is strengthened by trombones and similar heavy artillery, has impeded the recognition of the true value of the organ concertos which, together with much that is perfunctory, contain some of Handel's noblest music, not inferior to the great string concertos, though the latter are more satisfying in their general finish and symmetry.

The original works among these various collections are Op. 4, Nos. 1, 2, 4, and 6, and all six of Op. 7 with the exception of certain movements. (The Second Set, never given an opus number, contains nothing new apart from free transcriptions, with fresh material, in the first concerto, of movements taken from the Trio Sonata, Op. 5, No. 6.) We have therefore, no fewer than ten works for organ with orchestra, all belonging to Handel's maturity and possessing the advantage of having been designed, if not written, for performance by the composer himself. Their performance on an appropriate scale, and with scholarly solution of the various problems mentioned should establish them among Handel's finest contributions to instrumental music. They are in fact the only satisfactory concerted music for the organ: Bach's cantatas with organ obbligato present a strange paradox, for as Schweitzer has pointed out, it is inexplicable that Bach, whose writing for organ solo is incomparably more resourceful and characteristic than Handel's, gives us in these cantatas nothing typical of the organ, which merely plays in two parts of which one doubles the continuo bass. Handel, though producing a texture rarely differing from that of the harpsichord[1] (a notable exception is the chaconne of the Concerto in B flat, Op. 7, No. 1), achieves a genuine relationship between organ and orchestra, by no means the only instance of his superiority to Bach in imaginative grasp of tone-colours. That this should be so is surprising, for the English organs of Handel's day were considerably less developed than the great instruments of North Germany, where the pedal-organ was an elaborate structure containing numerous ranks. During Bach's career he had at his disposal organs of the greatest richness and variety. At Weimar, for example, he had an organ, admittedly of two manuals only, with one 16 foot stop, three 8 foot, two 4 foot, and mixtures on the great organ, with a choir organ of four 8 foot stops, two 4 foots, and a 2 foot flute, and a powerful pedal with one 32, three 16's, two 8's, and a 4. At Leipzig the organ at St. Thomas's was, after its rebuilding in 1721, a far larger instrument than could ever have been available to Handel in London, comprising as it did, three manuals controlling thirty-one stops and a pedal organ of five stops.

Yet, by a seeming paradox, the modest specifications of English organs may well have made possible in Handel's concertos a musical form which would have seemed unworkable to a composer familiar only with the more powerful German instruments. The baroque orchestra rarely exceeded thirty players, and only an organ of the soft-voiced chamber-type could reasonably combine with an orchestra lacking brass and percussion. Despite their frequent grandeur of style Handel's concertos are on the verge of chamber music, like

---

[1] Walsh published all three sets—and pirates published the first set—as 'Concertos for the Harpsichord or Organ'; there is every justification for playing them as harpsichord concertos.—*Ed.*

Bach's Brandenburg set, and although like Shakespeare's plays they will survive and indeed generally undergo the most insensitive misrepresentations a callous philistinism can contrive and an ignorant public be induced to admire, their classical beauty will only appear when, to paraphrase a famous remark of Plato, the scholars are all musicians, and the musicians all scholars.

While a case may be made for deliberate 'modernization', conductors and instrumentalists who distort Handel's style cannot expect serious consideration until they are able to show more convincingly than hitherto that their practices derive from something more solid than ignorance.

All these points are illustrated by the First Concerto, Op. 4, No. 1, (Händel-Gesellschaft, Vol. 28) in G minor and major, a chamber work of flawless lucidity and grace. Its opening movement, with two distinct ritornello themes and further new material given to the organ, is not really a conventional baroque design and the grave mood is near to Beethoven in the free creations of his later years. Nothing could be further from the truth of Handel's style than a *pomposo* treatment of this profound music. A splendid breadth marks the allegro that follows in the major key and though the solo episodes are conventional enough, the orchestral comments and sudden tuttis are as incalculable as Haydn. Handel uses sometimes a mere phrase of the ritornello, sometimes a whole portion, beginning each in a different place, and in fact displays a freedom of form possible only to a composer whose creative activity was like Nature itself. Among these organ concertos alone there are no two identical designs. This First Concerto after a brief adagio ends most unexpectedly with a kind of minuet and variations expanded from the Trio Sonata in F, Op. 5, No. 6. In this delicate piece the strings are marked *pp* or *p* by Handel, and the organ is at times accompanied only by the continuo. Taken as a whole, this concerto shows a highly original view of the four-movement baroque form; in key sequence alone it is hard to find a parallel for the scheme G minor— G major—E minor—G major.

The popular Concerto in B flat, Op. 4, No. 2, follows a more orthodox scheme and, it must be admitted, contains a certain amount of over-conventional passage work. A suggestion of immaturity in some of its material is supported by the fact that the opening movement is an expansion of material first used as a *symphonia* to the motet for soprano *Silete Venti* (H.–G., Vol. 38)[1] which Chrysander

[1] See p. 161.

assigns to the 'first English period'. Caution, however, is advisable in dismissing even the most perfunctory looking writing when the composer is Handel; many long stretches of semiquaver figuration, tedious when performed with mechanical rapidity, reveal unexpected subtleties in phrasing and rhythm when played with the true baroque freedom and rubato. Those who are inclined to dismiss as 'tedious divisions' the solo episodes in this B flat Concerto should be warned by the fantastic subtlety of phrasing in the ritornello of the first allegro (borrowed from the Trio Sonata, Op. 2, No. 4), a technical feat as witty as Tennyson's hendecasyllables ('O you chorus of indolent reviewers') and no less accomplished than Horace's latinized versions of Greek metres:

Ex. 85

It would be hard to overpraise the subtlety of this paragraph, with its repetitions, expansions and rhythmic tension between treble and bass, this last a technical device producing the same energy as Dryden's overrunning of the fundamental beat in his flowing couplets. Not all the enthusiasm of the apologists for such minor masters as Telemann can conceal the absence in their agreeable compositions of this vital energy and variety in metre, however near to Handel they may seem to superficial examination. Dyer's 'Grongar Hill' was a popular poem in the eighteenth century. Incidentally, the parallel between Dryden and Handel may be supported by an amusing coincidence of self-criticism: Handel in Vauxhall Gardens, 'You are right sir, it is very poor stuff; I thought so when I wrote it'—Dryden of some lines in his heroic plays, 'I knew they were bad enough to please, even when I wrote them.'

Of the remaining concertos in the first set, Op. 4, No. 3 in G minor is largely derived from a Trio Sonata (Op. 2, No. 6) and Flute Sonata (Op. 1, No. 2) and is a curious hybrid with solo violin and 'cello parts reclaimed from the original two violin parts in its first movement.[1] The Concerto ends with a kind of gavotte which seems to have been a favourite with Handel, as it appears first in one of his earliest operas, *Agrippina* (1709), then in the Sonata, Op. 1, No. 2, in the present work, and once again in a later Organ Concerto (Op. 7, No. 5). The first bars of the second movement here are almost identical with a theme (already quoted as Ex. 77*b*) occurring in an early Oboe Concerto written at the same time as *Agrippina* so the whole complex of associations, unimportant in itself, throws some light on the working of Handel's mind.

The well-known Concerto in F, Op. 4, No. 4, is really a three-movement work, in the form used by Bach for solo concertos, for the brief adagio in the relative minor may be regarded as a link between the middle movement and the fugal finale. Attractive though the music is,[2] especially in the quiet andante, the material is unusually square for Handel. An important indication of the type of organ the composer used is given by the direction at the beginning of the andante: strings *pp*—organ, open diapason, stopped diapason and flute, i.e. the three stops used together for the solo were not too loud for the *pp* of a small string orchestra. The further indication 'senza

[1] Which is heralded here by two introductory bars that also open the Concerto, Op. 3, No. 3.—*Ed.*
[2] A large part of the first movement is identical with the introduction to the second form of the chorus 'Questo è il cielo' in *Alcina.*—*Ed.*

cembalo' makes it clear that a harpsichord was used by Handel for continuo accompaniment to the organ in these concertos.

Op. 4, No. 5, also in F, is a close transcription of the Recorder Sonata, Op. 1, No. 11. Played on soft flute stops it would give an effect close to the original. The first movement has the perfection of simplicity, though the remaining movements are such close imitations of Corelli as to have little of Handel, charming though they are.

A certain confusion, not easily resolved, surrounds this Concerto and Op. 4, No. 6. This last bears the indication 'Harpa o Organo' and seems to be the concerto written for the famous harpist Powell and performed in *Alexander's Feast*; presumably the same work is referred to in the advertisement that appeared in the London *Daily Post*, 27 February 1741: 'A concerto of Mr. Handel's on the Harp by Mr. Parry' referring to a concert at Hickford's music room. Hawkins, however, says that the *Fifth* Concerto was originally a harp concerto written for the younger Powell whereas the *Sixth* was a solo for the recorder, as its compass reveals, and was composed in this form for one of Handel's friends. Hawkins may, of course, have made a blunder, but this seems improbable, as he certainly possessed the scores in question and was too precise a character to have omitted such an easily-made reference. Certainly the two works are very similar in style, and must be assigned to Handel's early years. The Sixth, in addition to the harp and/or organ and strings, employs two recorders.

Of the Second Set (published 1740) little need be said, for all except No. 1 are merely transcriptions of Nos. 11, 10, 1, 5, and 6 of the Concerti Grossi, Op. 6.

The first of the set is derived principally from the Trio Sonata in F, Op. 5, No. 6, but the first and second movements are re-composed into the new medium; in both forms we have here some first-rate Handel. It will be remembered that the last movement of the same Trio provided the conclusion to the Concerto, Op. 4, No. 1. The autograph score is marked 'Adagio ad libit', but Handel afterwards inserted here a larghetto based on that in Op. 6, No. 9, preceding it with a transcription of the second movement of the same work.

With the Third Collection (composed 1740–50) Handel produced almost entirely new material and, taken as a whole, this set contains his most important original works for the organ. They were not published until after the composer's death, and appeared in 1760 as Op. 7. No. 1, in B flat, is a work in the grand style, far less like

chamber music than are the more intimate concertos of the First
Set. The organ pedal is presented for the first time and the first and
second movements comprise a vast chaconne, on a simple ground
bass of the early baroque type. (It resembles Bach's pedal figure
in the prelude on *In dir ist Freude*.) On this foundation Handel
sets out a series of variations of deceptive simplicity but telling
effect. There is no attempt at profound expression and we see him
directing his music at the public attending the oratorios. Another
chaconne-like bass in the following largo takes gravity from its
D minor thoughtfulness but the final bourrée enlists the majestic
organ for purposes unblushingly frivolous in a tune surely made for
the 'mobile crowd' to whistle in the streets:

Ex. 86

Allegro

Op. 7, No. 2, in A, is more lyrical and less imposing; of its intended
four movements one is to be supplied by the performer.[1] In No. 3
still more is left to such precarious reliance on taste and invention,
for between the heavy footed opening movement[2] with its Hallelujah
Chorus motive and a lengthy piece based on a hornpipe, appears
the terse injunction 'Organo adagio e fuga ad libitum', a dangerous
offer to organists who not infrequently make the best of the opportunity provided. The Concerto ends with one of two minuets of
which the second is probably not by Handel. Impressive though
these large works are, there is a certain falling off in originality from
the less pompous style of the earlier concertos.

With No. 4 Handel strikes his elegiac mood in all its nobility in
the opening dialogue between 'cellos with bassoons *divisi* and the
organ. A magnificent energy pervades the allegro, which has a
ritornello of 18 bars simple in harmony and melody alike, and devoid
of a single turn of phrase which is not common property, yet unmistakably Handel; it is in fact based on a movement from Telemann's
Musique de Table. It is in such pieces as this that Handel confronts us
with the most baffling aspect of his greatness. As finale, after an

---

[1] Its finale is based on *La Coquette*, in the sixth suite of Gottlieb Muffat's
Componimenti musicali: a point which Chrysander oddly failed to notice.—*Ed.*

[2] The definite instruction to the organist not to play in a number of tuttis is a
noteworthy innovation. Leichtentritt (*Händel*, p. 814) detects stylistic affinities in
this movement with the pre-Haydn symphonies of the Mannheim and Viennese
schools.—*Ed.*

improvised slow movement, he resorts to the 3/8 piece in D minor already used in the Concerto, Op. 3, No. 6, and elsewhere.

In Op. 7, No. 5, it is possible to trace further aspects of Handel's creative workmanship. He begins with a striking unison theme of Italian type answered by a phrase evidently derived from the Trio Sonata, Op. 2, No. 1 (see Ex. 109).

The Trio movement is however closely related to the opening of another Trio, Op. 2, No. 8, in G minor, the same key as the Concerto, and the organ figure appears to be a conflation of the two ideas with the same rhythm. A few bars later Handel uses the sequence of sevenths found as continuation of the opening of the G minor Trio movement (by no means a common progression in Handel):

Ex. 87
   a) Trio
   b) Concerto

There is a dramatic tension in this powerful movement between the stern vigour of the unison theme and the chromatic inflexion of the solo episodes. It leads by way of an organ cadenza, adagio, to one of Handel's most impressive designs, a two-bar ostinato always in octaves against which the organ projects a series of variations. The usual treatment of this in a long crescendo is expressly forbidden by Handel's direction *piano continuando*, only the last variation being marked *forte*. After this the minuet and gavotte (this last an elaborated version of the one already used in Op. 4, No. 3) make something of an anticlimax. The Concerto originally ended with the minuet.

Op. 7, No. 6, consists of two movements only; with the improvised slow movement intended, it would form a three-movement concerto of Vivaldi type. As written, it provides little for the organ to do, being an extreme case of Handel's practice of leaving these concertos, intended for his own performance, in a fragmentary state.

Two further concertos may be mentioned, one a version for two

organs and orchestra of the opening movement from the D minor
Concerto (Op. 7, No. 4). In the same key is a work published by
Arnold (as No. 1 of his so-called 'First Collection')[1] who added
between the two movements the direction 'Organ Ad[agi]o e par
[*sic*] una Fuga All[egr]o ad libitum'. Both the extant movements
are fine vigorous music, based on a Telemann flute sonata,[2] and,
with a suitable insertion of genuine Handel or Telemann to complete
the scheme, this would make a fine concerto.

Of the performance of the organ concertos little more need be
said. The instruments built by such English makers as Renatus
Harris, unsurpassed in beauty of tone, were deficient in German
baroque sounds and it is perhaps for this reason that Handel wrote
nothing for organ solo comparable in importance even with the minor
works of Bach. Handel's concertos can, with few exceptions, be played
on the harpsichord with no serious loss, especially if the orchestra is
small. (It should never be large.) Rescoring to suit the over-blown
instruments of later organ builders is mere philistinism as has already
been suggested with perhaps excessive though scarcely unnecessary
emphasis.

Whereas Bach in his concertos gives every subtlety of counterpoint and detailed rhythm, Handel shows himself, especially in the
best of the organ concertos, to be the unequalled master of large-
scale metre, around whom the amiable minor figures of his age
cluster like the Myrmidons round Achilles.

[1] Of which No. 2 is a garbled version (with no organ part!) of the Double
Concerto in B flat mentioned on p. 223, while No. 3 is a seven-movement Concerto
in F, ending with the march from *Judas Maccabaeus*.—*Ed.*

[2] See p. 262.

CHAPTER VIII

THE KEYBOARD MUSIC

By KATHLEEN DALE

As a composer of clavier music Handel holds a curiously anomalous position among the great masters. He is universally recognized as a 'classic', but is familiar to music-lovers by only the merest fragment of his whole production: by a few movements whose attractions as separate pieces have proved more enduring than those of the musical context from which they have been torn. The main body of Handel's clavier works, although it is held in the greatest respect by musicians in general, is almost entirely ignored by performers. As music for playing in public it labours under several disadvantages. It embraces no single large-scale items such as would form the backbone of a complete Handel-recital programme; the long chaconnes are monotonous, the fugues lack preludes to invest them with status as concert pieces, the suites are uneven in interest. Thus it provides little incentive for study by performers and is barely kept alive for concert-goers.

Handel's contemporaneity with J. S. Bach and Domenico Scarlatti, which renders comparisons between the clavier works of the three men inevitable, only serves to accentuate the relative ineffectiveness for the piano of Handel's. His compositions as they now exist in print are not remarkable for great refinement of workmanship. Those he intended as teaching pieces for his pupils are naturally restricted in interest as regards keyboard technique. Those he designed more especially for his own playing have come down to us in notation that gives no idea of the improvisatory passage-work with which, according to contemporary evidence, he was wont to embellish them in actual performance. Moreover, his work as a whole displays neither the noble proportions and intellectual depth of Bach's, nor the irrepressible vivacity of Scarlatti's, nor the exquisitely sensuous tone-colouring of Rameau's and Couperin's.

Yet Handel's clavier music is distinguished by melodic spontaneity, infectious rhythms and great depth of expression. The unaccountable neglect into which the greater portion of it has fallen in this country may perhaps be ascribed in no small part to the unsatisfactory state of its accessibility in print. The actual musical material constituting this section of Handel's production is plentiful, but some is no longer available except in reference libraries, and the remainder is scattered in a number of publications in which the overlappings, duplications and editorial discrepancies are left to the reader to sort out as best he can. Only one of the editions of the Suites[1] now available gives the player expert and exhaustive guidance on the performance of the ornaments and arpeggioed chords which occur so frequently throughout the works and whose sympathetic interpretation is of vital artistic importance.

The 'Complete Edition' edited by Chrysander and published by the Händel-Gesellschaft, which includes in Vols. 2 and 48 all the clavier works current at the time of publication (1859 and 1894), is out of print. So also is the only modern performing edition (Universal) which prints the whole of the 'Four Collections' constituting the bulk of Handel's clavier compositions with an editorial commentary making clear the order and manner in which they were originally issued. There now remain only incomplete editions which give the practical musician an imperfect idea of the composer's work as a whole. Moreover, since the publication of the Händel-Gesellschaft edition several independent discoveries of manuscript copies of hitherto unknown clavier pieces by Handel have resulted in the addition of valuable items to the original number. Many of these finds have been published, and most of them are still obtainable in this country. Yet although they are of extraordinary interest in throwing fresh light upon Handel's methods of writing for the keyboard they are little known, even to specialists, and they were not even mentioned in the most recent English study of the composer, published in 1947. Until these new accessions have been embodied in the existing practical editions, and the results of modern Handelian research have been collated and made easily available to musicians, the study of the clavier works must continue to entail the difficulties as well as the rewards of an exploration into territory which is still incompletely uncharted.

The 'Four Collections', as printed in H.-G., Vol. 2, are made up as follows. The First comprises the eight suites known to users of Book I of current editions such as Augener's; the Second, the two chaconnes in G major with twenty-one and sixty-two variations respectively, seven more suites, among which is the one in B flat major containing the aria upon which Brahms based his 'Handel

[1] Bärenreiter-Verlag. Kassel and Basel, 1949: Eight Suites.

Variations', but not the suites in G minor and D minor, Nos. 15 and
16 of Book II of modern editions; the Third, the two suites last
mentioned, and ten separate pieces of varying size and type, sonatas,
capriccios, etc.; and the Fourth, the *Six Fugues or Voluntarys for
the organ or harpsichord*, first published in 1735. The Collections are
supplemented in H.–G., Vol. 48, by the *Six Fugues faciles pour
l'orgue ou pianoforte composées par le célèbre G. F. Händel*, which
were published thus, long after his death, by Diabelli. They have
been included (as 'fughettas') in modern editions, their authenticity,
at first in doubt, having been established by Max Seiffert, who
claimed to have found an earlier English print as their source.

Among the heterogeneous collection of instrumental works in
H.–G., Vol. 48, is a set of clavier compositions written by Handel as
a youth, and discovered in 1894 in a twenty-one-page manuscript
bound up with a copy of *My Lady's Banquet* (Walsh). These manuscripts *aus der Jugendzeit*, as they are termed by Chrysander, relate
to the years 1710–20, the period before the publication by Handel
himself of his First Collection of Eight Suites (1720). Some of them
give alternative versions of movements which appeared in the First
Collection, or later in the Second Collection which was printed by
Walsh in 1733 without Handel's permission. Others afford the only
available means of making acquaintance with pieces published at
home or abroad during Handel's lifetime and later, printed copies of
which are now unknown: e.g. the Suite in C minor *à deux clavecins*[1]
and the Partita in A major.[2] Others, again, provide examples both
of Handel's first and second thoughts upon some of his individual
compositions, and of the relationship of a few of them to his work
in other mediums: for instance, a Lesson in D minor,[3] which he
also used as the presto of the Suite in D minor (Coll. I, 3), as a
section of the overture to the opera *Pastor Fido*, and as the last
movements of the Oboe Concerto, Op. 3, No. 6, and Organ Concerto
in D minor, Op. 7, No. 4.

The whole set assumes greater importance when it is studied in
conjunction with Max Seiffert's essay 'Zu Händels Klavierwerken'[4]
and the chapter on Handel in his *Geschichte der Klaviermusik*,[5]

[1] Witvogel, Amsterdam. A reconstruction for two pianos by Thurston Dart is
published by the Oxford University Press (London, 1951).
[2] Senff, *c.* 1864.
[3] According to Seiffert, there is a still earlier version marked 'Gigue' in the Berlin
Staatsbibliothek (MS. fol. 4078 acc.).—*Ed.*
[4] *Sammelbände der internationalen Musikgesellschaft*, Vol. I, p. 131.
[5] Leipzig, 1899, pp. 443–61.

in which the writer traces the connexions between pieces *aus der Jugendzeit* and those in the Handel manuscripts preserved in Berlin, and gives many interesting facts derived from the last-named concerning the original planning of several of the suites. For example, that the *Courante e due minuetti* (No. 7 of the Third Collection) were at first intended for the Suite in F major (Coll. I, No. 2) which, without them, now approximates more nearly to a sonata than to a suite; that the *Harmonious Blacksmith* variations were once included, with minor alterations, in a *Sonata per cembalo*; that an early version of the Suite in E minor, without the opening fugue and with a different ending to the sarabande, dates from Handel's Hamburg period (1703–6), and that the sarabande of the Suite in G minor (Coll. I, No. 7) was composed for the Suite in G minor (Coll. II, No. 6) which contains the much-played gigue, but was removed therefrom to make way for a new courante derived thematically from the allemande.

Of the series of Handel's keyboard pieces published from manuscript sources during the present century, the largest and most varied consists of seventy-six items ranging in size from a chaconne with forty-eight variations to the tiniest of minuets. It was edited in 1928 from the Aylesford MSS. by W. Barclay Squire and J. A. Fuller-Maitland,[1] who stated in the preface that, with one exception (the overture to *Il Trionfo del Tempo* arranged for harpsichord), these pieces had never previously appeared in print, at any rate as keyboard music. Nevertheless, three can easily be identified as having been published as keyboard works in the Händel-Gesellschaft edition, even though not always under the same titles,[2] while various adaptations of other numbers have already been mentioned.[3] The two Aylesford volumes thus draw attention to Handel's innumerable self-borrowings, and they also provide interesting examples of his re-working of his own material. Vol. I contains two differing versions of the Gigue in G minor just mentioned, each considerably shorter

---

[1] Schott, Mainz.

[2] No. 9, Minuet in F, is the second minuet of the *Courante e due Minuetti* (Coll. III, No. 7); and other references to its use will be found on p. 216; No. 31, Sonata in G minor, is the allegro of *Preludio ed Allegro* (Coll. III, No. 9); No. 38, 'Chaconne for harpsichord with two sets of keys', here written on two pairs of staves, is identical with the Chaconne in F major (Coll. III, No. 5). As regards No. 1, an Overture in G minor, the opening ten bars, which are included at the end of the *Jugendzeit* manuscript, are printed in the Foreword to H.–G., Vol. 48, with a note by Chrysander saying that this fragment appears 'extensively treated but still incomplete' in an English manuscript of 1730.

[3] See pp. 211 and 216.

than the version current today, one with an arpeggio prelude, and both containing fresh types of figuration. The Air, No. 25, is evidently the original form of the second movement of the Sonata (Coll. III, No. 12). In Vol. II there is a Courante in C minor, the first half of which is nearly identical with, but the second half almost entirely different from, the sarabande of the *Suite à deux clavecins*, while the piece as a whole bears no likeness to the courante actually belonging to this Suite, though it is closely akin to the preludium.

Evidence of more fundamental alterations by Handel to his own works is supplied in a book containing three of his early suites edited in 1930 by Werner Danckert.[1] This publication is unfortunately no longer obtainable, but its contents were summarized by Professor Abraham in his article 'Handel's Clavier Music'.[2] The music-type examples he quoted therein, which show the transformation of a youthful Suite in C major into one more mature in D minor (Coll. III, No. 2), make clear the kind of revision to which Handel was in the habit of submitting his early compositions.

Other newly discovered pieces dating from the beginning of his career are the *Zwölf Fantasien und vier Stücke*[3] published in 1942 by Georg Walter from manuscript copies that were formerly in the possession of the Swiss publisher Hans Georg Nägeli, and are now in the Central Library, Zürich. Only the first of the Fantasias was published, as a 'sonata', during the composer's lifetime, at Amsterdam in 1732, and was later included as No. 11 of the Third Collection. Handel is reported as having said that he wrote it in his earliest youth, and for this reason the whole set of Fantasias is considered by Georg Walter to belong to the same period. These movements, which are all of slight dimensions, display formal outlines and types of keyboard writing which are also distinctive of Handel's later works, and demonstrate the early development of his style.

These many recent additions to Handel's *œuvre* do not quite complete the tale of the clavier compositions known to have been written by the composer. In an article, 'Unbekannte Klavierkompositionen von G. F. Händel',[4] published at the time he edited the Fantasias, Georg Walter gave a thematic list, made by Hermann Nägeli, of five partitas and two sonatas in manuscript which had formerly belonged to his father but are now lost. The opening theme

---

[1] *Unbekannte Meisterwerke der Klaviermusik* (Bärenreiter, Kassel).

[2] In *Music and Letters*, October 1935.

[3] Hug & Co., Zürich.

[4] In *Schweizerische Musikzeitung*, May 1942.

of one of the partitas proves to be the same as that of the Suite in D minor *aus der Jugendzeit* (H.–G., Vol. 48, pp. 170–175). Perhaps the others in the list may even yet be identified as having been utilized by Handel in his works in other mediums.

Handel's clavier music is a reflection in miniature of the large-scale compositions which form the summit of his art. As the works of a composer accustomed to giving musical expression in operas and oratorios to a wide range of human situations and emotions, these small instrumental pieces bear the impress of the universality of his style. The preludial movements to the suites demonstrate his power of creating on the keyboard an impression of timeless serenity or of impending tragedy, his fugue-subjects are character sketches, now sympathetic, now quizzical, his sarabandes breathe a spirit of infinite consolation, his gigues might set a whole company dancing. The performer of this music may well be more keenly aware of its underlying expressive qualities than of the actual forms and textures of the pieces he is interpreting. Yet if the expressive qualities are paramount, the forms and textures have a fascination and an interest of their own.

The suites, which constitute the solid core of Handel's output for the clavier, are no mere successions of dance-movements in stereo-typed binary form. They include specimens of all the different kinds of structures exemplified throughout his works for the instrument, whether or not they belong properly to the suite: the several varieties of Scarlattian sonata-type, the French overture, chaconne, passacaglia, dance-movements and airs with (and without) 'doubles', and pieces in one continuous sweep, sometimes with a strong suggestion of the ritornello plan. The suites as a whole are character-ized by great freedom in planning. Only a minority follow the con-ventional four-movement sequence of allemande, courante, sara-bande and gigue. The others, which range in length from three to seven movements, do not conform to any systematic scheme; they may begin with a short prelude, a full-sized overture or a fugue, and end with a passacaglia, a minuet or a presto 'lesson'. In the Suite in G major (Coll. II, No. 8), two of the seven pieces are dance-movements in unusual types of rondo form.

Although the suites display features in common with those of Bach and of Gottlieb Muffat they differ from them in several notable respects. Generally speaking, they consist of fewer movements. Bach's sometimes contain as many as nine; Muffat's, up to ten. Moreover, both these composers used a greater variety of *types* of movement. Handel never included Bach's polonaise, anglaise, passepied, burlesca or scherzo, Muffat's hornpipe, rigaudon or bourrée, or genre pieces with French titles after the manner of Couperin. In incorporating the chaconne and the *gavotte en rondeau* in his suites, however, Handel showed that he was not immune from the influence of the French *clavecinistes*, and with his habitual use of the Italian species of courante he introduced a lively southern element into his schemes. Strangely enough, he did not find a place in the suites for one of his favourite Italian dance-movements, the siciliana, as he did in the chamber sonatas and the concerti grossi.

Unlike Muffat's suites, all but two of Handel's remain in one key and mode throughout. The principal exception is the F major (Coll. I, No. 2) already referred to in connexion with its sonata-like construction. This suite is distinguished from all the others, not only by its key system, which hovers between the tonic major and relative minor, but also by the grouping of the four movements into two pairs, each comprising an adagio and an allegro linked to one another by an inconclusive cadence: a structural plan which finds a near parallel in the Concerto grosso in the same key, Op. 6, No. 2. Handel showed a marked preference for the minor mode. He used it for eleven out of the seventeen published suites and for four of the *Six Fugues*. Four of the suites are in D minor, a key which seems to have exercised a special attraction over him, for not only did he write a complete alternative version of the Suite in D minor of the First Collection, but yet another, six-movement Suite in the same key, which is also to be found in the *Jugendzeit* manuscript (H.–G., Vol. 48, pp. 170–175). In general, his choice of tonality was conventional. In the whole of the clavier music only one work is written in a key not in everyday use: the Suite in F sharp minor (Coll. I, No. 6).

Where Handel's suites differ most strongly from those of his contemporaries in any country is in the sense of homogeneity imparted to them by thematic connexions between two or more movements of the same suite. This method of treatment did not originate with Handel. It had been in use for centuries,[1] but was generally restricted to the allemande and the courante. Handel eagerly adopted the idea for unifying the suites and used it with varying degrees of subtlety. Professor Abraham dealt very fully with this aspect

[1] Originating in the pavane-galliard and other, still earlier, pairs of dances commonly based on rhythmic alterations of the same basic material.

of Handel's composition in the article referred to earlier. In discussing how far the practice might be regarded as the outcome of
calculation or of improvisation, he gave so many examples of the
types of similarities occurring between both the thematic material
and the figuration of successive movements that the subject needs
little further consideration here. Moreover, in the editorial commentary to the recent (1949) Bärenreiter edition of the first eight
suites, Rudolf Steglich, who considers Handel's thematic inter-
connexions to have been intentional, gives a number of diagrammatic
music-examples in support of his contention.

From the theoretical point of view, Handel's practice has everything to recommend it. Artistically, it is not without its risks. If
carried beyond a certain point, it tends to produce a feeling of monotony. It may even be one of the reasons why the suites as whole
works have lost currency in the concert-room. In the three-movement Suite in G minor (Coll. II, No. 6), for instance, the likeness
between the allemande and the courante is so pronounced that,
effective as is each movement individually, when the two are played
consecutively the courante is little more than a pale reflection of its
robust predecessor. That the tremendous and original gigue should
have broken away from the Suite to become an independent show-
piece for pianists may be due as much to the lack of mutual contrast
between its pair of companions as to its own sizeable dimensions and
irresistibly virtuosic style.

Even Handel himself appears to have felt the inadvisability of
cultivating too strong a sense of uniformity within a single suite.
A comparison of the manuscript (H.–G., Vol. 48, pp. 152–161)
and the definitive versions of the Suite in D minor (Coll. I, No. 3)
shows that not only did he decide to reject the sarabande and minuet,
as well as the final gigue which is thematically a continuation of the
preceding air and variations, but that he substituted an entirely fresh
and only distantly related allemande and courante for the closely
allied pair he had originally written. In these two superseded
movements he had gone to the length of allowing the musical substance to run as nearly parallel as is possible in pieces respectively
in quadruple and triple time, as in the oldest known pairs of dances.
Every two bars of the courante correspond rhythmically to one bar
of the allemande, while the harmonic foundation and melodic outline
of each movement remain virtually similar throughout their whole
extent. In the Partita in A major (*Jugendzeit*), too, he extended the
thematic relationship between the allemande and courante to embrace

the sarabande and gigue, so that the four movements seem to be facets of the same musical crystal.

Although he used the conventional binary form for the majority of the dance-movements in the suites, Handel occasionally modified it by incorporating within it a feature suggesting ternary form: the partial restatement of the principal theme in the original key towards the end of the piece. The allegro and the air of the Suite in G major (Coll. II, No. 8) exemplify this procedure, while the courante and the gigue of the same suite, like the allegro spiritoso of Muffat's Suite No. 3 in D, are even more definitely tripartite in comprising a threefold statement of almost the whole of their thematic material; a structural plan which may also be seen in the little Sonata in A major in the Nägeli collection. Only one instance of genuine ternary form is to be found in the suites; the sarabande of the B flat major (Coll. II, No. 7). The sarabande of the Partita in A major is of the same type, and the expressive style of both these essentially tuneful pieces resembles that of a *da capo* vocal aria. Indeed, the A major sarabande bears a strong likeness to the sarabande-rhythmed aria 'Lascia ch'io pianga' in *Rinaldo*. The gavotte which forms the third movement of the Sonata in C (Coll. III, No. 12) and is likewise in ternary form, with a varied reprise, is, however, purely instrumental in character.

Among other movements in the less usual forms, two are unique, not only in the suites themselves but in all Handel's clavier works. One is the gigue of the Suite in E minor (Coll. II, No. 5), a piece with the unusual time-signature of 24/16, composed entirely of one theme which is presented in a different guise at each of its four appearances. After the opening seven-bar statement, the same material recurs with the right-hand and left-hand figuration reversed. On being transposed into the relative major and extended to nine bars to facilitate its return to the tonic, it undergoes the same process of being turned upside down and inside out. Despite this carefully calculated plan the piece runs in an unbroken rhythmical sweep, never losing its initial momentum. It almost foreshadows the type of continuous variation used by Haydn in his piano sonatas and in the Capriccio in G major. The other unusual movement is the set of variations in the Suite in D minor (Coll. I, No. 3), the air of which, with its leisurely flowing line and superabundance of ornament, is submitted to clarification instead of to the customary elaboration during the ensuing 'doubles'. The manuscript version of the Suite (H.–G., Vol. 48, pp. 153–161) gives the air in its native simplicity, without a single auxiliary-note to disguise the contour of the melody. The 'doubles', which outnumber those of the definitive version by two, differ from them only in details of figuration. In both sets the melodic line is maintained by the right hand, but in one of the additional 'doubles' of the early version it is transferred entirely to the left, and constitutes the only instance in all Handel's sets of clavier variations of the placing of the theme in the lowest part of the texture.

Handel's variations in general are of a melodically decorative kind. Whether they are 'doubles', as in the *Harmonious Blacksmith* set, or the virtuosic 'divisions' of the big chaconnes, they seldom present the theme in any strikingly new light, harmonically or metrically. The chaconnes, although they display none of the subtlety in planning which distinguish Couperin's and Purcell's, show some diversity in their formal schemes. Of the two in G major (Coll. II), the one with sixty-two variations remains obstinately in the major mode throughout and relies for contrast solely upon variety of figuration. The other, with twenty-one variations, includes a central block of eight in the minor, and by thus falling into three clear-cut sections escapes undue monotony. The Chaconne in C with forty-eight variations (Aylesford, No. 15),[1] too, although it pursues its relentlessly diatonic way entirely in the major mode, assumes a tinge of chromaticism during five consecutive variations towards the end. Of an altogether less rigid kind are two so-called chaconnes in G minor (Aylesford, Nos. 5 and 45), another in F major (Coll. III, No. 5) and an 'Air for two-manual harpsichord' (Aylesford, No. 36), all of them continuous movements in which the theme recurs in fresh array and in different keys between free episodes. These movements are closely allied in type to a number of Handel's other pieces bearing a variety of titles but all distinguished by their ritornello attributes. Among them are an Allegro in A minor (Aylesford, No. 18), belonging to a family of pieces already described on p. 211, a Capriccio in G minor (Coll. III, No. 3) and a Lesson in A minor (Coll. III, No. 6); the short allegro of the *Preludio ed Allegro* in G minor (Coll. III, No. 9) in which a two-bar figure recurs twenty-four times and in five keys; the first movement of the Sonata in C (Coll. III, No. 12), whose opening motive makes nine appearances in either the upper or lower strands of the texture;

[1] This is a re-working of one with twenty-seven variations which was originally the finale of a Suite in C major dating from Handel's Hamburg period, c. 1706, and published by Danckert in the volume mentioned above.

and above all, two of the composer's most extended single pieces: the Sonata in G major for a two-manual harpsichord (Aylesford, No. 35), with an unquenchable, ubiquitous refrain that vividly recalls the aria 'Vo far guerra' from the opera *Rinaldo*; and the Gigue in G minor, thematically the most closely-knit of these pieces, and incidentally the only dance-movement throughout the suites to run its course unobstructed by double-bars and repeats.

The minuet from the Suite in G major (Coll. II, No. 8) is one of three mutually differing, unrelated pieces that stand alone in Handel's output for the clavier by reason of their construction in a series of strips or panels. The minuet proceeds from start to finish in regularly alternating phrases: the first in octaves so strongly syncopated as to suggest that a line of verse running in the composer's thoughts was responsible for their rhythmic pattern, and the second in flowing semiquavers. Similar in build, but totally different in expressive character is the presto *Carillon* of the Nägeli collection, clearly designed for a two-manual harpsichord, for in the playing of the scurrying repeated notes (like those in Debussy's *Snow is dancing*) on a single keyboard, the two hands can hardly get quickly enough out of each other's way. This miniature genre piece, and the even slighter, bourrée-like *Impertinence* (Aylesford, No. 51) are the only clavier works to which Handel gave descriptive titles, though it seems not unlikely that he had definite pictures in his mind's eye when he composed pieces so full of character as the desolate-sounding Fugue in A minor—the keyboard equivalent of the choral fugue 'They loathed to drink of the river' in *Israel in Egypt*—and the mysterious, otherworldly preludes to the suites of the First Collection. The third of the 'panelled' movements, an andante (Aylesford, No. 34) which is the second of two movements headed 'Concerto' and actually appears, in F, in the Concerto, Op. 3, No. 4, is, in its subdued way, as impressionistic in style as the *Carillon*. It is dominated by a single rhythmic figure $\frac{3}{8}$ ♫♫♫♩ which forms the initial bar or bars of ten successive phrases varying in length from twelve to two bars, and, like the andante of the Concerto grosso in B flat, Op. 6, No. 7, which also grows out of one rhythmic motive **c** ♩♪ | ♩.♩ ♩♫ similarly treated, is pervaded by a sense of profound tranquillity. The texture of the 'Concerto', in which the homophonic element predominates over the polyphonic and the musical interest is concentrated in the treble line, is characteristic of much of Handel's clavier music. In his fugues and in the movements

in fugal style he wrote a type of firmly-knit counterpoint which
is magnificently adapted to the purposes of the keyboard, for it is free
from the intricate overlappings and wide gaps in the texture caused
by the exigencies of strict part-writing such as often make Bach's
works of this kind very difficult to perform. Some of Handel's two-
part and three-part inventions are models of linear purity: for
instance, the allegro of the Suite in G minor (Coll. I, No. 7) and the
Sonatina in B flat (Coll. III, No. 10), both of which are in two parts,
the three-part gigue of the E minor Suite (Coll. I, No. 4) and that
of the B flat major (Coll. II, No. 7). In the main, however, he
cultivated a flexible style of part-writing in which the number of
voices is indeterminate, the highest takes precedence over the others,
and the basses are seldom as melodically expressive as are Bach's
and Couperin's. The basses of the preludes to the Sixth, Seventh
and Eighth Suites are outstanding exceptions. Canonic imitations
between the parts often occur at the beginnings of the sections of the
pieces in binary form, but (except in the strenuously contrapuntal
pieces) the inner voices are inclined to be decorative rather than
integral. Pungent clashes resulting from the essential movement of
individual parts are so rare as to be startling when they occur, as they
do in the gigue in F sharp minor (Coll. I, No. 6), bar 5 after the
double-bar; in the andante of the Suite in G minor (Coll. I, No. 7),
bars 3–5, and in the overture to the same Suite, presto section, bar
14 after the double-bar.

Handel's harmonic schemes are, on the whole, conventional and
predominantly diatonic in character. In some of his movements in
the minor mode: for instance, the Fugue in A minor and the prelude
to the Suite in F minor (Coll. I, No. 8), the chromatic possibilities
inherent in the two forms of the tonic minor scale are realized to the
very utmost. Elsewhere, a string of decorative chromaticisms now
and again breaks the spell of diatonic monotony, as in the courante of
the E major Suite (Coll. I, No. 5), the sarabande and gigue of the
E minor (Coll. II, No. 5) and in a short piece in G minor in the first
Aylesford volume (No. 27). A sudden, expressive Neapolitan sixth
occasionally lends a dramatic touch to stately pieces in slow-moving
tempo, such as the sarabande of the Partita in A and the prelude to
the Suite in F sharp minor. But nowhere in Handel's pieces are there
to be found harmonic audacities comparable with those that enliven
the pages of Rameau's, Couperin's and Domenico Scarlatti's, and the
modulations are limited almost exclusively to nearly-related keys.
The distinguishing feature of Handel's clavier music is a melodic

and rhythmic vitality which more than counterbalances the harmonic uneventfulness. His melodies are pre-eminently vocal in type and remain long in the mind's ear. When they are less cantabile in character they are nevertheless endowed with nearly as powerful an ear-haunting quality, for the immanent vocal outlines are never wholly obscured by the keyboard figuration surrounding them.

Rhythmically, the music is markedly plastic. Many of the short movements in binary form, which might so easily be merely sectional and perfunctory in style, manifest a striking sense of continuity by reason of their construction in phrases of uneven bar-lengths, by the overlapping of periods and the rarity of definite cadences. Among the innumerable cases in point are the allemandes and courantes of the Suites in A major and D minor and the courante and sarabande of the E minor (all in Coll. I), which despite their enforced division into two balancing halves, make an impression of 'perpetual motion' as phrase grows out of phrase with quiet inevitability. Rhythmic complexities are far to seek. The persistent syncopation already noted in the minuet of the Suite in G major is one of the very few examples of this phenomenon, others of which may be found in the aria in C minor (Aylesford, No. 52) and in the countersubject of the fugue in F sharp minor (Coll. I, No. 6). Cross-bar rhythm, and series of suspensions across the bar-line, occur very rarely: in the gigues of the Suite in E minor (Coll. II, No. 5) and of the Partita in A major, and in the fugue of the Suite in E minor (Coll. I, No. 4).

Handel, like Purcell, showed great partiality for dotted beats and for characteristic rhythmic figures, which he sometimes maintained throughout an entire piece. The presto section of the overture to the Suite in G minor (Coll. I, No. 7), for instance, races along with scarcely a break in the dotted quaver metre, and the same metrical pattern recurs at the end of the Suite in the theme of the passacaglia. The gavotte in the Sonata in C (Coll. III, No. 12) moves with great precision owing to the accenting of auxiliary-notes on the first and third beats of groups of bars in succession, and one variation each in the Chaconnes in G (Coll. II, No. 9) and in C (Aylesford, No. 15) runs in polonaise rhythm. The movements in which trochaic metre prevails are beyond reckoning. Among them, the gigue in the Suite in B flat (Coll. I, No. 7) and the tripping allemande of the Nägeli collection (p. 28) are the most irresistible as music for dancing.

In respect of its layout for the keyboard Handel's music is far less interesting to the performer than is that of his greatest contemporaries. It is almost entirely lacking in novel types of figuration such as Bach devised for some of the preludes of the 'Forty-Eight' and for the later *Goldberg* variations; it is little concerned with the kind of tone-painting that was carried to a fine art by the French *clavecinistes*, or with the possibilities of sheer technical brilliance that Domenico Scarlatti exploited more thoroughly than any composer of his time. But although Handel's keyboard music is far removed in spirit from the reckless abandon and superb technical efficiency of Scarlatti's, it does show features in common with it. As some of these are already apparent in the early Fantasias which are thought to have been written before Handel went to Italy and became personally acquainted with Domenico, it can hardly be decided whether they are the outcome of Scarlatti's influence or whether the two men cultivated the same kinds of technique independently.

Among those features in Handel's pieces that recall Scarlatti's style are (a) sudden changes between major and minor: allemande in A major (Coll. I, No. 1) bars 6–7; (b) figures containing repeated notes: Fantasia (Nägeli, No. 3); (c) ostinato figures in the right hand over a changing bass: Fantasia (Nägeli, No. 9) bars 33–35, and minuet from the Suite in B flat (Coll. III, No. 1) towards the end; (d) rapid passages containing rising or falling fifths giving the effect of 'consecutives': Fantasias (Nägeli) No. 1, bars 42–45 and No. 11, bars 11–13, and Allemande (Nägeli, p. 28) bars 24–26; (e) threefold echo effects: Minuet in G minor (Aylesford, No. 3); (f) repetitions of short patterns and the lingering upon characteristic figures for expressive purposes: Allemande (Aylesford, No. 41) second half, Fantasia (Nägeli, No. 10) bars 18–19, Sonata in A major (Nägeli, p. 30) last line of piece.

Cross-hand passages, which are a commonplace of Scarlatti's pieces, were never favoured by Handel. The nearest approach to them in his works is to be found in the gigue in G minor (Coll. II, No. 6), where the two hands are for a short time closely interlocked (bars 90–94). In both this movement and the gigue in F minor (Coll. I, No. 8) there are successions of leaps wider than the octave, which are rare in Handel's quick pieces and lend these two a Scarlattian tinge.

The style of some of Handel's more loosely-woven fugues is closer to Scarlatti's than to Bach's, particularly in the retaining of the original key for many entries of the subject and answer during the central section, and in the decorative, homophonic texture. His finest fugues, Nos. 1, 4, 5, and 6 of the Fourth Collection, make no concessions whatever to decorative keyboard style. Contrapuntally closely-wrought and fiercely argumentative, they display the master at his most recondite, and in the intensity of their expressive qualities they bear witness to the strength of his musical inspiration.

Handel's contribution to the concert-performer's repertory is comparatively slight, but he left to the non-professional pianist a rich legacy of satisfying and eminently companiable music.

CHAPTER IX

THE CHAMBER MUSIC

By JOHN HORTON

OF Handel's works in the baroque sonata forms, three collections
were published in his lifetime. The first of these, the Twelve
Sonatas for solo instruments with continuo, Op. 1, appears with
additional material as the '15 Sonatas' in the H.–G., Vol. 27. The
same volume contains the sets of trio sonatas (Op. 2 and Op. 5)
together with the very early sonatas for two oboes with continuo.
To these must be added a number of solo and trio sonatas, some
included in H.–G., Vol. 48, others in various editions of more recent
date. Manuscripts of works of this type attributed to Handel are
still coming to light, but some of those already published are of
doubtful authenticity.

A considerable proportion of the movements, particularly in the
later duet sonatas, are arrangements by the composer himself of
instrumental or vocal numbers from his other compositions[1] which
were doubtless considered to have served their turn in their original
forms but were thought acceptable to amateurs in the guise of
chamber music for instruments. Certain movements also appear
again among the harpsichord and organ works. In view of the
complete effectiveness of Handel's adaptations there seems to be no
reason why they should not be taken on their merits as baroque
trio sonatas; indeed, these were in some cases evidently the original
forms. The reader will scarcely need to be reminded that as the
third (continuo) part normally implied 'cello or viola da gamba as
well as harpsichord, the 'trio' sonata employed four performers.

That Handel's own adaptations by no means exhausted the demand
for some of his most popular music reduced to these convenient
domestic terms is shown by the series of so-called *Sonatas, or
Chamber Aires* brought out by Walsh about 1740. There were seven
volumes of these, presumably arranged by the publisher's hacks,
and the solo instrument specified was the German flute or the violin
with harpsichord. The pieces were described as 'being the most
celebrated Songs and Ariets, Collected out of all the Late Oratorios

[1] Many such cross-references have been noted in earlier chapters.—*Ed.*

and Operas Compos'd by Mr. Handel'. They were mere transcriptions for the modestly-equipped amateur, and no further reference need be made to them.

Several of the authentic chamber works rank among the finest
baroque sonatas extant, and proudly bear the imprint of Handel's
personality. The various instruments specified—German flute
(*traverso*), English flute or treble recorder (*flauto*), oboe, violin,
viola da gamba, and harpsichord—are ingeniously exploited, the
part-writing in contrapuntal passages often produces that transparent sonority of which Handel held the secret, the continuo gives
rise to harmonic patterns of monumental grandeur, and there is a
firm but flexible control of structure.

Most of these works follow in a fairly conservative way the plan
developed by Corelli out of the *sonata da chiesa*; that is to say, they
contain four movements, the first weighty in matter and manner,
the second more animated and often written in *fugato* style, the third
lyrical and often in the metre of the sarabande, and the fourth a
moto perpetuo, generally in the style of a gigue. The tradition of
the church sonata is preserved in the absence of dance-titles from
these movements, though, as with Corelli, dance-idioms often per-
vade the whole work. Handel's debt to Corelli is also to be observed
in his treatment of the continuo, especially when, as frequently
happens, the bass line is allowed to join on equal terms with the
solo instruments, using the same thematic figures and taking a lively
share in the contrapuntal texture. Side by side with works of the
church sonata type stand others that inherit characteristics of the
chamber sonata, with its greater fluidity in number of movements,
its tendency to be made up of, or at least to terminate in, a series of
short, specifically-labelled dance pieces, and its generally lighter
calibre and more homophonic style. Sets of variations occur rarely
in the sonatas.

An almost invariable key-system is followed: a few examples, like
the six-movement Op. 5, No. 3, in E minor, have all their movements in the same key and mode, but it is usual to find a change to
the relative or the tonic major or minor, as the case may be, for the
third movement. It is part of the lyrical character of this movement
to modulate freely, and it may end on the dominant of the main key
of the work in preparation for the final movement. The first movement also frequently ends on the dominant, thereby emphasizing
its function of a prelude, and adding impetus to the energetic allegro
that follows.

R

The *Six Sonatas or Trios for 2 hoboys with a thorough bass for the harpsicord* (H.–G., Vol. 27, p. 57 *et seq.*) are believed to date from Handel's boyhood in Halle. Chrysander assigns them to the year 1696 or thereabouts, and describes how they were acquired in Germany by Lord Polwarth who brought them to England and gave them to his flute-master, Weidemann. Their rediscovery called forth from Handel the often-quoted remark 'I used to write like the devil in those days, and chiefly for the oboe, which was my favourite instrument'. Weidemann's own copy of the three instrumental parts was found in the Library of Buckingham Palace by W. G. Cusins, written in a German hand of about 1700. No contemporary score is known. If these works have come down to us unrevised from Handel's childhood, they are among the most remarkable examples of precocity in all music. In their opening slow movements they show already the typical Handelian spaciousness and solidity, as well as a mature grasp of instrumental idioms in the imitative writing (see Ex. 88, from No. 3 in E flat). The emotional range is considerable; contrast the radiant cheerfulness of No. 5, the pastoral tranquillity of No. 4, and the pathos of No. 2. All six sonatas are laid out on a uniform plan of adagio—allegro—slow movement—allegro, with a change of mode for the slow movement; but within this framework there is a wide variety of formal treatment. Thus in Nos. 1 and 5 the first allegro passes without break into a rhapsodical slow movement of short duration. In Nos. 3, 4, and 6 the expressive slow movements are all cast in the mould of the

Ex. 88

sarabande. The third movement of No. 2 is an unpretentious minuet. Interesting chromatic touches that are apt to occur at cadence points (like the close of the first movement of No. 2) are typical of German baroque composers like Froberger, just as the crisply articulated subjects of some of the *fugato* movements (the posthorn tunes, for example, in the second movements of Nos. 5 and 6) recall the lively materials of Pachelbel's fughettas.

Of somewhat later date is the Sonata in C for viola da gamba and cembalo *concertato*, in four movements (H.-G., Vol. 48). This was probably written about 1705 in Hamburg, where the viola da gamba was much cultivated. The style is immature. The cembalo part is written out in full, with no figured bass, and the arpeggio accompaniment of the adagio (third movement) is of particular technical interest. In two later MSS. (c. 1750 and 1780), which are not in the composer's autograph, there are directions for performance on the violin or the viola da braccio.

Three Sonatas (A minor, E minor, B minor) for flute (traverso) and bass (H.-G., Vol. 48), published by Walsh in a volume with another flute sonata by Brivio and two violin sonatas by Geminiani and Somis, may date from the Halle period. The first two movements of the E minor Sonata are identical with those of the Oboe Sonata, Op. 1, No. 8, except for a transposition. The last two movements, which are thematically connected, are related to other works in Op. 1 (Nos. 1a and 2). The opening adagio of the B minor Sonata is an eloquent, impassioned piece.

Autograph manuscripts of three Sonatas for recorder and figured bass are among the Handel collection in the Fitzwilliam Museum, Cambridge. All three have recently been edited by Mr. Thurston Dart,[1] who considers them to date from the period of Handel's travels in Italy in his early twenties. The three movements of the B flat Sonata are used elsewhere in Handel's works, the finale being a version of the gigue that ends the Violin Sonata in A. The D minor Sonata has been assembled by Mr. Dart from three movements scattered among the Fitzwilliam manuscripts. The remaining Sonata, also in D minor, occurs, in the key of B minor and with two additional movements, as the traverso Sonata, No. 9 of the Fifteen Solo Sonatas.

The fifteen *Solos for a German flute, a hoboy, or violin, with a thorough bass for the Harpsicord or Bass Violin* (H.-G., Vol. 27), are based on a set of twelve sonatas originally published in 1724 by

[1] Fitzwilliam Sonatas, ed. Thurston Dart. Schott, 1948.

Witvogel of Amsterdam, and reproduced shortly afterwards 'corrected' by Walsh of London as Handel's Op. 1. Arnold and Chrysander printed the additional works. The instrumentation is not always specified, and in some cases is uncertain, but the usual allocation is Nos. 1a, 1b, 5 and 9 to the German flute (traverso), Nos. 2, 4, 7, and 11 to the English flute (recorder), Nos. 6 and 8 to the oboe, and six sonatas—Nos. 3, 10, 12, 13, 14, and 15—to the violin.[1] Recently, however, No. 6 has been shown by Mr. Thurston Dart to have been designed for the viola da gamba.[2]

The miscellaneous nature of this collection is further indicated by the variety of forms employed. While most of the sonatas follow the plan of the *sonata da chiesa*, several of them—Nos. 1a, 5, 7, and 9 —have more than four movements and include dance-movements, whether specified or otherwise. It will be noted that all four of these works were apparently written for the German or English flute. The violin sonatas differ considerably in degree of elaboration: thus Nos. 10 and 15 are modest in scope and keep closely to the simple Corellian models, but No. 14, a fully written out virtuoso piece, with abundance of double and triple stopping and brilliant passagework, bears an obvious relationship to such a work as Corelli's Op. 5, No. 3.

The two Traverso Sonatas, Nos. 1a and 1b, appear to be different drafts of the same work. Their opening slow movements are almost identical, but 1a—probably the later version, as it is in several respects the more highly developed—has a brief adagio link between first and second movements. The second movement of No. 1b is an attractive allegro in close imitative style, well suited to wind instruments, with short, clear-cut motives and many repeated notes. The corresponding movement of No. 1a is a binary andante developed from an idea that must have pleased the composer, as he used it on several occasions elsewhere. Its first two bars are identical with those of the sarabande of Corelli's Sonata Op. 5, No. 8, and the whole theme[3] may perhaps be regarded as coming from a common stock drawn upon by composers in the baroque period. In this sonata Handel transforms the theme into a gavotte (presto) for the fifth movement (Ex. 89 (a) and (b)); and the transformation became

---

[1] Mr. Edgar Hunt has pointed out that these instruments are the same as those dealt with in a compendium of popular instruction, *The Modern Music Master*, published in 1730 (see *Proceedings of the Royal Musical Association*, Session *LXXV* (1948–9), pp. 46–7).

[2] See Preface to Sonata in G minor, ed. Thurston Dart. Schott, 1950.

[3] See p. 228.

a still greater favourite, reappearing in the Organ Concertos, Op. 4, No. 3, and Op. 7, No. 5. The slow movement of No. 1*b* is a modest little piece 13 bars long. In No. 1*a* the largo is built on the magnificent rising phrase we meet with again in the Violin Sonata, Op. 1, No. 13 (see Ex. 91). The fourth movement of both works is a gigue-like allegro. Op. 1, No. 2, has second and fourth movements identical with the second and fifth of No. 1*a*, except for an upward transposition of a third to suit the recorder. The opening larghetto and the short third movement of No. 2 are particularly effective on the recorder.

Ex. 89

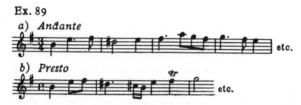

The comparatively limited resources of the treble recorder are well exploited also in Op. 1, No. 4 (A minor). Even the narrow range of tone-colour is cunningly disguised by interesting detail in the continuo part (Ex. 90), and the sense of unity that pervades the four movements makes this one of the classics of recorder literature. The opening movement of Op. 1, No. 7 (C major), also for recorder, is strong in harmonic interest. This work has the looser structure of the *sonata da camera*; there are five movements, of which the fourth is a gavotte, and the third in the style of a chaconne.[1]

Ex. 90

The Traverso Sonata in G, No. 5, also contains this movement, transposed a fourth lower, and has a bourrée and a favourite minuetto (which appears also as a keyboard piece and in the Concerto, Op. 3, No.

[1] For another working of the same bass, also in A minor, see the aria 'Tears are my daily food' in the fourth version of the sixth Chandos Anthem, *As pants the hart* (H.–G., Vol. 36, p. 237). Similarly, the bass of the larghetto of No. 4 (Ex. 90) is identical with that of 'Se non giunge' in the solo cantata *Filli adorata.*—*Ed.*

4) as its fourth and fifth movements. Another Traverso Sonata, No. 9 in B minor, has no fewer than seven movements, whose miscellaneous character suggest the suite rather than the chamber sonata. The second of these movements is in hornpipe metre (the minor original of a favourite piece in the D major *Water Music*) and the final one is a minuet written out in 6/8 time. As already noted, there is an earlier version of this work in D minor for recorder. The fifth movement stands in close relationship to the first of the doubtfully authentic keyboard fughettas, and the 6/8 minuet has been printed as No. 55 of the Aylesford pieces.

Of the remaining sonatas assigned to wind instruments in the Händel-Gesellschaft edition, Op. 1, No. 6, formerly regarded as an oboe sonata, must on the evidence available be restored to the viola da gamba, to which it is better suited on technical grounds. Its opening movement begins like a familiar air from the F major *Water Music* but at once takes a different course. Op. 1, No. 8 (C minor) is an interesting work, though small in scale; it makes effective oboe music. Certain features, including the angular fugal theme of the second movement, suggest a comparatively early date of composition. The little bourrée that forms the fourth movement is delightful. Op. 1, No. 11 (F major), for recorder, is almost identical with the Organ Concerto, Op. 4, No. 5, except that orchestral ritornelli are interpolated in the latter.

It would be impossible to mistake Op. 1, No. 3, in A, for anything but violin music. The second movement (allegro) has a continuity of texture that would have been hard to make convincing on any woodwind instrument of the period, and there are passages of double and triple stopping. Equally characteristic are the five rhapsodical bars that form the third movement. The graceful gigue that closes the work has become one of the violinist's most popular recital-pieces.

The influence of Corelli, and perhaps of Corelli's pupil Geminiani,[1] can be detected in the violinistic writing of Op. 1, No. 10 (G minor), which, with its sequential passages, its series of 6/3 chords, and the use made in the solo part of the sonorities of all four strings, might well have come from the pen of the older master. Nos. 12 (F major) and 15 (E major) are of slighter interest. No. 14 (A major) is a virtuoso work, evidently written for a player far beyond the ordinary in technical accomplishment. No. 13 (D major), although it makes

[1] It has been suggested that the six violin sonatas were written for Matthew Dubourg (1703–1767), a pupil of Geminiani.

fewer technical demands, is perhaps the greatest work, from the standpoint of purely musical value, in the whole collection. The opening bars make inspired use of the ringing sonorities of the open strings of the violin (Ex. 91). The remaining movements are a finely-knit fugal allegro, with boldly contrasting subject and counter-subject,[1] a poignant larghetto, and a virile dance-movement, later used in *Jephtha*, as finale. The whole constitutes one of the most completely unified of all Handel's instrumental compositions.

Ex. 91

The *Sonatas or Trios for two violins, flutes, or hoboys with a thorough bass for the harpsicord or violoncello (Op. II)* include the original *VI Sonates à deux Violons deux hautbois ou deux Flûtes traversières et Basse Continue . . . . Second ouvrage* published by Witvogel at Amsterdam in 1724 and reproduced by Walsh in 1733. These are Nos. 1*b*, 2, 4, 5, 6, and 7 of the Händel-Gesellschaft edition; Nos. 1*a*, 3, 8, and 9 were added in that edition by Chrysander from transcripts in the royal collection at Dresden.[2] All the sonatas are in four movements, and their style, rich and elaborate, suggests that they are works of Handel's maturity. A large number of the movements occur in other of Handel's works.

No. 1*b* (B minor) is a transposed version of 1*a* (C minor); Chrysander regards the latter as the original version. If so, it is possible that the sonata was first laid out for treble recorder and violin with bass, the violin being obligatory in the slow movement with its double stopping. The B minor version would be an adaptation for transverse flute with violin. The opening largo (andante in the B minor version) (see Ex. 109) is splendidly economical of material and with its imitative contrapuntal style makes effective chamber music.

---

[1] Both used subsequently in the chorus 'From the censer curling rise' in *Solomon* (see p. 122).

[2] A version of No. 6, with a separate figured bass part marked *Organo*, is given in H.–G., Vol. 48. This was taken from a contemporary MS., not in the composer's handwriting, said to date from about 1730 and containing *VI Sonate a 2 Violini et Basso. Par Signor Hendel.* Nos. 1, 2, 3 and 4 correspond to Op. 2, Nos. 6, 5, 4 and 1*a*. Nos. 5 and 6 of the manuscript (in B flat major and G minor respectively) are dismissed by Chrysander as spurious.

Similar devices are employed in the following allegro, where in addition
the continuo is drawn into the imitative texture (Ex. 92; the passage
quoted comes from the close of the movement, and shows the culmination of a process of interval-extension in the melodic sequences that
contributes to the feeling of energy). The andante (largo in the B
minor version) betrays its origin in an aria, and can be traced to
Keiser's *Octavia*.[1] The final allegro is adapted from a duet in the
sixth Chandos anthem, *As pants the hart* ('Why so full of grief, O
my soul?').

Ex. 92

Op. 2, No. 2 is a straightforward, solidly built work of no special
distinction. The first, second and fourth movements owe much of
their vitality to a contrapuntal texture full of vivid imitation. The
theme of the opening andante recalls 'The flocks shall leave the
mountains' in *Acis*. The third movement is a sarabande with upper
parts moving sedately above a bass suggestive of the 'broken grounds'
of the seventeenth century. The finale is based on one of Handel's
favourite themes (cf. p. 211).

Op. 2, No. 3, in F major, is another work evidently written with
virtuoso performers in mind. In the first movement there is much of
the bold writing across the four strings of the violin in which the
Italian violinist composers took such delight. The second movement
is fugal, with the bass joining in on equal terms; harmonically as
well as contrapuntally there is an exciting growth of tension up to a

[1] See p. 265.

climax, where all three parts break off in the midst of a semiquaver passage, to end after a dramatic pause with a coda of intense pathos (Ex. 93) setting the mood for the following adagio and subtly recalled in the final bars of that movement. The finale, an example of bravura writing, is a version of part of the overture to *Athaliah*, which is practically identical with the allegro and allegro non presto of Op. 5, No. 4. This Sonata is another of the dominating peaks of Handel's chamber music.

Ex. 93

The articulation of Op. 2, No. 4, in B flat, suggests that Handel conceived the work originally for a pair of flutes. Its four movements provide a fascinating study in phrasing, and afford evidence enough, if it is still required, to dispel any belief that Handel's music is rhythmically obvious. The larghetto shows how a master can give new life to a threadbare material—in this instance, sequences of thirds and sixths—and produce a moving effect by the simplest means. This movement, with the preceding allegro, was used also in the overture to *Esther*, and the allegro in the second of the B flat Oboe Concertos described by Mr. Lam on p. 209, while the final allegro is better known in a slightly different form as the second movement of the Organ Concerto, Op. 4, No. 2.

Op. 2, No. 5, in F major, for traverso, violin and bass has less distinction. There are five movements. The first is an adaptation of the overture to the fourth Chandos Anthem, and the fourth, a solid fugal allegro, is derived from the overture to the eighth Chandos Anthem, *O come let us sing*. The finale is a gigue of which two versions are given in the Händel-Gesellschaft edition, and which was used again in the last movement of the overture to *Parnasso in Festa* (1734).

Nos. 6 and 7 (both G minor) both have weighty opening slow movements[1] and lengthy, well-developed allegro second movements, followed by short arioso slow movements. The finales are in dance-forms: that of No. 6, with the hornpipe syncopations that Handel gratefully took over from the native English tradition of light music, is a favourite movement occurring elsewhere.[2]

No. 8 (again in G minor) is a favourite with violin duet players and understandably so; the partners are treated as impartially as any Faustina and Cuzzoni, and there is much splendid part-writing, as in Ex. 94, taken from near the end of the opening andante where the first violin provides a bass to the second.

Ex. 94

While the preceding work represents a fine type of baroque chamber music, Op. 2, No. 9, in E major, the last of the set, belongs

[1] That of No. 6, closely related to 'Vouchsafe O Lord' in the Chandos *Te Deum*, was afterwards scored as the first movement of the Organ Concerto, Op. 4, No. 3.—*Ed.*

[2] See Ex. 77*b*.—*Ed.*

rather to the rococo age, and in its day must have seemed advanced in style and technique. After a graceful ornate adagio comes an allegro based on a very lively syncopated motive.[1] The indication 'allegro' for the third movement as given in the Händel-Gesellschaft edition is obviously incorrect; the piece is a short, pathetic andante or adagio. The finale opens conventionally, but as it progresses the violin part becomes more florid, and eventually breaks into arpeggios over a steadily moving bass, suggestive of a chaconne, while the second violin recalls the syncopated rhythm of the second movement (Ex. 95). The harmonic enterprise shown at this point is in keeping with the general brilliance of the work, and fitly crowns a remarkable volume of instrumental music.

Ex. 95

Considerably less musical interest attaches to the seven *Sonatas or trios for two violins or German flutes, with a thorough bass for the harpsicord or violincello (sic)*, published as Op. 5 by Walsh in 1739. These are slighter works than the fine duet-sonatas of Op. 2, and are in the nature of loosely assembled suites rather than typical

[1] Romain Rolland states that this is an English traditional tune, but I have not been able to identify it as such.

baroque sonatas. Their essentially popular character is emphasized by the comparatively modest demands they make on the performers, and also by the large number of adaptations they contain. Op. 5, No. 1, in A major, begins with an andante derived from two early concertos (see Ex. 107), which also appears in the fifth Chandos Anthem and as the introduction to 'I will magnify Thee' in *Belshazzar*. The remaining four movements include two allegros,[1] separated by a brief larghetto, and a short gavotte (also used in *Ariodante* and *Terpsicore*) as finale. Op. 5, No. 2, in D major runs to seven movements, the first two being taken respectively from the early *Te Deum* in D major and the Utrecht *Te Deum*. Then comes an allegro in hornpipe rhythm sandwiched between two statements of an exquisite musette, the whole of this material being from *Ariodante*. The last two movements are a march and a gavotte. Op. 5, No. 3, in E minor, begins with what is virtually a French overture, taken from the sixth Chandos Anthem; the Händel-Gesellschaft edition give alternatives for the fugal allegro, the second —identical with that in the first version of the same anthem—being taken from a manuscript in Buckingham Palace. The other movements are a sarabande, also in *Terpsicore*; an allemande opening like the one in a D minor Suite for harpsichord (Coll. II, No. 3); a rondo; and a gavotte, likewise taken from *Terpsicore*. Op. 5, No. 4, in G major, is built on a more grandiose scale. Much of its material is to be found also in *Parnasso in Festa*, *Athaliah* and *Terpsicore*[2]. The passacaille from *Terpsicore* that forms the introduction to the second movement is superficially in the manner of Purcell, but has little of Purcell's depth and urgency. The last two movements are a gigue from *Terpsicore* and the popular minuet from *Alcina*. Op. 5, No. 5, (G minor) is an odd assemblage of a weighty French-overture largo, an attractive larghetto from *Athaliah* (accompaniment to 'Jerusalem, thou shalt no more'), two fugues almost identical with No. 6 of the *Six Fugues* and the one in the Fourth Suite for harpsichord, an air from *Terpsicore*, and a bourrée. Op. 5, No. 6 (F major) draws freely on the third and sixth Chandos Anthems. After the opening largo come an allegro and an adagio that are variants of the corresponding movements of Sonata Op. 2, No. 3. A

---

[1] Of which the first comes from the second of the early Oboe Concertos in B flat described on p. 209, and also appears as the second movement of the second version of the fifth Chandos Anthem.—*Ed.*

[2] The additional part for viola, given in the Buckingham Palace manuscript and printed in small notes by Chrysander, in all movements except the minuet, is taken from the orchestral version of the same pieces.

fugal allegro is followed by an andante with a variation, for which the Buckingham Palace manuscript is the source[1] and, as an alternative, a minuet. Op. 5, No. 7, in B flat, contains a flowing larghetto, a bustling allegro, an adagio, a gavotte, and a minuet which is also found as a trio for two recorders and a violin in *Terpsicore*.

Two additional sonatas were discovered some twenty years ago in the library of Count Schönborn at Wiesentheid-Unterfranken in Bavaria, and published in a performing edition by Fritz Zobeley.[2] They are described in the manuscript parts, which are not in the composer's autograph, as 2 *Concerten par le Sieur Handel*. The term 'concerto' is accounted for by the addition of *concertante* parts for 'cello to what were probably written originally as ordinary trio sonatas. The Count was a keen amateur cellist, and it is supposed that Handel added the parts at his request. The D minor work is laid out for flute, violin, solo 'cello, and continuo, and is in four movements; in the first, the flute plays an *arioso* to the accompaniment of an ostinato figure shared by violin and 'cello, the whole being supported by continuo chords on the beats. The second movement is a three-part *fugato*, the third a largo in which the chief interest is in the obbligato 'cello part, and the finale is a gigue. The D major piece begins with a richly scored, swinging andante, marked *con concento*. The style of the following allegro is diffuse and suggests that the work, if it is authentic Handel, belongs to an early period of composition. The largo is the conventional Corellian slow movement; the solo 'cello plays throughout with the continuo. The finale is brisk and tuneful, but again bears marks of immaturity. Zobeley considers that these two works may date from about 1715. They are certainly not representative of Handel's chamber music at its best, but they are none the less welcome additions to the repertory of amateur performers who can count on the help of a good 'cellist.

---

[1] This movement, with an additional variation, is also found (in G major and 3/8 time) in the Organ Concerto, Op. 4, No. 1; the largo and fugal allegro were recast as the first Organ Concerto of the 'Second Collection'.

[2] Published by Schott in the series 'Antiqua'. See also Zobeley's article in *Händel-Jahrbuch* for 1931, pp. 104–116.

CHAPTER X

SOME POINTS OF STYLE

By GERALD ABRAHAM

THE first great paradox of Handel's music—that, gifted with his enormous fertility, he should have needed or bothered to borrow from others less gifted—is closely linked with the second: that, despite his obvious individuality, he was so much the man of his time that these borrowings are completely assimilated, and suspected as such only when someone comes across the original. When a Telemann cantata has been ascribed to J. S. Bach as in the case of 'Gott der Hoffnung erfülle euch',[1] it has been published as 'doubtful' and Spitta could declare roundly[2] that it was 'quite un-Bachlike and certainly not genuine'; when Arnold in 1797 published as Handel's an organ concerto[3] of which both movements are based on movements of a flute sonata by Telemann (*Musique de Table*, Prod. I, No. 5) no one seems to have regarded it as 'quite un-Handelian', nor did anyone until Seiffert later came to edit the Telemann original for the 'Denkmäler deutscher Tonkunst'.[4] Nor was that simply because Handel has, as usual, worked wonders with borrowed material.[5] The explanation is that Handel was completely the man of the age, a supreme figure embodying every aspect of its music in his own work, while Bach—at least equally great, just as firmly rooted in the age—embodies only certain aspects of its music, the essentially German ones. Whatever Bach learned from Italian and French masters—and he certainly learned a great deal from Italians—he remained through and through a German composer writing German music; Handel began as a German composer writing German music with an Italian accent, and developed into a cosmopolitan composer

[1] Bach Gesellschaft, Jg. XLI.
[2] *J. S. Bach* (Leipzig, 1873–80), p. 779.
[3] H.–G., Vol. 48, p. 57.
[4] Vol. 61–2. A practical edition of the Sonata is published separately as No. 5 of Breitkopf's series of 'Kammersonaten'.
[5] Which justified him in the eyes of his contemporaries. 'Borrowing is allowable (*eine erlaubte Sache*)', says Mattheson in *Der vollkommene Capellmeister* (1739), 'but one must pay interest, i.e. one must so contrive and work out the imitations that they take on a fine and better appearance than the things from which they are borrowed'.

writing Italian music with a German command of solid technique and an occasional trace of English accent, caught mainly from Purcell. Every composer of the period is closely related to Handel in many points of style. (Perhaps one should qualify that assertion by saying 'every older composer' or 'more conservative composer'; the generation of the young Viennese, the Mannheimers, C. P. E. Bach and the age of sentiment and the *galant* style overlapped his later years.)[1] But they come close to Bach only when, as Handel himself does in dozens of pieces—from the first movement of the Flute Sonata, Op. 1, No. 1, or 'Sünder, schaut mit Furcht und Zagen' from the Brockes *Passion*, to the last chorus of *Theodora*[2]—they remind us of their roots in late seventeenth-century Germany.

In Handel's case the roots, of course, go much deeper than cosmopolitan Hamburg and the already Italianized style of Keiser. In particular we should not undervalue, as Chrysander did,[3] the three years of study with Friedrich Wilhelm Zachow. Zachow was a minor master of the chorale prelude and of fugue; there can be little doubt that it was through him that Handel became one of the heirs of the tradition of Scheidt and Pachelbel, and learned among other things, the art of improvisation on the organ and such technical devices as the combination of a sustained *cantus firmus*-like theme with a web of counterpoint. It is entirely characteristic of Handel that he should have employed this latter technique, devised as a purely constructive principle or for the purpose of decorating a *cantus firmus*, for the quite different purpose of dramatic effect in great choral frescoes such as 'Let all inspired' in the ninth Chandos Anthem and the end of 'Praise the Lord with harp' in *Solomon*.

Zachow made his pupil copy out examples of the work of mastercraftsmen and one such copy-book of Handel's, for the year 1698, was preserved for many years, only to be lost by Lady Rivers early in the nineteenth century; but we know that its contents included

---

[1] It is true that Handel occasionally leans toward the new spirit and style, in such things as 'Un momento di contento' in *Alcina*, 'His mighty arm' in *Jephtha*, and parts of *Solomon*; but his conservatism is very evident when one compares his course of development with that of Christoph Graupner, two years his senior, who wrote typical baroque operas such as *Antiochus und Stratonica* (1708) for Hamburg (see Seleucus's aria 'Zu den Wolcken, zu den Sternen' from this opera in H. C. Wolff's collection of 'Deutsche Barockarien', published by Bärenreiter in 1943) but by the middle of the century was pouring out symphonies which in material and treatment (for instance, in the first movement of the G major Symphony, printed by Riemann in his *Musikgeschichte in Beispielen*) belong to the new age.

[2] See, for instance, the references on pp. 17, 31, 154, 166, 172, 178 and 207.

[3] *G. F. Händel*, I, pp. 21–43.

compositions by Froberger, Poglietti, J. K. Kerll, Georg Muffat (father of Gottlieb), J. K. F. Fischer, N. A. Strunck, Kuhnau, Pachelbel and Zachow himself. Among living composers, Buxtehude too was evidently one of Handel's models for technique.

Mattheson tells us that when the eighteen-year-old Handel first came to Hamburg in 1703 he 'set very long arias and absolutely endless cantatas, which lacked the right finish or the right taste, though the harmony was perfect; was however soon quite differently fashioned in the high school of opera. He was clever on the organ: cleverer than Kuhnau, in fugues and counterpoints, particularly *ex tempore*: but he knew very little of melody before he came into the Hamburg opera'. Yet at least one of Zachow's church cantatas, 'Ruhe, Friede, Freud und Wonne',[1] provides ample evidence that Handel could have already learned something of Italian operatic methods and conventions—and Italianate melody—from his first master:[2] David's aria 'O du werter Freudengeist',[3] is archetypal of Handel in both its instrumental and its vocal melodies:

Ex. 96

O du wer - ter Freu - den - geist

But it must be admitted that this vein is exceptional in Zachow. Handel learned to write Italian music because Italian or Italianate music was everywhere about him, at Hamburg almost as much as in Italy itself. At Hamburg only his friend Johann Mattheson maintained a more Teutonic style;[4] the predominant master, Reinhard Keiser, was almost completely under the spell of Agostino Steffani, whose chamber duets unquestionably exercised a strong direct

[1] No. 4 of the twelve published by Seiffert in *Denkmäler deutscher Tonkunst* Vol. 21-2.

[2] See the detailed study of this cantata by Alfred Heuss, 'F. W. Zachow als dramatischer Kantatenkomponist', in *Zeitschrift der internationalen Musikgesellschaft*, Jg. X, pp. 228-35, and Mr. Lam's comment on *Laudate pueri* on p. 157.

[3] *Denkmäler deutscher Tonkunst*, Vol. 21, p. 71.

[4] Judging from the arias from *Henrico IV* and *Boris Goudenow* published by H. C. Wolff in his 'Deutsche Barockarien'.

influence on Handel himself. An enumeration of the actual Italians
who probably or certainly helped to mould Handel's style would make
a formidable list, but it would undoubtedly have to be headed with the
names of Steffani, Alessandro Scarlatti and Corelli. An aria such as
Elmiro's 'Ah, crudel', in Scarlatti's *Rosaura* (1690)[1] takes us straight
to the heart of what is commonly taken to be Handelian melody:

Ex. 97

Mention of Keiser brings us back once more to the question of
Handel's 'borrowings'. His indebtedness to Keiser's *Octavia* has
already been mentioned by Professor Dent, Mr. Herbage and Mr.
Horton,[2] but two additional points are worth making: Handel's
borrowings both from others and from his own earlier works are
often limited to instrumental introductions, and, even when he
did not improve borrowed ideas immediately, he was apt to improve
them later and to go on improving them. The latter point is the less
important; it may be illustrated by the almost note-for-note appropri-
ation of the ritornello of 'Ruhig sein' in Keiser's *Octavia* for the
ritornello of 'Vaghe fonte' in *Agrippina*, quoted in parallel by
Sedley Taylor,[3] and also in the ritornelli of 'Crede l'uom' in *Il
Trionfo del Tempo* ('Mortals think' in the English version) and the
middle section of 'Volate più dei venti' in *Muzio Scevola*. The
process of improvement is already begun when the same music
reappears in the third movement of the Trio Sonata, Op. 2, No. 1,

[1] *Publikationen der Gesellschaft für Musikforschung*, XIV, p. 215.
[2] See pp. 18, 73, and 256.   [3] Op. cit., p. 171.

and when the same basic idea comes to the surface again in 'Comfort ye' in *Messiah*, after long rest in the depths of the composer's unconsciousness, the transformation is complete. Nothing remains but the essential idea—transfigured.

The point that Handel often borrowed or repeated mere introductions is more important, for it appears to throw light on a peculiar aspect of his creative processes. Sometimes, of course, as when he lifts the introduction to 'Disserratevi o porte d'Averno' from *La Resurrezione* to serve as the introduction to an aria in *Alexander Balus*, he is obviously only saving himself a little trouble. But the transference of the Keiser-'Vaghe fonte' idea to the Trio Sonata is in a rather different class; the melody itself is abandoned and not heard again, but the basic idea of the quietly throbbing repeated chords goes on and seems to generate a fresh melody, indeed a whole entirely fresh movement. Far from being exceptional, that is an exceedingly common procedure with Handel. We know from a dozen contemporary sources that he was a masterly improviser, and it is clear that a large proportion of his published work originated in private improvisation, however polished and worked up after being set on paper. There is ample internal evidence that Handel frequently began to compose by playing the harpsichord, starting from the first favourite cliché that came under his fingers—whether his own, someone's else's, or common property of the age, he probably neither knew nor cared—and allowing it to grow into something that was usually in the end absolutely his and his alone. Hasty and superficial critics have observed identical openings and too often assumed that what follows is identical too; that is by no means always the case.

One of the commonest of such gambits appears in an early form in the finale of the youthful Recorder Sonata in C, Op. 1, No. 7:

Ex. 98

This was first revised for 'Placa l'alma' in *Alessandro*, then taken up, bass and all, vastly improved and quite differently continued in the penultimate movement of the Oboe Concerto, Op. 3, No. 2:

Ex. 99

while a rhythmically identical but melodically modified form of the original theme provides the basis of a movement which exists in substantially identical forms, as part of the *Pastor Fido* overture, finale of the Oboe Concerto, Op. 3, No. 6, finale of the Organ Concerto, Op. 7, No. 4, and finale of the Third Suite for harpsichord:[1]

Ex. 100

The same gambit may serve for different tempi; the opera *Giustino* (1737) and the final minuet of the Trio Sonata, Op. 5, No. 6, which Handel passed for the press in 1738 (the dates are not insignificant), show two versions in the same key, even beginning with identical basses, but diverging completely—the one vocally, the other instrumentally—directly afterward:

Ex. 101

Larghetto

Ex. 102

Allegro moderato

[1] See. p. 235 for two earlier keyboard versions.

Also in the slower tempo, the idea opens the sarabande of the Fourth Suite for harpsichord, and the air of the D minor Suite (Coll. II, No. 3), continuing in each case with a soaring curve collapsing in a diminished-fifth drop:

Ex. 103

Ex. 104
Lentement

The ritornello of 'Thrice happy the monarch' in *Alexander Balus* returns to the brisk pace and abruptly cut off perfect fifth of the prototype, but develops quite differently. Sometimes this generating motive appears only after a bar or two (as in the minuet of the Trio Sonata, Op. 5, No. 4, in Ex. 77*b*, in 'Gioja sì speri sì' in *Scipione*); sometimes it crops up unexpectedly in the middle of a movement (e.g. the courante of the harpsichord Suite in G minor, Coll. II, No. 6, where it immediately runs away with the improviser's fingers.) The fact that the motive consists of little more than conventional ornamentation of the rhythmic figure ♪ ♩ in no way lessens its importance as a generator—a generator, that is, of natural *continuations*, not necessarily (indeed very seldom) of further material spun from its own nature as would be the case with a Beethoven theme.

There are a great number of such recurrent generating motives in Handel. To take only a few examples: there is the siciliana motive which generates among other things the middle sections of 'In tanti affanni' in *Armida abbandonata* and 'Affanni del pensier' in *Ottone*, and 'Ye sons of Israel, mourn' in *Esther*; there is the sarabande motive of the D minor Suite for harpsichord (Coll. III, No. 1) and 'The glorious company of the Apostles' from the Chandos *Te Deum*, with its modified form in 'Praise ye the Lord' in *Solomon*; there is the specifically instrumental adagio gambit in the early Sonatas, Op. 1, Nos. 2 and 6, the Organ Concerto, Op. 4, No. 3, the Concerto grosso, Op. 6, No. 1, and elsewhere.[1] A specially interesting one is traced in the third footnote on p. 211.

Again, Handel has favourite fugue subjects such as the curious one

[1] The idiom is derived from Stradella: cf. Eurinda's aria, 'Sepellitevi', in his *Floridoro*, printed by Heinz Hess in *Die Opern Alessandro Stradellas* (Leipzig, 1906), p. 75.

used for 'Alla salma infedel' in the solo cantata *O Numi eterni* (cf. Ex. 63*b*), 'They are brought down and fall'n' from the tenth Chandos Anthem (*The Lord is my light*) (Ex. 57) and the second movement of the G minor Concerto grosso, Op. 6, No. 6; though based on the same subject, these pieces have nothing else in common except the key of G minor. It is something more than coincidence that No. 27 of the so-called 'Aylesford pieces' for harpsichord, in which this theme also appears, is in the same key.

But Handel's favourite openings are not always melodic; Professor Dent has pointed out[1] his habit, especially in early works, of 'thinking upwards from the bass rather than downwards from the melody' and he often begins with one modification or another of some favourite bass convention. A striking illustration of this method of composition is offered by the openings of the early Sonatas, Op. 1, Nos. 8 and 9, for oboe and flute respectively, of which the first four bars are composed on exactly the same bass—and indeed with partly identical melodies—though the movements as wholes take totally different courses, conditioned by the different, not the common, factors in the opening melodies. The melody of No. 8 is here transposed a semitone down to facilitate comparison:

Ex. 105

Variants of the bass gambit are numerous; I quote another from *Alcina* ('Dì, cor mio'):

Ex. 106

[1] See p. 25.

And one of the Aylesford pieces for harpsichord, the Sonata, No. 32, enables us to watch Handel in the middle of the process of composing on this same bass. Mr. Lam has discussed on pp. 210–11 alternative forms, in B flat, of a movement, the opening of which appears thus in the early Violin Concerto or 'Sonata' (H.-G., Vol. 21, p. 108; Seiffert, No. 11):

Ex. 107

The keyboard Sonata shows this transferred to the minor, with the bass reduced to its skeleton form:

Ex. 108

From this, Handel derives the apparently new melody of the Trio Sonata, Op. 2, No. 1:

Ex. 109

The B flat version of Ex. 107 in the Oboe Concerto, and the A major version which opens the Trio Sonata, Op. 5, No. 1, and was used again in 'I will magnify Thee' (fifth Chandos Anthem and *Belshazzar*), all adopt the dotted form of the melody on the third beat of bar 1. From Handel's preference for the A major form in the vocal works, I would argue against Chrysander[1] and Mr. Lam that Op. 5, No. 1, is *later* than the Oboe Concerto.

Some of the cases cited earlier may suggest that Handel differentiated very little between vocal and instrumental music. In essence, that is true enough. Yet he actually distinguishes between vocal and

[1] *G. F. Händel*, Vol. III, p. 155.

instrumental styles even more clearly than Bach. A fugue subject may be used both instrumentally and vocally but it will be used quite differently, as in the cases just mentioned or the one cited by Mr. Herbage and Mr. Horton in *Solomon*.[1] The opening of the chorus 'Il Nume vincitor' in *La Resurrezione* will reappear in the *Water Music* but it will there generate quite a different continuation, just as the tinier motive quoted in Exs. 101 and 102 takes quite different courses in opera aria and instrumental piece. The masque *Terpsicore*[2] contains several examples of vocal pieces followed or preceded by dances based on the same material but treated in instrumental style: Apollo's 'Hai tanti rapido, leggiero il pie', the little duet 'Col tuo piede', the chorus 'Replicati al ballo il canto'. One might put it that the normal relationship between vocal and instrumental movements in Handel is that between 'O grant a leader' from the first chorus of *Deborah* and the first movement of the Oboe Concerto, Op. 3, No. 3 (fresh working of the same material) than that between 'And the glory of the Lord' and the second movement of the B flat Concerto *a due cori*[3] (simple transference to instruments in a new key and with a 14-bar cut). The next movement of this same B flat Concerto, based on 'See, from his post' in *Belshazzar*—both the concertos *a due cori* are pastiches of popular oratorio choruses, it will be remembered—reverts to Handel's more usual practice: the substance of the music is completely retained, uncut, but given an instrumental dress—*transcribed* in the modern sense.[4]

Handel's revisions always repay the closest study, whether of his own or of borrowed material, whether necessitated by transference of the musical substance to another medium or simply by the desire for finer technical finish. There is often much to be learned from the cases of transference such as that last mentioned or the transformation of 'Cease, ruler of the day' in *Hercules* (1744) into the great final chorus ('O love divine') of *Theodora* (1749): the overlap obliterating the former caesura at the end of the ritornello, the general tightening up and closer weaving of the whole texture. Again, in the largo third movement of one version of the Flute Sonata, Op. 1, No. 1[5] and the opening movement of the Violin Sonata, Op. 1, No. 13 (see Ex. 91), we have a parallel case to the instances (already mentioned) of

---

[1] See pp. 122 and 255.

[2] H.–G., Vol. 84.

[3] H.–G., Vol. 47, p. 130; No. 27 of Seiffert's 'practical edition'.

[4] See Chrysander's study, 'Händels Instrumentalkompositionen für grosses Orchester', in *Vierteljahrsschrift für Musikwissenschaft*, Jg. 3, particularly pp. 183–5.

[5] H.–G., Vol. 27, p. 4.

composition on identical basses and to those discussed by Mr. Lam on p. 211: movements beginning identically but then taking quite different courses. But in this case one can say with confidence that the differences—only partially conditioned by the change of instrument—are much later revisions; the substantially identical parts are given a finer polish in the violin version, and what follows in the violin version—though longer—is far more shapely, far more consequent and better knit. There is a similar difference between the superb D minor piece in the *Water Music*, described by Mr. Lam on p. 220, and the straggling larghetto of the Oboe Sonata, Op. 1, No. 6, which Handel evolved from the same opening phrase. The improvising type of composer, like Handel—or, to take a very different character, Chopin—is always needing to revise what he has already 'finished'; he does at the end what the more careful planner, the Beethoven type, does in the early, sketch stage. But, as Professor Lewis has shown,[1] the second thoughts are not always in every respect the better, and the improviser sometimes goes back to his original conception: sometimes, what appears to be revision is only alternative improvisation. When Handel fails to revise, we are sometimes left with careless workmanship. It is tempting to suggest that his finest music came when his natural, easy, Mediterraneanized inspiration and his solid German technique were in perfect equilibrium, as in his own favourite chorus from *Theodora*, 'He saw the lovely youth'. Yet the broad, slapdash element in Handel's workmanship is not unconnected with what one may call 'theatrical perspective'. Work for the theatre demands just this kind of treatment; elaborate workmanship is thrown away; Handel's music always sounds far better than it bears inspection.

The relationship of dramatic and non-dramatic elements in Handel's music is similar to that between vocal and instrumental; there is much common ground but there are many vital differences. There can be little question that Handel was essentially a dramatic composer, and the present book therefore begins its consideration of the music with a chapter on the operas; Mr. Herbage has shown how the same dramatic principle of building up a character in a succession of arias, each crystallizing one of his typical moods or states of mind, often carefully organized in key,[2] is employed in the

[1] See Exs. 65 and 66.

[2] Beginning with Leichtentritt, recent German writers on Handel have devoted much study to the tonal organization of the operas, in particular; sometimes they seem to prove too much, but Handel's key-plans were clearly far from haphazard.

oratorios. But the arias of opera and oratorio are not all to be claimed as dramatic on the ground that each embodies a dramatic emotion, with or without a modifying or contrasting shade; there are the numerous 'simile' arias which, as Professor Dent has pointed out, stand in the way of the action instead of clinching it. On the other hand, a good many instrumental movements which we think of as 'absolute' music were possibly conceived as expressions of an *Affekt*, stylized expressions of an emotion; Handel's friend Mattheson in *Das forschende Orchestre* (1721) expressed the view that instrumental music had the power to 'stir all the emotions by sounds alone (without the addition of any words or verses)', and went on in *Der vollkommene Capellmeister* (1739) to examine the emotional implications of the various types of dance and their characteristic rhythms. Here again Bruno Flögel, in his thorough study of the types of Handel's opera arias, has shown how the andante variety of minuet-aria is connected with the *affetto amoroso*;[1] we must not be so absurd as to equate all Handel's andante minuets with amorous expression, yet the connexion ought to be borne in mind.

Just as Handel is in instrumental music tempted farthest from the common ground of his general style by the sense of his hands on a keyboard, evoking a certain amount of pure keyboard figuration, he is roused to harmonic adventure when the dramatic element in opera or oratorio rises above the simple alternation of recitative-dialogue and *Affekt*-laden aria. And that happens a good deal oftener than is supposed by those who still believe that Handel's operas were 'concerts in costume'; the least known of all the aspects of his work is that remarkable series of scenas —not so called, though that is what they are: mixtures of *secco* and accompanied recitative, *arioso* and aria—already foreshadowed in Fernando's 'Verhängnis, willst du denn nur mich Verlass'nen fallen' in *Almira* (1705), and reaching outstanding heights in Bajazet's death scene in *Tamerlano*, the mad scene in *Orlando*, and Dejanira's 'Where shall I fly?' in *Hercules*. Professor Dent has spoken[2] of Handel's 'sudden flashes' of unexpected modulation, and the accompanied recitatives—not only in Handel but in his operatic rivals—are always liable to change key dramatically and to develop unusually intense harmonies. (Jephtha's 'Deeper, and deeper still' is, of course, a classic instance.) The cantata *O Numi eterni* contains outstanding early examples and

---

[1] 'Studien zur Arientechnik in den Opern Händels' in *Händel-Jahrbuch*, Jg. 2, 1929, p. 81.
[2] See p. 34.

Hercules is specially marked by harmonically striking passages (e.g.
'No longer, Fate' in Act I, and the end of 'Tyrants now no more shall
dread' in Act III).

Again, as Mr. Lam has remarked, Handel's handling of the
orchestra is far more varied in the operas and the more operatic
oratorios than anywhere else. It ranges from the most perfunctory
Italian doubling of the voice-part by violins, without even a continuo
bass, as in Poppea's famous 'Bel piacere' in *Agrippina*[1]—though in
this case the bare unison seems to heighten the kittenish capricious-
ness of the melody:

Ex. 110

Bel pia - ce - re 'e go - de - re fi - do a - mor
Ques-to fà con - tento il cor, ques- to fa con-
-tento il cor, fà con - tento il cor

to the sumptuous and imaginative combinations which accompany
Cleopatra's seduction scene in the second act of *Giulio Cesare*
(double orchestra, including harp and theorbo in one of them) and
the other Cleopatra's 'Hark! He strikes the golden lyre' in *Alexander
Balus* (with flute, harp, mandoline, and organ).

Despite his undeniable tendency to conform to convention, to
types and patterns, Handel is unconventional—and brilliantly
unconventional—far more often than is popularly supposed. Of all
the great masters, he is the one at present in most danger of petri-
faction into a monument: partly, of course, because of the monumental quality that is such an obvious but splendid feature of much
of his work, of many nobly polished, serene arias as well as of
massive double choruses and the like. But the unconventionalities
of melody, harmony, rhythm, and scoring that leap out at every
period of Handel's career reveal the constant liveliness of his mind.
It is really our reverence for Handel that is in danger of petri-
faction, not Handel's art.

[1] Handel later gave it, in A major, to Almirena in the third act of *Rinaldo*.

CATALOGUE OF WORKS

By

William C. Smith

INTRODUCTION

At the time of Handel's death he had in his possession the original autograph manuscripts of most of his works, fair copies of many of them, and a large number of the early printed editions. From the time he left his native land, during his stay in Italy, and throughout his life in England, he was methodical enough to preserve his manuscripts or to see that they were looked after by Johann C. Schmidt and his son, John Christopher Smith, or others. All this material passed to J. C. Smith and eventually, some time before 1774, Smith presented the autograph manuscripts and some of the copies to His Majesty King George III. This fine collection is now housed in the Department of Printed Books, British Museum, as part of the King's Music Library, which was deposited there on permanent loan by His Majesty King George V in 1911.

The King's Music Library, formed by King George III and Queen Charlotte, was considerably added to by purchases and presentations during the following reigns, and on the Handel side was enriched by the accession of a number of manuscripts formerly owned by Robert Smith of St. Paul's Church Yard, whose collection was sold in May 1813; by manuscripts from the Aylesford collection (sold in 1918) presented by W. Barclay Squire, which include much material not existing elsewhere; and by four valuable manuscript indexes and catalogues of Handel's works, which formerly belonged to Victor Schœlcher and Julian Marshall, and were presented by Mrs. R. Carter and Miss Marshall. A number of copies of printed editions of Handel's works, including a complete set of the Händel-Gesellschaft edition with the prefaces and introductions in English, have been added to the King's Music Library from time to time. The student has therefore this unrivalled collection of the composer's works available for study in one place—and few, if any, of the other great masters have been so fortunately treated by posterity.

Besides the works in the King's Music Library, the British Museum contains much Handel material in its general collections. The Department of Printed Books—Music Section—is rich in early editions, and includes a vast amount of more modern publications, British and foreign, while the general library has many of the early libretti, an important field for the research worker. The Department of Manuscripts has many miscellaneous items containing music by Handel (including some autographs) which have been gathered together over many years from different sources, among them the Granville collection of manuscript copies, purchased in 1915, and miscellaneous manuscripts from the Royal College of Music—the printed music of the College still being retained at South Kensington.

The Fitzwilliam Museum, Cambridge, has a number of very valuable autograph manuscripts, fragments and sketches, which supplement those in the King's Music Library. In 1902 the Fitzwilliam acquired the H. Barrett Lennard collection of early manuscript copies. The National Library of Scotland possesses the fine collection of early editions formerly owned by Julian Marshall and the late Earl Balfour. The Rowe Music Library, King's College, Cambridge, has much material, including the collection made by A. H. Mann and enriched by the many gifts of early editions.

Victor Schœlcher's comprehensive collection of early printed editions and much Handel literature is in the Conservatoire de Musique, Paris; and it is of interest to record that Schœlcher's manuscript catalogue of the collection, which was not available outside the Conservatoire, has been recently photographed, translated and reproduced in typescript at the expense of, and through the arduous personal efforts of, James S. Hall, O.B.E., F.R.C.S., of Walmer, who has enriched my collection with a complete copy of this monumental work in four volumes.

Schœlcher's collection of Handel manuscripts (mostly contemporary copies, some with the composer's autograph additions) which passed from J. C. Smith by will to Lady Rivers, his step-daughter, and then to Kerslake, a Bristol bookseller, was sold to Friedrich Chrysander prior to 1885 and subsequently purchased by a public fund for the State and University Library of Hamburg, where the collection is still.

Many other public libraries at home and abroad have Handel collections, small or large, which cannot be listed here; and the fine private collections of the Earl of Malmesbury, Sir Newman Flower, Gerald Coke and others have not been generally drawn upon in the preparation of this catalogue.

Handel, who must have kept his copyists busy, seems to have made presents of copies of his works to some of his friends, or allowed them to have copies made. Charles Jennens, the compiler of the words of 'Messiah', was an early subscriber to the printed editions, and thus started building up his collection, which also included a large number of manuscript copies. When he died in 1773, all his pictures, prints, drawings, models, &c., went to Mr. Curzon (Assheton Curzon) a relative by marriage, and passed again by marriage into the family of Earl Howe; but Jennens left his music books with his musical instruments to another relative, Heneage, Third Earl of Aylesford. Jennens was also related by marriage to the family of Sir Clement Fisher, whose descendants, Sir Edward Littleton and his brother Fisher Littleton, were enthusiastic collectors of Handeliana. The Littleton collection was sold in London a few years ago, part of it going to the U.S.A., and I have some items from it.

The Malmesbury, the Shaftesbury and the Granville collections all owed their existence to Handel's friendship and associations with the founders of them. The Aylesford collection was dispersed, the principal sale taking place in May 1918, much of the collection being subsequently acquired by Sir Newman Flower, some manuscripts going to the Library of Congress, Washington, and a few as already mentioned being purchased by W. Barclay Squire.

Apart from these well known sources and collections, from time to time in the last century and a half, a considerable number of Handel manuscripts (including some autographs) have passed through the London sale rooms, and although I have notes of the particulars of many of these, not until an exhaustive search is made and a record prepared, shall we know the full story of how widely spread was the interest in the composer's works, and in some cases, what those works really included.

Similarly, with regard to the bibliography of the early printed editions, the information is still incomplete, as copies are frequently turning up differing from existing known editions, that supplement what we know, not only of the publication of the works, but also of who took part in them, and what changes Handel made in the music, from time to time, to suit the circumstances and available resources at the moment—a wide and complicated problem outside the scope of the present work.

The following catalogue has been prepared to provide as simply as possible the essential facts about the composition, performance and publication of each item. It includes as far as possible, every known genuine work, with the exception of numerous minor works, extracts, fragments and unidentified items scattered about in public and private collections in various parts of the world, and also, no doubt, a number of minor publications published abroad that have escaped notice. As a rule only original works are included, and no information is given of the various collections, adaptations and arrangements published by Walsh and others, although some items (e.g. 'The Minuet Songs') have been inserted which are not original works in the form given; and a few doubtful items have been included for one reason or another. Some more recently published works attributed to Handel, have been excluded because they are considered to be extremely doubtful and in some cases definitely spurious. The many marches, songs, dance tunes, &c., appearing in ballad operas, pasticcios and song books, &c., of the eighteenth century have also been ignored.

The detail under each work has been set out in this order, as far as it can be applied:—

Title—librettist or author of words—date, and place of production, or composition—location of the autograph, or parts of such—location of important manuscript copies—publisher, with short title in brackets, and date of the first authentic edition in any form, followed by similar details of more complete or important editions (this is necessary in many cases, particularly of the oratorios and operas, of which the first issues only contained as a rule the overture, songs, &c.)—references to Arnold's collected edition—references to the Händel-Gesellschaft edition.

It must be borne in mind that Walsh, father and son, both published as J. or John Walsh, so that works after the death of the father, on March 13 1736, can be considered as having been issued by the son. As this firm frequently used the same title-page for different editions of a work, the brief titles given are not enough to enable one to determine in many cases whether a particular copy is of the first edition.

In most cases, only the pressmark of a manuscript is given in the catalogue, as details of the folios or pages can be obtained from the published catalogues of the collections concerned, but sometimes to avoid confusion these details have been given.

Printed catalogues are available of the King's Music Library, the

Department of Printed Books and the Department of Manuscripts, British Museum, the Fitzwilliam Museum, the Royal College of Music, printed music—a manuscript catalogue of the MSS. of the R.C.M. being available in the Department of Manuscripts, British Museum. The following abbreviations are used: B.M. (British Museum); R.M. (King's Music Library); R.C.M. (Royal College of Music); B.M. Add. MSS. (Manuscripts in the Department of Manuscripts); Eg. (Egerton MSS., British Museum Department of Manuscripts, including the Granville collection); Fitzwilliam works included in the printed catalogue by J. A. Fuller-Maitland and A. H. Mann, appear as 'Fitzwilliam'; the Barrett Lennard collection in the Fitzwilliam as Fitzwilliam (L.); Hamburg (the Schœlcher collection in the State and University Library); H.G. (Händel-Gesellschaft edition); fr., used in some cases, for part or parts of a work.

It has not been possible to give the many sources of information from which the material has been gathered, or to mention the numerous friends who have brought things to my notice over many years spent in Handelian research; but it is necessary to record the willing help obtained from the authorities of the Fitzwilliam Museum, the National Library of Scotland, the Rowe Music Library, Cambridge, the Bodleian Library, the State and University Library, Hamburg, my many former colleagues at the British Museum, and my very good friend James C. Hall, O.B.E., F.R.C.S., of Walmer, whose indefatigable zeal has brought much information to my notice, and provided me with photostats of many rare works in his collection, besides a copy of the Schœlcher catalogue previously referred to.

As much of the foundation work for this list was originally prepared for, and will appear in, the new edition of 'Grove's Dictionary of Music and Musicians', under the editorship of Eric Blom, I should like to thank Messrs. Macmillan & Co. and Mr. Blom for kindly allowing me to present much of the same material in its new form.

The catalogue as presented must of necessity be incomplete, and probably in some cases inaccurate, but no statements have been made without due consideration of all the available evidence.

ORATORIOS AND PASSION MUSIC

Alexander Balus. Thomas Morell. Covent Garden, 23 Mar. 1748. *Auto.* R.M.20.d.3; Fitzwilliam, *fr. MS. copies*: R.M.18.f.2; Fitzwilliam (L.); Hamburg. J. Walsh ('Songs in Alexander Balus'—Issued in two parts) 19 Apr. 1748, &c. J. Walsh ('Alexander Balus an Oratorio'—Overture, Songs, &c., from the three acts) 5 May 1748, when Acts II and III were also advertised as available. H. Wright ('Alexander Balus An Oratorio in Score') 10 Feb. 1787 (ready in the summer). Arnold, 160-164, *c.* 1795. H.G. 33.

Athalia. Samuel Humphreys, based on Racine. Oxford Theatre (Sheldonian), 10 July 1733. *Auto.* R.M.20.h.1; R.M.20.f.12, *fr.*; Fitzwilliam, *fr. MS copies*: R.M.18.d.4; R.M.18.c.6,8; Eg. 2933 (Granville); Fitzwilliam (L.); Hamburg. J. Walsh ('The Most Celebrated Songs') *c.* 1735. H. Wright ('Athalia'—Full Score) 10 Feb. 1787 (ready in the summer), published? no copy traced. Harrison & Co. ('The Overture and Songs . . . Corrected by Dr. Arnold') 1787. Arnold, 1-4, 1787. H.G. 5.

Belshazzar. Charles Jennens. King's Theatre, 27 Mar. 1745. *Auto.*
R.M.20.d.10; R.M.20.f.12, *fr.*; Fitzwilliam, *fr. MS. copies*: R.M.18.e.5;
R.M.19.a.2, *fr.*; R.M.19.e.8, *fr.*; Fitzwilliam (L.); Hamburg. J. Walsh
('Belshazzar an Oratorio'—Overture, Songs, &c.) 18 May 1745. Wright &
Co. ('Belshazzar. An Oratorio, in Score') 31 Mar. 1784. Arnold, 68-72,
1790. H.G. 19.
Deborah. Samuel Humphreys. King's Theatre, 17 Mar. 1733. *Auto.*
R.M.20.h.2; R.M.20.f.12, *fr. MS. copies*: R.M.18.d.3; B.M. Add. MSS.
31870, 34006; Eg. 2932 (Granville); Fitzwilliam (L.); Hamburg. J. Walsh
('The Most Celebrated Songs in . . . Deborah') *c.* 1735, and later issues, with
variations in contents. J. Walsh ('Deborah an Oratorio'—From the previous
issues of the Songs, 21 numbers, followed by 'Additional Airs, in ye late
Oratorios', 9 numbers) *c.* 1751 or later. Wright & Co. ('Deborah, An
Oratorio in Score') 31 Mar. 1784 (in a month). Arnold, 140-146, *c.* 1794-
1795. H.G. 29.
Esther. Probably by Alexander Pope assisted by John Arbuthnot, based
on Racine's 'Esther', with additional text by Samuel Humphreys. First
produced at Cannons, near Edgware for the Duke of Chandos, as 'Haman
and Mordecai' a masque, *c.* 1720. (*See* Operas, &c.) Revived under the
direction of Bernard Gates for the Philharmonic Society, as 'Esther an Oratorio
or Sacred Drama' at the Crown and Anchor Tavern in the Strand, 23 Feb.
1732, the children of the Chapel Royal and some other choristers from the
Choirs of the Chapel Royal and Westminster Abbey taking part, the instrumentalists principally members of the Philharmonic Society. (A contemporary
manuscript of the score of this performance, which was based on the original
production, with details of place and those taking part is in the William C.
Smith collection.) Performed, presumably, without Handel's authority, as
'Esther an Oratorio or Sacred Drama . . . the words by Mr. Pope'—'At the
Great Room in Villars-street, York Buildings,' 20 Apr. 1732, details and names
of those taking part not known. Given under Handel's direction, King's
Theatre, 2 May 1732, with the additional words by Humphreys and additional
music. 'The London Magazine', May 1732 gives an abbreviated libretto of
'Esther . . . As it is now acted at the Theatre Royal in the Haymarket with vast
applause'—a statement for which there appears to be no evidence elsewhere.
Auto. R.M.20.e.7; R.M. 20.g.9, *fr.*; Fitzwilliam, *fr. MS. copies*: R.M.18.d.2;
R.M.18.d.1; R.M.19.g.8; R.M.19.b.2 (Vocal Parts); R.M.18.c.5-7, *fr.*; R.M.
19.a.1; R.M.19.d.11; R.M.19.e.10 (String Parts); B.M. Add. MSS. 31560; Eg.
2931 (Granville); William C. Smith collection; Fitzwilliam (L.); Hamburg. J.
'Walsh ('The Most Celebrated Songs in . . . Queen Esther') 25 Nov. 1732; J.
Walsh ('Esther, an Oratorio'—A further issue of the Overture, Songs, &c.)
c. 1751. Wright & Co. ('Esther An Oratorio in Score') 21 April 1783. Arnold,
135-139, *c.* 1794. H.G. 41.
Israel in Egypt. Compiled from the Bible and Prayer Book version of the
Psalms. King's Theatre, 4 Apr. 1739. *Auto.* R.M.20.h.3; Fitzwilliam, *fr.*
(Songs interpolated in Israel in Egypt). *MS copies*: R.M.18.d.7; B.M. Add.
MSS. 5320; Eg. 2936 (Granville); Fitzwilliam (L.); Hamburg. J. Walsh,
'Handel's Songs Selected from His Latest Oratorios', 1748-59, includes 6
numbers from 'Israel in Egypt' and one wrongly attributed to that oratorio;
Walsh also published one number printed at the end of 'The Occasional

Oratorio', *c.* 1748 or later; and one in 'A 2d Grand Collection of Celebrated English Songs Introduced in the late Oratorios', 1763. William Randall ('Israel in Egypt An Oratorio, in Score') 3 Sept. 1771. Harrison & Co. ('Israel in Egypt'—Vocal Score) *c.* 1785. Arnold, 92-98, *c.* 1791. H.G. 16.

Jephtha. Thomas Morell. Covent Garden, 20 Feb. 1752. *Auto.* R.M. 20.e.9 (Published in facsimile, edited by F. Chrysander, Strumper & Co., Hamburg, 1885); R.M.20.g.14, *fr.*; Fitzwilliam, *fr. MS. copies*: R.M.18.f.7; B.M. Add. MSS. 31570; Fitzwilliam (L.); Hamburg. J. Walsh ('Jephtha An Oratorio'—Overture, Songs, &c.) 4 Apr. 1752. William Randall ('Jephtha an Oratorio, In Score') 5 Apr. 1770. Arnold, 116-121, *c.* 1792. H.G. 44.

Joseph and his Brethren. James Miller. Covent Garden, 2 Mar. 1744. *Auto.* R.M.20.e.10; Fitzwilliam, *fr. MS. copies*: R.M.18.e.8; R.M.19.a.2, *fr.*; Eg. 2939 (Granville); Rowe Music Library, Cambridge; Fitzwilliam (L.); Hamburg. J. Walsh ('Joseph and his Brethren'—Symphonies, Songs, &c.; issued in 2 parts) 4 May, 19 May 1744; complete, 24 May 1744. H. Wright ('Joseph An Oratorio in Score') 25 June 1785 (shortly will be printed; issued *c.* 1786). Arnold, 107-111, *c.* 1792. H.G. 42.

Joshua. Thomas Morell. Covent Garden, 9 Mar. 1748. *Auto.* R.M.20.e. 11; R.M.20.g.12, *fr.*; R.M.20.h.4, *fr.*; Fitzwilliam *fr. MS. copies*: R.M.18.f.3; Fitzwilliam (L.); Hamburg. J. Walsh ('Joshua an Oratorio'—Introduction, March, Songs, &c.) 2 Apr. 1748. William Randall ('Joshua an Oratorio in Score') 5 May 1774. Arnold, 56-60, *c.* 1789. H.G. 17.

Judas Maccabæus. Thomas Morell. Covent Garden, 1 Apr. 1747. *Auto.* R.M.20.e.12; Fitzwilliam, *fr. MS. copies*: R.M.18.f.1; R.M.18.f.10; Fitzwilliam (L.); Hamburg. J. Walsh ('Judas Macchabæus an Oratorio'— Overture, Songs, &c.) 30 Apr. 1747. William Randall ('Judas Macchabæus An Oratorio, in Score') 16 Jan. 1769. Arnold, 39-43, 1789. H.G. 22.

Messiah. Charles Jennens, compiled and adapted from the Bible and Prayer Book. Music Hall, Fishamble Street, Dublin, 13 Apr. 1742; public rehearsal, 8 Apr. *Auto.* R.M.20.f.2 (Published in facsimile: Sacred Harmonic Society, 1868; Edited by F. Chrysander, Strumper & Co., Hamburg, 1892.); R.M.20.g.6. *fr.*; Fitzwilliam, *fr. MS. copies*: St. Michael's College, Tenbury (Known as the Dublin Score, used as a conducting copy, considered to be mainly in the hand of J. C. Smith the elder, with additions and corrections by the composer); R.M.18.b.10; R.M.18.e.2; R.M.19.d.1, *fr.*; R.M.19.a.2, *fr.*; B.M. Add. MSS. 5062 (Transcribed by Henry Needler); Eg. 2937 (Granville); B.M. Add. MSS. 39774; Otto Goldschmidt copy (Rosenbach Company, Philadelphia, 1946); Fitzwilliam (L.); Hamburg; Foundling Hospital (which also possesses an early set of orchestral parts); Rowe Music Library, Cambridge. Records exist of a number of other manuscript copies of the score, of the 'Songs in Messiah', and of other extracts and fragments, in the British Museum and elsewhere. J. Walsh ('Songs in Messiah') *c.* 1749 or later. Randall and Abell ('Messiah An Oratorio in Score') 4 July 1767 (*Public Advertiser*—Ready to deliver to the subscribers ... 7th instant); 23 July (now ready, &c.); 3 August (now delivering to the subscribers). Arnold, 9-13, 1787-1788. H.G. 45.

Occasional Oratorio. Compiled from Milton's 'Psalms', Spenser, &c. perhaps by Thomas Morell. Covent Garden, 14 Feb 1746. *Auto.* R.M. 20.f.3; R.M.20.h.5, *fr.*; R.M.20.f.12, *fr.*; Fitzwilliam, *fr. MS. copies*:

R.M.18.e.7; Hamburg. J. Walsh ('The Occasional Oratorio'—Overture, Songs, &c.) 3 Apr. 1746. Wright & Co. ('The Occasional Oratorio in Score') 31 Mar. 1784 (in a month; probably issued in June). Arnold, 99-105, c. 1791. H.G. 43.

Passion nach dem Evang. Johannes. (Das Leiden und Sterben Jesu Christi in gebundener Rede als Oratorium.) From the Gospel of St. John, with arias by Christian Heinrich Postel. Hamburg, Holy Week, 1704. *MS.* copy: Pölchau Collection, Berlin (Liepmannsohn catalogues, 139 (1899), No. 197; 185, No. 512). H.G. 9.

Passion (Brockes—'Der für die Sünden der Welt gemarterte und sterbende Jesus aus den vier Evangelisten in gebundener Rede vorgestellet'). Barthold Heinrich Brockes. Hamburg? *c.* 1716. *Auto.* R.M.20.g.13, *fr. MS. copies:* R.M.19.g.3; R.M.19.d.3; B.M. Add. MSS. 39571; Pölchau Collection, Berlin; J. S. Bach copy, Berlin; Vienna (? copy presented by Queen Charlotte, wife of George III, to Haydn); Liepmannsohn catalogue 65 (1888) No. 227; Chrysander copy, 1724; Aylesford collection (sale catalogue, 1918, No. 242); Pitti Palace, Florence. H.G. 15.

La Resurrezione. Carlo Sigismondo Capece. Rome, Palazzo Bonelli, 8 Apr. 1708. *Auto.* R.M.20.f.5. *MS. copies:* R.M.19.d.4; Full Score (? in handwriting of J. C. Smith, the younger, with pencilled additions by Handel) Sotheby, 24 July 1916, and Ellis, sale catalogues, Nos. 251 and 277. Not published in Handel's lifetime; but one number, 'Hò un non sò che nel cor', was used by Handel in 'Agrippina', inserted in Alessandro Scarlatti's 'Pirro e Demetrio' (London, 1710-11), and was published as a popular song with various sets of English words, 1711, &c. Arnold, 169-171, *c.* 1796. H.G. 39.

Samson. Newburgh Hamilton, based on Milton's 'Samson Agonistes', 'Hymn on the Nativity', 'At a Solemn Music', &c. Covent Garden, 18 Feb. 1743. *Auto.* R.M.20.f.6; Fitzwilliam, *fr. MS. copies:* R.M.18.e.3; B.M. Add. MSS. 37323-5; Eg. 2938 (Granville); Rowe Music Library, Cambridge; Fitzwilliam (L.); Hamburg. J. Walsh ('Samson an Oratorio'—Overture, Songs, &c., issued in three parts as 'Songs in the Oratorio') 19 Mar., 2 Apr., 9 Apr. 1743. J. Walsh ('Samson an Oratorio'—The complete work) *c.* Sept. 1763. Arnold, 49-54, 1789. H.G. 10.

Saul. Charles Jennens. King's Theatre, 16 Jan. 1739. *Auto.* R.M.20.g.3; R.M.20.g.14, *fr.;* Fitzwilliam, *fr. MS. copies:* R.M.18.d.9; R.M.18.c.11, *fr.;* B.M. Add. MSS. 5319; Eg. 2935 (Granville); Fitzwilliam (L.); Hamburg. J. Walsh ('The Most Celebrated Songs', &c.—Two collections) 12 Feb., 17 Mar. 1739; (In one volume) 19 Mar. 1739. J. Walsh ('Saul an Oratorio'—A fuller edition of the Overture, Songs, &c.) *c.* 1748 or later. William Randall ('Saul An Oratorio in Score') 15 May 1773. Arnold, 111-116, *c.* 1792. H.G. 13.

Solomon. Thomas Morell? Covent Garden, 17 Mar. 1749. *Auto.* R.M. 20.h.4; R.M.20.f.12, *fr.;* Fitzwilliam, *fr. MS. copies:* R.M.18.f.5; R.M.18.b.5 (Act I); R.M.19.a.7, *fr.;* Fitzwilliam (L.); Hamburg. J. Walsh ('Solomon an Oratorio'—Overture, Songs, &c.) 17 Apr. 1749. Harrison & Co. ('Solomon an Oratorio'—Vocal Score) *c.* 1785. H. Wright ('Solomon An Oratorio in Score') 10 Feb. 1787 (ready in the course of the summer; probably not issued until 1789). Arnold, 85-92, *c.* 1790. H.G. 26.

Susanna. Librettist unknown. Covent Garden, 10 Feb. 1749. *Auto.*

T

R.M.20.f.8; Fitzwilliam, *fr. MS. copies*: R.M.18.f.4; Fitzwilliam (L.); Hamburg. J. Walsh ('Susanna an Oratorio'—Overture, Songs, &c.) 8 Mar. 1749. Wright & Co. ('Susanna. An Oratorio in Score') 31 Mar. 1784. Arnold, 131-135, *c.* 1793. H.G. 1.
Theodora. Thomas Morell. Covent Garden, 16 Mar. 1750. *Auto.* R.M.20.f.9. *MS. copies*: R.M.18.f.6; Fitzwilliam (L.); Hamburg. J. Walsh ('Theodora An Oratorio'—Overture, Songs, &c.) 20 June 1751. Harrison & Co. ('Theodora An Oratorio'—Vocal Score) *c.* 1785. H. Wright ('Theodora An Oratorio in Score') 10 Feb. 1787 (ready in the course of the summer). Arnold, 5-8, 1787. H.G. 8.
Il Trionfo del Tempo e del Disinganno. Cardinal Benedetto Pamfili. Rome, Palace of Cardinal Ottoboni, 1708. Recast for performances in London, Covent Garden, 23 Mar. 1737, as 'Il Trionfo del Tempo e della Verità'. *Auto.* R.M.20.f.10 (1737 version, incomplete); Fitzwilliam, *fr.* (1708, 1737 and 1757 versions). *MS. copies*: R.M.19.d.9 (1708 version, partly autograph); R.M.19.f.1 (Full score, 1737 version); R.M.18.e.5 (Three separate parts, 1737 version); R.M.18.c.8 (Full Score, 1737 and 1757 versions); R.M. 18.c.11 (Selection, 1737 version); B.M. Add. MSS. 31568 (1737 version); Eg. 2934 (Granville); Fitzwilliam (L.); Hamburg. No contemporary editions of the 1708 and 1737 versions, except one or two editions of an excerpt, 'Lascia la spina' as a song, 'The Address to Silvia', *c.* 1740. For details of the English version, 1757, *see* 'The Triumph of Time and Truth'. H.G. 24.
The Triumph of Time and Truth. Adapted and translated from the libretto of the preceding by Thomas Morell. Covent Garden, 11 Mar. 1757. *Auto.* R.M.20.f.10 (1737 version, used with English words for the 1757 version); R.M.20.a.3, *fr.*; Fitzwilliam, *fr. MS. copies*: R.M.18.f.8; R.M.18.c.8; Hamburg. J. Walsh ('The Triumph of Time and Truth An Oratorio'—Overture, Songs) 16 Apr. 1757. J. Walsh ('A Grand Collection of Celebrated English Songs Introduced in the late Oratorios'—Includes five numbers introduced into the 1758 version) 13 July, 1758. H. Wright ('The Triumph of Time and Truth—Complete Score) 10 Feb. 1787 (ready in the course of the summer; no copy traced). Arnold, 165-169, *c.* 1795. H.G. 20. *See* also the preceding item.

MISCELLANEOUS SACRED MUSIC

Ach Herr, mich armen Sünder. Church Cantata. *c.* 1696 or later. Early 19th century MS. Franz Commer's collection, Berlin? Karl Winterfeld, 'Der evangelische Kirchengesang', 1843-47. Vol. III. p. 159 and musical examples, No. 51a and 51b. Max Seiffert, 'Organum'. Series I. No. 12. 1926? 6 *Allelujahs* (*Alleluja-Amens*) *for Soprano. c.* 1735-45. *Auto.* R.M.20.f.12. Others, Fitzwilliam. H.G. 38, pp.166-172.

ANTHEMS

Chandos Anthems. c. 1717-20. (H.G. 34-36.) No. 1. O be joyful in the Lord. No. 2. In the Lord put I my trust. No. 3. Have mercy upon me. No. 4 and 4a. O sing unto the Lord a new song. No. 5 and 5a. I will magnify thee. No. 6a-d. As pants the hart. No. 7. My song shall be alway. No. 8. O come let us sing unto the Lord. No. 9. O praise the Lord with one consent. No. 10. The Lord is my light. No 11a and 11b. Let God arise. From the Prayer Book and metrical versions of the Psalms. *Auto*. R.M.20.d.6; R.M.20.d.7; R.M.20.d.8; R.M.20.g.1,4,6,8,10,14; B.M. Add. MSS. 30308 (No. 6c); Fitzwilliam (No. 9, *fr.* No. 6). *MS. copies*: R.M.19.g.1; R.M.18.b.7; R.M.19.e.7; R.M.19.e.3 and R.M.19.b.4 ('Miserere'—adaptation of No. 3); B.M. Add. MSS. 29417-29426; 28968; 29998; 31557-59; 30309; Eg. 2910-13 (Granville); Fitzwilliam (L.); W. H. Cummings sale catalogue, 1917, No. 816 (Quaritch catalogue, No. 355, 1919, No. 168); Novello and Co. (A volume of 5 anthems presented by George III to Dr. Aylward); St. Michael's College, Tenbury. Birchall and Beardmore ('Anthems with Simphonies'—Only 'As pants the Hart' published, the plates of which, with modifications, were used for Arnold's edition, No. 78, Anthem VIII) 12 June 1783. Wright and Wilkinson ('The Complete Score of Ten Anthems', &c— Does not contain, 'O be joyful in the Lord' (H.G. No. 1) another version of the 'Utrecht Jubilate', and the order compared with H.G. is 8, 10, 4, 5, 2, 9, 3, 7, 6, 11b) 1783-1784. Arnold, 72-84, *c.* 1790 (The ten numbers in Wright and Wilkinson, but in a different order, with No. 11a of H.G. and 'O praise the Lord ye angels of his', which is not a Chandos Anthem— *See* separate entry). Arnold, 20, pp. 1-3 ('Symphony to the Jubilate'—Anthem, H.G. No. 1) 1788. H.G. 34, 35 and 36, pp. 219-247.

Coronation Anthems for George II. No. 1 Zadok the Priest. (I Kings I. 38-40.) No. 2. Let Thy hand be strengthened. (Ps. LXXXIX. 13, 14, adapted.) No. 3. The King shall rejoice. (Ps. XXI. 1, 3, 5, Prayer Book version.) No. 4. My heart is inditing. (Ps. XLV. 1, 10, 12, Prayer Book version; Is. XLIX. 23.) Westminster Abbey, 11 Oct. 1727; rehearsal, 6 Oct. *Auto.* R.M.20.h.5. *MS. copies*: B.M. Add. MSS. 31504, *fr.*; Fitzwilliam (No. 1 only); Fitzwilliam (L.); Hamburg. J. Walsh ('Handel's Celebrated Coronation Anthems in Score'—Nos. 1, 4 and 2 only) *c.* 1743 or earlier; J Walsh ('Handel's Celebrated Coronation Anthems, &c.'—Nos. 1, 4, 2 and 3) Feb. 1743 (No. 3 previously published at the end of the Funeral Anthem). Arnold, 157-159, *c.* 1795; 171-172, *c.* 1796. H. G. 14.

Dettingen Anthem. ('The King shall rejoice'.) Ps. XXI. 1, 5-7; XX. 5. Chapel Royal, St. James's, 27 Nov. 1743; rehearsal, Whitehall Chapel, 18 Nov. *Auto.* B.M. Add. MSS. 30308. *MS. copies*: B.M. Add. MSS. 30309; Hamburg. Arnold, 156-157, *c.* 1795. H.G. 36, pp. 111-153.

Foundling Hospital Anthem. ('Blessed are they that consider the poor.') Adapted from Ps. XLI. 1-3, and other scriptural passages. Foundling Hospital, 27 May 1749. *Auto.* (partly) Foundling Hospital; R.M.20.f.12, *fr.* *MS. copies*: R.M.19.e.8; Christ Church Cathedral Library, Dublin (a different setting); R.C.M. MSS. No. 245. H.G. 36. pp. 154-216.

Funeral Anthem for Queen Caroline. ('The Ways of Zion do mourn.') Lamentations I. 4, and other scriptural passages. Henry VII's Chapel, Westminster, 17 Dec. 1737. *Auto.* R.M.20.d.9 (with Italian words added); R.M. 20.g.3 ('Saul', f. 98v., words only). *MS. copies*: R.M.19.a.15; B.M. Add. MSS. 5061 (Needler copy); Eg. 2913 (Granville); Fitzwilliam (L.); Reid Library, Edinburgh ('Trauer-Motetten'—German text). J. Walsh ('The Anthem which was Perform'd in Westminster Abby at the Funeral of . . . Queen Caroline . . . Vol. II.') Feb. 1743 or earlier. (Also contained the Coronation Anthem, 'The King shall rejoice', which was omitted from the next edition a little later.) H. Wright ('When the ear heard him. A favourite Quartetto Perform'd at Westminster Abbey in Commemoration of Mr. Handel. Taken out of his Anthem Composed for the Funeral of . . . Queen Caroline') 25 June 1785. German adaptation of the Funeral Anthem ('Empfindungen am Grabe Jesu, ein Oratorium') Leipzig, 1804. Arnold, 155-156, c. 1795. H.G. 11.

O be joyful. See Chandos Anthems, No. 1.

O praise the Lord, ye angels of his. Ps. CIII. 20, 21, 11, 17; CXV. 12; CXLV. 21. Presumably the Anthem performed before King George I and his family at the Chapel Royal, St. James's, 5 Jan. 1724. Arnold (incorrectly as No. 12 of the Chandos Anthems) 83-84, c. 1790. H.G. 36, pp. 1-26.

Wedding Anthem for Princess Anne and William, Prince of Orange. ('This is the day which the Lord hath made'.) Ps. CXVIII. 24; Ps. XLV. 14, 15; Prov. XXXI. 25, &c. Chapel Royal, St. James's, 14 Mar. 1734. *Auto.* Fitzwilliam, *fr. MS. copy*: Hamburg (partly autograph). H.G. 36, pp. 27-79.

Wedding Anthem for Frederick, Prince of Wales and Princess Augusta of Saxe-Gotha. ('Sing unto God, ye kingdoms of the earth'.) Ps. LXVIII. 32; CVI. 47, 48; CXXVII. 3-5; CXXVIII. 1-4; XLV. 17, &c. Chapel Royal, St. James's, 27 Apr. 1736. *MS. copy*: R.M.19.g.1. Arnold, 153-154, c. 1795. Performed also for the marriage of George, Prince of Wales and Princess Caroline of Brunswick at the Chapel Royal, St. James's, 8 Apr. 1795. Reissued with a new title-page by Arnold, 153-154, 1795. H.G. 36, pp. 80-110.

Deutsche Arien. 9 German Sacred Songs for Soprano, Figured Bass and accompaniment of Violin, Flute or Oboe. c. 1729. Words by Barthold Heinrich Brockes. No. 1. 'Künft'ger Zeiten eitler Kummer'. No. 2 Aria —'Das zitternde Glänzen der spielenden Wellen'. No. 3. 'Süsser Blumen Ambra-Flocken'. No. 4. 'Süsse Stille, sanfte Quelle'. No. 5. 'Singe, Seele, Gott zum Preise'. No. 6. Aria—'Meine Seele hört im Sehen'. No. 7. 'Die ihr aus dunkeln Grüften'. No. 8. In den angenehmen Büschen. No. 9. Flammende Rose, Zierde der Erden'. *Auto.* R.M.20.f.13. Drei Masken Verlag, Munich, edited by Herman Roth, 1921. (*See* Rochus von Liliencron Festschrift, 1910.)

Dixit Dominus. Ps. CX. *Auto.* R.M.20.f.1 (Rome, April 1707). *MS. copies*: R.C.M. Nos. 246, 248 and 249. H.G. 38, pp. 53-126.

Gloria in excelsis. c. 1740. Doubtful. *Auto.* R.M.20.g.10.

Gloria Patri. See Nisi Dominus.

Hec est Regina virginum. Antifona for Canto Solo with accompaniments for Strings and Organ. Composed for the festival 'Madonna del Carmine', Rome, c. 1707-08. MS. from the Colonna Library, owned by Rev. E. Goddard (sale 1878) and Dr. W. H. Cummings (*See The Musical Antiquary*, Jan. 1912, pp. 116-117).

Three Hymns. Words by Charles Wesley. c. 1750. No. 1. O Love divine how sweet thou art. (Tune—Fitzwilliam.) No. 2. Rejoice the Lord is King. (Gopsall.) No. 3. Sinners obey the Gospel Word. (Cannons.) *Auto.* Fitzwilliam. *MS. copy*: T. Jones sale, Feb. 13-16, 1826. S. Wesley ('The Fitzwilliam Music never published. Three Hymns . . . transcribed by Samuel Wesley ... To be had of Mr. S. Wesley ... and at the Royal Harmonic Institution, Regent Street') 1826. Goulding and D'Almaine ('Three Hymns from the Fitzwilliam Library arranged in Score,' &c.) c. 1827.

Laudati pueri, in F major. Ps. CXII. *c.* 1702. *Auto.* R.M.20.h.7. H.G. 38, pp. 1-18.

Laudati pueri, in D major. Ps. CXII. *Auto.* R.M.20.f.1 (Rome, 8 July 1707). Cummings, complete set of parts, with oboe parts in C. (*See The Musical Antiquary*, Jan. 1912, pp. 116-117.) H.G. 38, pp. 19-52.

Lobe den Herrn meine Seele. Cantata for four voices and instruments. 1719. *MS. copy*: R.M.18.b.13 ('Possibly a copy of an early work or wrongly attributed to Handel.'—Squire).

Magnificat. Disputed. *MS. copy*: in Handel's hand, R.M.20.g.6. *c.* 1738; *MS. copies*: R.C.M. Nos. 185 and 186 ('Magnificat Del R^d. Sg^r. Erba'). Published by Chrysander as 'Magnificat von D. Erba', Leipzig, 1888.

Nisi Dominus (Ps. CXXVII.) *and Gloria Patri.* Completed, Rome, 13 July 1707. Written for the Festival of Madonna del Carmine? *Auto.* Nisi Dominus, lost; Gloria Patri (Puttick and Simpson sale catalogue, Jan. 29-30, 1858) lost in a fire at Clifton, 1860. *MS. copies*: Nisi Dominus, R.M.19.d.2; Eg. 2458. *MS. copy*: Gloria Patri (Rev. E. Goddard sale, 1878; W. H. Cummings; Marquis Tokugawa of Kishu, Japan; Nanki Music Library, Tokyo). Published, Tokyo, 1928. Another copy of the preceding, University Library, Münster, Westphalia. H.G. 38, pp. 127-135, Nisi Dominus. Gloria Patri, prepared for H.G. 49 by Chrysander, but not published by him. Nisi Dominus and Gloria, edited by T. W. Bourne, Novello, Ewer & Co., 1898. Gloria Patri, Novello, Ewer & Co., *c.* 1891.

Salve Regina, for Soprano Solo and String Orchestra. *c.* 1707-12. *Auto.* Staatsbibliothek, Berlin (from Landsberg Collection, Rome). *MS. copy:* Staatsbibliothek, Berlin. H.G. 38, pp. 136-143.

Seuiat tellus inter vigores. Motet for a Treble Voice, with symphonies and accompaniments for Oboes and Strings. Date? Probably for performance at the Church of Madonna di Monte Santo at Rome, for the festival of Madonna del Carmine. Eg. 2458 (MS. from the Colonna Library, owned by Rev. E. Goddard (sale 1878) and Dr. W. H. Cummings. *See The Musical Antiquary*, Jan. 1912. pp. 116-117).

Silete venti. Motet. *c.* 1707 or later. *Auto.* R.M.20.g.9 (with Italian words, 'Spira una aura', to the solo 'Surgant venti', as an additional song in a later alteration of the 1732 version of 'Esther'). *MS. copy.* R.M.18.c.5,*fr.* H.G. 38, pp. 144-165.

TE DEUMS

Utrecht Te Deum and Jubilate. St. Paul's Cathedral, 7 July 1713. *Auto.* R.M.20.g.5. *MS. copies*: R.M.18.f.9; R.M.19.a.14 ('Jubilate'); B.M. Add. MSS. 5323; Eg. 2914 (Granville); Fitzwilliam (L.). J. Walsh ('Te Deum et Jubilate, for voices and Instruments. Perform'd before the Sons of the Clergy at the Cathedral-Church of St. Paul') *c.* 1731. Arnold, 15-17, 1788. H.G. 31. *See also* Chandos Anthems, No. 1.

Te Deum in D major. c. 1714 or later. Probably intended for the Chapel Royal. Burney ('Commemoration', p. 45) says, 'composed for the arrival of the Queen Caroline'. *Auto.* R.M.20.g.4; Fitzwilliam, *fr.* *MS. copies*: R.M.19.e.2; Eg. 2914 (Granville); Fitzwilliam. (L.). Arnold, 13 ('A Short Te Deum in Score Composed for her late Majesty Queen Caroline in . . .

1737') 1788. There seems to be no evidence for Arnold's statement. H.G. 37, pp. 1-24.

Te Deum, in Bb major. (Chandos.) *c.* 1719. *Auto.* R.M.20.d.7. *MS. copies:* R.M.19.g.1; B.M. Add. MSS. 29416; Eg. 2914 (Granville); Fitzwilliam; Fitzwilliam (L.); Copy in the Malmesbury collection dated 1719. Arnold, 14-15 ('Te Deum in Score Composed for . . . the Duke of Chandos, in . . . 1719') 1788. H.G. 37, pp. 25-108.

Te Deum in A major. A shortened and modified version of the preceding, prepared for use at the Chapel Royal. *c.* 1720-27. May have been used in 1727 on the accession of George II. *Auto.* R.M.20.g.4. *MS. copies:* R.M. 19.g.1; B.M. Add. MSS. 29998; Fitzwilliam (L.) is reported to have included a copy, not now in the collection. Arnold, 20 ('Te Deum in Score Composed for . . . the Duke of Chandos in . . . 1720') 1788. H.G. 37, pp. 109-138.

Dettingen Te Deum. Chapel Royal, St. James's, 27 Nov. 1743; rehearsal, Whitehall Chapel, 18 Nov. 1743. *Auto.* R.M.20.h.6. *MS. copies:* R.M.18.f.9; R.M.19.a.13; B.M. Add. MSS. 27745 (Organ part); Fitzwilliam (L.). J. Walsh ('Handel's Grand Dettingen Te Deum in Score . . . as Perform'd at the Cathedral-Church of St. Paul. Vol. IV') 1763 or earlier. Arnold, 17-19, 1788. H.G. 25.

OPERAS, PASTICCIOS[1] AND OTHER STAGE MUSIC

Admeto. Nicola F. Haym or Paolo B. Rolli, from the libretto, 'L'Antigona delusa da Alceste' by Aurelio Aureli. King's Theatre, 31 Jan. 1727. *Auto.* R.M.20.d.2, *ff.* 9-10, *fr. MS. copies:* R.M.19.c.1, 2; R.M.18.c.10, *fr.*; R.M. 19.a.1, *fr.*; B.M. Add MSS. 38002; Eg. 2924 (Granville); Fitzwilliam (L.); Hamburg. J. Cluer ('Admetus, An Opera'—Overture, Songs, &c.) 24 June 1727 or earlier. H.G. 73.

Agrippina. Vincenzo Grimani. Venice, Teatro San Giovanni Crisostomo, 26 Dec. 1709. *Auto.* R.M.20.a.3. *MS. copies:* B.M. Add. MSS. 16023; R.M.19.d.12 (Part of Act I); Fitzwilliam. Arnold, 146-149, *c.* 1795. H.G. 57. *See* also Oratorios—'La Resurrezione'.

Alceste. Incidental music for Tobias Smollett's play, some words of vocal parts attributed to Thomas Morell. Written for performance at Covent Garden, 1750, which did not take place. Some of the music used for 'The Choice of Hercules'. *Auto.fr.:* R.M.20.e.6; R.M.20.g.13; R.M.20.f.12. B.M. Add. MSS. 30310 (Act IV, &c.). *MS. copies:* R.C.M.251; Hamburg (with pencil notes by Handel). Arnold, 84-85 ('Alcides') *c.* 1790. H.G. 46b.

The Alchemist. Incidental music for Ben Jonson's play. Drury Lane, 7 Mar. 1732. Music not advertised for this performance, but for a revival, New Theatre, Haymarket, 20 Dec. 1733, as by Corelli, Vivaldi, Geminiani and Handel. *MS. copy:* B.M. Add. MSS. 31576 (as published by Arnold). J. Walsh ('The Tunes in the Alchimist for 2 Violins and a Bass'—Mostly from the overture to 'Rodrigo') *c.* 1732. Arnold, 64, *c.* 1790.

Alcina. Antonio Marchi, from Ariosto's 'Orlando Furioso'. Covent Garden, 16 Apr. 1735. *Auto.* R.M.20.a.4; R.M.20.a.7, *fr.*; Fitzwilliam,

[1] Handel's contribution to some of the works listed as pasticcios is uncertain, but only those have been included which contain some music by him or for which he was partly responsible. Ballad operas containing extracts of his work are omitted.

fr. MS. copies: R.M.19.a.12; B.M. Add. MSS. 31566; Fitzwilliam (L.); Hamburg. J. Walsh ('The Favourite Songs . . . Sold at the Musick Shops' —Two collections without Walsh's name) Spring, 1735. J. Walsh ('The Favourite Songs'—Two collections with Walsh's name) Aug. and Autumn, 1735. J. Walsh ('The Favourite Songs . . . First, Second and 3rd Collection') 11 Nov. 1736. J. Walsh ('Alcina an Opera'—Overture and 31 vocal numbers) *c.* Sept. or Oct. 1737. H.G. 86. (First issued as H.G. 27.)

Alessandro. Paolo A. Rolli from Ortensio Mauro's 'La Superbia d'Alessandro'. King's Theatre, 5 May 1726. Revived, King's Theatre 15 Nov. 1743 as 'Roxana, or Alexander in India', music by Handel probably with additions by G. B. Lampugnani; and at later dates as various pasticcios with some Handel items. *Auto.* R.M.20.a.5; R.M.20.d.2, *fr. MS. copies*: R.M. 18.c.10, 11, *fr.*; B.M. Add. MSS. 31563; Eg. 2923 (Granville); Fitzwilliam (L.); Hamburg. J. Cluer ('Alexander, an Opera'—Overture, Songs, &c.) 6 Aug. 1726. H.G. 72.

Alessandro Severo. Pasticcio, mainly from other works by Handel, with a new overture. Probably Apostolo Zeno. King's Theatre, 25 Feb. 1738. *Auto.* Fitzwilliam, *fr. MS. copies*: R.M.19.a.1, *fr.*; B.M. Add. MSS. 31569; 29386 (Minuet); Hamburg. J. Walsh ('The Favourite Songs') 8 Mar. 1738. J. Walsh ('Sonatas or Chamber Aires,' &c. Vol. III. pt. 7; Vol. IV. pt. 1, 2—Selections) 29 Apr. 1738; 18 Jan. 1739; 18 May 1739. J. Walsh ('Six Overtures for Violins,' &c. Seventh Collection; 'Six Overtures fitted to the Harpsichord', &c. Seventh Collection) 21 Oct. 1738; 18 Jan. 1739. H.G. 48, pp. 104-107 (Overture).

Almira. Friedrich C. Feustking, on an Italian libretto by Giulio Pancieri. Hamburg, Theater beim Gänsemarkt, 8 Jan. 1705. *MS. copies*: A very incomplete copy was in the Staatsbibliothek, Berlin; B.M. Add. MSS. 31555, *fr.* H.G. 55.

Amadigi. John. J. Heidegger? King's Theatre, 25 May 1715. *Auto.* sold in London 1870; Fitzwilliam, *fr. MS. copies*: R.M.19.g.2; R.M.19.c.5; R.M.18.c.1, *fr.*; Eg. 2917 (Granville); Fitzwilliam; Fitzwilliam (L.); Hamburg; St. Michael's College, Tenbury. J. Walsh ('Favourite Songs in Amadis and Theseus') advertised *c.* 1732, no copy traced. H.G. 62.

Arbace. Pasticcio, music probably from J. A. Hasse's opera, with recitatives by Handel; also attributed to Leonardo Vinci. Probably based on Pietro Metastasio's 'Artaserse'. King's Theatre, 5 Jan. 1734. *MS. copy*: (partly autograph?) Hamburg. J. Walsh ('The Favourite Songs in . . . Arbaces') 5 Feb. 1734.

Arianna. Pietro Pariati's 'Arianna e Teseo', with alterations. King's Theatre, 26 Jan. 1734. *Auto.* R.M.20.a.6. *MS. copies*: R.M.18.c.4, *fr.*; R.M. 19.d.11, *fr.*; Fitzwilliam (L.); Hamburg. J. Walsh ('The Favourite Songs in . . . Ariadne'—Two collections) 23 Feb.; 6 Apr. 1734. J. Walsh ('Ariadne an Opera'—Overture, Songs, &c.) Summer or autumn, 1737. H.G.83.

Ariodante. Antonio Salvi, based on Lodovico Ariosto's, 'Orlando furioso'. Covent Garden, 8 Jan. 1735. *Auto.* R.M.20.a.7; Fitzwilliam, *fr. MS. copies*: R.M.19.a.16; Eg. 2928 (Granville): Fitzwilliam; Fitzwilliam (L.); Hamburg. J. Walsh ('The Favourite Songs') 13 Sept. 1735 (just published). H.G. 85.

Arminio. Antonio Salvi, with alterations. Covent Garden, 12 Jan. 1737. *Auto.* R.M.20.a.8; Fitzwilliam, *fr. MS. copies*: Fitzwilliam (L.); Hamburg.

J. Walsh ('Arminius an Opera'—Overture, Songs, &c.) 12 Feb. 1737. H.G. 89.
Atalanta. Belisario Valeriani's 'La Caccia in Etolia', adapted. Covent
Garden, 12 May 1736. *Auto.* R.M.20.a.9. *MS. copies:* R.M.18.c.5, *fr.*;
Fitzwilliam (L.); Hamburg. J. Walsh ('Atalanta an Opera'—Complete
except for recitatives) 9 June 1736. H.G. 87.
Der beglueckte Florindo. See Florindo and Daphne.
Berenice. Antonio Salvi. Covent Garden, 18 May 1737. *Auto.* R.M.
20.a.10. *MS. copies:* Fitzwilliam (L.); Hamburg. J. Walsh ('Berenice an
Opera'—Complete except for recitatives) 15 June 1737. H.G. 90.
Cajo Fabricio. Pasticcio, music probably from J. A. Hasse's opera, with
recitatives by Handel. Apostolo Zeno. King's Theatre, 4 Dec. 1733. *MS.
copy:* Hamburg (partly autograph ?).
Catone. Pasticcio, music probably from J. A. Hasse's opera, with recita-
tives by Handel. Pietro Metastasio, English words by Samuel Humphreys.
King's Theatre, 4 Nov. 1732. *MS. copy:* Hamburg. J. Walsh ("The
Favourite Songs in the Opera call'd Cato') 25 Nov. 1732.
Daphne. See Florindo and Daphne.
Deidamia. Paolo A Rolli. Lincoln's Inn Fields Theatre, 10 Jan. 1741.
Auto. R.M.20.a.11; Fitzwilliam, *fr. MS. copies:* R.M.18.c.11, *fr.*; Eg.2930
(Granville); Hamburg. J. Walsh ('Songs in the new Opera . . . Deidamia'
—First collection—Overture and Act I) 29 Jan. 1741. Acts II and III were
advertised with the score ('Deidamia an Opera'—Containing most of the
work except for some recitatives and choruses) 21 Feb. 1741. H.G. 94.
Didone. Pasticcio, music from Leonardo Vinci, with alterations, recitatives
by Handel. Based on Pietro Metastasio. Covent Garden, 13 Apr. 1737. *MS.
copy:* B.M. Add. MSS. 31607 (with a few entries by Handel). This copy
belonged to Samuel Arnold, who claimed on it to possess also a 'half score in
which the notes of ye Voice Part of all the Recitatives except . . . 2. . . . are
written by Mr. Handel, also the Song, "Se vuoi ch'io mora" . . . written entirely
in Score by him'. Giovanni Alberto Ristori is also credited with having
composed an opera, 'La Didone abbandonata', produced in London, 1737,
of which the words of some arias are in the Fitzwilliam Museum (Catalogue,
pp. 180-182). There is therefore some doubt about the details of the
production of 13 April 1737, and no definite evidence whether the work was
published, although an anonymous 'Didone abbandonata' is advertised in
Randall's Catalogue, 1776.
Die durch Blut und Mord erlangete Liebe: oder Nero. See Nero.
Emilia. See Flavio.
Ernelinda. Pasticcio. Francesco Silvani's, 'La fede tradita e vendicata',
adapted. King's Theatre, 26 Feb. 1713. May or may not be the work of
which Act II is at Hamburg, and to which Handel contributed.
Ezio. Pietro Metastasio, English words by Samuel Humphreys. King's
Theatre, 15 Jan. 1732. *Auto.* R.M.20.a.12. *MS. copies:* R.M.19.a.5, *fr.*;
Fitzwilliam (L.); Hamburg. J. Walsh ('Ætius an Opera'—Overture, Songs,
Final Chorus) 14 Feb. 1732. H.G. 80.
Faramondo. Apostolo Zeno, considerably modified. King's Theatre,
3 Jan. 1738. *Auto.* R.M.20.a.13. *MS. copies:* R.M.19.a.1, *fr.*; Fitzwilliam
(L.); Rowe Music Library, Cambridge; Hamburg. J. Walsh ('Faramondo
an Opera'—Complete except for recitatives) 4 Feb. 1738. H.G. 91.

Fernando Re di Castiglia. *See* Sosarme.

Flavio. Nicola F. Haym, after Corneille's 'Le Cid', and a libretto by Stefano Ghigi. King's Theatre, 14 May 1723. *Auto.* R.M.20.b.1 (with the title 'Emilia Opera' on *f*.5, which was what Handel evidently intended calling this work). *MS. copies*: R.M.18.c.10, *fr.*; B.M. Add. MSS. 31572; Fitzwilliam (L.); Hamburg. 'Publish'd by the Author': J. Walsh, John and Joseph Hare ('Flavius an Opera'—Overture, Songs, &c.) 21 June 1723. H.G. 67.

Floridante. Paolo F. Rolli. King's Theatre, 9 Dec. 1721. *Auto.* R.M. 20.b.2 (wanting the final chorus, sold by Sotheby & Co., 16 Mar. 1737). *MS. copies*: R.M.19.f.4; R.M.19.c.10; R.M.18.c.3, 10, *fr.*; Fitzwilliam; Fitzwilliam (L.); Hamburg. 'Publish'd by the Author': J. Walsh, John and Joseph Hare ('Floridant an Opera'—Overture, Songs, &c.) 28 Mar. 1722; J. Walsh, John and Joseph Hare ('Additional Songs In Floridant') *c.* 1722. H.G. 65.

Florindo and Daphne. Heinrich Hinsch, after an unknown Italian work. Hamburg, Theater beim Gänsemarkt, Jan. 1708. Owing to the length of the work it was performed in two parts:—'Die beglueckte Florindo' and 'Die verwandelte Daphne'. (Librettos, Library of Congress.) The music, which is lost, composed 1706 and performed after Handel left Hamburg.

Giulio Cesare. Nicola F. Haym. King's Theatre, 20 Feb. 1724. *Auto.* R.M.20.b.3; Fitzwilliam, *fr. MS. copies*: R.M.19.c.6,7; R.M.19.f.3, *fr.*; R.M.18.c.9,10, *fr.*; Eg. 2919 (Granville); Fitzwilliam (L.); Hamburg. J. Cluer and B. Creake ('Julius Cæsar: an Opera'—Overture, Songs, &c.) 24 July 1724, announced 11 July to be published 13 July. Pirated editions of 'The Favourite Songs', attributed to J. Walsh and John and Joseph Hare, had been issued previously. Arnold, 43-47, 1789. H.G. 68.

Giustino. Nicolo Beregani, with alterations. Covent Garden, 16 Feb. 1737. *Auto.* R.M.20.b.4; Fitzwilliam, *fr. MS. copies*: Fitzwilliam (L.); Hamburg. J. Walsh ('Justin an Opera'—Overture, Songs, &c.) 30 Mar. 1737. H.G. 88.

Haman and Mordecai. Masque, first version of the oratorio 'Esther'. Probably Alexander Pope, assisted by John Arbuthnot, based on Racine's 'Esther'. For the Duke of Chandos, at Cannons, near Edgware, on some unknown date, although without definite evidence it has been attributed to 29 Aug. 1720, when the Duke's domestic chapel was opened and an anthem performed. *Auto.* R.M.20.e.7. *MS. copy*: B.M. Add. MSS. 31560; Eg.2931 (Granville). H.G. 40. *See* also Oratorios, &c.—Esther.

Hermann von Balcke. Pasticcio. Partly in German, partly in Italian. Music from operas by Handel, with additional airs and recitatives by Johann Jeremias du Grain. Author of libretto, unknown. Intended for performance at Elbing, 1737, but was not produced. The music has disappeared. Libretto afterwards used for a school play in German, Latin and Polish, without music, by George Daniel Seiler, performed Elbing, 1737. (Some details from the late Dr. A. Loewenberg.)

Imeneo. Librettist? Lincoln's Inn Fields Theatre, 22 Nov. 1740. *Auto.* R.M.20.b.5; R.M.20.g.11, *fr.*; Fitzwilliam, *fr. MS. copies*: R.M.18.c.11; Eg. 2929 (Granville); Hamburg. J. Walsh ('The Favourite Songs in the Operetta . . . Hymen'—Songs) 18 Apr. 1741. Reissued by Walsh as the 'Opera of Hymen', *c.* 1760. H.G. 93. For the English concert version as 'Hymen', *see* Secular Choral Works.

Jupiter in Argos. 'Dramatical Composition . . . intermix'd with Chorus's, and two Concerto's on the Organ', including items from other works by Handel. Antonio Maria Lucchini's 'Giove in Argo' with modifications and additions. King's Theatre, 1 May 1739. *Auto.* R.M.20.d.2.*fr.*; Fitzwilliam, *fr. MS. copies:* R.M.19.d.11, *fr.*; Sir Newman Flower collection (Aylesford *MS.*). Music used for an entirely new libretto, 'Perseus and Andromeda', an operatic masque by Albert G. Latham, broadcast by the B.B.C. 8 Oct. 1935, vocal score, O.U.P., 1935.

Lotario. Antonio Salvi's 'Adelaide', adapted. King's Theatre, 2 Dec. 1729. *Auto.* R.M.20.b.6; Fitzwilliam, *fr. MS. copies:* R.M.19.a.5, *fr.*; R.M.19.c.9, *fr.*; Eg. 2927 (Granville); Fitzwilliam (L.); Hamburg. Cluer's Printing Office ('Lotharius, an Opera'—Overture, Songs, &c.) 13 Feb. 1730. H.G. 77.

Lucio Papirio. Pasticcio. Apostolo Zeno. King's Theatre, 23 May 1732. *MS. copy,* Hamburg (partly autograph).

Lucio Vero. Pasticcio mainly from other works by Handel. Apostolo Zeno, adapted. King's Theatre, 14 Nov. 1747. J. Walsh ('The Favourite Songs in . . . Lucius Verus') 24 Nov. 1747; ('A Second Set of the Favourite Songs', &c.) 1 Dec. 1747.

Muzio Scevola. Pasticcio. Act III only by Handel; Act I by 'Sigr Pipo' (most probably Filippo Amadei); Act II by G. B. Bononcini. Paolo A. Rolli. King's Theatre, 15 Apr. 1721. *Auto.* R.M.20.b.7 (Act III). *MS. copies:* R.M.19.c.8; R.M.19.c.9; B.M. Add. MSS. 16108; Fitzwilliam; Fitzwilliam (L.); Hamburg (Act III.). Richard Meares ('The Most Favourite Songs in . . . Muzio Scævola') 23 Aug. 1722; J. Walsh, John and Joseph Hare (The Fävourite Songs' in . . . Muzio Scævola) 25 Aug 1722 ('publish'd this vacation'). H.G. 64.

Nero. 'Die durch Blut und Mord erlangete Liebe oder: Nero'. Friedrich Feustking. Hamburg, Theater beim Gänsemarkt, 25 Feb. 1705. Music lost. Copies of the libretto: Sir Newman Flower and the Library of Congress.

Oreste. Pasticcio. Mainly from other works by Handel, with partly new overture. Librettist? Covent Garden, 18 Dec. 1734. *Auto.* Hamburg. *MS. copies:* B.M. Add. MSS. 31555, *fr.*; Fitzwilliam (L.). Score or Songs not published. J. Walsh (Overture, in 'Six Overtures for Violins, &c', 7th collection) 21 Oct. 1738; (Two Minuets, in 'Sonatas or Chamber Aires for a German Flute', &c. Vol. II, pt. VII.) 3 June 1735; J. Walsh ('The Lady's Banquet, Sixth Book'—Includes the two minuets, on pp. 5 and 9) 23 Aug. 1735; J. Walsh ('A Collection of Lessons for the Harpsicord . . . 4th Book'— A reissue of 'The Lady's Banquet, Sixth Book') 17 Jan. 1758. H.G. 48, pp. 102-103.

Orlando. Grazio Braccioli, based on Ludovico Ariosto's 'Orlando Furioso', English words by Samuel Humphreys. King's Theatre, 27 Jan. 1733. *Auto.* R.M.20.b.8. *MS. copies:* R.M.19.f.5; R.M.18.c.7, *fr.*; B.M. Add. MSS. 31564, 31565; Fitzwilliam (L.); Hamburg. J. Walsh ('Orlando an Opera'— Overture, Songs, &c.) 6 Feb. 1733. H.G. 82.

Ormisda. Pasticcio. Music attributed to Francesco Conti, &c., produced by Handel. Apostolo Zeno. King's Theatre, 4 Apr. 1730. *MS. copies:* B.M. Add. MSS. 31551. Hamburg (partly autograph). J. Walsh and Joseph Hare ('The Favourite Songs . . . in Ormisda'—no composer given) 25 Apr. 1730. One number ('Sentir si dire') appears in J. Walsh and Joseph Hare's 'Solos for a German Flute . . . by Mr. Handel', Vol. II, pt. I, 17 Oct. 1730, but no composer's name is given to this number in the work, the other numbers being described as by Handel. Ten numbers are also included in J. Walsh and Joseph Hare's 'Parthenope For a Flute . . . To which is added . . . Songs in . . . Ormisda', &c., but without any composer's name.

Ottone. Nicola F. Haym, adapted from Stefano B. Pallavicino's 'Teofane'. King's Theatre, 12 Jan. 1723. *Auto.* R.M.20.b.9; R.M.20.b.10; Fitzwilliam, *fr. MS. copies*: R.M.18.c.10, *fr.*; B.M. Add. MSS. 31572, 33238, 31571; Eg. 2918 (Granville); Bodleian (5 Songs with 'graces' for the singer in Handel's hand); Fitzwilliam (L.); Hamburg (Act III only). 'Publish'd by the Author', J. Walsh, John and Joseph Hare ('Otho an Opera'—Overture, Songs, &c.) 19 Mar. 1723. J. Walsh, John and Joseph Hare ('The Monthly Mask of Vocal Musick'—Contains 4 additional songs, also issued as 'Additional Songs in Otho') April 1723. J. Walsh and Joseph Hare ('The Quarterly Collection of Vocal Musick'—Contains 5 songs introduced into the Feb. and Mar. performances, 1726) 1726. H.G. 66.

Partenope. Silvio Stampiglia, modified. King's Theatre, 24 Feb. 1730. *Auto.* R.M.20.b.11; R.M.20.d.2, *fr. MS. copies*: R.M.19.a.5, *fr.*; Fitzwilliam (L.); Hamburg. J. Walsh and Joseph Hare ('Parthenope an Opera'—Overture, Songs, &c.) 4 Apr. 1730. H.G.78.

Il Pastor Fido. Giacomo Rossi, based on Battista Guarini's pastoral play. Queen's Theatre, 22 Nov. 1712. Second version, King's Theatre, 18 May 1734. Third version, preceded by the ballet 'Terpsicore', Covent Garden, 9 Nov. 1734. *Auto.* R.M.20.b.12, *fr.*; R.M.20.g.13, *fr.*; Fitzwilliam, *fr. MS. copies*: R.M.19.e.4 (Score of 1712 version, with pencil notes by Handel); R.M. 18.c.4 (Selections from the version with 'Terpsicore'); R.M.19.d.11 (Selections from the version with 'Terpsicore', incorrectly described as 'Songs and other Pieces in Ptolemy' and printed by Arnold (159-160) as 'Masque'); B.M. Add. MSS. 16024 (Score, 1712 version); B.M. Add. MSS. 31571; Fitzwilliam (L.—Score, 'Terpsicore' separate); Hamburg (Score—'Terpsicore' separate). J. Walsh ('The Favourite Songs in . . . Pastor Fido No. 1'; 'A Second Collection of the most Favourite Songs in . . . Pastor Fido') 30 Nov. 1734 or a little earlier. Arnold, 159-160 ('A Masque') *c.* 1795. H.G. 59, 84.

Poro. Pietro Metastasio's, 'Alessandro nell' Indie' adapted, English words by Samuel Humphreys. King's Theatre, 2 Feb. 1731. *Auto.* R.M.20.b.13; R.M.20.d.2, *fr. MS. copies*: R.M.19.a.5, *fr.*; Fitzwilliam; Fitzwilliam (L.); Hamburg. Printing Office in Bow Church Yard ('The Favourite Songs in . . . Porus'—a pirated edition) 17 Feb. 1731; J. Walsh ('Porus an Opera'—Overture, Songs, &c.) 2 Mar. 1731; J. Walsh ('The Favourite Songs in . . . Porus'—an old title page of J. Walsh and Joseph Hare's, adapted) 3 Mar. 1731. H.G. 79.

Radamisto. Nicola F. Haym, altered from 'L'Amor tirannico', an anonymous drama with music, published Rome, 1713, based on Tacitus, 'Annals', Book XII. chapter 51, which has been ascribed to Domenico Lalli and Matteo Noris. King's Theatre, 27 Apr. 1720. *Auto.* R.M.20.c.1; R.M.20.d.2, *fr.*; Berlin, *fr. MS. copies*: R.M.18.c.9, *fr.*; B.M. Add. MSS. 31562; 39180; Fitzwilliam; Fitzwilliam (L.); Hamburg. 'Publisht by the Author': Richard Meares and Christopher Smith ('Il Radamisto Opera'—Overture, Songs, &c.) 15 Dec. 1720; ('Arie aggiunte di Radamisto') 14 Mar. 1721. H.G. 63.

Riccardo Primo. Paolo A. Rolli mostly, other sources not identified.

King's Theatre, 11 Nov. 1727. *Auto.* R.M.20.c.2. *MS. copies*: R.M.18.c.10, 11, *fr.*; B.M. Add. MSS. 31573; Eg. 2925 (Granville); Fitzwilliam (L.); Hamburg. J. Cluer ('Rich^d ye 1st King of England'—Overture, Songs, &c.) 17 Feb. 1728. H.G. 74.

Rinaldo. Giacomo Rossi, from a sketch by Aaron Hill after Torquato Tasso's 'Gerusalemme liberata', English translation by Aaron Hill. Queen's Theatre, 24 Feb. 1711. *Auto.* R.M.20.c.3 (Fragments of the 1711 and 1731 versions); R.M.20.f.11, *ff.* 19-21,26-28 (Two additional songs, 1717); Fitzwilliam, *fr. MS. copies*: R.M.19.d.5 (Full Score, 1711 version, with numerous autograph pencil alterations for the 1731 version); R.M.18.b.12, *fr.*; R.M.18.c.9, *fr.*; Eg. 2915 (Granville—1711 version with songs of the 1731 version at the end); Fitzwilliam (L.), Hamburg. Gerald Coke owns a manuscript copy of 4 additional songs, 1717, formerly in the Aylesford collection. J. Walsh and John Hare ('Songs in the Opera of Rinaldo') 24 Apr. 1711; ('Arie dell' Opera di Rinaldo') 21 June 1711. J. Walsh ('The Additional Favourite Songs', &c.—12 numbers from the previous issues) 21 Apr. 1731. H.G. 58, 58a.

Rodelinda. Antonio Salvi, adapted by Nicola F. Haym. King's Theatre, 13 Feb. 1725. *Auto.* R.M.20.c.4; R.M.20.d.2, *fr.*; Fitzwilliam, *fr. MS. copies*: B.M. Add. MSS. 31571, *fr.*; Eg. 2921 (Granville); Fitzwilliam (L.); Hamburg. J. Cluer ('Rodelinda: an Opera'—Overture, Songs, &c.) 6 May 1725. H.G. 70.

Rodrigo. Librettist unknown. Florence, *c.*1707 or 1708. *Auto.* R.M. 20.c.5; R.M.20.d.2, *f.*9, *fr.*; Fitzwilliam, *fr. MS. copies*: Fitzwilliam (L.); 'Roderigo et Silla', an MS. score sold at the J. S. Hawkins sale, London, May 29-30, 1843, present location unknown. Not published, as 'Rodrigo', but 'The Tunes in the Alchimist', J. Walsh, *c.*1732, are mostly from the Overture to 'Rodrigo'. H.G. 56.

Roxana,or Alexander in India. See Alessandro.

Scipione. Paolo A. Rolli, based on Apostolo Zeno's 'Scipione nelle Spagne'. King's Theatre, 12 Mar. 1726. *Auto.* R.M.20.c.6; R.M.20.d.2, *fr.*; Fitzwilliam, *fr. MS. copies*: *fr.*:—R.M.18.c.10; R.M.18.c.11; R.M.18.b.4; R.M.19.a.1; Eg. 2922 (Granville—1726 version with 1730 additions); Fitzwilliam (L.), Hamburg. J. Cluer ('Scipio an Opera'—Overture, Songs, &c.) 27 May 1726. H.G. 71.

Semiramide. Pasticcio, music probably principally by Antonio Vivaldi, with recitatives by Handel. Pietro Metastasio, based on. King's Theatre, 30 Oct. 1733. *MS. copies*: Hamburg (Score, with recitatives in Handel's hand); B.M. Add. MSS. 31572 (One number, 'Dal labbro tuo vezzoso'). No evidence of publication.

Serse. Niccolò Minato, as altered by P. Licurio, i.e. Silvio Stampiglia, with further alterations. King's Theatre, 15 Apr. 1738. *Auto.* R.M.20.c.7; Fitzwilliam, *fr. MS. copies*: Fitzwilliam (L.); Hamburg. J. Walsh ('Xerxes an Opera'—Practically complete, except for recitatives) 30 May 1738. H.G. 92.

Silla. Librettist unknown. Composed 1714 or earlier, no evidence of performance, although it has been suggested that it was performed for Lord Burlington at his London residence. *Auto.* R.M.20.c.8, *fr.*; Fitzwilliam, *fr. MS. copies*: R.M.19.d.7; B.M. Add. MSS. 31555, *fr*; Fitzwilliam (L.); 'Roderigo et Silla', an MS. score sold at the J. S. Hawkins sale, London, 29-30 May 1843, present location unknown. H.G. 61.

Siroe. Pietro Metastasio, altered by Nicola F. Haym. King's Theatre, 17 Feb. 1728. *Auto*. R.M.20.c.9 (includes fragments from a libretto, 'Flavio Olibrio' by Apostolo Zeno and Pietro Pariati); Fitzwilliam, *fr. MS. copies*: R.M.18.c.10,11, *fr.*; Eg. 2926 (Granville); Fitzwilliam (L.); Hamburg. J. Cluer ('Siroe an Opera'—Overture, Songs, &c.) 13 July 1728. H.G. 75.

Sosarme. Matteo Noris, altered from his 'Alfonso Primo', English words by Samuel Humphreys. The libretto was originally called 'Fernando Re di Castiglia', and the action took place at Coimbra. The first two acts were set to this book, but the title, characters and place were changed, with corresponding alterations in the words. King's Theatre, 15 Feb. 1732. *Auto*. R.M.20.c.10. *MS. copies*: Fitzwilliam (L.); Hamburg. J. Walsh ('The Favourite Songs in . . . Sosarmes') 11 Mar. 1732; ('A Second Collection of the most Favourite Songs in . . . Sosarmes') 29 Apr. 1732; ('Sosarmes an Opera'—Overture, Songs, &c.) *c*.1733. Arnold, 20-23, 1788. H.G. 81.

Tamerlano. Agostino Piovene, adapted by Nicola F. Haym, with some numbers in Handel's autograph score, from 'Il Bajazet', another version of the Piovene work, produced at Reggio, 1719, with music by Francesco Gasparini, in which Francesco Borosini took the role of Bajazet as also in Handel's 'Tamerlano'. King's Theatre, 31 Oct. 1724. *Auto*. R.M.20.c.11; R.M.20.d.2, *fr. MS. copies*: R.M.18.c.10, *fr.*; Eg. 2920 (Granville); Fitzwilliam (L.); Hamburg. J. Cluer ('Tamerlane an Opera'—Overture, Songs, &c.) 14 Nov. 1724. H.G. 69.

Teseo. Nicola F. Haym. Queen's Theatre, 10 Jan. 1713. *Auto*. R.M. 20.c.12, *fr*; R.M.20.c.5, *fr. MS. copies*: R.M.19.e.6; R.M.19.g.4; R.M.19.d.8; R.M.19.c.9, *fr.*; Eg. 2916 (Granville); Fitzwilliam; Fitzwilliam (L.). J. Walsh ('Favourite Songs in Amadis and Theseus') advertised *c*. 1732, no copy traced. J. Walsh? ('The Favourite Songs in Theseus'—4 leaves not paginated, containing 2 songs—copy N.L.S.) date? J. Walsh, 'Apollo's Feast', Vol. II and III (*c*. 1734), contain 3 numbers attributed to 'Teseo'. J. Cluer and B. Creake, 'A Pocket Companion for Gentlemen and Ladies', 2 vol. 1724-5, contains 6 numbers from 'Teseo'. A number of sheet songs from the opera appeared, *c*. 1715-20. The overture was published in J. Walsh, John and Joseph Hare's 'Six Overtures for Violins', &c. 3rd collection, *c*. 1725; 'Fitted to the Harpsicord', *c*. 1728. Arnold, 30-34, 1788. H.G. 60.

Tolomeo. Nicola F. Haym. King's Theatre, 30 Apr. 1728. *Auto*. R.M.20.d.1; R.M.20.d.2, *fr. MS. copies*: R.M.18.c.10, *fr.*; Fitzwilliam (L.); Hamburg. J. Walsh and Joseph Hare ('The Favourite Songs in . . . Ptolomy') 14 Sept. 1728; J. Walsh ('Ptolomy an Opera'—Overture, Songs, &c.) *c*. 1733. H.G. 76.

Venceslao. Pasticcio, with recitatives by Handel. Apostolo Zeno, English words by Samuel Humphreys. King's Theatre, 12 Jan. 1731. *MS. copy*: Hamburg (partly autograph). J. Walsh and Joseph Hare ('The Favourite Songs in . . . Venceslaus') 27 Jan. 1731.

OPERAS REFERRED TO IN VARIOUS MANUSCRIPTS BUT WHICH WERE NEVER
COMPLETED OR APPEARED AS SUCH

Alfonso Primo. The libretto of 'Sosarme' was from Matteo Noris's 'Alfonso Primo'.

Fernando Re di Castiglia. See 'Sosarme'.

Flavio Olibrio (*or Genserico*). Fragments of a libretto by Apostolo Zeno and Pietro Pariati exist in the autograph MS. of 'Siroe' (R.M.20.c.9), and a deleted reference to the work occurs after the overture to 'Tolomeo' in the autograph MS. of that opera (R.M.20.d.1). Portions of an opera 'Olibrio' are in the Fitzwilliam Museum.

Honorius. Onorico is a character in 'Olibrio'. (Fitzwilliam.)

Tito. The overture to 'Ezio' was intended for 'Titus, l'Empereur,' and is followed in the autograph MS. of 'Ezio' (R.M.20.a.12) by an incomplete score from 'Tito' (Act I. sc. 1), and other fragments of the intended work are in (R.M.20.d.2.)

SECULAR CHORAL WORKS (SERENADES, ODES, ETC.)

Aci, Galatea e Polifemo. Serenata or Cantata. Author of libretto unknown. Naples, 19 July 1708, presumably for the marriage of the Duke of Alvito. *Auto.* R.M.20.a.1, and Eg.2953,*ff.* 98-101 (dated 16 June 1708); R.M.20.e.3, *fr.* Parts of the work were used by Handel in the 1732 Italian and English version of 'Acis and Galatea', and one number from the 1708 version, 'Del 'aquila l'artigli' ('Dell'aquila gli artigli') appeared in the Walsh editions, 1732, &c. H.G. 53. *See* also the following item.

Acis and Galatea. Serenata or Masque. Words attributed to John Gay, with additions by John Dryden, Alexander Pope and John Hughes. Cannons, near Edgware, *c.* 1718-20. Another version by Handel in Italian and English based on the 1708 and Cannons versions, with new material, King's Theatre, 10 June 1732, but this polyglot version soon afterwards gave way to the entirely English version which was extremely popular during the rest of the century. Performances, not under Handel's direction: Lincoln's Inn Fields, 26 Mar. 1731; New Theatre, Haymarket, 17 May 1732. *Auto.* R.M.20.a.2; R.M.20.d.2, *fr.*; R.M.20.e.3, *fr.*; Fitzwilliam, *fr.* *MS. copies*: R.M.19.f.7 (1732 version); R.M.18.c.5 (Selection, 1732 version); R.M.18.c.7 (Additional Songs, 1732 version); R.M.19.d.10 (Additional Songs, &c., 1732 version); R.M.18.c.11,*fr.* B.M. Add. MSS. 36710 (English version, presumably of 26 Mar. 1731); B.M. Add. MSS. 5321; 31561; Eg. 2940 (Granville); Eg. 2953 (with four leaves autograph of the 1708 version); Schœlcher (Catalogue) mentions a copy of the English version bearing the signature of William Antrobus and the date 'ye 9th November, 1720'; Fitzwilliam (L. Acis and Galatea); Hamburg (Acis and Galatea). J. Walsh, John and Joseph Hare ('The Favourite Songs in the Opera call'd Acis and Galatea') Oct. 1722 or a little earlier; no composer's name is given. (Some of the numbers were issued separately, and also appeared previously in 'The Monthly Mask of Vocal Music', Apr.-July 1722.) J. Walsh and Joseph Hare ('The Songs and Symphony's in the Masque of Acis and Galatea'—Several issues of the preceding 'Favourite Songs', with variations) *c.* 1725, &c. J. Walsh ('Acis and Galatea A Serenade'—Reissues of the preceding) 13 Dec. 1739. J. Walsh ('Acis and Galatea A Mask'—First complete edition; issued in parts), 24 Aug-19 Nov. 1743; complete in one volume, 28 Nov. 1743. (*See* William·C. Smith: 'Concerning Handel'.) Arnold, 28-30, 1788. H.G. 3, 53. *See* also 'Aci Galatea e Polifemo'.

Alexander's Feast. Ode. John Dryden, adapted, with additions by Newburgh Hamilton. Covent Garden, 19 Feb. 1736. *Auto.* R.M.20.d.4; R.M.20.f.12,*fr.* *MS. copies*: R.M.19.a.10 (Organ part as performed in 1736, omitting the Concertos in Pt. I and II); R.M.19.a.1 (Organ part, with Concertos, &c.); B.M. Add. MSS. 31567 ('Il Convito d'Alessandro'—An Italian version); Fitzwilliam (L.); Hamburg. J. Walsh ('Alexander's Feast or the Power of Musick. An Ode') 8 Mar. 1738 or a little earlier. The well known Houbraken portrait of Handel, which includes the opening scene of 'Alexander's Feast', was first issued in connexion with this work. The Ode is followed by 'Cecilia, volgi un sguardo', a cantata, performed at the beginning of Act II; and 'Sei del ciel dono perfetto', an additional song (*Auto*. R.M. 20.e.4 and H.G. 52*a*. No. 6). J. Walsh also issued these two numbers as 'Handel's Cantata, with Recitatives, Songs and Duets', 26 Feb. 1743. Arnold, 65-67, 1790. H.G. 12.

L'Allegro, il Penseroso ed il Moderato. John Milton, adapted and the third part ('Il Moderato') by Charles Jennens. Lincoln's Inn Fields, 27 Feb. 1740. *Auto.* R.M.20.d.5; R.M.20.f.11, *fr.*; Fitzwilliam, *fr. MS. copies*: R.M.19.c.4; R.M.18.d.8; R.M.19.b.1 (Solo Voice Parts); *fr.*: R.M.18.c.11; R.M.19.d.10; R.M.19.a.2; R.M.19.e.10 (String Parts); Scores: Eg. 2941 (Granville—preceded by the Concerto Grosso. Op. 6. No. 10, played in the work); Fitzwilliam (L); Hamburg. J. Walsh ('Songs in L'Allegro ed il Penseroso') 15 Mar. 1740; ('Songs in L'Allegro ed il Penseroso . . . 2d Collection') 7 May 1740. J. Walsh ('L'Allegro, Il Penseroso ed Il Moderato'—The two previous collections together) 13 May 1740; J. Walsh ('L'Allegro', &c.— The two collections, but with the numbers arranged in correct order of the libretto) 2 Feb. 1741; J. Walsh ('Additional Songs in L'Allegro il Penseroso'— As pp. 19-24 of 'The British Orpheus. A Collection of Favourite English Songs', No. II, and also sold as a separate item) 1742. William Randall ('L'Allegro, il Pensieroso, ed il Moderato'—Complete score) 18 May 1770. Arnold, 150-153, *c.* 1795. H.G. 6.

The Choice of Hercules. Musical Interlude, produced as a new act to 'Alexander's Feast', includes music written for 'Alceste'. Text extracted and adapted probably by Thomas Morell or Tobias Smollett, from a poem with the same title, first published anonymously in Joseph Spence's 'Polymetis', 1747, based on Xenophon's 'Memoirs of Socrates' ('Memorabilia') Bk. II. This poem has been attributed to William Duncombe, but with more reason to Robert Lowth, Bishop of Oxford and London; but Handel's libretto has little similarity to the poem. Covent Garden, 1 Mar. 1751. *Auto.* R.M.20. e.6. *MS. copies*: R.M.18.d.6; Fitzwilliam (L.); Hamburg. J. Walsh ('The Choice of Hercules'—Overture, Songs, &c.) 4 May 1751. William Randall ('The Complete Score of the Choice of Hercules') 15 May 1773. Arnold, 55-56, *c.* 1789. H.G. 18.

Hercules. Musical Drama. Thomas Broughton, based on Ovid, 'Metamorphoses', Bk. IX and Sophocles, 'The Trachinians'. King's Theatre, 5 Jan. 1745. *Auto.* R.M.20.e.8. *MS. copies*: R.M.18.e.6; R.M.19.a.9 (Parts of the Trachinian and the Priest of Jupiter); R.M.19.a.11 (Part of Iole); Fitzwilliam, *fr.*; Fitzwilliam (L.); Hamburg. J. Walsh ('Hercules in Score—Overture, Symphonies, Songs, &c.) 9 Feb. 1745. Arnold, 34-39, 1788-89. H.G. 4.

Hymen. Serenata. English concert version of the opera 'Imeneo'. Librettist unknown. Music Hall, Fishamble Street, Dublin, 24 Mar. 1742. *See* also Operas, &c.—Imeneo.

Ode for St. Cecilia's Day. John Dryden. Lincoln's Inn Fields Theatre, 22 Nov. 1739. *Auto.* R.M.20.f.4; Fitzwilliam, *fr.* *MS. copies*: R.M.18.d.6; R.M.19.a.2, *fr.*; Fitzwilliam (L.); Hamburg. J. Walsh ('The Songs in the Ode wrote by Mr. Dryden for St. Cecilia's Day') 13 Dec. 1739. William Randall ('The Complete Score of the Ode for S^t. Cecilia's Day') 18 Feb. 1771. Arnold, 105-106, *c.* 1792. H.G. 23.

Ode for the Birthday of Queen Anne. ('Eternal Source of Light divine'.) Serenata. Author of words unknown. Most probably, Windsor, 6 Feb. 1714. *Auto.* R.M.20.g.2. *MS. copies*: R.M.19.e.1; B.M. Add. MSS. 35347; Fitzwilliam; Fitzwilliam (L.); Hamburg. Arnold, 54, *c.* 1789. H.G. 46a.

Il Parnasso in Festa. Serenata in honour of the marriage of the Princess Royal (Anne) and the Prince of Orange. Much of the music from 'Athalia'. Author of Italian text not known. English version by George Oldmixon. King's Theatre, 13 Mar. 1734. *Auto. fr.*: R.M.20.h.1; R.M.20.g.13; R.M. 20.d.2. *MS. copies*: R.M.19.d.2; R.M.18.c.4, *fr.*; R.M.18.c.8, *fr.*; R.M.19.d.11, *fr.*; Fitzwilliam (L.); Hamburg (partly in Handel's hand); Copy in J. S. Hawkins Sale, 29-30 May 1843. Not published in Handel's lifetime except J. Walsh (The Overture for the Harpsicord—Eighth Collection of Overtures) 2 Dec. 1743; (The Overture for Violins, &c.—Eighth Collection of Overtures) 19 July 1743. H.G. 54.

Semele. After the manner of an Oratorio. William Congreve, with alterations perhaps by Alexander Pope. Covent Garden, 10 Feb. 1744. *Auto.* R.M.20.f.7; Fitzwilliam, *fr.* *MS. copies*: R.M.19.d.6; R.M.18.e.4; R.M.19.b.3 (Seven separate parts); R.M.19.e.10 (String Parts); Hamburg. J. Walsh ('Semele as it is Perform'd at the Theatre Royal in Covent Garden' —Overture, Songs, &c.—Issued in three parts, advertised as 'Songs in Semele', &c. 25 Feb., 2 Mar., 10 Mar. 1744) 13 Mar. 1744. H. Wright (Score, advertised as being ready in the summer) 10 Feb 1787, no copy traced. Arnold, 24-28, 1788. H.G. 7.

MISCELLANEOUS SECULAR VOCAL WORKS

CANTATAS

72 Italian Cantatas for Voice and Continuo. (H.G. 50 and 51.) Various dates, early 18th century. *Auto.* (some numbers only): R.M.20.d.11; R.M.20.d.12; R.M.20.e.5; R.M.20.g.8; B.M. Add. MSS. 30310 (H.G. 50. No. 25); Bodleian Library (Nos. 10 and 72); Fitzwilliam (some numbers and fragments). *MS. copies* (some numbers only): R.M.19.a.7; R.M.19.e.7 (some with *auto.* notes); B.M. Add. MSS.: 14212, 14215, 14182, 29484, *ff*.45b-96, 31226, 31555, 31573, 31574, 5321, 14229; Eg. 2942 (Granville— 50 numbers, including 'Handel non può mia musa'); Fitzwilliam (L.—49 numbers). Arnold, 176-179 ('Thirteen Chamber Duetto's and Twelve Cantatas') 1797. H.G. 50, 51.

28 Italian Cantatas for various Voices and Instruments. (H.G. 52a and 52b.) Various dates, early 18th century. *Auto.* (some numbers only): R.M.20.d.13; R.M.20.e.1; R.M.20.e.2; R.M.20.e.3; R.M.20.e.4,5: R.M.20.f.12. *MS. copies*: (some numbers only): R.M.18.c.7; R.M.19.a.1; R.M.19.a.6; R.M.19.d.10;

R.M.19.e.7; R.M.19.d.11; B.M. Add. MSS. 31555, 31573. Arnold, 174–176 ('Two Trios and Four Cantatas in Score') c. 1797. H.G. 52a, 52b.

3 English Cantatas for Soprano, Violin, Violoncello and Basso Continuo. Attributed to Handel. c. 1720–30. 1. 'To lovely shades', Recit; 'My fair from hence is gone', Aria. &c, 2. 'With roving and with ranging', Aria, &c. 3. 'So pleasing the pains', Aria, &c. MS. Bibliotheca della Accademia di Santa Cecilia, Rome.

Cecilia, volgi un sguardo. See Secular Choral Works, &c.—Alexander's Feast.

Diana Cacciatrice. Unpublished Cantata. Date? *Auto. fr.*: Staatsbibliothek, Berlin; Gesellschaft der Musikfreunde, Vienna. See J. M. Coopersmith, 'Handelian Lacunæ'. (*The Musical Quarterly*, April 1935.)

Ero e Leandro. Unpublished Cantata. c. 1707. *Auto. fr.*: Koch Collection, Wildegg, Switzerland; Musikbibliothek Peters, Leipzig. See J. M. Coopersmith, 'Handelian Lacunæ'. (*The Musical Quarterly*, April 1935.)

Handel non può mia musa. For Solo Voice and Continuo; in praise of the composer. Cardinal Benedetto Pamfili. *Auto.* University Library, Münster, Westphalia. *MS. copies*: Eg. 2942 (Granville); Fitzwilliam. Performed, Handel Festival, Cambridge, 10 June 1935; Ramsgate, 19 Nov. 1951. (Translated by Dr. James S. Hall—Arranged by Ernest S. Stride.)

Look down, harmonious Saint. See 28 Italian Cantatas. H.G. 52a. No. 8.

Pastorella vagha bella. Cantata for Soprano or Tenor, Cembalo and Violoncello. Date? *MS.*: Musikbibliothek Peters, Leipzig. F. Kistner and C. F. W. Siegel (Edited by Max Seiffert, German words by H. J. Moser) 1935.

Quel fior che all' alba ride. Unpublished Cantata for Soprano Solo, similar in part to the Duet, H.G. 32a. No. 15. *Auto.* Fitzwilliam, 30 H. 11, pp. 38–39.

Venus and Adonis. Cantata for Voice and Continuo. Words by John Hughes, c. 1711. *MS. copy*: B.M. Add. MSS. 31993 (Two arias only— 'Dear Adonis' and 'Transporting Joy'). Augener, 1938, edited by William C. Smith, music arranged by Havergal Brian. Handel's first songs to English words.

DUETS AND TRIOS

22 Italian Duets with Continuo. (H.G. 32 and 32a.) Words of Nos. 3-14 by Ortensio Mauro; No. 18a, translation from Horace. Various dates, c. 1707-45. *Auto.* R.M.20.g.9 (11 numbers); Fitzwilliam (4 numbers and *fr.*); Staatsbibliothek, Berlin (2 numbers); *MS. copies* (various numbers): R.M.18.b.11; R.M.18.b.14; R.M. 19.f.2; R.M.19.e.7; R.M.19.a.7; B.M. Add. MSS. 5322 (11 numbers); Eg. 2943 (Granville—12 numbers); Fitzwilliam (7 numbers); Fitzwilliam (L—12 numbers); Hamburg (some numbers only); Ellis, Bond Street, Catalogue, No. 217, lists 'Vocal Duets, in Italian and English, contemporary manuscript', 3 vols., 600 pp. from the Barrett Lennard Collection; C. P. E. Bach owned a copy of 9 numbers. William Randall ('Thirteen Celebrated Italian Duets'—H.G. Nos. 3-13, 1 and 14) 8 Nov. 1777 (issued by Elizabeth Randall). Arnold, 176-179 ('Thirteen Chamber Duetto's and Twelve Cantatas') 1797. H.G. 32, 32a.

Spero indarna. Duet with Bass for Harpsichord. Date? *MS. copies*: B.M. Add. MSS. 5322; 31573.

2 Italian Trios with Continuo. 1. 'Se tu non lasci amore'. Ortensio Mauro.

U

1708. 2. 'Quel fior che all' alba ride'. Author of words? *c.* 1708. *Auto.* No. 1. Koch Collection, Wildegg, Switzerland, dated 12 July 1708, Naples. *MS. copies*: R.M.18.b.11; R.M.19.a.6 (No. 2); B.M. Add. MSS. 31496; 31723 (Bass part of No. 1); Eg. 2943 (Granville—No. 2); Eg. 2459 (No. 2); Fitzwilliam. R. Birchall ('Two Celebrated Italian Trios') 5 July 1784. (Plates 16-19 of this edition were used with modifications in Arnold's edition.) Arnold, 174-176 ('Two Trios and Four Cantatas in Score') *c.* 1796. H.G. 32, 32a.

SONGS

La bella Pastorella. ('E troppo bella troppo amorosa'). *Auto.* Cummings Sale Catalogue, 1917. No. 132. Facsimile copy, B.M. Add. MSS. 35027. C. Lonsdale, edited by W. H. Cummings, *c.* 1877.

A Collection of Choice English Songs (A Choice Collection of English Songs) Set to Musick by Mr. Handel. J. Walsh. 28 Aug. 1731. Also known as 'English Minuet Songs'; '20 Songs set to his (Handel's) Minuets'. Copy in the N.L.S. (Julian Marshall—Balfour collection) consists of the following 24 numbers — 1. 'As Celia's fatal arrows'. (The Unhappy Lovers.) 2. 'Return fair maid'. (A Favourite Minuet in Porus.) 3. 'When fearful Pastorella'. (The Bagpipe Song in Porus.) 4. 'Beneath a shady willow'. (The Dream.) 5. 'Oh cruel tyrant Love'. (Strephon's complaint of Love.) 6. 'Come to my arms'. (A Favourite Air by Mr. Handel.) 7. 'Chloe when I view thee smiling'. (A Song to a favourite Minuet.) 8. 'Bacchus one day'. (A Song to a favourite Minuet.) 9. 'Why will Florella'. (Florella. A Song by an Eminent Master.) 10. 'When I survey Clarinda's charms'. (A Song made to a favourite Minuet.) 11. 'We follow brave Hannibal'. (A Song to the March in Scipio.) 12. 'Strephon in vain'. (A Song made to a favourite Minuet in Rodelinda.) 13. 'The sun was sunk'. (The Poor Shepherd.) 14. 'Says my uncle, I pray you discover'. (Molly Mogg.) 15. 'Wine's a mistress gay and easy'. (Sung by Mr. Leveridge in the Entertainment of Love and Wine.) 16. 'Faithless ungrateful'. (The forsaken maid's complaint.) 17. 'Charming is your shape and air'. (The Polish Minuet, or Miss Kitty Greville's Delight. A Song sung by Mr. Ray at the Theatre Royal.) 18. 'See the yielding fair'. (A Two-part Song sung by Mr. Legar and Mr. Leveridge.) 19. 'Flatt'ring tongue, no more I hear thee'. (A Song by an Eminent Master.) '20. 'Thyrsis afflicted. (A Song to Mr. Handel's Trumpet Minuet—i.e. in 'the Water Music'.) 21. 'Hark how the trumpet sounds'. (The Soldier's call to the war—Set to the French Horn Minuet—i.e. in 'The Water Music'.) 22. 'Twas when the seas were roaring'. (The faithful Maid. Sung in the Comick Tragick Pastoral Farce or What d'ye call it.) 23. 'Oh lovely charmer'. (Favourite Minuet in the additional Songs of Floridant.) 24. 'Ye winds to whom Collin complains'. (An Answer to Collin's complaint, the tune by Mr. Handel.)

Some of these songs may be original works or vocal settings of minuets by Handel; others are arrangements of excerpts from operas, &c., and some may be attributed wrongly to Handel. Many were issued as sheet songs at one time or another before the collected edition, in which, in some cases, the earlier plates were used, and copies of the sheet song issues are in the British Museum (catalogued under their separate titles) and elsewhere, sometimes with other words and titles. Some numbers are also to be found in 'The Musical Miscellany', 'The British Musical Miscellany', 'The Universal

Musician', and other 18th century song books, also in Walsh's Collection of Minuets, &c.

The Death of the Stag. ('When Phœbus the tops of the hills does adorn'.) Hunting Song for two voices, 1740 or earlier. *MS. copies*: B.M. Add. MSS. 33351, 34074-5, 34126. Appeared as a sheet song in a number of editions from *c.* 1740 onwards (B.M. G.313.(93.), &c.) and in various collections ('Apollo's Cabinet', 1756, &c.). It was included in 'A Companion to the Magdalen-Chapel containing the Hymns', &c., *c.* 1780, as a Hymn on the Redemption ('When Jesus our Saviour came down from above').

The Forsaken Nymph. ('Guardian Angels now protect me'.) Song, attributed to Handel. *c.* 1739 or earlier. Henry Roberts, 'Calliope or English Harmony' Vol. 1. p. 62, 1739. Also in other early song books, and as a sheet song. Not the same as 'Guardian Angels' in 'The Triumph of Time and Truth'.

French Songs. 'Airs francois de G. F. Hendel'. 1. 'Sans y penser'. 'Chanson'. 2. 'S'il ne falloit que bien aimer'. 'Cantate Francoise par Mr. Handel' (with alterations in pencil in a later hand). 3. 'Petite fleur brunette' (with alterations in pencil). 4. 'Vous qui m'aviez procuré une amour eternelle' (with alterations in pencil). 5. 'Nos plaisirs seront peu durables'. 6. 'Vous ne scauriez flatter ma peine'. 7. 'Non, je ne puis souffrir.' 'Air'. *c.* 1707-09, *Auto.* R.M.20.d.11. *MS. copy*: B.M. Add. MSS. 31573 (Nos. 1, 2 and 4). C. Lonsdale, Nos. 6 and 7, edited by Adolf Ganz. *c.* 1850.

From scourging Rebellion. 'A Song on the Victory obtain'd over the Rebels by His Royal Highness the Duke of Cumberland. The words by Mr. (John) Lockman'. J. Walsh, 26 May, 1746. Also in 'The Vocal Musical Mask', Book IV. *c.* 1746; 'The London Magazine', July 1746, pp. 364-365, and sheet song editions.

3 German Songs. Lieder. 1. In deinem schönen Mund'. 2 'Endlich muss man doch entdecken'. 3. 'Ein hoher Geist muss immer höher denken'. Author of words? *c.* 1696-98. MS. owned by Rudolph Chrysander, Hamburg. Max Seiffert, 'Händels deutsche Gesänge' (Rochus von Liliencron Festschrift), Breitkopf & Härtel, Leipzig, 1910—where No. 3 is printed.

I like the am'rous youth that's free. Song. 'Sung by Mrs. Clive in the Comedy call'd the Universal Passion (By James Miller). Set by Mr. Handel.' Drury Lane, 28 Feb. 1737. Issued as a sheet song, *c.* 1737, and by J. Walsh, 'The British Orpheus', Book I. p. 2, 1741, and Henry Roberts, 'Clio and Euterpe', Vol. I. p. 98, 1758.

Love's but the frailty of the mind. Song. Sung by Mrs. Clive in (Congreve's) 'The Way of the World'. Drury Lane, 17 Mar. 1740; benefit of Mrs. Clive. *Auto.* Fitzwilliam. *MS. copy*: R.M.19.d.11. Early English Musical Magazine, Vol 1. No. 6, June 1891, edited by A. H. Mann.

The Morning is charming. Hunting Song, words by Charles Legh. 1751. *Auto.* Fitzwilliam; Legh family, Adlington Hall, Macclesfield. *Facsimile*, R. A. Streatfeild 'Handel'. Early English Musical Magazine, Vol 1. No. 6, June 1891, edited and arranged by A. H. Mann for four parts. Musical Times, Dec. 1942, edited by O. E. Deutsch.

Not Cloe that I better am. Song. J. Walsh, 'British Musical Miscellany', Vol. V. p. 121, 1736.

Stand round my brave boys. 'A Song made for the Gentleman Volunteers of the City of London. Set to Musick by Mr. Handel'. 1745. *MS. copy*: B.M. Add. MSS. 31573. John Simpson, 15 Nov. 1745. The London Magazine, Nov. 1745. Republished as a sheet song, with altered wording, at the time of the French Revolution. William C. Smith collection. *Yes, I'm in Love.* Song. Words by W. Whitehead. *c.* 1740. Anonymous sheet song issues, B.M. G. 314. (20.); G. 305. (263.)

CHAMBER MUSIC AND MISCELLANEOUS INSTRUMENTAL MUSIC

Concerto in D major, for two Violins, Harpsichord and Violoncello obligato. *c.* 1725 or earlier. *MS.*: Library of Count Schönborn, in Wiesentheid (Unterfranken). Schott, Mainz, edited by Fritz Zobeley, 1935.

Concerto in D minor, for Flute, Violin, Harpsichord and Violoncello obligato. c. 1725 or earlier. *MS.*: Library of Count Schönborn, in Wiesentheid (Unterfranken). Schott, Mainz, edited by Fritz Zobeley, 1935.

Concerto in E♭ major, for Solo Oboe, Strings and Harpsichord. c. 1715. *MS.*: Upsala University Library. Henry Litolff, edited by Fritz Stein, 1935.

15 Solos (Sonatas) for a German Flute, Oboe or Violin and Continuo. Op. 1. c. 1731. *Auto.* (some numbers and *fr.*): R.M. 20.g.13; R.M.20.g.14; Fitzwilliam. *MS. copy*: Calkin and Budd, Catalogue, 1844. J. Roger, Amsterdam ('Sonates pour un Traversiere un Violon ou Hautbois Con Basso Continuo'—12 Sonatas, H.G. Nos. 1b, 2-9, 14, 11 and 15, with some differences) *c.* 1731; B.M. copy has a manuscript note on Nos. 10 (H.G. 14) and 12 (H.G. 15): 'N.B. This is not Mr. Handel's'. J. Walsh ('Solos For a German Flute a Hoboy or Violin with a Thorough Bass for the Harpsicord', &c.—12 Sonatas, H.G. Nos. 1b, 2-12, from Roger's plates with differences) Nov. 1732 or earlier; B.M. copy (g.74.h) has a manuscript note on Nos. 10 and 12: 'Not Mr. Handel's Solo'. Arnold, 139-140 ('12 Sonatas or Solos', &c.—same numbers as Roger's edition) *c.* 1794. H.G. 27, pp. 2-56.

3 Solos for a German Flute and Bass. c. 1730. J. Walsh and Joseph Hare ('Six Solos Four for a German Flute and a Bass and two for a Violin with a Thorough Bass . . . Compos'd by Mr. Handel Sig^r: Geminiani Sig^r: Somis Sig^r: Brivio'—Nos. 1-3 are by Handel) 22 July 1730. H.G. 48, pp. 130-139.

6 Sonatas for two Oboes and Bass. c. 1696. *MS. copy*: R.M.18.b.3. See Burney, 'Commemoration', p. 3; G. F. Händel, 'Abstammung und Jugendwelt', Halle, 1935, p. 135. H.G. 27, pp. 58-90.

6 Sonatas for two Violins, Oboes or German Flutes and Continuo. Op. 2. c. 1730 or earlier. *MS. copies*: R.M.19.g.6; B.M. Add. MSS. 31575; R.C.M.260 (Nos. 1, 3-5). J. Roger, Amsterdam ('VI Sonates à deux Violons, deux haubois ou deux Flutes traversieres & Basse Continue . . . Second ouvrage') *c.* 1731. J. Walsh ('VI Sonates à deux Violons, deux haubois', &c.—From Roger's plates, with differences) *c.* 1732-33. Arnold, 47-48, 1789. H.G. 27, pp. 92-108, 115-141.

Sonata in G minor, for two Violins, Bass and Organ. Another version of Op. 2. No. 5. MS. copy, *c.* 1730, formerly owned by T. W. Bourne. H.G. 48, pp.118-129.

3 Sonatas for two Violins, Oboes or German Flutes with Continuo. Date?

MS. copy: Royal Collection, Dresden. H.G. 27, pp. 109-114, 142-154, included with Op. 2, to which they do not belong.

7 Sonatas or Trios for two Violins or German Flutes with a Thorough Bass for the Harpsichord or Violoncello. Opera Quinta. 1739. *Auto.* R.M.20.g.14,*fr. MS. copies*: R.M.19.f.6; R.M.19.g.6; B.M. Add. MSS. 31575; J. S. Hawkins sale, May 1843. J. Walsh ('Seven Sonatas or Trios,' &c.) 28 Feb. 1739. Arnold, 48-49, 1789. H.G. 27, pp. 156-200.

Sonata in B♭ major, for Oboe and Continuo. Date? *Auto.* Fitzwilliam ('Sonata pour l'Hautbois Solo'). Rudall Carte and Co., edited by A. H. Mann for Flute and Piano, *c.*1892; Schott and Co., arranged by T. Dart and W. Bergmann, for Oboe and Piano, 1948.

*Sonata in C major, for Viola da Gamba¹and Cembalo. c.*1705. *MS. copies*: Darmstadt (*See* A. Einstein, *Sammelbände der Internationalen Musik-Gesellschaft*, Jahr. IV. Heft 1. Oct.-Dec, 1902, pp. 170-172); Nägeli Collection, Zurich. H.G.48, pp. 112-117.

Sonata in D major, for Flute, Violoncello and Harpsichord? Date? Breitkopf and Härtel (for Flute, Violoncello and Pianoforte), edited by Max Seiffert ('Kammersonaten', No. 22) *c.*1924.

Sonata in D major, for Flute and Continuo. Date? *MS.* Archiepiscopal Library, Paderborn ('Traversiere solo Sig. Hendel'). Bärenreiter Verlag, Kassel, (for Flute and Pianoforte) edited by W. Hinnenthal, Bielefeld (1935), 1949.

Sonata in D major, for Violoncello and Continuo? Date? *J. C. Smith MS. copy?* William Ayrton, Sale, July 3, 1858. Present location, Vienna?

Sonata in E minor, for two German Flutes and Bass. Date? *MS. copy*: R.M.19.a.4 ('Sonata con due Flauti Travers: Del S^r. Hend(el)').

Sonata in G major, for Violin (and Harpsichord?) Date? *MS.* in Mempel's handwriting, Musikbibliothek Peters, Leipzig. Breitkopf and Härtel (for Violin and Pianoforte), edited by Max Seiffert ('Kammersonaten', No. 21) 1924.

3 Sonate a tre (two Violins and Continuo). Date? *MS. copy*: R.C.M. No. 260, Nos. 5-7 (Sacred Harmonic Society Catalogue, 1872. No. 1633). The MS. also contains four numbers from Op. 2.

The Fitzwilliam Sonatas, for Treble Recorder and Piano or Harpsichord (with Violoncello or Viola da Gamba ad lib.). Date? Schott, edited by Thurston Dart, from fragments in the Fitzwilliam Museum, including a version of the Sonata Op. 1, No. 9, H.G. 27. 1948.

Trio in F major, for Oboe, Bassoon, Bass and Harpsichord? *c.* 1703. *MS.*: Theological Academy, Paderborn. Breitkopf and Härtel (for Oboe, Bassoon, Bass and Pianoforte), edited by Max Seiffert ('Kammertrios', No. 24) 1938.

Trio in G minor, for Violin, Violoncello (Gamba) and Harpsichord? Early 18th century. MS. Royal Library, Copenhagen. Breitkopf and Härtel (for Violin, Violoncello (Gamba) and Pianoforte), edited by Max Seiffert ('Kammertrios', No. 23) 1934.

*Clock Music. c.*1740 or earlier. *MS. copies*: R.M.18.b.8 ('Sonata by Mr Handel For a Musical Clock', and other movements); R.M.19.a.1 ('Ten (or rather eleven) tunes for Clay's Musical Clock'). W. Barclay Squire, 'Handel's Clock Music' (*The Musical Quarterly*, Oct. 1919). H. Flammer, New York, edited by R. Purvis ('Suite for a Musical Clock for the Organ') 1952.

Forest Music for Treble and Bass (*Violin and Harpsichord*). Written for Mrs. Vernon (Dorothy Grahn), Clontarf Castle, Cork, 1742. Printed by F. Rhames, Dublin, edited by William Ware, 1803. Smollet Holden, Dublin, arranged in eight parts, for military band, *c.*1815. Henry Bussell, Dublin for piano, edited by Dr. John Smith, 1854. C. Lonsdale, London, for piano, *c.*1856.

Minuets and Marches, for Violin, Oboe or Flute; Violin and Bass; Harpsichord, Violin or Flute. Various dates. *Auto.* R.M.20.f.3,*f.*10; R.M.20.f.4,*f.*3v; *MS. copies*: R.M.18.b.8; R.M.19.a.4; R.M.18.b.4; B.M. Add. MSS. 31453. Many published for the first time in W. Barclay Squire and Fuller-Maitland's 'Pieces for Harpsichord', from Aylesford MSS. in the King's Music Library, which include a number of what appear to be original works, as well as arrangements from operas, instrumental music, &c. Some numbers also appeared in one or other of the following printed collections: J. Walsh and John Hare ('A Collection of Minuets, Rigadoons or French Dances for the Year 1720 . . . by Mr. Hendell, Mr. Lature and Mr. Hill . . . for the Violin or Hautboy') 5 Feb. 1720; J. Walsh and Joseph Hare ('Minuets for his Majesty King George IId's Birthday, 1727 . . . Composed by Mr. Handell . . . for a Violin or Hoboy') 11 Nov. 1727 or earlier; J. Walsh, Joseph Hare and John Young ('A General Collection of Minuets made for the Balls at Court. The Operas and Masquerades Consisting of Sixty in number Compos'd by Mr. Handell. To which is added Twelve celebrated Marches made on several occasions by the same Author . . . for the German Flute or Violin'—'The Basses to the General Collection', &c.) 19 Apr., 17 May, 1729; this collection was also advertised as 'A Choice Collection of 72 Marches, Minuets & Trumpet Tunes for the German Flute, Violin and Hautboy, with Bass', 22 July 1730; and as 'Handel's 72 Minuets and Marches'; J. Walsh ('Select Minuets Collected From the Operas, the Balls at Court, the Masquerades . . . For the Harpsicord, Violin or German Flute. Compos'd by Mr. Handel, Dr. Greene, Mr. M. C. Festing, Mr. Hudson') 31 Oct. 1739; J. Walsh ('A Second Book of Select Minuets . . . by Mr. Handel, St. Martini, Pasquali and Hasse') 11 Mar. 1745; J. Walsh ('Select Minuets by Mr. Handel, Hasse', &c.) 3 vols. 6 Sept 1759; ('Select Minuets', &c.), 4 vols. 7 June 1765; J Walsh ('Handel's Favourite Minuets . . . for the Harpsicord, German Flute, Violin or Guitar') 4 books, 13 Dec. 1762 (tomorrow will be publish'd); David Rutherford ('Musicæ Spiritus or a Collection of the choicest Airs Selected out of Mr. Handel's Works and other Celebrated Masters . . . for two German Flutes') *c.* 1750.

See also 'A Collection of Choice English Songs' (Minuet Songs).

ORCHESTRAL WORKS INCLUDING ORGAN CONCERTOS

6 Concerti Grossi for Flutes, Oboes, Bassoons, Strings and Continuo. Op. 3. No. 1 in B♭ major-G minor. No. 2 in B♭ major. No. 3 in G major. No. 4 in F major. No. 5 in D minor. No. 6 in D major-minor. Dates? *Auto.* R.M.20.g.13 (No. 6, *fr.*). *MS. copies*: R.M.19.g.7; R.M.19.e.1 (No. 4); R.M.19.g.6, *fr.*; B.M. Add. MSS. 31576 (*fr.*: Nos. 2, 4 and 5); Fitzwilliam (L.—Nos. 1, 2 and 4). J. Walsh ('Concerti Grossi Con Due Violini e Violoncello di Concertino

Obligati e Due Altri Violini Viola e Basso di Concerto Grosso Ad Arbitrio . . .
Opera Terza') 7 Dec. 1734 or earlier. Arnold, 172-174, *c*.1796. H.G. 21,
pp. 3-60.

    12 Concerti Grossi for Strings and Continuo. Op. 6. No. 1 in G major.
No. 2 in F major. No. 3 in E minor. No. 4 in A minor. No. 5 in D major.
No. 6 in G minor. No. 7 in B♭ major. No. 8 in C minor. No. 9 in F major.
No. 10 in D minor. No. 11 in A major. No. 12 in B minor. 1739. *Auto.*
R.M.20.g.11 (Nos. 1, 2, 5 and 6 have Oboe parts); Fitzwilliam, *fr. MS. copies*:
R.M.19.g.5; B.M. Add. MSS. 31576, *fr.* (Nos. 1, 2, 5, 6, 8-12); Eg. 2944
(Granville—Nos. 1-12); Eg. 2941 (Granville—No. 10); Fitzwilliam (L.). J.
Walsh ('Twelve Grand Concertos in Seven Parts for Four Violins, a Tenor
Violin, a Violoncello with a Through Bass for the Harpsicord') 21 Apr. 1740.
Arnold, 60-64, 1790. H.G. 30.

    6 Organ Concertos, with Oboes and Strings. Op. 4. No. 1 in G minor. No. 2
in B♭ major. No. 3 in G minor. No. 4 in F major. No. 5 in F major. No. 6
in B♭ major. *c.* 1735-6. *Auto*: R.M.20.g.12 (No. 1, No. 6—'Concerto per
la Harpa'); B.M. King's MSS. 317 (Nos. 2, 3 and 4); Fitzwilliam, *fr.*
MS. copies: R.M.20.g.13 (No. 6—Harp or Organ part in copyist's hand,
partly crossed out by Handel); R.M.19.a.1 (No. 6—Organ part, 'Concerto
per il Liuto e l'Harpa' and Organ. This concerto was played in Act I of
'Alexander's Feast', following the recitative 'Timotheus plac'd on high',
1736); Eg. 2945 (Granville); Fitzwilliam (L.). J. Walsh ('Six Concertos for
the Harpsicord or Organ') 4 Oct. 1738. The Instrumental Parts, J. Walsh
('Six Concertos for the Organ and Harpsicord; Also for Violins Hautboys and
other Instruments . . . Opera Quarta') 4 Oct. 1738 (in a few days); 2 Dec.
1738 (this day is published). Arnold, 121-124, *c.* 1793. H.G. 28, pp. 3-69.

    6 Organ Concertos, with Oboes and Strings. Second Set. No. 1 in F major.
No. 2 in A major. No. 3 in D minor. No. 4 in G major. No. 5 in D major.
No. 6 in G minor. *c.* 1739. *Auto.* R.M.20.g.12 (Nos. 1 and 2); R.M.20.g.14
(No. 1, *fr.* dated 2 April 1739). *MS. copy*: Eg. 2945 (Granville—Nos. 1 and 2).
J. Walsh ('A Second Set of Six Concertos For the Harpsicord or Organ')
8 Nov. 1740; The Instrumental Parts of Nos. 1 and 2, J. Walsh ('Two
Concertos for the Organ or Harpsicord with the Instrumental Parts for
Violins, Hoboys, &c. in Seven Parts . . . 2d Set') 31 Jan. 1760. Instrumental
parts for Nos. 3-6 not issued, presumably as the Organ Parts could be played
with the Instrumental Parts of the 'Twelve Grand Concertos', op. 6, Nos.
10, 1, 5 and 6, of which they were organ arrangements; Nos. 1 and 2 of the
'Concertos for the Organ' do not agree exactly with the Instrumental Parts
of Op. 6, Nos. 9 and 11, of which they were arrangements, No. 1 including
also movements from No. 6 of the 'Seven Sonatas or Trios', op. 5. H.G. 48,
pp. 2-50.

    6 Organ Concertos, with Oboes and Strings. Third Set. Op. 7. No. 1 in
B♭ major. No. 2 in A major. No. 3 in B♭ major. No. 4 in D minor. No. 5
in G minor. No. 6 in B♭ major. 1740-51. *Auto.* R.M.20.g.12; R.M.20.g.14
(No. 3, *fr.* and No. 6, *fr.*); Fitzwilliam, *fr. MS. copies*: R.M.18.c.6 (No. 4,
fr.); R.M.19.a.1 (No. 4, *fr.*); R.M.19.a.2 (Nos. 2 and 6); Eg. 2945 Granville—Nos. 1, 2 and 4). J. Walsh ('A Third Set of Six Concertos for the Harpsicord or Organ') 23 Feb. 1761; The Instrumental Parts, J. Walsh ('A Third
Set of Six Concertos for the Organ and Harpsicord with the Instrumental

Parts for Violins, Hoboys, &c. in 7 Parts . . . Opera 7ma') 23 Feb. 1761.
Arnold, 124-128 ('A Second Set of Six Concertos') *c.* 1793. H.G. 28, pp.
73-140.

Concerto Grosso in C major, for Oboes, Strings and Continuo. 1736. *Auto.*
R.M.20.g.11 (Dated 25 Jan. 1736. This Concerto was played at the begin-
ning of 'Alexander's Feast', Act II.) *MS. copies:* R.M.19.a.1 (Organo part);
B.M. Add. MSS. 31576, *fr*; Eg. 2946 (Granville); Fitzwilliam ('Concerto
per il Gravicembalo in C'); Fitzwilliam (L.); William C. Smith Collection,
Instrumental Parts from the Aylesford Collection. J. Walsh ('Select Harmony
Fourth Collection. Six Concertos in Seven Parts. For Violins and other
Instruments Compos'd by Mr Handel Tartini and Veracini', No. 1.) 11 Dec.
1740. Advertised as a separate work by Walsh, but no copy traced. Arnold,
98-99 ('Concertante In nine parts', &c.) *c.* 1791. H.G. 21, pp. 63-82.

Concerto in B♭ major, for Oboes, Strings and Continuo. Date? *MS. copy:*
B.M. Add. MSS. 31576. J. Walsh ('Select Harmony Fourth Collection,'
&c. No. 2—*See* preceding item) 11 Dec. 1740. H.G. 21, pp. 85-90.

Concerto in B♭ major, for Oboes, Strings and Continuo. Date? J. Walsh
('Select Harmony Fourth Collection', &c. No. 3—*See* preceding item)
11 Dec. 1740. H.G. 21, pp. 91-97.

Concerto in F major, for 2 Horns, 2 Oboes, Strings and Continuo. c. 1740.
Auto. fr. R.M.20.g.13 ('Largo' for two Horns, two Oboes, two Violins,
Viola ad libitum and Bass). A fragment based on the preceding item. H.G.
21, pp. 98-99.

*Concerto (Double Concerto) in B♭ major, for Oboes, Bassoons, Strings and
Continuo* (Concerto a Due Cori). *c.* 1740-50. *Auto.* R.M.20.g.11 (Wanting
the first three movements); B.M. Add. MSS. 30310 *ff.* 39-48 (Parts missing
from R.M.20.g.11). Arnold 179-180 ('Concertos &c. for the Organ . . . now
first Published 1797'—'Full Concerto II', with Horns in the last movement). H.G. 47, pp. 130-158.

Concerto in D major, for Horns, Strings and 2 Claviers. c. 1710-15. *MS.:*
Prince Bentheim-Tecklenburg, Rheda. Breitkopf and Härtel, edited by Max
Seiffert ('Concerti Grossi', No. 30) 1939.

Concerto in D minor, for 2 Organs, Bassoons and Strings. Date? Similar to
the first movement of Op. 7. No. 4. *See* 'Zeitschrift für Musikwissenschaft',
Nov. 1935. H.G. 48, pp. 51-56.

Concerto in D minor, for Organ and Strings. Date? *Auto.* R.M.20.g.14.
Arnold, 179 ('Concertos &c. for the Organ . . . now first Published 1797'—
'Concerto for the Organ'). H.G. 48, pp. 57-67.

*Concerto in F major, for 2 Oboes, Bassoon, 4 Horns, Strings and Continuo.
c.* 1749. Used in the 'Fireworks Music'. *Au^{t}o.* R.M.20.g.7. H.G. 47,
pp. 72-79.

*Concerto in D major, for 2 Oboes, Bassoon, 4 Horns, 2 Trumpets, Drums,
Strings and Continuo. c.* 1749. Used in the 'Fireworks Music'; similar to the
preceding except for transposition, and the addition of Trumpet and Drum
parts. *Auto.* R.M.20.g.7. *MS. copies:* R.M.19.a.2; R.M.18.b.9 (Parts for
Tromba I, II and Drums); William C. Smith Collection, imperfect set of
parts from the Aylesford Collection. H.G. 47, pp. 80-98.

*Concerto in F major, for 2 Oboes, Bassoon, 2 Horns, Strings and Continuo.
c.* 1715. *Auto.* B.M. Add. MSS. 30310, *ff.* 52-62 (Two movements, the first

unnamed, the second 'Alla Hornpipe', which also appear in the 'Water Music' in D major, for different instruments). Chrysander considered it an independent work. H.G.47, pp. 2-15. *See* also Water Music.

Concerto (Double Concerto) in F major, for Horns, Oboes, Bassoons, Strings and Continuo. c. 1740-50. *Auto.* R.M.20.g.6; Fitzwilliam, *fr.* H.G. 47, pp. 159-231. Chrysander subsequently published a different edition of H.G. 47, pp. 203-231, as 'Overture' ('Concerto III') in H.G. 47, supplement, pp. 203-241, which is similar to H.G. 48, pp. 68-100. This work is in Arnold, 180 ('Concertos &c. for the Organ now first Published 1797'—'Concerto Organo', pp. 46-80).

Concerto in G minor, for Oboe, with Strings and Continuo. c. 1703. J. Schuberth, Leipzig, *c.* 1860. H.G. 21, pp. 100-107.

Fireworks Music. Composed and performed for celebrations for the Peace of Aix-la-Chapelle (18 Oct. 1748) in the Green Park, 27 Apr. 1749; rehearsal at Vauxhall Gardens, 21 Apr. *Auto.* R.M.20.g.7; Fitzwilliam, *fr. MS. copies:* R.M.18.b.5 (Third Trumpet part); Fitzwilliam (L.—but now missing). J. Walsh ('The Musick for the Royal Fireworks in all its Parts viz. French Horns, Trumpets, Kettle Drums, Violins, Hoboys, Violoncello, & Bassoons. with a Thorough Bass for the Harpsicord or Organ') 24 June 1749 or a little earlier. J. Walsh ('The Musick for the Royal Fireworks Set for the German Flute Violin or Harpsicord'—Contains in addition a number of miscellaneous Marches, &c., by Handel, and one number not identified as being by or attributed to him) July 22, 1749, or a little later. Arnold, 24, 1788. H.G. 47, pp. 100-127.

Hornpipe in D major, for Violins, Violas and Bassi. 1740. *MS. copy:* R.M.19.d.11 ('Hornpipe compos'd for the Concert at Vauxhall, 1740'). H.G. 48, p. 144.

Overture in B♭ major, for Oboes, Strings and Continuo. Date? *MS. copies:* R.M.19.a.4 (Score); R.M.18.b.8 (Harpsichord). J. Walsh ('Handel's Overtures XI. Collection for Violins, &c. in 8 Parts'—No. 5 in this set is this Overture, unnamed), 21 Oct. 1758; and also in J. Walsh, 'Six Overtures Set for Harpsicord . . . Eleventh collection', published about the same time or a little earlier. The principal subject is similar to the Overture of 'Il Trionfo del Tempo e del Disinganno.' H.G. 48, pp. 108-111.

Overture in D major, for Flute, Oboes, Bassoons, Archlute, Strings and Continuo. Date? *Auto.* R.M.20.g.13, *ff.* 29-32v ('Ouverture'). Unidentified and unpublished.

Overture in D major, for 2 Clarinets and Corno di Caccia. c. 1740. *Auto.* Fitzwilliam, 30. H. 14, pp. 17-23. Mercury Music Corporation, New York, edited by J. M Coopersmith and Jan La Rue' ('Sonata in D major for 2 Clarinets and Horn') 1950; Schott & Co., edited and arranged by Karl Haas ('Overture (Suite) for two Clarinets (in B flat) and Corno di Caccia (Horn in F) or two Violins and Viola') 1952.

8 Sinfonie diverse. H.G. 48, pp. 140-143. Miscellaneous items; alternative versions. *MS. copies:* Formerly Lennard Collection; R.M.19.a.1, *ff.* 158v-159 (March).

Sonata a 5 (Concerto) in B♭ major, for Violin Solo, Oboes, Strings and Continuo. c. 1710. *Auto.* R.M.20.g.14.*ff.* 11-20 ('Sonata 5'). H.G. 21, pp. 108-116.

Water Music. c. 1717. *Auto.* B.M. Add. MSS. 30310, *ff.* 52-62 (Two movements in F major, for 2 Oboes, Bassoon, 2 Horns, Strings and Continuo. Attributed to 1715, and published in H.G. 47, pp. 2-15 as a Concerto in F major. The movements appear in the 'Water Music,' in D major, for different instruments); Fitzwilliam, *fr*. 30.H.10, p.11. *MS. copies*: Eg. 2946 (Granville); Fitzwilliam (L.); The Earl of Malmesbury's Collection has an MS of '23 airs' J. Walsh ('The Celebrated Water Musick in Seven Parts viz. Two French Horns Two Violins or Hoboys a Tenor and a Thorough Bass for the Harpsicord or Bass Violin') *c*. 1732-3; consists of 9 unnumbered pieces or groups of pieces containing 21 movements in all. The parts are Corno Primo, Corno Secondo, Violino e Hautboy Primo, Violino e Hautboy Secondo, Alto Viola, Violoncello e Cembalo and Bassoon; J. Walsh ('Handel's Celebrated Water Musick Compleat. Set for the Harpsicord. To which is added, Two favourite Minuets, with Variations for the Harpsicord, By Geminiani') 1743; this is an augmented edition containing 41 separate movements, one movement of the earlier issue being omitted. For details of movements issued as instrumental pieces and songs, some of them probably before the publication of the parts, see William C. Smith, 'The Earliest Editions of the Water Music' (*Concerning Handel*, Cassell & Co., 1948); and for the spurious edition by Daniel Wright in 1733, and other little known 18th-century editions, *see* William C. Smith, 'More Handeliana' ('*Music and Letters*', Dec. 1952). Arnold, 23-24, 1788. H.G. 47, pp. 18-70.

HARPSICHORD MUSIC

6 Fugues. Op. 3. No. 1 in G minor. No. 2 in G major. No. 3 in B♭ major. No. 4 in B minor. No. 5 in A minor. No. 6 in C minor. Date? *Auto*. R.M.20.g.14. *MS. copies*: R.M.18.b.8; R.M.19.a.3; The Earl of Malmesbury's Collection, 'Twelve Fugues for an Organ or Harpsicord'. J. Walsh ('Six Fugues or Voluntarys for the Organ or Harpsicord . . . Troisieme Ovarage') 23 Aug. 1735 or a little earlier. Arnold, 131, *c*. 1793. H.G. 2, pp. 161-174.

6 Fugues faciles (*Fughettas*). No. 1 in C major. No. 2 in C major. No. 3 in D major. No. 4 in C major. No. 5 in D major. No 6 in F major. Date? Longman and Broderip ('Twelve Voluntaries and Fugues For the Organ or Harpsichord with Rules for Tuning by the celebrated Mr Handel Book IV') *c*. 1776. Handel's name is not given except on the title-page, and on p. 1 to the 'Rules', &c. Other items than the Fugues in the volume were attributed in a later edition to Dr. Croft and Dr. Green. Chrysander in H.G. 2 considered the Fugues spurious and of later Viennese origin. H.G. 48, pp. 183-190. *See* preceding item, Malmesbury MS. collection of 'Twelve Fugues' which may or may not include the 'Fugues faciles.'

Suites de Pièces (*Lessons*). No. 1 in A major. No. 2 in F major. No. 3 in D minor. No. 4 in E minor. No. 5 in E major. No. 6 in F♯ minor. No. 7 in G minor. No. 8 in F minor. Date? *Auto*. R.M.20.g.13,14, *fr*.; Fitzwilliam, *fr*. *MS. copies*: R.M.18.b.8, *fr*.: B.M. Add MSS., *fr*.: 31467, 31573, 31577, 35040; Fitzwilliam, *fr*.; Complete copy, contemporary MS. attributed to J. C. Smith, Ellis sale catalogue, XXIV, No. 145, and Sotheby sale, July 24, 1916. 'Printed for the Author' ('Suites de Pieces pour le Clavecin . . . Premier

Volume London printed for the Author (by J. Cluer) And are only to be had at
Christopher Smith's . . . and by Richard Mear's', &c.) 14 Nov. 1720. In
his preface Handel stated that he had published them 'because Surrepticious
and incorrect copies of them had got abroad'. Arnold, 128-129 ('Lessons for
the Harpsichord') c. 1793. H.G. 2, pp. 1-60.
    Suites de Pièces (Lessons). Vol. II. No. 1 in B♮ major. No. 2 in G major.
No. 3 in D minor. No. 4 in D minor. No. 5 in E minor. No. 6 in G minor.
No. 7 in B♭ major. No. 8 in G major. No. 9 in G major (Chaconne and
Variations). Date? *Auto.* R.M.20.g.14, *f.*40 (Preludio, *see* Walsh edition).
MS. copies: R.M.18.c.2, *fr.*; R.M.18.b.4, *fr.*; R.M.19.a.3,4, *fr.*; B.M. Add.
MSS., *fr.*: 31467, 31573, 31577. J. Walsh ('Suites de Pieces Pour le Clavecin
...Second Volume') c. 1733. In this volume the 'Preludio' on p. 64 preceding,
the 'Chacoone' is the same as the 'Courante' in F major, H.G. II, p. 142.
An earlier issue of the 'Suites' was printed by Walsh, with the items in a
different order to that of the later Walsh (usually considered the first), and
commencing with the 'Preludio', p. 2 (p. 64 in the earlier issue). The title-
page of the earlier issue is the same as in later one, but has the imprint
blanked out. Why this issue was prepared and apparently replaced by the
more popular one is not known. (Copy in William C. Smith collection.)
Michel Charles Le Cene, Amsterdam ('Suites de Piéces pour le Clavessin
Composée par G. F. Hendel') c. 1733; this edition (no copy available) was
advertised in Le Cene's 'Catalogue des livres de Musique, Imprimés à
Amsterdam, as No. 490', which also appears on the title page of Walsh's
edition, which it may or may not have preceded. An edition of the 'Suite
No 9' was issued 'Imprimé aux dépens de Gerhard Fredrik Witvogel,'
Amsterdam ('Prelude et Chacoone Avec LXII Variations Composees par
M! Hendel, Opera primo') which may have appeared as early as 1731;
it has a different 'Prelude' to those given in the two Walsh editions referred
to above (B.M. f. 45.(1.). *See* Chrysander, 'G. F. Händel', Vol. III, p. 196.
Arnold, 129-130 ('A Second Set of Lessons for the Harpsichord') c. 1793.
H.G. 2, pp. 63-122.
    A Third Set of Lessons for the Harpsichord. Arnold, 130-131. *Klavierstücke.*
Dritte Sammlung. H.G. II, pp. 125-158. The items are entered separately.
    Capriccio in F major. Date? G. F. Witvogel, Amsterdam ('Capriccio pour
le Clavecin. Opera terza') 1732. J. Walsh ('The Lady's Banquet', Fifth Book,
as part of 'the celebrated Organ Concerto compos'd by Mr. Handel') c. 1734.
H.G. 2, pp. 144-147 ('Dritte Sammlung', No. 8). This and three other pieces
included in H.G. 2 were published by Witvogel on large single sheets, the
descriptions, 'Opera terza', &c. being his own.
    Capriccio in G minor. c. 1736. *Auto.* Fitzwilliam, 30.H.13, pp. 33-34.
The leading idea of this movement appears in 'Alexander's Feast' ('Now strike
the golden lyre again'). B. Goodison ('Lessons by Handel', pp. 10-11) 1787.
Arnold, 130-131 ('A Third Set of Lessons for the Harpsichord', No. 4)
c. 1793. H.G. 2, pp. 131-132 ('Dritte Sammlung', No. 3).
    Chaconne in F major. Date? *MS. copy:* R.M.19.a.3 ('Chaconne with 2
Setts of Keys'). Arnold, 130-131 ('A Third Set of Lessons for the Harpsi-
chord', No. 6) c. 1793. W. Barclay Squire and Fuller-Maitland ('Pieces for
Harpsichord'. Vol. 2. No. 38) 1928. H.G. 2, pp. 136-139 ('Dritte Sammlung',
No. 5).

308 HANDEL

Concertos for the Harpsichord or Organ. See Orchestral Works including
Organ Conceitos.

Courante (Preludio) e due Menuetti in F major. Date? *Auto.* R.M.20.g.
14,*f*.40 ('Courante'—unnamed). It was published in 'Suites de Pieces',
Vol. II, by Walsh as 'Preludio' (p. 64) preceding the 'Chacoone', but in the
key of G major. *MS. copy:* R.M.18.b.4 ('Menuet', No. 2). B. Goodison
('Lessons by Handel', p. 11. 'Minuet', No. 1) 1787. Arnold, 130-131 ('A
Third Set of Lessons for the Harpsichord', as 'Allegro' and 'Minuets' at
the end of Nos. 6 and 4) *c.* 1793. H.G. 2, pp. 142-143 ('Dritte Sammlung',
No. 7).

12 Fantasias and other pieces. Date? MS. Nägeli Collection, Zurich
Central Library. *See* Georg Walter, 'Unbekannte Klaviercompositionen von
G. F. Händel' (*Schweizerische Musikzeitung*, May 1942, No. 5); Chrys-
ander, 'G. F. Händel', Vol. III, p. 200. Hug & Co., Leipzig and Zurich ('Zwölf
Fantasien und Vier Stücke für Cembalo . . . herausgegeben von Georg
Walter') 1942. The first 'Fantasia' in this collection is the 'Sonata in C
major', H.G. II, pp. 151-153. The 'Vier Stücke' are 'Allemande' in D major,
'Sonata' in A major, an unnamed piece in D major, and 'Carillon' in D major.
Another MS. containing the 12 Fantasias is reported to have been in the
Staatsbibliothek, Berlin.

Fantasia in C major. Date? G. F. Witvogel, Amsterdam ('Fantasie Pour
le Clavecin. Opera Quinta'—*See* 'Capriccio in F major') 1732. J. Walsh
('The Lady's Banquet', Fifth Book—as part of 'the celebrated Organ Concerto
compos'd by Mr. Handel') *c.* 1734. B. Goodison ('Lessons by Handel',
pp. 7-9) 1787. Arnold, 130-131 ('A Third Set of Lessons for the Harpsichord',
No. 5) *c.* 1793. H.G. 2, pp. 133-135 ('Dritte Sammlung', No. 4).

2 Fugues in B minor and C minor. Date? Goulding, Phipps and D'Almaine
('A Set of Ten Miscellaneous Fugues . . . three by Handel . . . (arranged) by
J. Diettenhofer') *c.* 1803 or earlier; the other Handel Fugue in this collection
was arranged from 'Alexander's Feast'.

2 Fugen für zwey Personen auf einem Clavier. Date? Both in C major
and each with a short Prelude. Edited by Heinz Schüngeler and published
in 1944 by Heinrichshofens Verlag, Magdeburg and Leipzig, from a contemporary manuscript in the archives of the firm. No other source known.

Hornpipe in G major. Date? *MS. copy:* B.M. Add. MSS. 29371,*f*.76v.
('Mr. Handele Hornpipe'). Used in the Ballad Opera, 'The Female Parson',
1730. 'Rutherford's compleat Collection of 200 . . . Country Dances', &c.
Vol. 1. p. 35. c. 1756.

Lesson in A minor. Date? *Auto.* R.M.20.g.14,*f*.60 (First movement
only—'Harp', i.e. 'Harpeggio'). Arnold, 130-131 ('A Third Set of Lessons
for the Harpsichord', No. 3—without the arpeggio introduction) *c.* 1793.
H.G. 2, pp. 140-141 ('Dritte Sammlung', No. 6).

Lesson in D minor. Date? Probably a first version of the movement
'Presto', Suite III. H.G. 2, pp. 21-23. H.G. 48, pp. 191-193.

March in D major. Date? Arranged for Pianoforte by M. Rophino Lacy
from an MS. owned by Henry Barrett Lennard, C. Lonsdale, 1848.

Partie (Suite) in C major. c. 1706. *MS:* Staatsbibliothek, Berlin, 9162 in K
Bärenreiter, Kassel, edited by Werner Danchert in volume 'Unbekannte
Meisterwerke der Klaviermusik', 1930.

Partie (Suite) in G major. c. 1706. *MS*: Staatsbibliothek, Berlin, 9164, 1 in K. Edition as previous item.

Partie (Suite) in C minor, c. 1706. *MS*: Staatsbibliothek, Berlin, 9164, 3 in K. Edition as two previous items.

Partita (Suite) in A major. c. 1720. *MS.* (J. C. Smith?) Nägeli and afterwards, Mortier de Fontaine. B. Senff, Leipzig, edited by Fontaine, 1863 H.G. 48, pp. 176-182.

Pieces for Harpsichord. (*Stücke für Clavicembalo.*) Various dates, *c.* 1736 and earlier. Edited by W. Barclay Squire and J. A. Fuller-Maitland, Schott & Co., London (B. Schott Söhne, Mainz und Leipzig). 1928. A selection in two volumes from the many unpublished pieces in four MS. volumes, formerly in the Aylesford Collection, sold in May 1918, and now in the King's Music Library; the selection duplicated far more already published work than the editors supposed (see Kathleen Dale's chapter in the present volume, *passim*).

Prelude in D minor. Date? Additional to 'Suites de Pieces', Vol. I. No. 4. H.G. 48, p. 149. ('Klavierbuch aus der Jugendzeit'). *See* 'Sonatina in D minor'.

Preludio ed Allegro in G minor. Date? G. F. Witvogel, Amsterdam ('Preludio ed Allegro pour le Clavecin. Opera quarta') 1732. J. Walsh ('The Lady's Banquet', Fifth Book, as part of 'the celebrated Organ Concerto compos'd by Mr. Handel') *c.* 1734. H.G. 2, pp. 148-149 ('Dritte Sammlung', No. 9).

Some golden Rules for the attaining to play Through Bass. Date? *Auto.* Cummings Sale Catalogue, No. 133, 1917. An MS. note says that it was given to (Bernard) Granville.

Sonata in C major. Date? *MS. copy*; Nägeli Collection, Zurich ('Zwölf Fantasien', &c. Fantasia No. 1). G. F. Witvogel, Amsterdam ('Sonata pour le Clavecin. Opera Seconda') 1732. J. Walsh ('The Lady's Banquet', Fifth Book, as part of 'the celebrated Organ Concerto compos'd by Mr. Handel') *c.* 1734. H.G.2, pp. 151-153 ('Dritte Sammlung', No. 11).

Sonata in C major, in three movements. c. 1750. *Auto.* R.M.20.g.13, *ff.*40-41v.; Fitzwilliam, 30.H.11, pp. 45-49. H.G. 2, pp. 154-158 ('Dritte Sammlung', No. 12).

Sonatina in B♭ major. Date? *Auto.* Fitzwilliam, 30.H.13, p. 7. H.G. 2, p. 150 ('Dritte Sammlung', No. 10).

Sonatina (Concerto) in G major. c. 1730. *MS. copies*: R.M.18.b.8, *ff.* 12-13 ('Concerto'); R.C.M. 2097, *ff.* 35v-36 ('Sonatina per Cembalo'); Fitzwilliam, 32.G.18; W. Barclay Squire and Fuller-Maitland ('Pieces for Harpsichord'. Vol. I. pp. 59-61, 'Concerto') 1928.

Sonatina in D minor. c. 1710-20. This and the following four items from a manuscript in the Barrett Lennard Collection, which also contains variants of other works; published in H.G. 48, pp. 146-175, as 'Klavierbuch aus der Jugendzeit'—'Earliest Compositions for the Harpsichord'. (*See* also 'Prelude in D minor'.) *MS. copy*: B.M. Add. MSS. 31573. H.G. 48, pp. 150-151.

Suite in D minor. c. 1710-20. *See* previous item. H.G. 48, pp. 152-161.

Suite à deux clavecins, in C minor. c. 1710-20. *MS. copy*: B.M. Add. MSS. 31577, *ff.* 11-13. The part for one Clavecin only, supposed to belong to the Suite for two Harpsichords, which Witvogel printed at Amsterdam, no copy of which is available. Oxford University Press ('Suite', for two Pianos) edited, and Piano II by Thurston Dart, 1950. *See* Sonatina in D minor. H.G. 48, pp. 162-166.

Suite in G major. c. 1710-20. The second movement, 'Allegro', occurs as 'Capriccio' in Aylesford MS. R.M.19.a.3.*f.*29v.; and in E. F. Rimbault's 'The Pianoforte', &c., 1860, pp. 340-343, where it is stated to be an extract from a manuscript in the hand of J. C. Smith, said to have been written for the Princess Amelia, and containing many unknown pieces. *See* Sonatina in D minor. H.G. 48, pp. 166-169.

Suite in D minor. c. 1710-20. *See* Sonatina in D minor. H.G. 48, pp. 170-175.

Suite in D minor. (Allemande, Courante, Saraband and Gigue.) c. 1736. *Auto.* Fitzwilliam, 30.H.11, pp. 41-43. *MS. copy*: R.M.19.d.11 ('Lessons composed for the Princess Louisa', No. 1). Arnold, 130-131 ('A Third Set of Lessons for the Harpsichord', No.1) *c.* 1793. H.G. 2, pp. 125-127 ('Dritte Sammlung', No. 1).

Suite in G minor. (Allemande, Courante, Saraband and Gigue.) c. 1736. *Auto.* Fitzwilliam, 30.H.11, pp. 31-37; 30.H.12, p. 60 (Saraband and Gigue). *MS. copy*: R.M.19.d.11 ('Lessons composed for the Princess Louisa', No. 2). C. and S. Thompson ('A Favourite Lesson for the Harpsichord Composed for Young Practitioners . . . Never before Printed') *c.* 1770. Arnold, 130-131 ('A Third Set of Lessons for the Harpsichord,' No. 2) *c.* 1793. H.G. 2, pp. 128-130 ('Dritte Sammlung,' No. 2).

Voluntaries for the Organ or Harpsichord. Longman, Lukey & Co. (and their successors) issued four books of Voluntaries, &c. *c.* 1775 and afterwards, Book II of which was entitled 'Ten Select Voluntaries . . . Composed by Mr. Handel, Dr. Green', &c. *c.* 1775. This was also issued by Muzio Clementi & Co., *c.* 1802 or later. Book I of the series was advertised as 'Voluntaries by Dr. Green, Travers,' &c.; Book III, as by 'Boyce, Smith', &c., and in the later edition by Muzio Clementi as by 'Orlando Gibbons, Blow, Purcell', &c. Book IV, which includes the 'Fugues faciles' of Handel, is dealt with under that entry. Handel's share in Book II has not been identified, and there is no evidence that Books I and III contain any Handel items, but the matter is open to question.

Various Harpsichord arrangements given in H.G. 48, pp. 194-243 have not been listed here.

A Collection of Lessons for the Harpsicord Compos'd by Mr. Handel 4th Book, published by J. Walsh, 17 Jan. 1758, is simply a reissue of the Sixth Book of 'The Lady's Banquet', published 23 Aug. 1735, all the items in which with one exception, have been identified as arrangements from operas, 'Il Pastor Fido', 'Alcina', &c.

HARP MUSIC

Pastoraleet Thême avec Variations pour Harpe ou Pianoforte. Date? Matthias Artaria, Vienna, 1826. (Details supplied by Maria Korchinska.)

Concerto for the Harp. See Orchestral Works—6 Organ Concertos. Op. 4. No. 6.

CHRONOLOGY

1685. Born at Halle, 23 February.
1702. Entered Halle University, 10 February.
1703-6. At Hamburg opera (*John Passion, Almira,* and *Nero*).
1706-10. In Italy (*Rodrigo, La Resurrezione, Il Trionfo del Tempo, Agrippina*).
1710. Court *Kapellmeister* in Hanover; first visit to London.
1711. *Rinaldo*; return to Hanover.
1712. Second visit to London.
1715. First *Water Music*; reconciliation with George I.
1716. Visit to Hanover; Brockes *Passion* composed.
1717. Second *Water Music*.
1717-20. Associated with Duke of Chandos; *Haman and Mordecai, Acis and Galatea.*
1719. Foundation of 'Royal Academy of Music' for opera performances at the Haymarket; visit to Germany.
1720. First keyboard suites published; *Radamisto.*
1721. *Muzio Scevola* and *Floridante.*
1723. At Lower Brook Street, London.
1723-5. *Ottone, Giulio Cesare, Tamerlano* and *Rodelinda.*
1726. *Scipione* and *Alessandro.*
1727. English naturalization, 20 February; Anthems for the Coronation of George II; *Admeto* and *Riccardo Primo.*
1729. Visit to Italy and Germany; operatic partnership with Heidegger; *Lotario.*
1730-2. *Partenope, Poro, Ezio, Sosarme* and *Esther*; Sonatas, Op. 1, published.
1733. *Orlando Furioso* and *Deborah*; visit to Oxford (*Athalia*); visit to Italy.
1734. *Arianna*; *Il Pastor Fido* (second and third versions).
1735. *Ariodante* and *Alcina.*
1736. *Alexander's Feast*; *Atalanta* and Wedding Anthem for the Prince of Wales.
1737. *Arminio, Giustino, Berenice, Trionfo del Tempo* (second version), financial and physical collapse; cure at Aachen; Funeral Anthem for Queen Caroline.
1738. *Faramondo* and *Serse*; first set of Organ Concertos published.
1739. *Saul, Israel in Egypt* and *Ode for St. Cecilia's Day*; Concerti grossi, Op. 6, composed.
1741. *Deidamia* (last opera); *Messiah* composed; visit to Ireland (November).
1742. *Messiah* performed in Dublin (13 April); return from Ireland (August).
1743. *Samson* and Dettingen *Te Deum.*
1744. *Joseph* and *Semele.*
1745. *Hercules* and *Belshazzar*; fresh illness.

1746. *Occasional Oratorio.*
1747. *Judas Maccabaeus.*
1748-9. *Alexander Balus, Joshua, Susanna, Solomon, Fireworks Music.*
1750. *Theodora*; visit to Germany.
1751. *Jephtha* composed; onset of blindness (February).
1757. *The Triumph of Time and Truth.*
1759. Death at Lower Brook Street (14 April); burial in Westminster
       Abbey (20 April).

BIBLIOGRAPHY

(The primary source for Handel bibliography is Kurt Taut's *Verzeichnis des Schrifttums über G. F. Händel* which constitutes Jg. 6 of the *Händel-Jahrbuch* (Leipzig, 1933). The books and articles selected below deal with the music rather than with the man, though the most important biographical works are included. Dictionary articles and chapters in general histories have been excluded.

ABERT, HERMANN: 'Die Aufgaben der heutigen Händelforschung' (in *Händel-Jahrbuch*, Jg. 1, 1928).

—— 'Georg Friedrich Händel' (in *Gesammelte Schriften und Vorträge*, Halle, 1929).

—— 'Händel als Dramatiker' (in *Universitätsbund Göttingen: Mitteilungen*, Jg. 3).

ABRAHAM, GERALD: 'Handel's Clavier Music' (in *Music and Letters*, Vol. XVI, 1935).

ADEMOLLO, A.: *G. F. Haendel in Italia* (Milan, 1889).

ARKWRIGHT, G. E. P.: 'Handel's Cantata *Conosco che mi piaci*' (in *Musical Antiquary*, Vol. I, 1910).

ARMSTRONG, THOMAS: 'The *Messiah* Accompaniments' (in *Music and Letters*, Vol. IX, 1928).

ARNOLD, S.: 'On Handel's Oratorio Methods' (in *Musical Times*, Vol. XLIII, 1902).

BAIRSTOW, EDWARD C.: *Handel's Oratorio 'The Messiah'* (London, 1928).

BALFOUR, A. J.: 'Handel' (in *Edinburgh Review*, January 1887).

BENSON, J. A.: *Handel's Messiah: the Oratorio and its History* (London, 1923).

BERNHARDT, Reinhold: 'Die "Kalte Arie" in Mozarts *Messias*-Bearbeitung' (in *Die Musik*, Jg. XXII, 1930).

—— 'W. A. Mozarts *Messias*-Bearbeitung und ihre Drucklegung in Leipzig 1802-3' (in *Zeitschrift für Musikwissenschaft*, Vol. XII, 1929).

BERNOULLI, E.: *Quellen zum Studium Händelscher Chorwerke* (Leipzig, 1906).

BEYSCHLAG, ADOLF: 'Über Chrysanders Bearbeitung des Händel'schen *Messias* und über die Musikpraxis zur Zeit Händels' (in *Die Musik*, Jg. X, 1910-11).

BLANDFORD, W. F. H.: 'Handel's Horn and Trombone Parts' (in *Musical Times*, Vol. LXXX, 1939).

BOUCHOR, MAURICE: *Israël en Egypte* (Paris, 1888).

BOURNE, T. W.: 'Handel's Double *Gloria Patri*' (in *Monthly Musical Record*, Vol. XXVII, 1897).

BRENET, MICHEL: *Haendel* (Paris, 1912).

BURNEY, CHARLES: *An account of the musical performances in Westminster Abbey and the Pantheon, May 26, 27 and 29; and June 3 and 5, 1784* (London, 1785).

CHERBULIEZ, A. E.: *Georg Friedrich Händel* (Olten, 1949).

CHOP, MAX: *G. F. Händel: 'Der Messias'* (Leipzig, 1910).

CHORLEY, H. F.: *Handel Studies* (London, 1859).

CHRYSANDER, FRIEDRICH: 'Bemerkungen zu dem Aufsatze von W. G. Cusins über Händels *Messias*' (in *Allgemeine musikalische Zeitung*, Vol. X, 1875).[1]

—— 'Der Bestand der königlichen Privatmusik und Kirchenkapelle in London, 1710-1755' (in *Vierteljahrsschrift für Musikwissenschaft*, Vol. VIII, 1892).

—— 'Der erste Entwurf der Bassarie 'Nasce al bosco' in Händels Opera *Ezio*' (in *Allgemeine musikalische Zeitung*, Vol. XIV, 1879).

—— 'Die Originalstimmen zu Händels *Messias*' (in *Peters-Jahrbuch*, Jg. 2, 1896).

—— 'Francesco Antonio Urio' (in *Allgemeine musikalische Zeitung*, Vols. XIII and XIV, 1878-9).

—— 'Geschichte der Hamburger Opera (1703 bis 1706)' (in *Allgemeine musikalische Zeitung*, Vol. XV, 1880).

—— 'Goethes und Zelters Correspondenz über Händels *Messias*' (in *Allgemeine musikalische Zeitung*, Vol. XII, 1877).

—— *G. F. Händel* (three vols., Leipzig, 1858, 1860 and 1867).

—— *Händels Biblische Oratorien in geschichtlicher Betrachtung* (Hamburg, 1897).

—— 'Händels Instrumentalkompositionen für grosses Orchester' (in *Vierteljahrsschrift für Musikwissenschaft*, Vol. III, 1887).

—— Händels Orgelbegleitung zu *Saul*' (in *Jahrbücher für musikalische Wissenschaft*, I, 1863).

—— 'Händels Teufels-Arie' (in *Allgemeine musikalische Zeitung*, Vol. XVII, 1882).

—— 'Händels zwölf Concerti grossi für Streichinstrumente' (in *Allgemeine musikalische Zeitung*, Vols. XVI and XVII, 1881-2).

—— 'Mendelssohn's Orgelbegleitung zu *Israel in Ägypten* (in *Jahrbücher für musikalische Wissenschaft*, II, 1867).

[1] This series of comments followed the serial publication of Chrysander's translation of Cusins' study (see under 'Cusins') in the same journal.

CHRYSANDER, FRIEDRICH: 'Über Händels fünfstimmige Chöre' (in *Allgemeine musikalische Zeitung*, Vols. XIV and XV, 1879-80).

—— 'Zelter über Mozarts Bearbeitung des Händelschen *Messias*' (in *Allgemeine musikalische Zeitung*, Vol. XII, 1877).

—— 'Zwei Claviere bei Händel. Cembalo-Partituren' (in *Allgemeine musikalische Zeitung*, Vol. XII, 1877).

COOPERSMITH, J. M.: 'A List of Portraits, Sculptures, etc. of G. F. Händel' (in *Music and Letters*, Vol. XIII, 1932).

—— 'Handel Lacunae: a project' (in *Musical Quarterly*, Vol. XXI, 1935).

—— 'The Libretto of Handel's *Jupiter in Argos* (in *Music and Letters*, Vol. XVII, 1936).

CUMING, GEOFFREY: 'The Text of *Messiah*' (in *Music and Letters*, Vol. XXXI, 1950).

CUMMINGS, W. H.: '*God Save the King* and Handel' (in *Musical Times*, Vol. XLIII, 1902).

—— *Handel* (London, 1904).

—— 'Handel Myths' (in *Musical Times*, Vol. XXVI, 1885, Vol XXXV, 1894, and Vol XLVI, 1905).

—— *Handel, the Duke of Chandos, and the Harmonious Blacksmith* (London, 1915).

—— 'Handel's *Nisi Dominus*' (in *Musical Times*, Vol. XXXIX, 1898).

—— 'The *Messiah*' (in *Musical Times*, Vol. XLIV, 1903).

—— '*Muzio Scevola*' (in *Musical Times*, Vol. LII, 1911).

CUSINS, WILLIAM G.: *Handel's 'Messiah': an examination of the original and of some contemporary MSS.* (London, 1874).

DEAN, WINTON: 'The Abridgment of Handel' (in *Monthly Musical Record*, Vol. LXXX, 1950).

—— *Handel's Dramatic Oratorios and Masques* (London, 1959).

DELANY, Mary: *Autobiography and Correspondence of Mary Granville, Mrs. Delany* (six vols. London, 1861-2).

DENT, E. J.: 'Englische Einflüsse bei Händel' (in *Händel-Jahrbuch*, Jg. II, 1929).

—— *Handel* (London, 1934).

—— 'The English Influences on Handel' (in *Monthly Musical Record*, Vol. LXI, 1931).

DEUTSCH, O. E.: *Handel: A Documentary Biography* (London, 1955).

EHRLINGER, F.: *G. F. Händels Orgelkonzerte* (Erlanger dissertation) (Würzburg, 1941).

EINSTEIN, ALFRED: 'Zum 48. Bande der Händel-Ausgabe' (in *Sammelbände der internationalen Musikgesellschaft*, Vol. IV, 1902).

EISENSCHMIDT, JOACHIM: *Die szenische Darstellung der Opern Händels auf der Londoner Bühne seiner Zeit* (Wolfenbüttel 1940).

ELLINGER, GEORG: 'Händels *Admet* und seine Quelle' (in *Vierteljahrsschrift für Musikwissenschaft*, Vol. I, 1885).

FARMER, HENRY: *Handel's Kettledrums, and other papers* (London, 1950).

FLOWER, NEWMAN: *Catalogue of a Handel Collection formed by Newman Flower* (Sevenoaks, 1921), *George Frederic Handel: His Personality and His Times* (London, 1923; revised edition, 1947).

FREY, MARTIN: 'Neue Händel-Funde' (in *Die Musik*, Vol. XIX, 1927).

FULLER-MAITLAND, J. A.: *The Age of Bach and Handel* (*Oxford History of Music*, Vol. IV, 1902).

GARAT, JULES: *La sonate de Haendel* (Paris, 1905).

GARDNER, HUGH: 'The Pre-Mozartian *Messiah*' (in *Musical Times*, Vol. LXXVI, 1935).

GERVINUS, G. G.: *Händel und Shakespeare* (Leipzig, 1868).

—— 'Nomen et omen: Händel über Händel' (in *Allgemeine musikalische Zeitung*, Vol. VI, 1871).

—— 'Über Händels Werke' (in *Deutsche Musik-Zeitung*, Vol. III, 1862).

GOLDSCHMIDT, HUGO: 'Zur Frage der vokalen Auszierung Händel'scher Oratorien' (in *Allgemeine Musik-Zeitung*, Vol. XXXV, 1908).

HAGEN, OSKAR: 'Die Bearbeitung der Händelschen *Rodelinde*' (in *Zeitschrift für Musikwissenschaft*, Vol. II, 1920).

HAHN, ALBERT: 'Händels Trompeten' (in *Die Tonhalle*, Vol. I, 1868).

HERBAGE, JULIAN: *Messiah* (London, 1948).

—— '*The Messiah*: Handel's Second Thoughts' (in *Musical Times*, Vol. LXXXIX (1948).

HEUSS, ALFRED: 'Das *Semele*-Problem bei Congreve und Händel' (in *Zeitschrift der internationalen Musikgesellschaft*, Vol. XV, 1914).

—— 'Das Textproblem von Händels *Judas Maccabäus*' (in *Händel-Jahrbuch*, Jg. I, 1928).

—— 'Die Braut- und Hochzeitsarie in Händels *Susanna*' (in *Zeitschrift der internationalen Musikgesellschaft*, Vol. XIV, 1913).

—— 'Eine Händel-Beethoven-Brahms Parallele' (in *Die Musik*, Jg. VII, 1908).

—— 'Händels *Jephta* in der Bearbeitung von H. Stephani' (in *Zeitschrift der internationalen Musikgesellschaft*, Vol. XII, 1911).

—— 'Händels *Samson* in der Bearbeitung von F. Chrysander' (in *Zeitschrift der internationalen Musikgesellschaft*, Vol. X, 1909).

—— 'Über Händel im Allgemeinen und die *Debora* im Besonderen' (in *Allgemeine Musik-Zeitung*, Vol. XLIV, 1917).

HEUSS, ALFRED: 'Über Händels '*Salomo*' (in *Zeitschrift für Musik*, Jg. XCII, 1925).

HILLER, J. A.: *Der 'Messias' von Händel, nebst angehängten Betrachtungen darüber* (Leipzig, 1787).

KAHLE, FELIX: *Händels Cembalosuiten* (Eisenach dissertation, 1928).

KILBURN, N.: 'Additional accompaniments to Handel's *Acis*' (in *Sammelbände der internationalen Musikgesellschaft*, Vol. III, 1901).

KRETZSCHMAR, HERMANN: 'Georg Friedrich Händel' (in Waldersee's *Sammlung Musikalischer Vorträge*, V, 1884).

LARSEN, J. P.: *Handel's 'Messiah': Origins—Composition—Sources* (London, 1957).

LEICHTENTRITT, HUGO: *Händel* (Stuttgart, 1924).
—— 'Handel's Harmonic Art' (in *Musical Quarterly*, Vol. XXI, 1935).

LEUX, IRMGARD: 'Über die "verschollene" Händel-Oper *Hermann von Balcke*' (in *Archiv für Musikwissenschaft*, Vol. VIII, 1926).

MAINWARING, JOHN: *Memoirs of the Life of the late George Frederick Handel* (London, 1760).

MANSFIELD, O. A.: 'The Minuet in Handel's *Messiah*' (in *Musical Quarterly*, Vol. V, 1919).

MARSHALL, MRS. JULIAN: *Handel* (London, 1883).

MENDELSSOHN-BARTHOLDY, FELIX: Preface to London Handel Society edition of *Israel in Egypt* (London, 1844).

MENKE, W.: *The Trumpet of Bach and Handel* (London, N.D.).

MEYER, E. H.: 'Has Handel written Works for Two Flutes without a Bass?' (in *Music and Letters*, Vol. XVI, 1935).

MICHAEL, WOLFGANG: 'Die Entstehung der *Wassermusik* von Händel' (in *Zeitschrift für Musikwissenschaft*, Vol. IV, 1922).

MÜLLER, E. H. (ed.): *The Letters and Writings of G. F. Handel* (London, 1935).

MÜLLER-BLATTAU, J.: *Georg Friedrich Händel* (Potsdam, 1933).

MYERS, ROBERT M.: *Handel's 'Messiah'* (New York, 1948).

PROUT, EBENEZER: 'Handel's *Messiah*: Preface to the new edition' (in *Musical Times*, Vol. XLIII, 1902).
—— 'Handel's Orchestration' (in *Musical Times*, Vol. XXV, 1884).
—— 'Handel's Wind Parts to the *Messiah*' (in *Monthly Musical Record*, Vol. XXIV, 1894).

REDLICH, H. F.: 'Handel's *Agrippina*' (in *Music Review*, Vol. XII, 1951).

REDWAY, V. L.: 'Handel in Colonial and Post-Colonial America' (in *Musical Quarterly*, Vol. XXI, 1935).

REICHARDT, J. F.: *G. F. Händels Jugend* (Berlin, 1785).

REISSMANN, August: *Georg Friedrich Händel* (Berlin and Leipzig, 1882).

RENDALL, E. D.: 'Is Handel's *St. John Passion* genuine?' (in *Zeitschrift der internationalen Musikgesellschaft*, Vol. VI, 1905).

—— 'The Influence of Henry Purcell on Handel, traced in *Acis and Galatea*' (in *Musical Times*, Vol. XXXVI, 1895).

ROBINSON, PERCY: *Handel and his Orbit* (London, 1908).

—— 'A recently discovered "Urio" MS' (in *Bulletin de la Société 'Union musicologique'*, Vol. VI, 1926).

—— 'Handel, or Urio, Stradella and Erba' (in *Music and Letters*, Vol. XVI, 1935).

—— 'Handel up to 1720: a new chronology' (in *Music and Letters*, Vol. XX, 1939).

—— 'Handel's Early Life and Mainwaring' (in *Musical Times*, Vol. LXVI, 1925).

—— 'Handel's Influence on Bach' (in *Musical Times*, Vol. XLVII, 1906).

—— 'Handel's Journeys' (in *Musical Antiquary*, Vol. I, 1910).

—— 'Was Handel a Plagiarist?' (in *Musical Times*, Vol. LXXX, 1939).

ROCKSTRO, W. S.: *The Life of G. F. Handel* (London, 1883).

ROLLAND, ROMAIN: *Haendel* (Paris, 1910; English translation, London, 1916).

—— 'Les "Plagiats" de Haendel' (in *S.M.I.*, Vol. VI, 1910).

SCHERING, ARNOLD: 'Die Welt Händels' (in *Händel-Jahrbuch*, Jg. V, 1933).

—— 'Händel und der protestantische Choral' (in *Händel-Jahrbuch*, Jg. I, 1928).

—— 'Die Oboe bei Händel' (in *Die Oboe*, Vol. I, 1928).

—— 'Die Instrumentation Händels' (in *Das Orchester*, Vol. V, 1928).

—— 'Zum Thema: Händels Entlehnungen' (in *Zeitschrift der internationalen Musikgesellschaft*, Vol. IX, 1908).

—— 'Zweistimmiger Klaviersatz bei Bach und Händel?' (in *Zeitschrift für Musik*, Jg. LXX, 1903).

SCHOELCHER, VICTOR: *The Life of Handel* (London, 1857).

SCHRADE, LEO: 'Studien zu Händels *Alexanderfest*' (in *Händel-Jahrbuch*, Jg. V, 1933).

SCOTT, CYRIL: 'The Influence of Handel on Victorian Morals' (in *The Sackbut* Vol. IV, 1924).

SEIFFERT, MAX: 'Buxtehude-Händel-Bach' (in *Peters-Jahrbuch*, Jg. IX, 1903).

SEIFFERT, MAX: 'Die Gesamtausgabe der Werke Händels und Bachs und ihre Bedeutung für die Zukunft' (in *Zeitschrift der internationalen Musikgesellschaft*, Vol. I, 1900).

—— 'Die Mannheimer *Messias*-Aufführung, 1777' (in *Peters-Jahrbuch*, Vol. XXIII, 1916).

—— 'Die Verzierung der Sologesänge in Händels *Messias*' (in *Sammelbände der internationalen Musikgesellschaft*, Vol. VIII, 1907).

—— 'G. Ph. Telemanns *Musique de table* als Quelle für Händel' (in *Bulletin de la Société 'Union musicologique'*, Vol. IV, 1924).

—— 'Händels deutsche Gesänge' (in *Liliencron-Festschrift*, Leipzig, 1910).

—— 'Händels Oratorien in Chrysanders Neugestaltung' (in *Caecilia*, Vol. LX, 1903).

—— 'Händels Verhältnis zu Tonwerken älterer deutscher Meister' (in *Peters-Jahrbuch*, Jg. XIV, 1908).

—— 'Zu Händels Klavierwerken' (in *Sammelbände der internationalen Musikgesellschaft*, Vol. I, 1899).

SEILER, JOSEF: 'Ein Lieblingsmotiv Händels' (in *Neue Berliner Musikzeitung*, Vol. XXVI, 1872).

SEILER, Robert: *Die Ariengestaltung Händels im 'Messias'* (Erlangen dissertation).

SHAW, G. BERNARD: 'Haendel et l'Angleterre' (in *S.I.M.*, Vol. IX, 1913).

SIBLEY, J. C.: *Handel at Cannons* (London, 1918).

SMEND, JULIUS: 'Händel und das deutsche Kirchenlied' (in *Monatschrift für Gottesdienst*, Vols. XXX-XXXI, 1925-6).

SMITH, WILLIAM C.: *Concerning Handel* (London, 1948).

—— 'Handel's First Song on the London Stage' (in *Music and Letters*, Vol. XVI, 1935).

—— 'Handeliana' (in *Music and Letters*, Vol. XXXI, 1950).

—— 'More Handeliana' (in *Music and Letters*, Vol. XXXIV, 1953).

SPITZ, CHARLOTTE: 'Die Opern *Ottone* von Händel und *Teofane* von Lotti (in *Sandberger-Festschrift*, Munich, 1918).

SQUIRE, W. BARCLAY: *Catalogue of the King's Music Library. Part I: The Handel Manuscripts* (London, 1927).

—— 'Handel in Contemporary Song-books' (in *Musical Antiquary*, Vol. IV, 1913).

—— 'Handel in 1745' (in *Riemann-Festschrift*, Leipzig, 1909).

—— 'Handel's Clock Music' (in *Musical Quarterly*, Vol. V, 1919).

—— 'Handel's *Semele*' (in *Musical Times*, Vol. LXVI, 1925).

—— 'Handel's "Song in eight parts" ' (in *Musical Antiquary*, Vol. IV, 1913).

STEGLICH, RUDOLF: 'Betrachtung des Händelschen *Messias*' (in *Händel-Jahrbuch*, Jg. IV, 1931).

STEGLICH, RUDOLF: 'Der Schlusschor von Händels *Acis und Galatea*' (in *Händel-Jahrbuch*, Jg. III, 1930).

—— 'Die neue Händel-Opern-Bewegung' (in *Händel-Jahrbuch*, Jg. I, 1928).

—— 'Händels Oper *Rodelinde* und ihre neue Göttinger Buhnenfassung' (in *Zeitschrift für Musikwissenschaft*, Vol. III, 1920).

—— 'Händels *Xerxes* und die Göttinger Festspiele' (in *Zeitschrift für Musikwissenschaft*, Vol. VII, 1924).

—— (ed.) *Handel-Jahrbücher* (Jg. I-VI, Leipzig, 1928-33).

—— 'Schütz und Händel' (in *Zeitschrift für Musik*, Jg. LXXXIX, 1922).

—— 'Über Händels *Alexander Balus*' (in *Zeitschrift für Musik*, Jg. XCV, 1928).

STEPHANI, HERMANN: 'Händels *Judas Makkabäus*' (in *Die Musik*, Jg. VIII, Vol. 31, 1908-9).

STREATFEILD, R. A.: *Handel* (London, 1909).

—— *Handel Autographs at the British Museum* (London, 1912)

—— *Handel, Cannons and the Duke of Chandos* (London, 1916)

—— 'Handel in Italy, 1706-10' (in *Musical Antiquary*, Vol. I, 1909).

—— 'Handel, Rolli, and Italian Opera in London in the Eighteenth Century' (in *Music Quarterly*, Vol. III, 1917).

—— 'Handel's Journey to Hanover in 1716' (in *Musical Antiquary*, Vol. II, 1911).

—— 'Remarks on the powers of characterization shown by Handel in his operas and oratorios' (in *Zeitschrift der internationalen Musikgesellschaft*,Vol. VIII, 1907).

—— 'The Granville Collection of Handel manuscripts' (in *Musical Antiquary*, Vol. II, 1911).

SWINYARD, L.: 'Handel's Organ Concertos' (in *Musical Times*, Vol. LXXVI, 1935).

TAUT, KURT: *Verzeichnis des Schrifttums über Georg Friedrich Händel* (*Händel-Jahrbuch*, Jg. VI, 1933).

TAYLOR, SEDLEY: *The Indebtedness of Handel to works by other composers* (Cambridge, 1906).

THAYER, A. W.: 'Zur Händel-Chronologie: Wann war Händel in Hannover, und wann kehrte er aus Italien zurück?' (in *Allgemeine Musikalische Zeitung*, Vol. I, 1863).

TIERSOT, J.: '*Israël en Egypte*' (in *Le Ménestrel*, Vol. LVII, 1891).

—— 'Un Théme de Haendel dans la 9ième Symphonie de Beethoven' (in *S.I.M.*, Vol. VI, 1910).

VERNIER, GABRIEL: *L'Oratorio biblique de Handel* (Cahors, 1901).

VOLBACH, FRITZ: *Georg Friedrich Händel* (Berlin, 1898; revised edition, 1907).

—— 'G. F. Händel und die Eigenart seines Schaffens' (in *Die Musik*, Jg. VI, Vol. 21, 1906).

—— 'Die Grundzüge der Anwendung und Bedeutung der Koloratur bei Händel und Chrysanders Stellung zu derselben' (in *Allgemeine Musik-Zeitung*, Vol. XXV, 1898).

—— *Die Praxis der Händel-Aufführung* (Bonn dissertation) (Charlottenburg, 1899).

—— 'Händel als Instrumentalkomponist' (in *Der Dreiklang*, Vol. I, 1926).

—— 'Händel-Plagiator' (in *Allgemeine Musik-Zeitung*, Vol. XVI, 1890).

VÖLSING, ERWIN: *G. H. Händel's Englische Kirchenmusik* (Giessen dissertation) (Leipzig, 1940).

WALTER, GEORG A.: 'Das Händel-Erlebnis eines Sängers' (in *Händel-Jahrbuch*, Jg. I, 1928).

—— 'Unbekannte Klavierkompositionen von G. F. Händel' (in *Schweizerische Musikzeitung*, 1942).

WEINSTOCK, HERBERT: *Handel* (New York, 1946).

WHITTAKER, W. G.: 'Bach, Handel and Robinson (with a reply by P. Robinson)' (in *Musical Times*, Vol. LXXVI, 1936).

WINTERSGILL, H. H.: 'Handel's Two-length Bar' (in *Music and Letters*, Vol. XVII, 1936).

WILLIAMS, C. F. ABDY: *Handel: his Life and Works* (London, 1900).

WOLFF, H. C.: *'Agrippina': eine italienische Jugendoper Händels* (Wolfenbüttel, 1943).

WUSTMANN, RUDOLF: 'Zwei *Messias*-Probleme' (in *Zeitschrift der internationalen Musikgesellschaft*, Vol. IX, 1908).

YOUNG, PERCY M.: *Handel* (London, 1947).

—— *The Oratorios of Handel* (London, 1949).

ZOBELEY, FRITZ: 'Werke Händels in der Gräfl. von Schönbornschen Musikbibliothek' (in *Händel-Jahrbuch*, Jg. IV, 1931).

INDEX

Set in Great Britain by the Camelot Press Ltd.,
and reprinted lithographically by Latimer, Trend & Co. Ltd., Whitstable